9/05

New Words

edited by
Orin Hargraves

New Words

edited by
Orin Hargraves

OXFORD
UNIVERSITY PRESS
2004

Oxford University Press

Oxford   New York
Auckland   Bangkok   Buenos Aires   Cape Town   Chennai
Dar es Salaam   Delhi   Hong Kong   Istanbul   Karachi   Kolkata
Kuala Lumpur   Madrid   Melbourne   Mexico City   Mumbai
Nairobi   São Paulo   Shanghai   Taipei   Tokyo   Toronto

Copyright © 2004 by Oxford University Press, Inc.

Published by Oxford University Press, Inc.
198 Madison Avenue, New York, New York, 10016
http://www.oup.com

Oxford is a registered trademark of Oxford University Press

Library of Congress Cataloging-in-Publication Data

New words / edited by Orin Hargraves.
    p. cm.
Includes bibliographical references and index.
ISBN 0-19-517282-5 (hardcover : alk. paper)
 1. English language—New words—Dictionaries.   I. Hargraves, Orin.
PE1630.N49 2004
423'.1—dc22

                                        2004003037

Printing number: 9 8 7 6 5 4 3 2 1

Printed in the United States of America
on acid-free paper

Staff

Project Editor: Orin Hargraves
Senior Editor: Erin McKean
Managing Editor: Constance Baboukis
Editors: Christine Lindberg
Grant Barrett
Carol Braham
Enid Pearsons, *pronunciations*
Jesse Ingham
Marina Padakis
Editorial Assistant: Ryan Sullivan

Contents

Introduction

THE LEXICOGRAPHER who has an opportunity to edit a dictionary of new words apprehends the task at first as a kid in front of the candy store: with eager impatience to experience, joyfully, all the things within. Very soon, however, the forces of habit and tradition assert themselves, and the anticipation of unalloyed joy turns into a somewhat soberer experience. The words are indeed interesting and there is some satisfaction in being able to introduce them to the dictionary format; but on closer examination, the words prove every bit as demanding as their more established counterparts: scrutinizing examples of their usage often reveals them to mean more, less, or other than what you thought. They resist—as words often do—the pigeonholing that dictionary definition necessarily entails: once you think you've nailed them, they have a way of popping up somewhere in a completely different guise, as if to prove that you hadn't really sorted them out after all.

This tendency to be a little less regular in their habits is much more a characteristic of new words than ones long-standing in a language: new words have not yet been subjected to the discipline— some might say the tyranny—of established usage, and so they are free to roam about slightly more than their older cousins, both semantically and orthographically. To some degree, however, a new word's appearance in a dictionary is the beginning of the end of its freedom: while lexicography pays these novel formations the respect of recognizing them as worthy additions to the language, it does so for a price, and that price is the suggestion, if not the insistence, that the new words settle down somewhat in form and meaning and stop flailing about.

What we designate as "new words" are rarely in fact new in the strictest sense. Just as cells and genomes have managed to produce everything in creation from the ingredients they find at hand, so it is with languages: letters in combinations hitherto unseen in a language will always be found to have roots in words or parts of words that already exist, in other languages if not in the same one. New words are pieced together from the fragments or the whole parts of old ones, and in a few cases, what we call a new word is simply a revival of a word coined in English hundreds of years ago — in all likelihood, to designate a different thing—and now pressed into service again.

The resources available to lexicography today in deciding on candidates for inclusion in dictionaries are myriad and complex. The rigors that once governed the careful collection, analysis, and storage of linguistic evidence in a more paper-based age must now be applied to the explosion of data available for examination in electronic form. In the end, however, the criteria for inclusion in a dictionary of new words are much the same as they have always been: is there something genuinely innovative about the word hitherto unnoted in dictionaries? Has the word escaped a relatively narrow field of usage, such as youth slang or trade jargon, to enjoy more general currency? Is the word likely to enjoy continuing currency, or does it designate a fad or phenomenon that we will probably no longer need a word for next year?

These guidelines have influenced the selection of words in this dictionary, along with a few other considerations. In most cases we have consulted the American college dictionaries, which are the bellwether of American lexicography and usage, and we have made a point of including words that are not generally treated in them. This has resulted in the selection of some words that you will immediately apprehend as not being new at all. They are words that, to our minds, have simply been neglected in the college dictionaries, despite widespread usage for some time. Take *guestbook* (or, if you prefer, *guest book*). Everyone knows what the old-fashioned kind is, a place where guests at a museum, hotel, event, or other venue sign their names and perhaps leave comments. Today guestbooks can also be found online, where visitors to websites can leave their comments. Strangely, however, the word is not to be found in most American dictionaries today, and even the *Oxford English Dictionary* has so far failed to take note of it. There are dozens of other words that we feel instinctively should have received more general coverage in dictionaries before this time, including *birthdate* (spelled thus as a solid compound), *landfall* (with reference to hurricanes), *peace order*, and *soymeal*, to choose a few.

In this dictionary there is also a strong emphasis on American English, but we have included some words from other major English dialects, particularly from British English, if the words are gaining currency on this side of the Atlantic (e.g., *minder*), if they might be confused with a similar American term (e.g., *care worker*), and in a few cases, if the words stand a good chance of filling a gap in American English, which has so far failed to provide a handy equivalent (e.g., *noughties*). The ease with which any speaker of English today can read English language newspapers from around the world on the Internet makes it desirable for all speakers to broaden their acquaintance with other dialects. This same phenomenon, along with the globalization of broadcast media outlets, makes the borders between English dialects more permeable than they have ever been before; a word that proves extremely useful in one dialect finds it much easier today to slip across a national border and fill a gap in another variety of English.

The need for language to keep pace with changes and innovations in human activities is one of the main engines of neology (that is, the coining of new words), and to some degree the words appearing in this dictionary reflect the preoccupations of our times.

There are many new words from medicine and biotechnology: *aromatase, gene-altered,* and *seroprevalence,* to pick out only three at random. Information technology also provides us with new offerings almost every day: consider *autocomplete, filesharing, service pack,* and the many words in which *cyber-* is the first element. Our concerns with the environment and our impact upon it is reflected in dozens of new entries, including those for newly-identified threatened or invasive species, and those representing phenomena arising from environmental degradation and our attempts to remedy it: *brown cloud, global common,* and *tidal farm,* for example.

As we have already noted, old words are sometimes given new jobs, which may or may not be closely related to their original ones. Consider *ephedra*; it has been in American dictionaries since the turn of the 20th century, designating "any of various plants of the genus Ephedra, growing in dry regions and having branching stems with dry scalelike leaves." At the turn of the 21st century, a definition similar to this one still prevailed in the American college dictionaries, but today, anyone who has not been living in a cultural vacuum will tell you that *ephedra* is a drug-cum-dietary supplement that is sold as an aid to athletic performance and weight loss. Of course the link between the old and new meanings is the plant, which is the source of the drug.

In general we have included in this dictionary only the new senses of a word, but in cases where the new sense makes little sense without reference to an older one, as with *ephedra* (*hypoxia* is another example), both the original and the newer sense are defined here.

Like professional athletes at the top of their careers, fully-defined words in dictionaries coexist with a vast infrastructure of less prominent players, many of whom never rise to the top. Just as some baseball players spend their entire careers in the bush leagues, many words spend generations in dictionaries with the lowly status of run-ons or list words. *Run-ons*, sometimes called *derivatives* (as they are in this dictionary), are words that appear in a dictionary without a definition, at the end of a standard entry: they are usually a predictably-formed inflection or a word formed with a standard suffix that can be fully understood if its defined root is understood. A *list word* is a word that is readily formed with the addition of a prefix, and whose meaning can also be guessed, such as the words typically appearing in dictionaries at *non-*, *pre-*, *super-*, *un-*, *under-*, and the like. It happens frequently, however, that a word once adequately treated as a list word or derivative gains so much in meaning or currency that it merits a full-fledged definition — a promotion to the majors if you will, where it stands a good chance of enjoying a high-profile career indefinitely. Examples of such felicitous promotions in this dictionary include *counterterrorism*, *implantable*, *nonstruck*, and *prelife*.

We have tried to uphold the principle that language appearing in public should be comprehensible to the public, whether this is the intention of the author of the language or not. In pursuit of this, words that have come to the editor's attention from newspapers, road signs, and ephemeral literature, for which no dictionary at hand offers any help, have been included in this dictionary. Consider the sign on the outskirts of Hanover, Pennsylvania that says "Jake Brake prohibited in this area" (what is a *Jake Brake*?), or an advertisement in a Chicago newspaper: "All-brick townhouse under construction—you get to put the first scratch in the wide-plank cherry flooring. European kitchen and baths (bidet optional), wine cellar, hydraulic closet rods." What is a *European kitchen*, and if you live in Chicago, why do you need one? Other words in this dictionary that have been nabbed for making unglossed appearances in public include *basket bingo, carryback note, outparcel,* and *pole building*.

It remains only to point out a few conventions and features of this dictionary. Entries generally follow the same format as in other recent Oxford American dictionaries, which are explained in some detail in the following pages. The usual parts of speech identify words in traditional classes. All registered trademarks are so identified following the part of speech. *Combining form* designates a word that has achieved the status of a productive compound element.

The great luxury of this dictionary, from an editor's point of view, is the space allowed for examples. Illustrative examples are supplied wherever one could be found that helped to illuminate the meaning, usage, or import of the words. These examples are citations from current language; there are no "made-up" examples, and attributional evidence is supplied for the overwhelming majority of citations in the square brackets that follow them. A plurality of the citations are from the *Oxford English Dictionary*'s "incomings," access to which has been generously provided by Jesse Sheidlower of the *OED*. The newspaper database Proquest has been used in some cases, and for the most contemporary citations, Google News was used as a search engine. A few citations have also been drawn from Usenet, the part of the Internet that handles and stores postings to newsgroups. Usenet citations are identified by group and date, but not by author. The citations generally should not be construed as representing the opinions of the publisher or the editor; in fact they should not be construed as representing any opinion, as they are chosen for the context they supply to illuminate words, not for any other purpose.

Etymologies for words in this dictionary have not been researched and presented systematically; that task awaits their inclusion in a more general dictionary. When an etymology was already at hand from existing Oxford resources, or where there is specific etymological information of interest concerning the coining of a word, it has been included. Words that are compounds of known, productive roots, prefixes, and suffixes are generally not given etymologies here.

The task of tracking down the new words defined here has been an enjoyable although quite time-consuming task; it would have been impossible in the time frame allowed without the help of lists supplied for perusal by editors at Oxford University Press. For these in particular I would like to thank Erin McKean, head of Oxford's dictionary program in the U.S., and Catherine Soanes of Oxford dictionaries in the UK. The editorial team behind this dictionary has worked diligently to make it accurate, comprehensive, informative, and up-to-date. We hope that you will find it so, and that you will take the opportunity provided by these definitions to give the words a good workout and test their viability for truly enduring status in forthcoming general dictionaries.

ORIN HARGRAVES
Westminster, Maryland
January, 2004

Using This Dictionary

The "entry map" below explains the different parts of an entry.

a•dre•nal•ized /ə'drēnl‚īzd/ ▸ **adjective** affected with adrenalin.
■ informal excited, charged, or tense: *they possess an adrenalized vigor that distinguishes them from other bands.*

Subsenses signalled by ■
Syllabification
Pronunciation set off with slashes / /
Examples in *italic*

ad•ver•game /'advər‚gām/ ▸ **noun** a downloadable or Internet-based computer game that advertises a brand-name product by featuring it as part of the game: *born of desperation and ingenuity, advergames, as they are called by marketers, are emerging at a time when Web surfers largely ignore more conventional forms of advertising.* [**30 Aug. 2001** *New York Times*]
-DERIVATIVES **ad•ver•gam•ing noun**
-ORIGIN blend of *advertisement* and *game.*

Citation information in square brackets
Derivative section, derivative in **bold face**
Etymology section
Grammar information in square brackets [ ]

burn /bərn/ ▸ **verb** (past and past participle **burned** or **burnt**) [trans.] produce (a compact disc) by copying from an original or master copy.
▸ **noun 1** a hot, painful sensation in the muscles experienced as a result of sustained vigorous exercise: *a home gym means having your phone, CD collection, coffee machine, TV remote, and 2-year-old within arm's reach while you're working up a burn.* [**17 Aug. 1998** *New York Magazine*]
2 BURN RATE.

Cross references in BOLD SMALL CAPITALS

close en•coun•ter /'klōs en'kountər/ ▸ **noun** a putative encounter with a UFO or with aliens: *Taylor said he is now an official MUFON (Mutual UFO Network) investigator and would be interested in speaking to individuals who feel they have experienced a UFO sighting or perhaps a close encounter of some sort.* [**11 Dec. 1996** *Bloomington (Indiana) Herald-Times*]
-PHRASES **close encounter of the first** (or **second,** etc.) **kind** used to describe encounters involving increasing degrees of complexity and apparent exposure of the witness to aliens, with the first kind being a mere sighting and the fourth kind being abduction.

Phrases section, phrases in **bold face**

MAIN ENTRIES AND OTHER BOLDFACE FORMS

Main entries appear in boldface type, as do inflected forms, idioms and phrases, and derivatives. The words PHRASES and DERIVATIVES introduce those elements. Main entries and derivatives of two or more syllables show syllabification with centered dots.

PARTS OF SPEECH

Each new part of speech is introduced by a small right-facing arrow.

SENSES AND SUBSENSES

The main sense of each word follows the part of speech and any grammatical information (e.g., [trans.] before a verb definition). If there are two or more main senses for a word, these are numbered in boldface. Closely related subsenses of each main sense are introduced by a solid black box. In the entry for **adrenalized** above, the main sense of "affected with adrenalin" is followed by a related sense, "excited, charged, or tense."

EXAMPLE SENTENCES AND CITATIONS

Example sentences are shown in italic typeface; certain common expressions appear in bold italic typeface within examples. Attribution of citations is shown in square brackets.

CROSS REFERENCES

Cross references to main entries appear in small capitals. For example, in the entry **burn** seen previously, a cross reference is given in bold small capitals to the entry for BURN RATE.

USAGE NOTES

Usage notes give important extra-linguistic information about a word, its history, and its acceptability.

bar•be•que /'bärbiˌkyōō/ ▶ noun, verb a common misspelling of barbecue.

> USAGE: This common form arises understandably from a confused conflation of the proper spelling *barbecue*, the abbreviation *Bar-B-Q*, and sound-spelling. Its frequency (well over one million hits on web sites) does not quite justify it: in no other English word does *que* attain the status of a standalone, terminal syllable.

Pronunciation Key

This dictionary uses a simple respelling system to show how entries are pronounced, using the following symbols:

a   *as in* **hat** /hat/, **fashion** /'fasHən/, **carry** /'karē/

ā   *as in* **day** /dā/, **rate** /rāt/, **maid** /mād/, **prey** /prā/

ä   *as in* **lot** /lät/, **father** /'fäTHər/, **barnyard** /'bärn,yärd/

b   *as in* **big** /big/

CH   *as in* **church** /CHərCH/, **picture** /'pikCHər/

d   *as in* **dog** /dôg/, **bed** /bed/

e   *as in* **men** /men/, **bet** /bet/, **ferry** /'ferē/

ē   *as in* **feet** /fēt/, **receive** /ri'sēv/

e(ə)r   *as in* **air** /e(ə)r/, **care** /ke(ə)r/

ə   *as in* **about** /ə'bout/, **soda** /'sōdə/, **mother** /'məTHər/, **person** /'pərsən/

f   *as in* **free** /frē/, **graph** /graf/, **tough** /təf/

g   *as in* **get** /get/, **exist** /ig'zist/, **egg** /eg/

h   *as in* **her** /hər/, **behave** /bi'hāv/

i   *as in* **guild** /gild/, **women** /'wimin/

ī   *as in* **time** /tīm/, **fight** /fīt/, **guide** /gīd/

i(ə)r   *as in* **ear** /i(ə)r/, **beer** /bi(ə)r/, **pierce** /pi(ə)rs/

j   *as in* **judge** /jəj/, **carriage** /'karij/

k   *as in* **kettle** /'ketl/, **cut** /kət/

l   *as in* **lap** /lap/, **cellar** /'selər/, **cradle** /'krādl/

m   *as in* **main** /mān/, **dam** /dam/

n   *as in* **honor** /'änər/, **maiden** /'mādn/

NG   *as in* **sing** /siNG/, **anger** /'aNGgər/

ō   *as in* **go** /gō/, **promote** /prə'mōt/

ô   *as in* **law** /lô/, **thought** /THôt/, **lore** / lôr/

oi   *as in* **boy** /boi/, **noisy** /'noizē/

o͝o   *as in* **wood** /wo͝od/, **football** /'fo͝ot,bôl/, **sure** /SHo͝or/

o͞o   *as in* **food** /fo͞od/, **music** /'myo͞ozik/

ou   *as in* **mouse** /mous/, **coward** /'kouərd/

p   *as in* **put** /po͝ot/, **cap** /kap/

r   *as in* **run** /rən/, **fur** /fər/, **spirit** /'spirit/

s   *as in* **sit** /sit/, **lesson** /'lesən/

SH   *as in* **shut** /SHət/, **social** /'sōSHəl/, **action** /'akSHən/

t   *as in* **top** /täp/, **seat** /sēt/, **forty** /'fôrtē/

TH   *as in* **thin** /THin/, **truth** /tro͞oTH/

TH   *as in* **then** /THen/, **father** /'fäTHər/

v   *as in* **never** /'nevər/, **very** /'verē/

w   *as in* **wait** /wāt/, **quick** /kwik/

(h)w *as in* **when** /(h)wen/, **which** /(h)wiCH/

y   *as in* **yet** /yet/, **accuse** /ə'kyo͞oz/

z   *as in* **zipper** /'zipər/, **musician** /myo͞o'ziSHən/

ZH   *as in* **measure** /'meZHər/, **vision** /'viZHən/

FOREIGN SOUNDS

KH   *as in* **Bach** /bäKH/

N   *as in* **en route** /äN 'ro͞ot/, **Rodin** /rō'daN/

œ   *as in* **hors d'oeuvre** /ôr 'dœvrə/, **Goethe** /'gœtə/

Y   *as in* **Lully** /lY'lē/, **Utrecht** /'Y͵treKHt/

STRESS MARKS
Stress marks are placed before the affected syllable. The primary
stress mark is a short, raised vertical line ['] and signifies greater
pronunciation emphasis should be placed on that syllable. The secondary stress mark is a short, lowered vertical line [͵] and signifies a weaker pronunciation emphasis.

ABBREVIATIONS
Abbreviations and acronyms that are headwords in this dictionary
and are not supplied with a pronunciation are read by pronouncing their individual letters.

Aa

AAVE ▶ **abbreviation** Linguistics African-American Vernacular English.

Ab•kha•zi•a /äb'käzēə; ab'kāzH(ē)ə/ an autonomous territory in northwestern Georgia, south of the Caucasus mountains on the Black Sea; pop. 537,500; capital, Sokhumi. In 1992, Abkhazia unilaterally declared itself independent, sparking ongoing armed conflict with Georgia.

A•bra•ham•ic /ˌābrə'hamik/ (also **a•bra•ham•ic**) ▶ **adjective 1** denoting any or all of the religions that revere Abraham, the Biblical patriarch: Judaism, Christianity, and Islam: *this is an argument which carries enormous force, since followers of all three of the monotheistic faiths which grew out of the Abrahamic heritage revere this tradition, both in general and as it applies to Jerusalem.* [1998 *Jusoor*]
2 relating specifically to the prophet and Biblical patriarch Abraham: *several LDS scholars have noted extensive parallels between Facsimile 2 and recently discovered Abrahamic literature.* [2003 *LDS FAQ*]

ac•cess charge /'akses ˌCHärj/ (also **ac•cess fee** /'akses ˌfē/) ▶ **noun** a charge made for the use of computer or local telephone network facilities.

ac•cor•di•on sched•ul•ing /ə'kôrdēən ˌskejōoliNG/ ▶ **noun** the practice of continually adjusting the work schedule of part-time or temporary workers to accommodate a company's changing labor requirements.

ACH ▶ **abbreviation** AUTOMATED CLEARINGHOUSE.

a•cha•ry•a /ə'CHə-rēə/ ▶ **noun** (in India) a Hindu or Buddhist spiritual teacher or leader: *Saint Thomas was approached courteously by Hindu holy men, by brahmins, sadhus and acharyas, who wanted to know who he was and why he was loitering around these parts.* [1991 R. Mistry, *Such a Long Journey*]
■ an influential mentor.
–ORIGIN early 19th cent.: from Sanskrit *ācārya* 'master, teacher.'

ac•id re•flux /'asid 'rēˌfləks/ ▶ **noun** the flow of stomach contents back into the esophagus, usually after a meal.

■ (also **acid reflux disease**) this condition experienced chronically.

ACMOS ▸ noun a system of complementary medicine that combines principles of acupuncture with modern technology and biophysics.
–ORIGIN initialism from *Analysis of the Compatibility of Matter on the Organism and its Synergy.*

a•cous•tic shock /ə'ko͞ostik 'sнäk/ ▸ noun damaged hearing suffered by the user of a listening device as a result of sudden excessive noise.

ac•tion•a•ble /'aksнənəbəl/ ▸ adjective **1** Law giving sufficient reason to take legal action: *an actionable assertion.*
2 able to be done or acted on; having practical value: *insightful and actionable information on the effect advertising is having on your brand.*

ac•tive bar•ri•er /'aktiv 'barēər/ ▸ noun a barrier that allows passage of defined agents while preventing or impeding others, in particular:
■ a security barrier that responds to attempted entries with sensors or personnel. ■ a physical or chemical barrier that intercepts contaminants, debris, or the like.

ac•tive•wear /'aktiv,we(ə)r/ ▸ noun clothing designed for sports, exercise, and outdoor activities: *Lycra, a lightweight stretch yarn, is already a staple in men's activewear.* [5 **Dec. 1991** *Baltimore Sun*]

ac•u•point /'akyo͞o,point/ ▸ noun any of the supposed energy points on the body where needles are inserted during acupuncture or where manual pressure is applied during acupressure.

ad•bot /'ad,bät/ ▸ noun a computer program that caches advertising on personal computers from an Internet-connected server and then displays the advertising when certain linked programs are being used: *click on the startup tab to view all the things that get loaded when you start Windows, and then uncheck anything that looks like the adbot software.*

ad•dy /'adē/ ▸ noun (plural **-dies**) informal an address, especially an e-mail address: *I just sent a note to you and Jemily from my other addy.* [24 **Mar.** 2002 Usenet: alt.med.fibromyalgia]

a•do•bo /ə'dōbō/ ▸ noun (plural **-bos**) a spicy dish or sauce, in particular:

■ a Filipino dish of chicken or pork stewed in vinegar, garlic, soy sauce, bay leaves, and peppercorns. ■ a paste or marinade made from chili peppers, vinegar, herbs, and spices, used in Mexican cooking.
-ORIGIN Spanish, literally 'marinade.'

a•dre•nal•ized /ə'drēnl‚īzd/ ▶ **adjective** affected with adrenalin.
■ informal excited, charged, or tense: *they possess an adrenalized vigor that distinguishes them from other bands.*

ADSL ▶ **abbreviation** asymmetric digital subscriber line, a technology for transmitting digital information over standard telephone lines that allows high-speed transmission of signals from the telephone network to an individual subscriber, but a slower rate of transmission from the subscriber to the network.

a•dult child /ə'dəlt 'CHīld/ ▶ **noun** an adult considered in relation to childhood trauma associated with the parents: [usually plural] *adult children of divorce.*

ad•ult•es•cent /‚adl'tesənt; ə‚dəl-/ ▶ **noun** informal a middle-aged person whose clothes, interests, and activities are typically associated with youth culture: *The implication is that* Maxim *taps the 15-year-old in all men—a readership* Advertising Age *gave the ugly sobriquet "adultescents."* [**Nov.** 2000 *New York Press*]
-ORIGIN 1990s: blend of *adult* and *adolescent.*

ad•vanced place•ment /əd'vanst 'plāsmənt/ (abbreviation: **AP**) ▶ **noun** the placement of a student in a high school course that offers college credit if successfully completed: [as modifier] *advanced placement English and chemistry courses.*

ad•ven•ture /ad'venCHər; əd-/ ▶ **adjective** [attributive only] (of an activity) daring and exciting: *adventure sports.*

ad•ver•game /'advər‚gām/ ▶ **noun** a downloadable or Internet-based computer game that advertises a brand-name product by featuring it as part of the game: *born of desperation and ingenuity, advergames, as they are called by marketers, are emerging at a time when Web surfers largely ignore more conventional forms of advertising.* [**30 Aug.** 2001 *New York Times*]
-DERIVATIVES **ad•ver•gam•ing** noun
-ORIGIN blend of *advertisement* and *game.*

aer•o•med•i•cal /ˌe(ə)rō'medikəl/ ▸ **adjective 1** relating to medical issues associated with air travel.
2 relating to the use of aircraft in the delivery of medical care: *the Black Hawk is the Army's primary helicopter for air assault, air cavalry and aeromedical evacuation units.* [**14 Feb.** 2001 *Washington Post*]

af•fect•ed class /ə'fektid ˌklas/ ▸ **noun** a group adversely affected from a common cause, as defined by legislation, litigation, or prevailing practice: *when Bilott commented Hill was not part of the affected class because he resides in Parkersburg, and no quantifiable C8 levels were found in Parkersburg's drinking water, Albright commented "I'm delighted to hear that."* [**24 Sept.** 2003 *Parkersburg (WV) News*]

af•flu•en•tial /ˌafloō'enCHəl/ informal ▸ **adjective** rich and socially influential: *the daughter of an affluential businessman.*
▸ **noun** a rich and socially influential person: *the local affluentials have driven up property values.*
– ORIGIN 1970s: blend of *affluent* and *influential.*

af•flu•en•za /ˌafloō'enzə/ ▸ **noun** a psychological malaise supposedly affecting young wealthy people, symptoms of which include a lack of motivation, feelings of guilt, and a sense of isolation.
– ORIGIN 1970s: blend of *affluent* and *influenza.*

Af•fri•la•chi•an /ˌafri'lāCH(ē)ən/ ▸ **noun** an African American who is native to or resides in Appalachia: [as modifier] *Affrilachian poets.*

Af•ri•can Eve hy•poth•e•sis /'afrikən 'ēv hīˌpäTHəsis/ ▸ **noun** another term for EVE HYPOTHESIS.

af•ter•care /'aftərˌke(ə)r/ ▸ **noun** childcare for the period between the end of the school day and the end of the parent's working day: [as modifier] *an aftercare facility at the local YMCA.*

a•gent /'ājənt/ ▸ **noun** Computing an independently operating computer program, typically one set up to locate specific information on the Internet and deliver it on a regular basis: *in the future, there will be almost as few humans browsing the Net as there are people using libraries today. Agents will be doing that for most of us.* [**Mar.** 1995 *Wired*]

ag•gra•va•tion /ˌagrə'vāSHən/ ▸ **noun** (in homeopathy) the temporary reappearance or worsening of symptoms that a remedy is intended to eliminate, assumed to be caused by too strong a dose.

ag•gre•ga•tor /ˈagriˌgātər/ ▸ noun Computing an Internet company that collects information about other companies' products and services and distributes it through a single Web site.

a•hi /ˈähē/ ▸ noun the Japanese name for yellowfin tuna.

air•pot /ˈe(ə)rˌpät/ ▸ noun a container for storing and dispensing coffee or other beverages that maintains a constant temperature by use of thermal glass insulation.

a•ji•no•mo•to /ˌäjēnōˈmōtō/ ▸ noun another name for monosodium glutamate, used especially in Asian cooking.
–ORIGIN Japanese, literally 'source of flavor.'

aj•o•wan /ˈajəˌwän/ ▸ noun an annual plant (*Trachyspermum ammi*) of the parsley family, with feathery leaves and white flowers, native to India.
■ the aromatic seeds of the ajowan plant, used as a culinary spice.
■ the essential oil of the ajowan plant.
–ORIGIN from Hindi *ajvāyn*.

Al•ber•ta Clip•per /alˈbərtə ˈklipər/ ▸ noun Meteorology a fast-moving winter weather system originating in the lee of the Canadian Rockies that typically brings snow, high winds, and cold temperatures across the northern U.S.

al•bon•di•gas /ˌälbônˈdēgäs/ ▸ noun small meatballs, prepared in the Mexican, Spanish, or South American way.
–ORIGIN Spanish, from Arabic *al-bunduq*, 'hazel nut.'

ale•cost /ˈälˌkäst/ ▸ noun a wild plant with small daisy-like flowers that has culinary and folk-medicinal uses. (Also called **costmary**).
•*Chrysanthemum balsamita*, family Compositae.

a•li•as•ing /ˈälēəsiNG/ ▸ noun Computing the distortion of a reproduced image so that curved or inclined lines appear inappropriately jagged, caused by the mapping of a number of points to the same pixel.

A-life /ˈā ˌlīf/ ▸ noun short for artificial life (the production or action of computer programs or computerized systems that stimulate the characteristics of living organisms): *Not surprisingly, the mimetic potentials of A-life are finding application in the arts, most notably in the emerging field of interactive art.* [**Sept. 1995** *Scientific American*]

A-list /'ā ˌlist/ (or **B-list** /'bē ˌlist /) ▸ **noun** a real or imaginary list of the most (or, for B-list, second-most) celebrated or sought-after individuals, especially in show business: [as modifier] *an A-list celebrity.*

al-Nak•ba /al 'nakbä/ ▸ **noun** the Arabic term for the events of 1948, when many Palestinians were displaced from their homeland by the creation of the new state of Israel.
‑ORIGIN from Arabic, literally 'the disaster.'

al•pra•zo•lam /al'präzəˌlam/ ▸ **noun** a tranquilizer that is prescribed for anxiety disorders. It has addictive properties and is subject to illicit abuse.

al Qae•da /al 'kīdə; 'kādə/, (also **al-Qa'i•dah, al-Qae•da**) a militant Islamic fundamentalist group. Founded in the late 1980s to combat the Soviets in Afghanistan, its goal is to establish a pan-Islamic caliphate by collaborating with Islamic extremists to overthrow non-Islamic regimes and to expel Westerners and non-Muslims from Muslim countries.
‑ORIGIN Arabic, literally 'the base.'

al-Qods /al kôdz/ ▸ **noun** the Arabic name for Jerusalem: *Israeli Premier Ariel Sharon is returning home Wednesday evening cutting short his visit to India following the twin bombings in Al-Qods.* [**9 Sept.** 2003 *Irib (Iran)*]

alt. (also **alt-**) ▸ **combining form** denoting a version of something that is intended as a challenge to the traditional version: *an alt.classical quartet.*
‑ORIGIN 1990s: abbreviation of *alternative*, influenced by the *alt.* prefix of some Usenet newsgroups.

al•tar call /'ôltər ˌkôl/ ▸ **noun** a summons to the altar at a Christian worship service to those wishing to show their commitment: *I never responded to an altar call, or if my pastor gave an altar call, I didn't think it applied to me.*

al•tar girl /'ôltər ˌgərl/ ▸ **noun** a girl who acts as a priest's assistant during a service, especially in the Roman Catholic Church.

alt.coun•try /'ôlt 'kəntrē/ (also **alt-coun•try**) ▸ **noun** a style of country music that is influenced by alternative rock.

AMBER A•lert /'ambər əˌlərt/ (also **Am•ber A•lert**) ▸ **noun** an emergency response system that disseminates information about a

missing person (usually a child), by media broadcasting or electronic roadway signs: *our state's AMBER Alert became operational
last September.*

■ a public announcement or alert that uses this system: *the
AMBER alert gave a description of the suspected abductor.*
-ORIGIN acronym from America's Missing: Broadcast Emergency
Response, named after Amber Hagerman, a child kidnapped in
Texas in 1996.

am•bu•lo•ce•tus /ˌambyələˈsētəs/ ▸ noun a large carnivorous amphib-
ian (*Ambulocetus natans*, order Cetacea) of the Eocene epoch, an
early ancestor of today's whales.
-ORIGIN 1990s (following the discovery of bones in Pakistan):
modern Latin, from Latin *ambulare* 'to walk' + *cetus* 'whale.'

am-dram /ˈam ˌdram/ ▸ noun mainly British [treated as singular or plural] informal amateur dramatics: *the inherent cheesiness of this scenario is
grotesquely accentuated by the performances, poised somewhere between slapstick and below-average am-dram.* [**10 Oct.** 2003 *Guardian
(UK)*]

amp /amp/ informal ▸ verb (often **amp something up**) **1** play (music)
through electric amplification: *their willingness to amp up traditional
songs virtually began the folk-rock genre.*
2 [as adj.] (**amped** or **amped up**) informal full of nervous energy: *in
one of tomorrow's marquee TV games (ESPN, 6 pm), third-ranked
Ohio State (5-0) visits an amped-up Madison for a date with 4-1 Wisconsin.* [**10 Oct.** 2003 *Seattle Times*]

Am•pa•kine /ˈampəˌkīn/ ▸ noun (trademark) any of a class of synthetic
compounds that facilitate transmission of nerve impulses in the
brain and appear to improve memory and learning capacity.
-ORIGIN 1990s: from *AMPA* (an acronym denoting certain receptors in the brain) + Greek *kinein* 'to move.'

am•scray /ˈamˌskrā/ ▸ verb leave quickly; scram: *just admit your error
and depart or even better, just amscray and be done with it.* [**23 Oct.**
2001 Usenet: comp.os.linux.advocacy]
-ORIGIN Pig Latin.

an•a•bol•ic ste•roid /anəˈbälik ˈsterˌoid; ˈstiər-/ ▸ noun any of various
synthetic derivatives of testosterone, especially those taken as a
dietary supplement to promote muscular development or athletic
performance: *football players or weight-lifters who take super-high*

doses of anabolic steroids—synthetic androgens—in an attempt to build strength and muscle mass. [20 June 1995 *New York Times*]

an•ac•ro•nym /ə'nakrə,nim/ ▶ noun an acronym or initialism whose source is unknown to most people (e.g. *Nicam, scuba*).
–ORIGIN 1980s: from Greek *an-* 'without' + *acronym.*

an•as•tro•zole /an'astrə,zōl/ ▶ noun a nonsteroidal aromatase inhibitor used in the treatment and prevention of breast cancer; it has fewer adverse side effects than tamoxifen.

an•a•tom•i•cal•ly cor•rect /,anə'tämik(ə)lē kə'rekt/ ▶ adjective (of a doll) having the sexual organs plainly represented.

An•drew•sar•chus /,androō'särkəs/ ▶ noun a very large carnivorous mammal (*Andrewsarchus mongoliensis*, order Creodonta) of the Eocene epoch.
–ORIGIN modern Latin: from the name of the U.S. paleontologist Roy Chapman *Andrews* (1884-1960), who led the expedition on which the animal's fossils were found, + Greek *arkhos* 'ruler.'

an•dro•pause /'andrə,pôz/ ▶ noun a collection of symptoms, including fatigue and a decrease in libido, experienced by some middle-aged men and attributed to a gradual decline in testosterone levels.
–DERIVATIVES **an•dro•pau•sal** /,andrə'pôzəl/ adjective
–ORIGIN 1960s: from Greek *andro-* 'man,' on the pattern of *menopause.*

an•dro•stene•di•one /,andrōstēn'dīōn/ ▶ noun an androgenic steroid from which testosterone and certain estrogens are derived in humans.

an•eu•ploid /'anyoō,ploid/ ▶ adjective Genetics having particular genes or chromosomal regions present in extra or fewer copies than in the normal type: *it is now apparent that the majority of aneuploid colon cancer cells missegregate their chromosomes with high frequency, that is they exhibit chromosome instability.* [July 2001 *EMBO Reports*]
–DERIVATIVES **an•eu•ploi•dy** noun

an•gi•o•sta•tin /,anjēō'statn/ ▶ noun Medicine a drug used to inhibit the growth of new blood vessels in malignant tumors.

an•gry white male /'aNGgrē ,(h)wīt 'māl/ ▶ noun derogatory a politically conservative or antiliberal white man.

an•i•mal /'anəməl/ ▸ **adjective** [attrib.] Embryology relating to or denoting the pole or extremity of an embryo that contains the more active cytoplasm in the early stages of development. The opposite of VEG-ETAL.

An•thro•po•cene /'anTHrəpə‚sēn/ ▸ **noun** the current geological age, viewed as having begun about 200 years ago with the significant impact of human activity on the ecosphere: *in this post-human, or as some geologists might call it, post-anthropocene, era, California will again become governed by geologic and climatic processes.* [**Autumn 2003** Trevor Paglin, *Remnants of California*]
-ORIGIN 2000: Reportedly coined by chemist Paul *Crutzen* (1933–) on the pattern of Holocene, Pleistocene, etc.

an•ti•a•li•as•ing /‚antē'ālēəsiNG; ‚antī-/ **noun** ▸ the reduction of jagged edges on diagonal lines in digital images. [often as modifier] *by combining with the antialiasing function, it enables a smooth and high-speed drawing which was not achievable with previous software processing.* [**2 Oct. 2003** *Japan Corporate News*]
-DERIVATIVES **an•ti•a•li•as** verb

an•ti•dote /'anti‚dōt/ ▸ **noun** (in homeopathy) a substance that cancels or opposes the effect of a remedy.
▸ **verb** (**an•ti•dot•ed, an•ti•dot•ing**) [trans.] counteract or cancel with an antidote: *what remedy will antidote Bryonia?*
-DERIVATIVES **an•ti•dot•al** /‚anti'dōtl/ adjective

an•ti•glob•al•i•za•tion /'antē‚glōbələ'zāsHən; ‚antī-/ ▸ **noun** opposition to the agendas and actions of groups perceived to be favoring globalization, such as the IMF, the World Trade Organization, and the G8 countries: [as modifier] *antiglobalization protesters.*

an•ti•re•tro•vi•ral /‚antē‚retrō'vīrəl; ‚antī-/ ▸ **adjective** working against or targeted against retroviruses, especially HIV: *smugglers in Ethiopia are passing off illegally imported concoctions as antiretroviral drugs used to treat people with Aids.* [**7 Oct. 2003** *News24 (South Africa)*]
▸ **noun** an antiretroviral drug: *culturally sensitive interventions aimed at improving access to antiretrovirals among HIV-infected aboriginal persons.* [**10 Oct. 2003** *Vancouver Sun*]

an•ti•roll /‚antē'rōl; ‚antī-/ ▸ **adjective** designed to prevent vehicles from rolling over when turning: *if the track is very bumpy, then antiroll bars are not your best bet.*

an•ti•ter•ror•ism /ˌantē'terə,rizəm; ˌantī-/ ▸ **noun** the prevention or abatement of terrorism: *a meeting of experts on antiterrorism* | [as modifier] *antiterrorism measures.*
–DERIVATIVES **an•ti•ter•ror•ist** adjective

ANWR ▸ **abbreviation** the Arctic National Wildlife Refuge, a wilderness area in Alaska.
■ a Congressional bill that would open up this area to oil exploration and drilling: [as modifier] *to date, ANWR language has not gained enough bipartisan backing to overcome filibuster threats by several senators.* [**6 Aug.** 2003 *Kenai (AK) Peninsula Clarion*]

an•y•time min•ute /'enē,tīm ,minit/ ▸ **noun** (on cellular phones) a minute's worth of conversation charged at a flat rate, rather than according to the time of day: [usually plural] *one low monthly cost and one simple plan with unlimited anytime minutes.* [**13 Oct.** 2003 *PRNewswire (press release)*]

An•y•town /'enē,toun/ ▸ noun (also **Anytown U.S.A.**) a real or fictional place regarded as being typical of American small-town appearance or values: *the party was looking for that elusive candidate from Anytown.*

Ao•ra•ki/Mount Cook /ou'rakē ,mount 'kŏŏk/ **noun** official name (since 1999) for Mount Cook, the highest peak in New Zealand: 12,349 feet (3,764 m).

APEC /'ā,pek/ ▸ **abbreviation** Asia-Pacific Economic Cooperation; a trade group of about 20 Pacific Rim countries, established in 1989.

a•pi•ther•a•py /ˌāpi'THerəpē/ ▸ **noun** the use of products derived from bees as medicine, including venom, honey, pollen, and royal jelly.

ar•a•mid /'arəmid/ ▸ **noun** any of a class of synthetic polymers, related to nylon, that yield fibers of exceptional strength and thermal stability.
–ORIGIN 1970s: from *ar(omatic)* + *(poly)amid(e)*.

ar•chive /'ärkīv/ ▸ **noun** a complete record of the data in part or all of a computer system, stored on an infrequently used medium.
▸ **verb** create an archive of (computer data): [intrans.] *we began archiving in June* | [trans.] *neglecting to archive our files was a costly oversight.*

arc•to•phile /'ärktə,fīl/ ▸ **noun** a person who collects or is very fond of teddy bears.

-DERIVATIVES **arc•to•phil•i•a** /ˌärktə'filēə/ noun; **arc•toph•il•ist** /ärk'täfilist/ noun; **arc•toph•il•y** /-filē/ noun
-ORIGIN 1970s: from Greek *arctos* 'bear' + *philos* 'loving.'

a•re•li•gious /ˌāri'lijəs/ ▸ adjective not influenced by or practicing religion: *liberals are defending the same application to the sexual mores of today's secular and areligious culture.* [**Aug.** 1994 *Wanderer*]

a•re•no•sol /ə'rēnəˌsôl; -ˌsäl/ ▸ noun a soil type consisting mainly of sand with very little organic matter and supporting limited amounts of specialized vegetation.

ar•e•ol•o•gy /ˌe(ə)rē'äləjē/ ▸ noun the study of the planet Mars.
-DERIVATIVES **ar•e•o•log•i•cal** /ˌe(ə)rēə'läjikəl/ adjective; **ar•e•ol•o•gist** noun & adjective
-ORIGIN late 19th cent.: from *Ares* (Greek equivalent of the Roman war god Mars) + *-ology* (denoting a subject of study or interest).

ar•gan oil /'ärgən ˌoil; 'ärˌgan/ ▸ noun an aromatic culinary oil expressed from the seeds of the evergreen argan tree, native to an area of southwestern Morocco.
•The tree is *Argania spinosa*, family Sapotaceae.

arm can•dy /'ärm ˌkandē/ ▸ noun informal a sexually attractive companion accompanying a person, especially a celebrity, at social events: *the athletes and their arm candy clustered around the bar.*

a•ro•ma•tase /ə'rōməˌtās/ ▸ noun an adrenal enzyme that converts androstenedione and estrone to estrogen; inhibiting its action is one approach to breast cancer prevention and treatment.

art car /'ärt ˌkär/ ▸ noun a car or other four-wheel motor vehicle decorated as a work of art: *today's Action Photo is a picture of a military-themed art car made up like a helicopter.* [2003 Wingedanimal.com]

ar•ti•fi•cial climb•ing /ˌärtə'fiSHəl 'klīmiNG/ ▸ noun the sport of climbing on an indoor or outdoor wall whose surface simulates a mountain: *artificial climbing can be done regardless of the weather.*

ar•ti•fi•cial life /ˌärtə'fiSHəl 'līf / ▸ noun see **A-life.**

ash•tang•a /asH'täNGə/ (also **as•tang•a** /as-/) ▸ noun a type of yoga based on eight principles and consisting of a series of poses

executed in swift succession, combined with deep, controlled breathing.
-ORIGIN from Hindi *aṣṭaṇ* or its source, Sanskrit *ashṭaṅga* 'having eight parts,' from *ashtán* 'eight.'

as•i•a•go /ˌäsēˈägō/ ▸ noun a strong-flavored cow's milk cheese made in northern Italy.
-ORIGIN named after *Asiago*, the plateau and town in northern Italy where the cheese was first made.

A•sian long-horned bee•tle /ˈāZHən ˈlôNG ˌhôrnd ˈbētl; ˈläNG/ ▸ noun a large black beetle with white spots whose larvae feed on hardwoods. Infestations in the U.S. have led to large-scale destruction of trees in order to eradicate the pest.
•*Anoplophora glabripennis*, family Cerambycidae.

A•sian swamp eel /ˈāZHən ˈswämp ˌēl/ ▸ noun a freshwater eel that can breathe air and traverse land. Its introduction in the southeastern U.S. threatens some native aquatic fauna.
•*Monopterus albus*, family Synbranchidae.

ask /ask/ ▸ noun [in singular] **1** a request, especially for a donation: *Somebody inside the university will want to make the ask, because it's prestigious, it will make him look good.*
2 the price at which an item, esp. a financial security, is offered for sale: [as modifier] *ask prices for bonds.*

ASP ▸ abbreviation application service provider, a company providing Internet access to software applications that would otherwise have to be installed on individual computers.

ass-back•ward /ˈasˈbakwərd/ (also **ass-back•wards**) informal ▸ adverb in a manner contrary to what is usual, expected, or logical: *I never did like to do anything simple when I could do it ass-backwards.*
▸ adjective contrary to what is usual, expected, or logical: *they are taking an ass-backward approach to crime.*

as•sist•ed liv•ing /əˈsistid ˈliviNG/ ▸ noun housing for the elderly or disabled that provides nursing care, housekeeping, and prepared meals as needed.

A•sta•na /əˈstänə/ a city in Kazakhstan, the capital since 1997; pop. (1990) 281,400. Former name **Akmola**.

as•tang•a /as'täNGə/ ▸ **noun** variant spelling of ASHTANGA.

as•tro•bi•o•lo•gy /ˌastrōbī'äləjē/ ▸ **noun** the science concerned with life in space.

a•sym•met•ri•cal war•fare /ˌāsə'metrikəl 'wôrˌfe(ə)r/ ▸ **noun** warfare involving surprise attacks by small, simply armed groups on a nation armed with modern high-tech weaponry.

@ ▸ **symbol for** 'at', used in e-mail addresses between the user's name and the domain name: *murrayj@oup-usa.org*.

At•kins di•et /'atkinz ˌdī-it/ ▸ **noun** a diet high in protein and fat and low in starch, prescribed for weight loss.
–ORIGIN 1972; after its originator, cardiologist Dr. Robert C. *Atkins* (1930-2003) and his book, *Dr. Atkins' Diet Revolution*.

at-risk /ˌat 'risk/ ▸ **adjective** vulnerable, especially to abuse or deliquency: *a church-run school for troubled youths will stop serving the most at-risk children and instead focus on education.* [4 **Oct.** 2003 *Newsday*]

at sign /'at ˌsīn/ ▸ **noun** the symbol @.

at•tach•ment /ə'taCHmənt/ ▸ **noun** a computer file appended to an e-mail: *the law firm's investigation was expanded a few weeks ago to include whether Stubblefield broke any city policies or copyright laws when he sent an e-mail to city department heads that included an attachment of an MP3 song file.* [13 **Oct.** 2003 *Huntsville (AL) Times*]

au•ric•u•lo•ther•apy /ôˌrikyəlō'THerəpē/ ▸ **noun** a form of acupuncture applied to points on the ear in order to treat other parts of the body.
–ORIGIN 1970s: from Latin *auricula* 'external part of the ear' + *therapy*.

Ausch•witz Lie /'ousHvits 'lī/ (also **Ausch•witz lie**) ▸ **noun** the assertion that the Holocaust did not take place or that the number of deaths is exaggerated: *he was accused of using the Internet to spread the Auschwitz Lie.*
–ORIGIN from *Auschwitz*, a concentration camp in Poland.

Aus•tral•ian pine /ô'strālyən 'pīn/ ▸ **noun** any of various Australian trees of the genus *Casuarina* that have become invasive pests in subtropical areas of the U.S.

auto- 14

auto- ▶ combining form relating to cars: *autocross.*
–ORIGIN abbreviation of *automobile.*

au•to•com•plete /ˌôtōkəm'plēt/ ▶ noun a software function that gives users the option of completing words or forms by a shorthand method on the basis of what has been typed before: *it would allow me to write plug-ins that hook into the editing process so that features like autocomplete, spell-checking, and other niceties could be added.* [16 Sept. 2003 *Microsoft Systems Journal*]
▶ verb [trans.] complete (a word or form) in this way.
–DERIVATIVES **au•to•com•ple•tion** noun /-kəm'plēsʜən/

au•to•dial /'ôtō͵dī(ə)l/ ▶ noun a function of telephonic equipment that allows for automatic dialing of preprogrammed or of randomly selected numbers: *have a telephone with autodial by your bed.* [19 Sept. 2003 *Advertiser (Australia)*]
▶ verb (-dialed, -dial•ing; Brit. -dialled, -dial•ling) [intrans.] automatically dial a telephone number, with or without human prompting: *the first time I discovered it had autodialed and been on-line for over 2 hours.* [4 June 1999 Usenet: alt.windows98]

au•to•dial•er /'ôtō͵dī(ə)lər/ ▶ noun an electronic device that dials telephone numbers randomly or from a list and may also leave messages and request information.

au•to•e•rot•ic as•phyx•i•a /'ôtō-i'rätik as'fiksēə/ ▶ noun asphyxia (suffocation) that results from intentionally strangling oneself while masturbating, in an attempt to heighten sexual pleasure by limiting the oxygen supply to the brain.

au•tog•ra•phy /ô'tägrəfē/ ▶ noun an autobiography: *as playwright Arthur Miller wrote in his splendid autography, "Timebends".* [10 Dec. 1999 Usenet: rec.arts.movies.erotica]

Au•to•mat•ed Clear•ing•house /'ôtə͵mātid 'kli(ə)riNG͵hous/ ▶ noun the clearing and settlement system used by U.S. commercial banks and other institutions.

au•to•pa•thog•ra•phy /ˌôtōpə'тнägrəfē/ ▶ noun an autobiography dealing primarily with the influence of a disease, disability, or psychological disorder on the author's life.
–ORIGIN blend of *autobiography* and *pathography.*

aw•ful•ize /'ôfə͵līz/ ▶ verb to imagine (something) to be as bad as it can possibly be: [intrans.] *I bravely boarded, managed to find a seat,* *stash my overnight bag, and engage in some steady awfulizing.* | [trans.] *one way to make yourself miserable is awfulizing a situation, or imposing impossible standards upon yourself and others.*

AYT ▸ abbreviation Computing informal (in e-mail or chatrooms) are you there?

az•a•role /ˈazəˌrōl/ ▸ noun a small tree related to the hawthorn, cultivated in southern Europe for its small, yellow or reddish fruit. •*Crataegus azarolus*, family Rosaceae.

A•zores High /ˈāzôrz ˈhī/ ▸ noun Meteorology a semipermanent area of high pressure located over the Azores in winter and early spring. Compare with BERMUDA HIGH.

Bb

ba•by•moth•er /'bābē,məᴛʜər/ (or **ba•by•fa•ther** /'bābē,fäᴛʜər/) ▸ **noun** black English the mother (or father) of one or more of one's children: *I knew his babymother, Miss Richards, as we went to school and grew up together.* [**19 Dec. 1999** Usenet: rec.music.reggae]

ba•cha•ta /bä'ᴄʜätä/ ▸ **noun** a style of romantic music originating in the Dominican Republic: *shantytown residents enjoy merengue, but they also have their own music, called* bachata. [**1995** P. Manuel, *Caribbean Currents*]
■ a bachata song.
-ᴏʀɪɢɪɴ Caribbean Spanish, literally 'a party, good time.'

back cat•a•log /'bak ,katl,ôg; -,äg/ (also **back catalogue**) ▸ **noun** all the works previously produced by a recording artist or record company: *Tori Amos has sifted through her Atlantic back catalog to pick the tracks that will comprise her first best-of compilation.* [**26 Sept. 2003** *Billboard*]
■ a similar archived collection of movies or television programs.

back•door sell•ing /'bak,dôr 'selɪɴɢ/ ▸ **noun** the selling by wholesalers directly to the public, seen as detrimental to retailers: [as modifier] *no stranger to supplier backdoor selling tactics, purchasing now has to thwart efforts of some technology suppliers who use electronic communication tools to get around established buying policy.* [**18 June 1998** *Purchasing*]

back•drop /'bak,dräp/ ▸ **verb** (**back•dropped, back•drop•ping**) give a background of: *in the oval at the head of the driveway there is an ornate fountain, and at its center, backdropped with golden spray, a statue of a young girl.* [**1988** N. Christopher *Desperate Characters*]

back•pay /'bak,pā; ,bak'pā/ ▸ **noun** payment for work done in the past that was withheld at the time, usually because of a dispute: *Hickman should be provided backpay plus any expenses and be compensated for any emotional pain, suffering or mental anguish, according to the EEOC lawsuit.* [**1 Oct. 2003** *Kansas City Star*]
ᴜꜱᴀɢᴇ: Though still somewhat more frequent as an open compound that most dictionaries have not defined, *backpay* is now gaining considerable ground as a solid compound, with an attendant shift in stress to the first syllable.

back•stab•bing /'bak,stabiNG/ ▸ **noun** the action or practice of criticizing someone in a treacherous manner while feigning friendship: *its rejection, by stubborn short-sightedness and conspiratorial backstabbing, is a triumph for petty-mindedness.* [14 **Mar.** 1996 *Independent (UK)*]
▸ **adjective** (of a person) behaving in such a way.
-DERIVATIVES **back•stab** verb; **back•stab•ber** noun

back•sto•ry /'bak,stôrē/ ▸ **noun** (plural **back•sto•ries**) a history or background created for a fictional character in a film or television program: *Oscar's giant self-narrated backstory, as queasy in its sexual rollings and pitchings as the voyage on which he's telling it.* [Jan. 1994 *Film Comments*]
■ similar background information about a real person or thing that promotes fuller understanding of it: *the little-known backstory about evolution is that the theory arose in the 19th century out of an emphasis on the world's failings.* [18 **Sept.** 2003 *World Magazine*]

bac•te•rize /'baktə,rīz/ ▸ **verb** [trans.] (**be bacterized**) treat with bacteria: [as adjective] *plots sowed with seeds bacterized with Pseudomonas from both locations had a higher percentage of healthy plants (81%) than those sowed with non-bacterized seeds.* [2003 (scientific paper from Auburn University Web site)]
-DERIVATIVES **bac•te•ri•za•tion** /,baktərə'zāsHən/ noun

bag /bag/ ▸ **verb** (**bagged, bag•ging**) [trans.] informal fit (a patient) with an oxygen mask or other respiratory aid: *"Bag him," cries out the first attendant. The patient is put on oxygen.* [Jan. 1995 *Hospital News (Canada)*]

ba•guette /ba'get/ ▸ **noun** a slim, rectangular handbag: *Fendi has revived its accessories business with a series of small shoulder bags— "Baguettes"—which cost, on average, $1,500 apiece.* [14 **Nov.** 1999 *New York Times Magazine*]

bail /bāl/ ▸ **verb** [intrans.] informal abandon a commitment, obligation, or responsibility: *naturally, after 12 years of this (grade school plus high school), including Sunday Mass with the family (always a fraught event), I bailed.* [**Apr.** 2000 *New York Press*]
■ (**bail on**) let (someone) down by failing to fulfill a commitment, obligation, or responsibility: *he looks a little like the guy who bailed on me.*

Baka /'bäkə/ ▸ noun (plural same) 1 a member of a nomadic Pygmy people inhabiting the rain forests of southeastern Cameroon and northern Gabon.
2 the Bantu language of the Baka.
-ORIGIN the name in Baka.

bald•head /'bôld,hed/ ▸ noun (among Rastafarians) a person who is not a Rastafarian.

bal•lo•tin /'balətin/ ▸ noun a decorative cardboard box, slightly larger at the top and with broad flaps, in which chocolates are sold: *famed for its gold ballotin boxes, Godiva sells more than 200 different chocolate pieces, featuring fillings like Turkish filbert butter, cashew mousse, mandarin orange, and crème fraiche.* [**May 1994** *Hispanic*]
-ORIGIN French, from *ballot* 'a small package of goods.'

bal•sam ap•ple /'bôlsəm 'apəl/ ▸ noun another name for BITTER GOURD.

bam•my /'bamē/ (also **bam•mie**) ▸ noun (plural **bam•my or bam•mies**) (in the West Indies) a flat roll or pancake made from cassava flour: *Jassette Lyle shows-off her homestyle steamed fish served with bammy, okra, string beans and tomatoes.* [**13 Sept. 2003** *Jamaica Observer*]
-ORIGIN probably from a West African language.

ban•deau /ban'dō/ ▸ noun (plural **ban•deaux** /-'dōz/) a woman's strapless top formed from a band of fabric fitting around the bust: [as modifier] *a bandeau bikini top.*

ban•do•bast /'bandə,bast/ ▸ noun variant spelling of BUNDOBUST.

Ban•ja Lu•ka /'banjə 'lookə/ a town in northern Bosnia–Herzegovina; pop. 195,000 (1991).

ban•ner /'banər/ (also **ban•ner ad** /'banər ,ad/) ▸ noun an advertisement appearing across the top of a web page: *to get a new banner now, click Step 1.* | [as modifier] *advertise and promote your site on thousands of web sites all around the world for free utilizing our award winning banner exchange engine and free web tools!*

bar•be•que /'bärbi,kyoo/ ▸ noun, verb a common misspelling of barbecue.
USAGE: This common form arises understandably from a confused conflation of the proper spelling *barbecue*, the abbreviation *Bar-B-Q*, and sound-spelling. Its frequency (well over one million hits on web sites) does not quite justify it: in no other English word does *que* attain the status of a standalone, terminal syllable.

Bar•ca•Loung•er /'bärkə,lounjər/ ▸ **noun** trademark a type of deeply padded reclining chair: *national resolve fares badly when the fighting is far away and most of the people are mere spectators, watching from the BarcaLounger.* [3 **Sept.** 1990 *Time*]
-ORIGIN 1970s: from the name of Edward J. *Barcolo*, who acquired the original license to manufacture the chairs, and *lounger.*

bar•do /'bär,dō/ ▸ **noun** (in Tibetan Buddhism) a state of existence between death and rebirth, varying in length according to a person's conduct in life and manner of, or age at, death.
▪ an indeterminate, transitional state: *she is wandering adrift in a bardo of intense negativity, blame, disappointment, criticism and denial.* [31 **Mar.** 1993 *Santa Fe Reporter*]
-ORIGIN Tibetan *bár-do*, from *bar* 'interval' + *do* 'two.'

bare•back•ing /'be(ə)r,bakiNG/ ▸ **noun** vulgar slang the practice of having anal intercourse without a condom: *when he sought other HIV-positive partners online to engage in barebacking, gay chatmeisters pounced.* [**Aug.** 2001 *Out*]

barf bag /'bärf ,bag/ ▸ **noun** a bag provided for airplane passengers for use in case of vomiting associated with motion sickness.

bar•i•a•trics /,barē'atriks/ ▸ **noun** the branch of medicine that deals with the study and treatment of obesity.
-DERIVATIVES **bar•i•a•tric** adjective
-ORIGIN 1960s: Greek *baros*, 'weight'+ *iatric.*

bar•i•at•ric sur•ger•y /'barē'atrik 'sərjərē/ ▸ **noun** surgical removal of parts of the stomach and small intestines to induce weight loss.

ba•ri•sta /bə'rēstə/ ▸ **noun** a person who serves in a coffee bar: *ask what a particular brew tastes like, and your well-trained* barista *may begin gushing such adjectives as* carbony, malty, caramelly, rounded, spicy, *and* harmonious. [**June** 1994 *Minnesota Monthly*]
-ORIGIN 1980s: Italian, 'barman.'

bark•i•tec•ture /'bärki,tekCHər/ ▸ **noun** humorous the art or practice of designing and constructing doghouses.▪ the style in which a doghouse is designed or constructed: *the property also included an elaborate doghouse that was a stunning example of pampered pooch barkitecture.*
-ORIGIN 1990s: fanciful blend of *bark* and *architecture.*

Bar•num ef•fect /'bärnəm i,fekt/ ▸ **noun** Psychology the tendency to accept certain information as true, such as character assessments or

horoscopes, even when the information is so vague as to be worthless.
-ORIGIN named after P. T. Barnum (1810–91), U.S. showman renowned for his promotion of sideshow oddities; the word *Barnum* was in use from the mid 19th cent. as a noun in the sense 'nonsense, humbug.'

bar•rique /bə'rēk/, French ▸ noun a wine barrel, especially a small one made of new oak in which Bordeaux and other wines are aged: *the most obvious difference between old and new school is the use of barriques, a bone of contention that has been chewed over since new French barriques of 225 litres were introduced by Gaja in 1969.* [**May 1993** *Wine (UK)*]
-ORIGIN late 18th cent.: French.

-bash•er /-ˌbasHər/ ▸ combining form forming nouns denoting a person who harshly criticizes, debunks, or commits violence against the named party: *Jerry Hough, a Duke university professor and a leading Kremlinologist at the Brookings Institution, is both an artful theorizer and a passionate theory basher.* [**10 April 1988** *Washington Post*] *John H. Fund argues that Republican presidential candidate Patrick Buchanan is indeed a trade-basher, and his trade policies are ineffective and narrow-minded in a global economy.* [**3 March 1992** *Wall Street Journal*]

ba•shert /bä'sHert/ ▸ noun (in Jewish use) a person's soulmate, especially when considered as an ideal or predestined marriage partner: *I am a 24 yr teacher in florida who is looking for her bashert.* [**26 June 1995** Usenet: alt.personals.jewish]
-ORIGIN Yiddish, 'fate, destiny.'

bas•i•lo•sau•rus /ˌbasələ'sôrəs/ ▸ noun a large marine cetacean (*Basilosaurus isis*) of the Eocene epoch, having a long, slender body and vestigial fore and hind limbs. Fossils were discovered in the early 1990s.
-ORIGIN modern Latin, from Greek *basileus* + *sauros* 'lizard.'

bas•ket bin•go /'baskit ˌbiNGgō/ ▸ noun a fund-raising event in which players buy tickets to play bingo for prizes of gift baskets that are made up by donors.

bas•ket-weav•ing /'baskit ˌwēviNG/ ▸ noun humorous a college course that is thought to be very easy or that imparts mainly useless knowledge.

bass-ack•wards /'bas 'akwərdz/ ▸ **adverb** & **adjective** jocular a politer form of ass-backwards.

bat•tered child syn•drome /'batərd 'CHīld ˌsindrōm/ ▸ **noun** the set of symptoms, injuries, and signs of mistreatment seen on a severely or repeatedly abused child.

bat•tered wom•an syn•drome /'batərd 'wo͞omən ˌsindrōm/ ▸ **noun** the set of symptoms, injuries, and signs of mistreatment seen in a woman who has been repeatedly abused by a husband or other male figure.

bat•ter•ing par•ent syn•drome /'batəriNG 'pe(ə)rənt ˌsindrōm; 'par-/ ▸ **noun** the set of symptoms and signs indicating a psychological disorder in a parent or child-care provider resulting in a tendency toward repeated abuse of a child.

bat•tler /'batlər; 'batl-ər/ ▸ **noun** a person who refuses to admit defeat in the face of difficulty: *His job on the line, a new Gray Davis is emerging: A trash talking battler taking swings at opponents, rallying friends, and daring the Terminator to a showdown debate.* [27 **Sept.** 2003 *AP*]

USAGE: *Battler* is long and firmly established in Antipodean English and summarizes a national character trait for many Australians; it is increasingly common now both in British and American English.

ba•zil•lion /bə'zilyən/ ▸ **cardinal number** informal a very large exaggerated number: *you were going a bazillion miles per hour!*
-ORIGIN 1980s: probably a blend of *billion* and *gazillion* (also a large exaggerated number).

b-ball /'bē ˌbôl/ ▸ **noun** informal basketball.
-ORIGIN 1980s: contraction.

BBIN ▸ **abbreviation** Bangladesh, Bhutan, India, and Nepal, considered as a group with regard to development, public health, and economic issues.

beard /bi(ə)rd/ ▸ **noun** informal a person who carries out a transaction, typically a bet, for someone else in order to conceal the other's identity.
■ a person who pretends to have a romantic or sexual relationship with someone else in order to conceal the other's true sexual orientation: *here was his dear Hans Zoroaster, surrounded by seven*

of his beauties, and here was his old friend and beard, Adriana la Chaise. [1977 Larry Kramer, *Faggots*]

beat•er /'bētər/ ▸ noun informal a dilapidated but serviceable car: *if you provide the kids with a car, give them an old beater.*

Bea•tle /'bētl/ adjective characteristic of the Beatles: *a Beatle jacket.*

bed-block•ing /'bed ˌbläkiNG/ ▸ noun British the long-term occupation of hospital beds, chiefly by the elderly, due to a shortage of suitable care elsewhere: [as modifier] *doctors fear the problem will lead to a bed-blocking crisis in Birmingham as elderly flu victims take up hospital spaces.* [29 Sept. 2003 icBirmingham.co.uk]

beef /bēf/ ▸ noun informal a criminal charge: *I don't have any sympathy for anyone on a third time drunk driving beef.* [9 June 2003 Usenet: alt.prisons]

Bee•mer /'bēmər/ (also **Bea•mer**) ▸ noun informal a car or motorcycle manufactured by the company BMW.
–ORIGIN 1980s (originally U.S.): representing a pronunciation of the first two letters of *BMW* (Bayerische Motoren Werke AG) + *-er.*

Beige Book /'bāzH ˌbook/ ▸ noun a summary and analysis of economic activity and conditions, prepared with the aid of reports from the district Federal Reserve Banks and issued by the central bank of the Federal Reserve for its policy makers before a Federal Open Market Committee meeting.

beit din /'bāt 'din/ ▸ noun a rabbinical court that decides questions on the basis of Talmudic law: *would a beit din close Napster down?*

Bel•fast sink /'belˌfast 'siNGk/ ▸ noun British a deep rectangular kitchen sink with a drain at one end, traditionally made of glazed white porcelain.

Bel•li•ni /bə'lēnē/ ▸ noun (plural **Bel•li•nis**) a cocktail consisting of peach juice mixed with champagne.
–ORIGIN from the name of Venetian painter Giovanni *Bellini* (*c.* 1430–1516): the cocktail is said to have been invented in Venice during a major exhibition of the artist's work in 1948.

Belt•way ban•dit /'beltˌwā ˌbandit/ ▸ noun informal a company that does a large percentage of its business by winning lucrative federal government contracts.

-ORIGIN with reference to Interstate 495 encircling Washington DC and popularly called the *Beltway*.

ben•e•fi•cials /ˌbenəˈfiSHəlz/ ▸ plural noun insects that are a boon to gardeners: *this long-blooming perennial produces bright yellow 2-inch daisies that are highly attractive to five key kinds of beneficials (ladybugs, lacewings, hover flies, tachinid flies, and miniwasps)*. [**May 2001** *Organic Gardening*]

beng•a /ˈbeNGgə/ ▸ noun a style of African popular music originating in Kenya, characterized by a fusion of traditional Kenyan music and a lively arrangement of guitars, bass, and vocals.
-ORIGIN 1980s: from Luo (a Kenyan language).

ben•to /ˈbentō/ ▸ noun (plural **ben•tos**) a lacquered or decorated wooden Japanese lunchbox.
■ a Japanese-style packed lunch, consisting of such items as rice, vegetables, and sashimi (raw fish with condiments).
-ORIGIN Japanese.

Ber•mu•da High /bərˈmyōōdə ˈhī/ ▸ noun Meteorology a semipermanent area of high pressure located over Bermuda in summer and fall that steers many storm systems westward across the Atlantic. Compare with **AZORES HIGH**

best-of /ˈbest ˌəv; əv/ ▸ noun a list or collection comprising the best examples of something: *Mariani is arguably the most influential food-wine critic in the popular press. Since 1988, foodies have flocked like sheep to his best-ofs.* [**28 Sept. 2003** *Philadelphia Inquirer*]
▸adjective denoting such a collection or list: *Crenshaw's 1982 album made most critics' best-of lists.* [**19 Dec. 1994** *Denver Post*]

be•suit•ed /biˈsōōtid/ ▸ adjective (of a person, especially a man) wearing a suit: *Ted Kennedy had become the personification of Bloated Washington, heaving his besuited bulk from stump to stump.* [**24 Oct. 1994** *New Yorker*]

be•ta-ad•ren•er•gic /ˈbātə ˌadrəˈnərjik/ ▸ adjective of, relating to, or being a beta receptor (stimulation of which results in increased cardiac activity): *observing the effects of beta-adrenergic stimulation in aging rats.*

BEV ▸ abbreviation Linguistics black English vernacular, any of various nonstandard forms of English spoken by black people.

BGH ▸ abbreviation bovine growth hormone.

bhik•khu /ˈbikoͦo/ ▸ noun a Theravada Buddhist monk: *the Blessed One was once living at Gayaslsa in Gaya with a thousand bhikkhus.* [(**undated**) *the Fire Sermon*]
–ORIGIN Pali.

bhik•khu•ni /biˈkoͦoneͤ/ ▸ noun a member of the now extinct order of Theravada Buddhist nuns.
–ORIGIN Pali.

bhu•na /ˈboͦonə/ (also **bhoo•na**) ▸ noun a medium-hot, dry curry originating in Bengal, prepared typically by frying meat with spices at a high temperature: *lamb bhuna.*
–ORIGIN 1950s: from Bengali, Urdu *bhunnā* 'to be fried,' ultimately from Sanskrit *bhrajj* 'to fry, parch, roast.'

bib•li•cist /ˈbibləsist/ ▸ noun mainly British a person who interprets the Bible literally: [as modifier] *this contempt owes little to Leviticus or Romans; yet biblicist attitudes within the Church of England give it respectability.* [**30 Sept. 1994** *Church Times (UK)*]
–ORIGIN mid 19th cent.: from *biblic(al)* + *-ist.*

USAGE: This term has very limited circulation in American English as a substitute for "biblical scholar." It would probably come under fire as politically incorrect if used to denote Christian fundamentalists, who are generally designated as such or as *evangelicals.*

bi•coast•al /bīˈkoͦstl/ ▸ adjective living on, taking place in, or involving both the Atlantic and Pacific coasts of the U.S.: *a bicoastal businessman.*
–DERIVATIVES **bi•coast•a•lite** /bīˈkoͦstlˌīt/ noun

bid cal•ler /ˈbid ˌkôlər/ ▸ noun one who announces the bids and recognizes bidders at an auction: *an auction company shall include the name and license number of each auctioneer who will act as a bid caller in an auction.* [**2003** *bill of the Texas legislature*]

big air /ˈbig ˈe(ə)r/ ▸ noun a high jump in sports such as skateboarding, snowboarding, and BMX: *a well-shaped hit will let you get big air over a long distance, with very little jolting on the transition once you hit the landing* [**1 Nov. 1997** Usenet: rec.skiing.snowboard]

big crunch /ˈbig ˈkrənCH/ ▸ noun Astronomy a contraction of the universe to a state of extremely high density and temperature, hypothesized as a possible scenario for its demise.

big hit•ter /'big 'hitər/ ▸ **noun** another term for HEAVY HITTER.

big•o•rex•i•a /ˌbigə'reksēə/ ▸ **noun** informal another term for MUSCLE DYS-MORPHIA.
-DERIVATIVES **big•o•rex•ic** adjective & noun
-ORIGIN *big* + Greek *orexis* 'appetite,' on the pattern of *anorexia*.

Big Rip /'big 'rip/ ▸ **noun** a theory about the end of the universe holding that the accelerating forces driving its expansion will eventually rend all currently organized matter.
-ORIGIN early 21st cent.: on the pattern of *Big Bang.*

big tent /'big 'tent/ ▸ **noun** used in reference to a political party's policy of permitting or encouraging a broad spectrum of views among its members: *the struggle to change Wyoming takes place inside the Republican Party and its "big tent."* [**6 July 1998** *High Country News*]

bio- /'bīō/ ▸ **combining form** relating to or involving the use of toxic biological or biochemical substances as weapons of war: *bioterrorism.*

bi•o•a•cou•stics /ˌbīōə'kōōstiks/ ▸ **plural noun** [treated as singular] the branch of acoustics concerned with sounds produced by or affecting living organisms, especially as relating to communication.

bi•o•as•tro•naut•ics /ˌbīōˌastrə'nôtiks/ ▸ **noun** the study of the effects of space flight on living organisms.

bi•o•cli•ma•tol•o•gy /ˌbīōˌklīmə'täləjē/ ▸ **noun** the study of climate in relation to living organisms and especially to human health.
-DERIVATIVES **bi•o•cli•mat•o•log•i•cal** /-ˌklīmətl'äjikəl/ **adjective**

bi•o•com•put•ing /ˌbīōkəm'pyōōtiNG/ ▸ **noun** the design and construction of computers using biochemical components: *while biocomputing includes ways to do rudimentary computing with DNA itself, scientists have begun looking at ways to do computations in whole cells by engineering part of the cells' DNA and the machinery controlled by those genes.* [**1 June 2000** *New York Times*]
■ an approach to programming that seeks to emulate or model biological processes. ■ computing in a biological context or environment.

bi•o•con•ver•sion /ˌbīōkən'vərzHən/ ▸ **noun** the conversion of organic matter, such as animal or plant waste, into a source of energy through the action of microorganisms.

bi•o•die•sel /ˌbīō'dēzəl; -səl/ (also **bi•o•die•sel fuel** /ˌfyōōəl/) ▸ noun a synthetic fuel produced from oilseed rape (canola) or other animal or vegetable oils: *the state is studying whether it's feasible to heat some state buildings with biodiesel fuel.* [**18 Sept.** 2003 *Press Herald (ME)*]

bi•o•e•lec•tron•ics /ˌbīōilek'träniks; -ˌēlek-/ ▸ noun **1** the study and application of electronics in medicine and biological processes. **2** the integration of biological principles in electronic technology: *I anticipate that the major near-term impact of bioelectronics on computer hardware will be in the area of volumetric memory.* [**Mar.** 1995 *Scientific American*]
-DERIVATIVES **bi•o•e•lec•tron•ic** adjective; **bi•o•e•lec•tron•i•cal•ly,** adverb

bi•o•film /'bīōˌfilm/ ▸ noun **1** a thin but robust layer of mucilage adhering to a solid surface and containing a community of bacteria and other microorganisms: *one tap water study showed* Legionella *could survive over a year inside pipe biofilms, emerging in wholly infectious form once the faucet was turned on full force.* [1995 L. Garrett, *The Coming Plague*]
2 a biopic: *Scorsese—currently in Montreal filming "The Aviator," a biofilm about the Hollywood years of Howard Hughes—will direct an "American Masters" profile on Bob Dylan.* [**28 Sept.** 2003 *Washington Post*]

bi•o•in•di•ca•tor /ˌbīō'indiˌkātər/ ▸ noun an organism whose status in an ecosystem is analyzed as an indication of the ecosystem's heath: *spruce, which is the main tree species in Austria, was used as bioindicator.* [2003 Austrian Federal Forest Research Centre Web site]
-DERIVATIVES **bi•o•in•di•ca•tion** /-ˌindi'kāSHən/ noun

bi•o•in•for•mat•ics /ˌbīōˌinfər'matiks/ ▸ plural noun [treated as singular] the science of collecting and analyzing complex biological data such as genetic codes.
-DERIVATIVES **bi•o•in•for•mat•ic** adjective

bi•o•log•i•cal /ˌbīə'läjikəl/ ▸ noun a therapeutic substance, such as a vaccine or drug, derived from biological sources: [usu. plural] *Starrate is an international biotechnology company with interests in Biologicals, Agriculture, and Pharmaceutical products.*

bi•o•ma•ter•i•al /ˌbīōmə'ti(ə)rēəl/ ▸ noun synthetic or natural material suitable for use in constructing artificial organs and prostheses or to replace bone or tissue: *biomaterials to repair or replace dam-*

aged human tissue and body parts. [17 **Sept.** 2003 *Portland Business Journal*]

bi•o•me•te•o•rol•o•gy /ˌbīōˌmētēəˈräləjē/ ▸ **noun** the study of the relationship between living organisms and weather.

bi•o•met•ric read•er /ˈbīəˈmetrik ˈrēdər/ ▸ **noun** an electronic device that determines identity by detecting and matching physical characteristics.

bi•o•met•rics /ˌbīəˈmetriks/ ▸ **plural noun** [treated as singular] the science and methodology of identifying people by means of unique biological characteristics. Such biological markers include facial features, fingerprints, and voice.
-DERIVATIVES **bi•o•met•ric adjective**

bi•o•met•ric sig•na•ture /ˈbīəˈmetrik ˈsignəCHər; -ˌCHo͞or/ ▸ **noun** the unique pattern of a bodily feature such as the retina, iris, or voice, encoded on an identity card and used for recognition and identification purposes.

bi•o•pi•ra•cy /ˌbīōˈpīrəsē/ ▸ **noun** the practice of commercially exploiting naturally occurring biochemical or genetic material, especially by obtaining patents that restrict its future use, while failing to pay fair compensation to the community from which it originates: *three multinational companies are being accused of "biopiracy" after taking out patents covering uses of three plants commonly used for herbal medicine treatments in India.* [8 **May 1998** *Independent*]
-DERIVATIVES **bi•o•pi•rate noun**

bi•o•sat•el•lite /ˌbīōˈsatlˌīt/ ▸ **noun** an artificial satellite that serves as an automated laboratory, conducting biological experiments on living organisms.

bi•o•sur•ge•ry /ˌbīōˈsərjərē/ ▸ **noun** the medical use of maggots to clean infected wounds, especially in cases where a patient is resistant to conventional antibiotic treatment: *Perhaps the latest term designed to lessen the gag factor—biosurgery—will finally do the trick and give medicinal maggots their long overdue makeover.* [**June 1999** *Scientific American*]

bi•o•tech /ˈbīōˌtek/ ▸ **noun** of, related to, or created by biotechnology. ▸ **adjective** genetically modified: *biotech corn.*
-ORIGIN shortened form of *biotechnology.*

bi•o•te•lem•e•try /ˌbīōtəˈlemitrē/ ▸ **noun** the detection or measurement of human or animal physiological functions from a distance using a telemeter: *a review of underwater biotelemetry, with emphasis on ultrasonic techniques.*
-DERIVATIVES **bi•o•tel•e•me•tric** /ˌbīōˌteləˈmetrik/ **adjective**

bi•o•ter•ror•ism /ˌbīōˈterəˌrizəm/ ▸ **noun** the use of infectious agents or other harmful biological or biochemical substances as weapons of terrorism: *to engage in bioterrorism requires only a sophisticated understanding of the properties of various edible plants, medicinal herbs, toxins and venoms, and infectious and pharmaceutical agents.* [**May 1991** *Atlantic Monthly*]
-DERIVATIVES **bi•o•ter•ror•ist** noun

bi•o•ther•a•py /ˌbīōˈTHerəpē/ ▸ **noun** (plural **bi•o•ther•a•pies**) the treatment of disease using substances obtained or derived from living organisms.

bi•o•war•fare /ˌbīōˈwôrfe(ə)r/ ▸ **noun** biological warfare; the use of toxins of biological origin or microorganisms as weapons of war.

bi•o•weap•on /ˈbīōˌwepən/ ▸ **noun** a biological weapon: *Questions of Security: Fears Mount on Smallpox as Bioweapon* [**19 Oct.** 2001 *Wall Street Journal (headline)*]

Bir•ken•stock /ˈbərkənˌstäk/ ▸ **noun** trademark a type of shoe or sandal with a contoured cork-filled sole and a thick leather upper.
■ [as modifier] denoting people concerned with political correctness or conservationist issues: *home builders are no longer content to leave environmentalism to the Birkenstock crowd.*
-ORIGIN 1970s: from the name of the manufacturer.

birth•date /ˈbərTHˌdāt/ ▸ **noun 1** date of birth: *her baptismal record puts her birthdate as 26 Apr 1741.*
2 the anniversary of a date of birth, especially for someone dead: *the communists' symbolic vote to clear the name of Stalin—who ordered the deaths of millions of people—came six days after Stalin's birthdate.* [**29 Dec.** 2000 *Baltimore Sun*]

birth•ing cen•ter /ˈbərTHiNG ˌsentər/ ▸ **noun** a medical facility specializing in childbirth that is less restrictive and more homelike than a hospital: *lavish maternity wards were designed not only to compete with "birthing centers" staffed by nurse-midwives and located outside hospitals, but also to generate business for other hospital departments.* [**7 July** 2002 *Philadelphia Inquirer*]

birth•ing room /'bərTHiNG ˌrōōm; ˌrōōm/ ▸ noun a room in a hospital or other medical facility that is equipped for labor and childbirth and is designed to be comfortable and homelike.

bitch-slap /'biCH ˌslap/ ▸ verb (**bitch-slapped, bitch-slap•ping**) slang deliver a stinging blow to (someone), typically in order to humiliate them: *we all know how the full court ruled. It bitch-slapped Clinton and his DOJ because it has grown weary of the constant delays and stonewalling.* [**17 July 1998** Usenet: alt.current-events.clinton.whitewater]
-ORIGIN 1990s: originally black English, referring to a woman hitting or haranguing her male partner.

bit•ter gourd /'bitər 'gôrd; 'gōōrd/ ▸ noun the warty, green-colored, unripe fruit of an annual tropical vine, used in Asian cooking. •*Momordica Charantia,* family Cucurbitaceae.
USAGE: The fruit of this vine is also called *karela* in Indian cooking, and *balsam apple* in nonculinary contexts.

bi•zar•ro /bi'zärō/ ▸ adjective informal bizarre: *a whacked out frontman for a bizarro fringe rock n' roll band beats the businessmen at their own game!* [**1994** *Hypno*]

black bot•tom pie /'blak ˌbätəm 'pī/ ▸ noun pie with a bottom layer of chocolate cream or custard and a contrasting top layer, usually of whipped cream.

blad•dered /'bladərd/ ▸ adjective British informal extremely drunk: *I got so bladdered I don't actually remember much about my 18th birthday.* [**21 Apr. 2003** Usenet: rec.arts.tv.uk.eastenders]

blade /blād/ ▸ verb informal skate using in-line skates: *he walks like Jack Hooker, his shoulders rolling slightly, his arms moving with the smooth swivel of his hips, his body blading through air as he crosses the parking lot of the motel.* [**Nov. 1997** *Esquire*]
-DERIVATIVES **blad•er** noun
-ORIGIN shortened form of the verb *rollerblade,* from the generic use of the trademark *Rollerblades.*

blame•storm•ing /'blāmˌstôrmiNG/ ▸ noun group discussion regarding the assigning of responsibility for a failure or mistake.
-ORIGIN 1990s: on the pattern of *brainstorming.*

bleed•ing edge /'blēdiNG 'ej/ ▸ noun the very forefront of technological development: *an architecture that many people believe is still too*

bleeding edge for large mission-critical systems. [**9 Sept. 1993** *Computer Weekly (UK)*]
-ORIGIN 1980s: on the pattern of *leading edge, cutting edge.*

bling-bling /'bliNG ˌbliNG/ ▸ **noun** informal expensive, ostentatious clothing and jewelry, or the wearing of them: *behind the bling-bling: are diamonds worth it?*
-ORIGIN 1990s: perhaps imitative of light reflecting off jewelry, or of jewelry clashing together.

blip•vert /'blipˌvərt/ ▸ **noun** a television commercial of a few seconds' duration.
-ORIGIN from *blip* + *(ad)vert(isement)*.

B-list /'bē ˌlist/ ▸ **noun** see **A-list.**

blis•ter a•gent /'blistər ˌājənt/ ▸ **noun** a chemical weapon that burns and blisters the skin or other tissues: *another 29,000 tons of nerve and blister agents are stored at eight other locations around the United States.* [**24 Apr. 1996** *City Paper (Baltimore)*]

bloat•ware /'blōtˌwe(ə)r/ ▸ **noun** software that requires an amount of disk storage space that is grossly incommensurate with its utility: *none of the programs on this page is bloatware, so they can be downloaded fairly quickly.*

BLOB /bläb/ ▸ **noun** Computing binary large object; a stored block of data without referents to the database management system except size and location
-ORIGIN acronym.

blog /bläg/ ▸ **noun** a weblog: *most blogs are run by twentysomething Americans with at least an unhealthy interest in computers—a bias that is still reflected in the content of most sites.* [**5 Oct. 2000** *Guardian (UK)*]
▸ **verb** [noun] (**blogged, blog•ging**) add new material to or regularly update a weblog.
-DERIVATIVES **blog•ger noun**

blog•o•sphere /'blägəˌsfi(ə)r/ ▸ **noun** the world of weblogs: *the blog's dullness was inspired—if that is the correct word—by Mr. Walker's careful study of the blogosphere.* [**15 May 2003** *New York Times*]

blonde mo•ment /'bländ 'mōmənt/ ▸ **noun** humorous an instance of being silly or scatterbrained.

-ORIGIN late 20th cent.: from the stereotypical perception of blonde-haired women as unintelligent.

blood film /'bləd ˌfilm/ ▸ **noun** a specimen of blood on a glass slide, used for microscopic investigation of possible abnormalities or pathogens: *these values alone are insufficient to tell whether the anemia is regenerative or non-regenerative; evaluation of the blood film is crucial.* [**Oct. 1999** *Lab Animal*]

blue dog Dem•o•crat /'blo͞o ˌdôg 'demaˌkrat/ (also **Blue Dog Dem• o•crat**) ▸ noun a Democrat from a Southern state who has a conservative voting record: *he said it would take a remarkable offer to get him to consider giving up a congressional career that has spanned 12 terms, beginning as a Blue Dog Democrat.* [**24 Sept.** 2003 *Times Picayune (LA)*]

Blue•tooth /'blo͞oˌto͞oTH/ ▸ noun trademark a standard for the short-range wireless interconnection of cell phones, computers, and other electronic devices.
-ORIGIN 1990s: said to be named after King Harald *Bluetooth* (910–985), credited with uniting Denmark and Norway, as Bluetooth technology unifies the telecommunications and computing industries.

blunt /blənt/ ▸ noun black slang a hollowed-out cigar filled with marijuana: *Bob and I was walking down the Ave. smoking on a blunt and we saw this crab.* [**Sept. 1989** *Atlantic Monthly*]

BMI ▸ abbreviation BODY MASS INDEX.

boat neck /'bōt ˌnek/ ▸ noun a type of wide neckline on a garment that passes just below the collarbone.

bo•ba tea /'bōbə ˌtē/ ▸ noun another term for BUBBLE TEA.

Bo•bo /'bōˌbō/ ▸ noun (plural **Bo•bos**) informal a person having both the values of the counterculture of the 1960s and the materialism of the 1980s; a bourgeois Bohemian.
-ORIGIN 1990s: abbreviation.

bod•i•ly /'bädl-ē/ ▸ adverb in one mass; as a whole: *the committee arrived, bodily, and demanded access to the transcripts.*

bod•y dys•mor•phic dis•or•der /'bädē disˈmôrfik disˌôrdər/ (abbrev.: **BDD**) ▸ noun a psychological disorder in which a person becomes obsessed with imaginary defects in their appearance.

bod•y im•age /'bädē ˌimij/ ▸ **noun** the subjective picture or mental image of one's own body: *another entrenched assumption is that perception of one's body results from sensory inputs that leave a memory in the brain; the total of these signals becomes the body image.* [**Apr. 1992** *Scientific American*]

bod•y•kit /'bädēˌkit/ (also **bod•y kit**) ▸ **noun** a packaged set of decorations and fittings for customizing a car or motorcycle body: *I'm looking for a Bodykit for my 94 Civic 4 door.* [**9 Oct. 1999** Usenet: rec.autos.makers.honda]

bod•y mass in•dex /'bädē ˌmas ˌindeks/ (abbrev.: **BMI**) ▸ **noun** (plural **bod•y mass in•di•ces** /'indəsēz/ or **in•dex•es**) a weight-to-height ratio, calculated by dividing one's weight in kilograms by the square of one's height in meters and used as an indicator of obesity and underweight.

bod•y me•chan•ics /'bädē məˌkaniks/ ▸ **plural noun** [treated as singular or plural] exercises designed to improve posture, coordination, and stamina.

boer•bull /'bôrbo͞ol; 'bo͞or-/ (also **boer•bul**) ▸ **noun** S. African a large dog crossbred from the mastiff and indigenous African dogs.
-ORIGIN 1960s: from Afrikaans *boerboel*, from *boer* (commonly applied to indigenous plants and animals) + *boel*, from Dutch *bul* (as in *bulhond* 'mastiff').

bo•gart /'bōgärt/ ▸ **verb** [trans.] informal selfishly appropriate or keep (something, especially a marijuana cigarette): *the gorilla took a long hit and handed the joint to me. I accepted it graciously, without Bogarting, and passed it back to my friend.* [**1980** Armistead Maupin, *More Tales of the City*]
-ORIGIN 1960s: from U.S. actor Humphrey *Bogart* (1899–1957), who often smoked in films.

BOGOF /'bägôf/ ▸ **abbreviation** buy one, get one free.

bo•keh /bō'kā/ ▸ **noun** Photography the visual quality of the out-of-focus areas of a photographic image, especially as rendered by a particular lens: *I wanted to make a quick, visual survey of the foreground and background bokeh of a variety of lenses.* [**6 Nov. 1999** Usenet: rec.photo.equipment.35mm]
-ORIGIN from Japanese.

bok•ken /'bäkən/ ▸ **noun** a wooden sword used as a practice weapon in kendo, the Japanese martial art of fencing.

bol•li•to mi•sto /bô'lētō 'mēstō/ ▸ **noun** (plural **bol•li•ti mi•sti** /bô'lētē 'mēstē/) an Italian dish of mixed meats, such as chicken, veal, and sausage, boiled with vegetables in broth.
–ORIGIN Italian, literally 'boiled mixed (meat).'

bomb /bäm/ ▸ **noun** informal **1** (**da** (or **the**) **bomb**) an outstandingly good person or thing: *the site would really be da bomb if its content were updated more frequently.*
2 a marijuana cigarette; a joint.

book•mark /'boŏk,märk/ ▸ **verb** [trans.] Computing make a record of (the address of a file, Internet page, etc.) to enable quick access by a user: *its database pool is expected to grow over time, and is well worth bookmarking.* [**Aug.** 1997 *NetGuide*]
▸**noun** any of a collection of Web site addresses saved in a computer file for easy retrieval: *you can access any work instantly from the main menu and designate up to 99 bookmarks.* [**Apr.** 1994 *CD-ROM World*]

boo•mer•ang kid /'boŏmə,raNG ,kid/ (also **boo•mer•ang•er** /'boŏmə ,raNGər/) ▸ **noun** informal a young adult who goes back to live with a parent after a period of independence: *I have a boomerang kid at home just when I'm ready to retire!*
–ORIGIN allusion to a *boomerang*, which is thrown so as to return to the thrower.

boost•er•ish /'boŏstəriSH/ ▸ **adjective** supporting or promoting something enthusiastically, and often uncritically: *out-of-work La Portans, inspired by black humor, slapped the city's boosterish slogan "La Porte's on the Move" on their cars as they left for good.* [**12 Mar.** 1986 *Wall Street Journal*]

boot-cut /'boŏt ,kət/ ▸ **adjective** (of jeans or other trousers) flared very slightly below the knee, so as to be worn comfortably over boots.

boot•strap /'boŏt,strap/ ▸ **verb** [trans.] start up an enterprise, especially one based on the Internet, with minimal resources: *they are bootstrapping their stations themselves, not with lots of dot-com venture capital.*

boo•ty call /'boŏtē ,kôl/ ▸ **noun** informal a sexual invitation or rendezvous.
■ a person regarded for this: *Here I was, thinking this sophisticated man is so into me, but to him, I was just a booty call.* [**Dec.** 2001 *Cosmopolitan*]
–ORIGIN 1990s: from *booty* (slang for 'buttocks') and *call.*

boo•ty•li•cious /ˌbo͞otl'isHəs/ ▸ **adjective** slang sexually attractive.
–ORIGIN early 21st cent.: from *booty* (slang for 'buttocks'), on the pattern of *delicious*.

bor•ga•ta /bôr'gätə/ ▸ **noun** (plural **bor•ga•tas** or **bor•ga•te** /bôr'gätē/) an organized branch of the Mafia.
–ORIGIN 1960s: from Italian *borgatà* 'district, village.'

Bos•man rul•ing /'bäzmən 'ro͞oliNG/ ▸ **noun** a European Court ruling that obliges professional soccer or other sports clubs to allow players over the age of 25 to move freely between clubs once their contracts have expired.
–ORIGIN 1990s: named after Jean-Marc *Bosman* (1964–), a Belgian soccer player who brought a legal case that resulted in the ruling.

bot /bät/ ▸ **noun** a computer program that behaves like a human user in some specific capacity: *often, a bot looks like any other human user, and you might not be able to tell you're hanging out with software.* [**Apr. 1995** *Wired*]

-bot ▸ **combining form** used to form nouns denoting a computer program or robot with a very specific function: *she wanted to direct the female's behavior. She envisioned controlling a robot that could replace the female and fool a male completely. So, she created the fembot.* [**2 Dec. 2000** *Science News*]

Bo•tox /'bō͟täks/ ▸ **noun** trademark a drug prepared from the bacterial toxin botulin, used medically to treat certain muscular conditions and cosmetically to remove wrinkles by temporarily paralyzing facial muscles.
–DERIVATIVES **Bo•toxed** adjective
–ORIGIN 1990s: from *bo(tulinum) tox(in)*.

Bo•tox par•ty /'bō͟täks ͟pärtē/ ▸ **noun** a social event at which guests receive Botox injections from a doctor and mingle with each other for mutual support.
–ORIGIN on the pattern of *Tupperware party*.

bot•tle bill /'bätl ͟bil/ ▸ **noun** any of several U.S. state laws that require refundable deposits on beverages sold in recyclable bottles and cans.

bot•tle jack /'bätl ͟jak/ ▸ **noun** a large bottle-shaped jack used for lifting heavy objects.

bot•tom feed•er /'bätəm ˌfēdər/ ▸ **noun** informal, derogatory one who panders to the lowest taste or eschews ethical considerations in
pursuit of profit: *one result of televising executions will be that the bot-
tom-feeders in the media create shows with gory close-ups and horrible
sound bites.* [**Apr.** 2001 *Brill's Content*]

bou•tique ho•tel /bo͞o'tēk hō'tel/ ▸ **noun** a small stylish hotel, typically one situated in a fashionable urban location.

bo•vine growth hor•mone /'bōvīn 'grōTH ˌhôrmōn/ (abbreviation:
BGH) ▸ **noun** a natural hormone in cattle that helps regulate growth
and milk production and that may be produced artificially and
given to dairy cattle to increase the yield of milk. Also called **bo•
vine so•ma•tro•pin** /'bōvīn ˌsōmə'trōpin/.

bow ech•o /'bō ˌekō/ ▸ **noun** Meteorology a bow-shaped radar signature
associated with fast-moving storm systems accompanied by damaging winds.

box /bäks/ ▸ **noun** informal a personal computer or workstation: *I'm
having networking problems where windows boxes can route through
my Linux gateway, but my Linux boxes can't.* [**19 Jan.** 2003 Usenet:
comp.os.linux.networking]

box cut•ter /'bäks ˌkətər/ ▸ **noun** a tool consisting of a metal sheath
with a retractable razor blade, used for cutting the tops of cardboard boxes: *the man suspected of hiding box-cutters on two airline
flights warned federal authorities in an e-mail.* [**18 Oct.** 2003 *WLOX*]

boy band /'boi ˌband/ (or **girl band** /'gərl ˌband/) ▸ **noun** a pop group
composed of attractive young men (or young women) whose music and image are designed to appeal primarily to a young teenage audience.

bra•ce•ro /brä'se(ə)rō/, ▸ **noun** (plural **bra•ce•ros**) a Mexican laborer
allowed into the United States for a limited time as a seasonal
agricultural worker.
■ any other temporary migrant worker to or from a Spanish-
speaking country: *now that their country is considerably more developed than its threadbare neighbor they do not welcome those Haitians
who filter across the frontier, except as braceros, cane-cutters who work
in conditions not far removed from slavery.* [**24 Feb.** 1992 *New Yorker*]
-ORIGIN 1970s: Spanish, literally 'laborer,' from *brazo* 'arm.'

brach•y•ther•a•py /ˌbrakē'THerəpē/ ▸ **noun** the treatment of cancer,
especially prostate cancer, by the insertion of radioactive implants

directly into the tissue: *Jerry's doctors used brachytherapy, a radiation treatment pioneered by Memorial Sloane-Kettering, to destroy his tumor without damaging the healthy tissue around it.* [**14 Apr.** 1997 *New York Magazine*]

Bra•dy Bill /'brādē ,bil/ (also **Bra•dy Law** /'brādē ,lô/) ▸ noun common name for the Brady Handgun Violence Protection Act, a law enacted by the U.S. Congress in 1993 that requires a waiting period for handgun purchases and background checks on those who wish to purchase them.
-ORIGIN named for former White House press secretary James S. Brady (1940–), who campaigned for the bill after being shot and seriously wounded in the 1981 assassination attempt on President Ronald Reagan.

brain fin•ger•print•ing /'brān ,fiNGgər,printiNG/ ▸ noun the recording and analysis of an individual's neurological responses to images and words flashed on a screen, especially to determine if the person is telling the truth.

brand ex•ten•sion /'brand ik,stensHən/ ▸ noun an instance of using an established brand name or trademark on new products, so as to increase sales: *the Pathfinder Armada is Nissan's first full-size SUV, and a literal brand extension of the automaker's smaller, midsize Pathfinder* [**29 Sept.** 2003 *AdAge*]

brand train /'brand ,trān/ (or **brand sta•tion** /'brand ,stāsHən/) ▸ noun a subway train or station in which most or all advertisements are sponsored by a single company or organization: *brand trains are an expensive but effective way to advertise your product.*

brane /brān/ ▸ noun Physics an extended object with any given number of dimensions, of which strings in string theory are examples with one dimension. Our universe is a 3-brane.
-ORIGIN abbreviation of *membrane*.

brane world /'brān ,wərld/ (also **brane-world**) ▸ noun Physics a world model in which our space-time is the result of a 3-brane moving through a space-time of higher dimension, with all interactions except gravity being confined to the 3-brane.

Bra•zil•ian /brə'zilyən/ (also **Bra•zil•ian wax•ing** /brə'zilyən 'waksiNG/) ▸ noun a style of waxing a woman's pubic hair in which almost all the hair is removed, with only a very small central strip remaining.

break•beat /'brāk‚bēt/ ▸ **noun** a repeated sample of a drumbeat, usually forming a fast syncopated rhythm, used as a basis for dance music: [as modifier] *the current European sped-up breakbeat techno, which sounds more like HiNRG played on metal shop machine tools.* [**Fall 1992** *Vibe*]
■ dance music featuring breakbeats.

break•through pain /'brāk‚THrōō ‚pān/ ▸ **noun** (usually in connection with cancer) severe pain that erupts while a patient is already medicated with a long-acting painkiller: *to treat breakthrough pain, your physician may prescribe medications that can be taken by injection; sublingually, which means the medication dissolves under your tongue; rectally; or transmucosally, which means the medication is absorbed in your mouth.* [**12 Sept.** 2002 National Pain Foundation Web site]

breath•ar•i•an /breTH'e(ə)rēən/ ▸ **noun** a person who believes that it is possible, through meditation, to reach a level of consciousness where one can obtain all the nutrients one needs from the air or sunlight: *An Indian swami sat in a corner, near an enigmatic Haitian "breatharian" who is admired by all because he lives, supposedly, on air alone.* [**July 2001** *Observer (UK)*]

breed•er doc•u•ment /'brēdər ‚däkyəmənt/ ▸ **noun** a document, genuine or fraudulent, that can serve as a basis to obtain other identification documents or benefits fraudulently: *"A driver's license can become a 'breeder document' for other documents for establishing false identities and gaining access to social services and voter registration," Tancredo said last week upon introducing H.R. 3052, the State Accountability and Identity Fraud Elimination Act of 2004.* [**17 Sept.** 2003 *WorldNetDaily*]

bre•sao•la /bre'sōlə; bri'zō-/ ▸ **noun** an Italian dish of raw beef cured by salting and air-drying, served typically in slices with a dressing of olive oil, lemon juice, and black pepper.
–ORIGIN Italian, from *bresada*, past participle of *brasare* 'braise.'

brew•ski /'brōōskē/ ▸ **noun** (plural **brew•skis** or **brew•skies**) slang a beer: *maybe y'all can knock back a few brewskies and talk about all the money Verio is raking in from their pet spammers.* [**2 July** 2003 Usenet: news.admin.net-abuse.email]
–ORIGIN 1980s: from *brew* + a fanciful ending, perhaps after the common Slavonic surname suffix *-ski.*

bricks and mor•tar /'briks ən 'môrtər/ ▸ **noun** used to denote a business that operates in the physical world rather than (or as well as) over the Internet: [as modifier] *the bricks-and-mortar banks.*

bride•zil•la /brīd'zilə/ ▸ **noun** an overzealous bride-to-be who acts irrationally or causes offense: *I like to think I wasn't a bridezilla in the months, days, and hours leading up to our wedding.*

bridge mix /'brij ˌmiks/ ▸ **noun** a mixture of various bite-size candies, especially nuts, raisins, and chocolates.

Bril•lo /'brilō/ (also **Bril•lo pad** /'brilō ˌpad/) ▸ **noun** hair that is wiry or tightly curled: [as modifier] *he's a twenty-something guy with creamy pumpernickel skin and Brillo dreads.* [**1997** L. Yablonsky, *The Story of Junk*]
-ORIGIN from the trademark *Brillo*, used for soaped, steel wool scouring pads.

broast /brōst/ ▸ **verb** [trans.] cook (food) by a combination of broiling and roasting: [as adjective] (**broasted**) *broasted chicken.*
-ORIGIN 1980s: blend of *broil* and *roast.*

broc•ci•flow•er /'bräkəˌflouər/ (also **broc•co•flow•er**) ▸ **noun** a light green vegetable that is a cross between broccoli and cauliflower: *this recipe calls for brocciflower but I can't find it here.*
-ORIGIN blend of *broccoli* and *cauliflower.*

broc•co•li rabe /'bräk(ə)lē ˌräb/ (also **broc•co•li raab, broccoli rape** /'bräk(ə)lē ˌrāp/) ▸ **noun** a leafy green vegetable with broccoli-like buds and bitter-flavored greens.

bro•chure•ware /brō'sнoͦor,we(ə)r/ ▸ **noun** Web sites or Web pages produced by converting a company's printed marketing or advertising material into an Internet format, typically providing little or no opportunity for interactive contact with prospective customers: *certainly the wealth of brochureware on the Internet makes comparison shopping there much easier than physically visiting or even telephoning each vendor.* [**Aug. 1997** *NetGuide*]

bron•to•there /'bräntəTHi(ə)r/ ▸ **noun** a large ungulate mammal (*Embolotherium andrewsi*) of the Eocene epoch with a hornlike bony growth on the nose.
-ORIGIN modern Latin, from Greek *brontē* 'thunder' + *thērion* 'wild beast.'

brown cloud /'broun 'kloud/ ▸ **noun** a visible pall of air pollutants that persists over a city or other area: *the Asian brown cloud* | *Throughout the day, air shifts in the Valley cause variances in the brown cloud.*

brown goods /'broun ˌgo͞odz/ ▶ plural noun television sets, audio equipment, and similar household appliances: *our supply chain needs to accommodate highly perishable products, as well as white and brown goods.* [5 **Sept.** 2003 *Food Navigator (France)*]

brown tree snake /'broun 'trē ˌsnāk/ ▶ noun a nocturnal tree snake of Pacific origin that has escaped captivity as a pet to threaten native fauna in many Pacific Rim locations.
•*Boiga irregularis*, family Colubridae.

brush•stroke ▶ noun **1** the stroke of a brush, especially a hairbrush or a paintbrush: *she talked in a tone of voice that was calculated to be just as soothing as the brushstrokes through the silky strands, despite the unsettling words.* [8 **Oct. 1998** Usenet: soc.sexuality.spanking]
■ the mark or effect created by this: *an errant brushstroke doesn't necessarily destroy a painting.*
2 an individual action that contributes to an overall effect or work: *you write in broad, inaccurate brushstrokes, and seem incapable of grasping the meaning of your own words.* [14 **Oct. 1996** Usenet: misc.activism.militia]

B2B ▶ abbreviation business-to-business, denoting trade conducted via the Internet between businesses.

B2C ▶ abbreviation COMM business-to-consumer, denoting trade conducted via the Internet between businesses and consumers.

bub•bie /'bo͝obē; 'bəbē/ ▶ noun informal (in Jewish use) one's grandmother: *a comedy about an old-fashioned bubbie who concerns herself with her sophisticated granddaughter's love life.* [22 **Jan.** 1992 *Tucson Weekly*]
–ORIGIN from Yiddish *bubeleh* 'grandmother.'

bub•ble tea /'bəbəl ˌtē/ ▶ noun a cold, frothy drink made with iced tea, sweetened milk or other flavorings, and usually with sweet black balls or "pearls" made from tapioca. Also called BOBA TEA, PEARL TEA.

buck•et hat /'bəkit ˌhat/ ▶ noun a simple soft cloth hat with a brim: *on stage with J. Lo, he wore black leather pants, no shirt, gold medallion and Burberry plaid bucket hat.* [7 **Sept.** 2001 *Hartford Courant*]

buck•et•load /'bəkitˌlōd/ ▶ noun a large quantity: *he scoops up business donations by the bucketload.* [11 **Sept.** 2000 *Washington Post*]

buck•le bun•ny /'bəkəl ˌbənē/ ▸ noun informal a woman who is a follower or devotee of rodeos and cowboys.

build•out /'bildˌout/ ▸ noun the growth, development, or expansion of something: *the rapid buildout of digital technology.*

bul•let point /'boolit ˌpoint/ ▸ noun any of several items in a list printed with a bullet before each for emphasis: *businesspeople are always describing the future with bullet points.* [**June 1998** *Fast Company*]

bun•do•bust /'bəndəˌbəst/ (also **ban•do•bast** /'bandəˌbast/ˌ) ▸ noun Indian arrangements or organization: *the security arrangements and the police bundobust near the temple.* [**8 Sept.** 2003 *Deccan Herald (India)*]
-ORIGIN Urdu, from Persian *band-o-bast* 'tying and binding.'

bun•ker bust•er /'bəNGkər ˌbəstər/ (also **bun•ker-bust•er**) ▸ noun a bomb designed to penetrate deep into the ground or rock before exploding or detonating.

bun•ny-boil•er /'bənē ˌboilər/ ▸ noun informal a woman who acts vengefully after having been spurned by her lover: *most of them, she says, were happily married men who could rely on her not to turn into a bunny-boiler.* [**19 Aug.** 2001 *Observer (UK)*]
-ORIGIN with reference to the movie *Fatal Attraction* (1987), in which a rejected woman boils her lover's pet rabbit.

bun•ny hug•ger /'bənē ˌhəgər/ (also **bun•ny-hug•ger**) ▸ noun informal, chiefly derogatory **1** an animal lover or supporter of animal rights: *ugly to the bone is exactly what mute swans are, and don't let any bunny hugger tell you otherwise.* [**14 Sept.** 2003 *Baltimore Sun*]
2 an environmentalist or conservationist.

bun•yan•ize /'bənyəˌnīz/ ▸ verb [trans.] cause (someone) to appear heroic or larger than life: *How are you going to allow teachers to finish their work if you keep bunyanizing them?*
-ORIGIN late 20th cent.: after Paul *Bunyan*, legendary American giant lumberjack.

bup•kis /'boopkis; 'bəp-/ ▸ noun informal nothing at all: *you know bupkis about fundraising.*
-ORIGIN from Yiddish.

bu•pro•pi•on /byoo'prōpēən/ ▸ noun an antidepressant drug ($C_{13}H_{18}ClNO$) that is also given to relieve the symptoms of nicotine withdrawal. Also called **ZYBAN** (trademark).
-ORIGIN 1970s: from *butane* + *propionic*.

bur•ka (also **bur•qa**) /'bŏŏrkə/ ▸ noun a long, loose garment covering the whole body, worn in public by many Muslim women.
-ORIGIN from Urdu and Persian *burḳaʿ*, from Arabic *burḳuʿ*.

burn /bərn/ ▸ verb (past and past participle **burned** or **burnt**) [trans.] produce (a compact disc) by copying from an original or master copy.
▸noun 1 a hot, painful sensation in the muscles experienced as a
result of sustained vigorous exercise: *a home gym means having
your phone, CD collection, coffee machine, TV remote, and 2-year-old
within arm's reach while you're working up a burn.* [17 **Aug.** 1998
New York Magazine]
2 BURN RATE.

burn•er /'bərnər/ ▸ noun a device for producing a compact disc by
copying from an original or master copy.

burn rate /'bərn ˌrāt/ ▸ noun the rate at which an enterprise spends
money, especially venture capital, in excess of income: *the corporation lays off workers to cut burn rate.*

bur•qa /'bŏŏrkə/ ▸ noun variant spelling of BURKA.

Bush•ism /'bŏŏsh,izəm/ ▸ noun informal 1 a linguistic gaffe of President George H. or George W. Bush: *French people love to repeat the
well-known idiocy by George W. Bush, a Bushism now famous in
France: "The main problem with the French is that they have no word
for 'entrepreneur'."* [7 **Sept.** 2003 *Washington Post*]
2 the policies or political philosophy of President George H. or
George W. Bush: *Bushism is feel-good politics, adding self-satisfaction
to the material comfort of the comfortable.* [1990 G. Will, *Suddenly*]

bush•meat /'bŏŏSH,mēt/ ▸ noun the meat of African wild animals:
*sustainable ways of hunting bush meat in Western Africa could be
developed with the help of a new computer model, researchers hope.*
[9 **Sept.** 2003 *New Scientist (UK)*]

busi•ness mod•el /'biznis ˌmädl/ ▸ noun a design for the successful
operation business, identifying revenue sources, customer base,
products, and details of financing: *over the last six months or so,
many of the free sites have either shifted their business model or have
gone out of business completely.* [2003 Mplans.com]

Bu•tey•ko meth•od /bŏŏ'tākō ˌmeTHəd / ▸ noun a technique of controlled breathing that is claimed to alleviate asthma.

-ORIGIN 1990s: named after Ukrainian physiologist Konstantin *Buteyko* (1923–), who devised the technique.

butt heads /ˈbət ˈhedz/ ▸ **verb phrase** informal engage in conflict or be in strong disagreement: *the residents continue to butt heads with the mall developers.*

but•toned-up /ˈbətnd ˈəp/ ▸ **adjective** reserved and not inclined to reveal information: *in keeping with Fleischer's buttoned-up style, his decision did not leak out until after he told Bush's senior staff at the 7:30 a.m. meeting yesterday.* [**20 May 2003** *Washington Post*]

but•ton up /ˈbətn ˈəp/ ▸ **phrasal verb** secure to the maximum degree against attack: *the tank had been buttoned up and had not been seriously damaged, but all four of the crew were rendered unconcious with serious concussion.* [**28 Sept. 1995** Usenet: sci.military.moderated]

buzz•y /ˈbəzē/ ▸ **adjective** (**buzz•i•er, buzz•i•est**) informal (especially of a place or atmosphere) lively and exciting: *a buzzy bar with live music.*

Cc

ca•cha•ca /kə'sHäsə/ ▸ noun a Brazilian white rum made from sugar cane: *the clear, 80-proof cachaca tastes nothing like typical rums.* [**March 1999** *Paper*]
-ORIGIN mid 19th cent.: Brazilian Portuguese, from Portuguese *cacaça* '(white) rum.'

CAFE ▸ abbreviation Corporate Average Fuel Economy.

cai•pi•ri•nha /ˌkīpē'rēnyä; ˌkīpə'rinyə/ ▸ noun a Brazilian cocktail made with cachaca, lime or lemon juice, sugar, and crushed ice: *it was another all-night party in Rio de Janeiro, and Eric Petterson and Charles Milite were sipping caipirinhas and watching women dance the samba.* [**14 May 1990** *New York Magazine*]
-ORIGIN Brazilian Portuguese, from *caipira* 'yokel.'

call cen•ter /'kôl ˌsentər/ ▸ noun an office set up to handle a large volume of telephone calls, especially for telemarketing, order taking, and providing customer service: *AT&T Co plans to announce a software system that links a person working at home to a company's call center, using inexpensive local telephone lines.* [**29 Jan. 1991** *Wall Street Journal*]

cam•boy /'kamˌboi/ ▸ noun a boy or man who poses for a webcam.

cam•girl /'kamˌgərl/ ▸ noun a girl or woman who poses for a webcam: *many camgirls and camboys say they haven't revealed to their parents the full extent of their online conversations.* [**2 Sept. 2001** *Washington Post*]

camp•er /'kampər/ ▸ noun informal a person in a specified mood: *one night, I sat down around 6:30 and closed my eyes, and in came, over the next half-hour, all these ideas. And by 7 o'clock I was a happy camper.* [**10 March 2002** *New York Times*]

Can•a•darm /'kanəˌdärm/ ▸ noun the popular name for a robotic manipulation system designed for use in zero gravity; it has accompanied numerous space missions as a component on space shuttles.
-ORIGIN 1970s: blend of *Canada* (where it was manufactured) and *arm.*

can•cer clus•ter /'kansər ˌkləstər/ ▸ **noun** a statistically higher than average occurrence of cancer among the residents of a particular geographic area: *Jackson had come to town to dramatize the plight of Hispanics in McFarland who seemed to be living in a cancer cluster; there had been 14 cancer deaths in a four-block area.* [27 **May 1988** *Washington Post*]

can•yon•ing /'kanyəniNG/ (also **can•yon•eer•ing** /ˌkanyə'ni(ə)riNG/) ▸ **noun** the sport of exploring a canyon by rappelling, rafting, jumping into a waterfall, etc.: *Swiss adventure tour companies canceled their canyoning excursions yesterday after at least 19 tourists died when caught in a flash flood near this Swiss Alpine resort.* [29 **July 1999** *Baltimore Sun*]

cap /kap/ ▸ **noun** Finance short for capitalization: [as modifier] *mid-cap companies* | *small-cap stocks.*

ca•peesh /kə'pēsh/ ▸ **exclamation** informal do you understand?: *Upstairs is off limits. Capeesh?* [1992 P. Auster, *Leviathan*]
-ORIGIN 1940s: from Italian *capisce* third person singular present tense of *capire* 'understand.'

cap•el•li•ni /ˌkapə'lēnē/ ▸ **plural noun** pasta in the form of very thin strands: *eight clams and a few weeks later it was* capellini *in white clam sauce at an excellent southern Italian restaurant around the corner from my house.* [1997 J. Steingarten, *The Man Who Ate Everything*]
-ORIGIN 1950s: Italian, diminutive of *capello* 'hair.'

cap•sule en•do•scope /'kapsəl ˌendəˌskōp/ ▸ **noun** another term for VIDEO PILL.
-DERIVATIVES **cap•sule en•dos•co•py** /'kapsəl enˌdäskəpē/ **noun**

car•bo-load /'kärbō ˌlōd/ ▸ **verb** eat large amounts of carbohydrates, as in preparation for athletic endurance: *I am pretty sure that I have not actually lost much aerobic fitness, and if I carbo-loaded I would be back where I was.* [2003 Usenet: misc.fitness.weights]
-DERIVATIVES **car•bo-load•ed** adjective: *if you need some energy then drink half a bottle of a carbo-loaded drink about 30 minutes before your workout.*

car•bon sink /'kärbən ˌsiNGk/ ▸ **noun** Ecology a forest, ocean, or other natural environment viewed in terms of its ability to absorb carbon dioxide from the atmosphere: *these gas-dependent species had less dense wood, and could transform forests into carbon sinks which*

*would emit chemicals that further exacerbated the carbon dioxide im-
balance and ozone crisis.* [1995 L. Garrett, *The Coming Plague*]

carbs /kärbz/ ▸ **plural noun** informal dietary carbohydrates: *create a format that serves your needs, creating columns for calories, carbs, protein,
fat and sodium.* [**Oct. 1990** *Ironman*]

car•di•nal sin /ˈkärdnəl ˈsin; ˈkärdn-əl/ ▸ **noun** chiefly humorous a serious
error of judgment: Quantum Leap *gets canceled for the biggest cardinal sin of them all: It dared to be intelligent.* [11 **June 1993**
Entertainment Weekly]

card read•er /ˈkärd ˌrēdər/ ▸ **noun 1** an electronic sensor that reads
a magnetic strip or barcode on a credit card, membership card,
etc: *each feature a card reader—a slot in the Citibank phone for debit
and automatic teller machine (ATM) cards* [**Mar. 1994** *Popular Science*]
2 an electronic device that reads and transfers data from various
portable memory storage devices: *if your computer doesn't have a
memory card slot, companies such as Lexar offer accessory card readers that plug into your computer and let you download data from memory cards.* [**4 June 2000** *New York Times Magazine*]
3 a reader of tarot cards or other cards in fortune telling: *Dave
shows us that some card readers use a little trick to get a jump-start on
their subjects.* [2001 CraftyGal.com]

care work•er /ˈke(ə)r ˌwərkər/ ▸ **noun** British a person employed to support and supervise vulnerable, infirm, or disadvantaged people,
or those under the care of the state: *his school has three additional
teachers and four care workers to support its special needs children.* [15
Mar. 1991 *Times Educational Supplement*]

car•go pants /ˈkärgō ˌpants/ ▸ **plural noun** loose-fitting casual cotton
pants with large patch pockets halfway down each leg: *What do
you predict will be the biggest urban sportswear trend for Fall '97? Bold
knit sweaters, jersey-weight knits and cargo pants with an emphasis on
large, distinct logos and deep earth-toned color blocks.* [**Oct. 1997**
Source]

car•pen•ter pants /ˈkärpəntər ˌpants/ ▸ **plural noun** loose-fitting pants
with many pockets of various sizes and loops for tools at the tops
or sides of the legs: *"Just browsing," I say, clinging to my last shred
of cool while I look for the lingerie top and carpenter pants that I'd seen
on a 13-year-old.* [23 **Sept. 2003** *Portland (OR) Tribune*]

car•rot•wood /'karət͵wŏŏd/ ▸ **noun** a tree of the soapberry family, native to southeast Asia, that threatens mangrove swamps and other habitats in the U.S. because of its invasive habit.
•*Cupaniopsis anacardioides*, family Sapindaceae.

car•ry•back note /'karē͵bak ͵nōt/ ▸ **noun** a negotiable promissory note representing the value of real estate when the seller has provided the financing.

carve•out /'kärv͵out/ ▸ **noun** 1 an entity separated from a larger one and given separate treatment, in particular:
■ a small company created from a larger one: *others are discovering that they can earn attractive returns by focusing on companies that are breaking up—through spin-offs, split-offs, and "carveouts."* [**5 Dec. 1994** *Business Week*]
■ a class of medical procedures treated separately with regard to insurance coverage: *to set up a carveout, the employer selects a network of specialists to provide this service and to track use of the services and patient-care outcomes.* [**23 Mar. 1998** *Washington Business Journal*]
■ a class of employees treated separately with regard to benefits.
2 the activity of effecting such a separation.

cash ma•chine /'kaSH mə͵SHēn/ ▸ **noun** another term for ATM.

ca•si•ta /kə'sētə/ ▸ **noun** (especially in the Southwest) a small house or other building: *guests stay in one of the 120 adobe-like casitas (little houses), which are tucked away on meandering paths bordered by spiny cholla cacti and delicate-leaved paloverde shrubs.* [**April 1989** *Food and Wine*]
–ORIGIN early 19th cent.: from Spanish, diminutive of *casa* 'house.'

ca•su•al Fri•day /'kaZHŏŏəl 'frī͵dā; -dē/ ▸ **noun** Friday as a designated day of the week when organizations allow employees to dress more casually than on other workdays: *the popularity of Casual Fridays isn't surprising: casual clothes are more comfortable and say more about who we really are than dressed-for-success ensembles.* [**Mar. 1996** *Homemaker's Magazine (Canada)*]

cat•e•go•ry kill•er /'kati͵gôrē ͵kilər/ ▸ **noun** a large store, typically one of a chain, that specializes in a particular type of discounted merchandise and becomes the dominant retailer in that category: *Many merchants are afraid that so-called retail "category killers"—*

giant chains that could rub out the smaller businesses—would push downtown Golden into oblivion. [25 **Oct.** 1995 *Denver Post*]

ca•the•dral ceil•ing /kəˈTHēdrəl ˈsēliNG/ ▸ **noun** a pointed or slanting ceiling of a room that rises through more than one floor.

ca•va•quin•ho /ˌkävəˈkēnyō/ ▸ **noun** (plural **ca•va•quin•hos**) a type of small, four-stringed guitar resembling a ukulele, popular in Brazil and Portugal.
-ORIGIN Portuguese.

cav•o•lo ne•ro /ˈkävəˌlō ˈne(ə)rō/ ▸ **noun** an Italian variety of kale with very dark-colored leaves.

CCU ▸ **abbreviation** ▪ cardiac care unit. ▪ coronary care unit. ▪ critical care unit.

CDM ▸ **abbreviation** cold dark matter: [often attrib.] *the story also said that recent findings had placed the validity of some details of the Big Bang theory at risk—namely the cold dark matter, or CDM, theory. Now some new astronomical observations have deepened the doubt.* [**May 1991** *Popular Science*]

CDMA ▸ **abbreviation** Electronics Code Division Multiple Access, a generic term denoting a wireless interface based on code division multiple access technology.

C8 ▸ **noun** a popular designation for ammonium perfluorooctanoate, a detergentlike chemical used in the manufacture of fluoropolymers. It is the subject of litigation concerning its potentially harmful presence in some drinking water supplies.

Ce•leb•ra /səˈlebrə/ ▸ **noun** trademark a synthetic drug (a COX-2 inhibitor) used in the management of arthritic pain.
-ORIGIN 1990s: an invented word.

ce•leb•re•al•i•ty /səˌlebrēˈalitē/ (often as **ce•leb•re•al•i•ty TV**) ▸ **noun** television shows that feature well-known people or celebrities interacting in real situations contrived for purposes of entertainment: *celebreality, the junk genre du jour, turns the notion of reality TV upside down.* [5 **Jan.** 2003 *New York Times*]
-ORIGIN blend of *celebrity* and *reality*.

cel•lu•lar blind /ˈselyələr ˈblīnd/ ▸ **noun** a window blind with a single or double layer of collapsible voids that provide insulation when the blind is extended.

cell•y /'selē/ (also **cell•ie**) ▸ **noun** (plural **cell•ies**) slang **1** a cell phone: *tonight the two of them are on a mission to score some weed. So Timmy whips out his celly to beep White Mike* [**2002** N. McDonell *Twelve*] ■ a person who uses a cell phone.
2 (among prisoners) cellmate: *my celly was badly beaten by a man in for double life.* [**2 Nov. 1994** Usenet: alt.prisons]

cell yell /'sel ‚yel/ ▸ **noun** informal loud talking on a cell phone: *cell yell— as train executives prefer to term the din—is the stimulating chat of telephone users who assume others are deaf to their stock tips, dining choices, office numbers and professions of love.* [**20 May 2001** *New York Times*]

ce•roc /sə'räk/ ▸ **noun** chiefly British a type of modern social dance having elements of rock and roll, jive, and salsa: *in the past three months a thriving social scene has developed around ceroc, and romance has often flourished between the lawyers, accountants and bankers who attend the classes.* [**9 July 1995** *Independent on Sunday (UK)*]
-ORIGIN 1990s: invented word, apparently coined in English from French *ce* 'this' + *roc* 'rock.'

cgi ▸ **abbreviation** common gateway interface (a script standard for writing interactive programs generated by visitors to web pages, such as forms and searches).

cgi-bin /'sē‚jē'ī ‚bin/ ▸ **noun** a server directory where cgi programs are stored: [as modifier] *cgi-bin files.*

cha•lu•pa /chə'lōōpə/ ▸ **noun** a fried tortilla in the shape of a boat, with a spicy filling: *One can select from enchiladas, chalupas, quesadillas, burritos as well as exotic tropical seafoods.* [**May 1991** *Connecticut*]
-ORIGIN late 19th cent.: Spanish, ultimately related to Dutch *sloep* 'sloop.'

cha•mise /CHə'mēz; SHə-/ (also **cha•mi•so** /CHə'mē‚sō/) ▸ **noun** (plural **cha•mis•es** or **cha•mi•sos**) an evergreen shrub (*Adenostoma fasciculatum*) of the rose family, with small narrow leaves, common in the chaparral of California.
-ORIGIN mid 19th cent.: from Mexican Spanish *chamiso*.

chan•nel-hop /'CHanl ‚häp/ ▸ **verb** chiefly British [intrans.] (**chan•nel• hopped, chan•nel•hop•ping**) informal **1** another term for channel-surf (as with a television's remote control): *he watched a good deal of television with half an eye, channel-hopping compulsively, for he*

was a member of the remote-control culture. [**1988** Salman Rushdie, *Satanic Verses*]
2 travel across the English Channel and back frequently or for only a brief trip: *as a special treat why not channel hop and have Sunday lunch in France?* [**Spring 1990** *France Magazine*]
-DERIVATIVES **chan•nel-hop•per** noun; **chan•nel-hop•ping** noun

Chap•ter 7 /'CHaptər 'sevən/ ▸ noun protection from creditors granted to individuals or companies who legally file for bankruptcy, providing for liquidation of certain assets to pay debts: [often attrib.] *a federal judge on Sept. 4 converted the case from Chapter 11 reorganization to a Chapter 7 liquidation.* [**24 Sept.** 2003 *Raleigh Triangle Business Journal*]

Chap•ter 13 /'CHaptər THər'tēn/ ▸ noun protection from creditors granted to individuals who legally file for bankruptcy, providing for repayment of debts by a court-approved plan: [often attrib.] *Morenci has not had a grocery store since Market Square went into Chapter 13 receivership and closed in April.* [**23 Sept.** 2003 *Adrian (MI) Daily Telegram*]

char•ac•ter code /'kariktər ˌkōd/ ▸ noun Computing the binary code used to represent a letter or number in a file or datastream: *for convenience, we call such embedded information—and all other aspects of a bit stream's representation, including byte length, character code and structure—the encoding of a document file.* [**Jan.** 1995 *Scientific American*]

charge•back /'CHärjˌbak/ ▸ noun a demand by a credit-card provider for a retailer to make good the loss on a fraudulent or disputed transaction: *Visa and Mastercard have been fining porn sites as much as $100,000 a month when chargebacks from disputed transactions have exceeded one percent of total transactions.* [**24 Aug.** 2000 *NewScan Daily*]
▪ (in business use) an act or policy of allocating the cost of an organization's centrally located resources to the individuals or departments that use them: *chargeback, always popular with IT departments that want users to know what they are getting for their money, is becoming one of the most sought-after management utilities and it has never really left the mainframe world.* [**16 Sept.** 2003 it-analysis.com]

chat group /'CHat ˌgro͞op/ ▸ noun a group of people who communicate regularly via the Internet, usually in real time but also by e-mail: *the Justice Department views IM mostly as a cyberstalking tool allowing members of chat groups and IM services to anonymously track other online visitors.* [**18 Sept.** 2003 *USA Today*]

chat•ter•bot /'CHatər,bät/ ▸ **noun** a computer program designed to interact with people by simulating human conversation: *one useful thing Andrette knows how to do is to tell you what movies are playing near you, and even in this simple task the chatterbot became confused because I gave my zip code too early in the process.* [**14 June 1999** *Tasty Bits from the Technological Front*] –ORIGIN 1990s: blend of *chatter* and *(ro)bot.*

Chat•tis•garh /'CHətēs,gär/ a state in central India, formed in 2000 from the southeastern part of Madhya Pradesh; capital, Raipur.

check•sum /'CHek,səm/ ▸ **noun** an error checking device consisting of a number automatically generated from data in such a way that any change to the data results in a change to the number: *the first record header contains the checksum of the login ID of the local administrator.* [**1996** W. McCarthy, *Murder in Solid State*]

chees•y /'CHēzē/ ▸ **adjective** (**chees•i•er, chees•i•est**) hackneyed, kitschy, or otherwise distasteful: *on the club's back wall one finds embarrassingly cheesy renderings of full-figured gals.* [**11 Mar. 1991** *New Yorker*]

chef /SHef/ ▸ **verb** (**cheffed, chef•fing**) [intrans.] (**cheffing**) informal work as a chef: *for when they finish cheffing, they gather themselves together and they drink their owners' best wines, and often through the wee-est of hours.* [**Jan. 2000** *Esquire*] –ORIGIN early 19th cent.: French, literally 'head.'

che•la•tion ther•a•py /kē'lāSHən ,THerəpē/ ▸ **noun** a therapy for mercury or lead poisoning that binds the toxins in the bloodstream by circulating a chelating solution: *Dr. Pittman and The Carolina Center use Chelation therapy to treat patients diagnosed with mercury toxicity, administering the chelating drugs EDTA and DMPS.* [**8 Sept. 2003** *BusinessNews Triangle (press release)*] ■ a therapy that attempts to remove calcium deposits from the arteries on the same principle.

chem•i•cal /'kemikəl/ ▸ **noun** an addictive or abusable drug: *put away the snowboards, sunscreen and the recreational chemicals. Spring Break is over.* [**1998** R. L. Fleming, Jr., *She's All That*]

chev•on /'sHevən/ ▸ **noun** the flesh of goats as food; goat meat: *the entree was crisp-on-the-outside succulent-inside haunch of spring chevon.* [**Feb.** 1995 *Mother Earth News*]
-ORIGIN from French *chèvre,* 'goat,' on the pattern of *mutton.*

Chi•ca•go•land /sHi'kägō₁land/ ▸ **noun** Chicago and its suburbs, considered as a unit: [often as modifier] *a thoughtful unpretentious matchmaking service for Chicagoland singles.* [**7 Mar.** 1991 *New York Review of Books*]

Chick•en Lit•tle /'cHikən 'litl/ ▸ **noun** an alarmist or doomsayer: *my beloved capital sounds more and more these days like a barnyard filled with Chicken Littles.* [24 **June** 1992 *Wilmington News Journal*]
-ORIGIN 1990s: from the name of a character in a children's story who repeatedly warns that the sky is falling.

chick flick /'cHik ₁flik/ ▸ **noun** informal a movie that appeals to women: *they urge their wives to pick the movie sometimes, even when it almost guarantees a night with a weepy chick flick.* [15 **June** 1998 *Louisville Courier-Journal*]

chick lit /'cHik ₁lit/ ▸ **noun** informal, chiefly derogatory literature, mainly modern, that appeals to women: *the astounding success of Bridget Jones's Diary has spawned a publishing phenomenon: "chick lit," a modern, post-feminist take on the mass-appeal romance novel.* [18 **June** 2001 *U.S. News and World Report*]

child•mind•er /'cHīld₁mīndər/ ▸ **noun** British a childcare worker or babysitter.
-DERIVATIVES **child-mind•ing noun**

Chil•e•an sea bass /'cHilēən 'sē ₁bas/ ▸ **noun** see PATAGONIAN TOOTHFISH.

chi•mi•ne•a /₁cHimə'nāə; -'nēə/, ▸ **noun** a free-standing clay fireplace or oven that consists of a hollow bulbous body, open at the front, in which a fire may be lit, tapering to a short chimneylike smoke vent: *and most of the new outdoor hearths are true fireplaces (meaning the permanent brick kind), not the moveable "chimineas" that were all the rage a few years back.* [14 **Feb.** 2003 *Wall Street Journal*]
-ORIGIN 1990s: Spanish, 'chimney.'

chi•nois /sHēn'wä/ ▸ **noun** a cone-shaped sieve with a closely woven mesh for straining sauces.
-ORIGIN from French, 'Chinese,' because of its supposed resemblance to a Chinese hat.

chlor•pyr•i•fos /klôr'pirə‚fäs/ ▸ **noun** a broad-spectrum organophosphate insecticide, widely used in food crop agriculture and as a termiticide: *some treatment facilities use activated charcoal filters which remove some chlorpyrifos residues from water because it is easily absorbed.* [9 **June** 2000 EPA Web site]

choc•o•late vine /'CHäk(ə)lit ‚vīn; 'CHôk-/ ▸ **noun** a fast-growing, shade-tolerant woody twining vine, native to Asia and introduced as an ornamental in the U.S. It has escaped cultivation and threatens native plants in some woodland habitats.
• *Akebia quinata*, family Lardizabalaceae.

cho•ki•dar /'CHôki‚där/ ▸ **noun** variant spelling of CHOWKIDAR.

chow•ki•dar /'CHôki‚där/ (also **cho•ki•dar** /'CHôki‚där/) ▸ **noun** (in India) a watchman or gatekeeper: *I asked the chowkidar guarding my house, Shabeer, to find taxis for Danny and Mariane, who was setting off for a separate interview.* [6 **June** 2003 *Wall Street Journal*] -ORIGIN from Urdu *caukīdār*, from *caukī* 'toll house' + *-dār* 'keeper.'

Chris•ma•tion /kriz'mäsHən/ ▸ **noun** a rite in the Orthodox and Eastern Catholic churches that is comparable and similar to confirmation in the Roman Catholic church.
-ORIGIN *chrism* (holy oil) + *-ation*

chro•ma•key /'krōmə‚kē/ ▸ **noun** a technique by which a block of a particular color in a video image can be replaced either by another color or by a separate image, enabling, for example, a weather forecaster to appear against a background of a computer-generated weather map.
▸ **verb** (**chro•ma•keys, chro•ma•keyed, chro•ma•key•ing**) [trans.] manipulate (an image) using this technique.

chro•mo•ther•a•py /‚krōmə'THerəpē/ ▸ **noun** another name for COLOR THERAPY.
-DERIVATIVES **chro•mo•ther•a•pist** noun

chron•o•ther•a•py /‚kränə'THerəpē/ ▸ **noun** treatment of an illness or disorder that takes into account the body's natural rhythms and cycles: *the concept of using the body's genetically programmed ebbing and flowing to diagnose, treat and even prevent some diseases is the focus of chronotherapy.* [21 **Sept.** 2003 *Baltimore Sun*]

chy•ron /'kīrän/ ▸ noun trademark an electronically generated caption superimposed on a television or movie screen.
–ORIGIN 1970s: The Chyron Corporation, its manufacturer.

cig•a•rette pants /,sigə'ret ,pants/ ▸ plural noun women's pants with straight, very narrow legs: *a creamy silk shantung trench coat over a pair of cigarette pants in kelly green shantung.* [7 **Nov.** 1991 *Washington Post*]

cir•cu•lar po•lar•i•za•tion /'sərkyələr ,pōlərə'zāsHən/ ▸ noun Physics polarization of an electromagnetic wave in which either the electric or the magnetic vector executes a circle perpendicular to the path of propagation with a frequency equal to that of the wave. It is frequently used in satellite communications.

cit•y /'sitē/ ▸ noun [with modifier] informal a place or situation characterized by a specified attribute: *at Thursday's practice, Rypien went down in a heap, threw his helmet, cursed, grabbed his ankle and left practice. Panic city.* [24 **Jan.** 1992 *Washington Post*]

civ•il com•mit•ment /'sivəl kə'mitmənt/ ▸ noun post-sentence institutional detention of a sex offender with the intention of preventing a reoffense: *a 75-year-old convicted sex offender being held in civil commitment was denied supervised release by a Milwaukee judge Thursday.* [26 **Sept.** 2003 *Milwaukee Journal Sentinel*]

civ•il con•vic•tion /'sivəl kən'viksHən/ ▸ noun (in military use) a current or former criminal conviction under civil law of an enlisted person: *when imposing a suspension or revocation because of an off-installation offense, the effective date should be the same as the date of civil conviction.* [2003 Fort Belvoir Web site]

civ•il un•ion /'sivəl 'yo͞onyən/ ▸ noun a legally recognized union of a same-sex couple, with rights similar to those of marriage: *the state, which recently passed a bill creating civil unions that give gay couples the rights of marriage, was praised and trumpeted throughout the day.* [1 **May** 2000 *New York Times*]

cla•fou•tis /kla'fo͞otē/ ▸ noun (plural same) a tart made of fruit, typically cherries, baked in a sweet batter.
–ORIGIN French, from dialect *clafir* 'to stuff.'

claw•back /'klô,bak/ ▸ noun the recovery of money already disbursed: *all Schedule Performance Fees are earned and final upon achievement* *of the stated milestone and are not subject to any clawback by the Government.* [2003 Department of Energy contract (Hanford Site)] ▸verb (also **claw back**) retrieve or recover funds already allocated or dispersed: *all three plans would also clawback benefits at retirement. That is, retirees would not receive both their full Social Security benefit and the proceeds of the individual account.* [3 June 2002 Congressman Elijah E. Cummings]

clean room /'klēn ,rōōm; ,rōōm/ ▸ noun an environment free from dust and other contaminants, used chiefly for the manufacture of electronic components: *Daw Technologies Inc. said it received a contract valued at more than $5.7 million to build a cleanroom for a semiconductor manufacturer.* [19 Jan. 1994 *Wall Street Journal*]

click rate /'klik ,rāt/ (also **click-through rate** /'klik 'THrōō ,rāt/) ▸ noun Computing the percentage of people viewing a Web page who access a hypertext link to a particular advertisement: *despite recent layoffs and a decline in the click rate of banner ads, Advertising.com still expects to prosper this year.* [21 Jan. 2001 *Baltimore Sun*]

clicks and mor•tar /'kliks ən 'môrtər/ ▸ noun used to refer to a traditional business that has expanded its activities to operate also on the Internet: *clicks and mortar has often been dismissed by analysts who suggest that real world outfits that move online will end up cannibalising their existing business.* [2 Dec. 1999 *Guardian (UK)*] ■ [usually attrib.] a business or business model that involves both Internet selling and physical stores: *many investors are optimistic about the company's use of the "clicks and mortar" strategy, in which walk-in customers use a Borders intranet site to search for titles and order books once they are in the store.* [21 Nov. 1999 *New York Times*]

click•stream /'klik,strēm/ ▸ noun Computing a series of mouse clicks made by a user while accessing the Internet, especially as monitored to assess a person's interests for marketing purposes: *clickstreams, as they are called, enjoy a digital afterlife in commercial databases, where raw statistics about our on-line behavior are transformed into useful information and then warehoused for future application, sale or barter.* [Mar. 1996 *Scientific American*]

click-through /'klik ,THrōō/ ▸ noun Computing the ratio of clicks that an Internet ad receives to page views of the ad: *a Web site's dynamics should be reflected in the average rate of click-through across many advertising banners.* [July 1996 *Internet World*]

cli•mate change /'klīmit ,CHānj/ ▸ noun long-term, significant change in the climate of an area or of the earth, usually seen as resulting from human activity; often used as a synonym for global warming: *U.S. and Soviet experts inaugurated a year-long scientific dialogue yesterday on the implications of global climate change* [12 May 1998 *Washington Post*]

cli•mate jump /'klīmit ˌjəmp/ ▸ **noun** a sudden and drastic change in climate: *the data analyses showed that there is clear interdecadal climate variation in China, particularly the climate jump in 1960s.* [(undated) Li Chongyin, *Anomalous Characteristics of Atmospheric Circulation Associated with Interdecadal Climate Variation in China*]

climb•ing eu•on•y•mus /'klīmiNG yo͞o'änəməs/ ▸ **noun** another name for WINTER CREEPER.

clin•i•cal e•col•o•gy /'klinikəl i'käləjē/ ▸ **noun** an earlier name for ENVIRONMENTAL MEDICINE.

clip•per /'klipər/ (also **clip•per chip** /'klipər ˌCHip/) ▸ **noun** a microchip that inserts an identifying code into encrypted transmissions, allowing them to be deciphered by a third party having access to a government-held key: *the Clinton Administration has been pushing for the development of the Clipper Chip, a technology that would enable the government to "wiretap" scrambled digital communications.* [30 May 1994 *Time*]

clon•al•i•ty /klō'nalitē/ ▸ **noun** the fact or condition of being genetically identical, as to a parent, sibling, or other biological source: *the lack of genetic diversity may be a combination of both isolation and clonality.* [6 Dec. 1997 *New Scientist (UK)*]

closed cap•tion /'klōzd 'kapsHən/ ▸ **noun** one of a series of subtitles to a television program, accessible through a decoder.
▸ **verb** (**closed-caption**) [trans.] [usually as noun **closed-captioning**] provide (a program) with closed captions.

close en•coun•ter /'klōs en'kountər/ ▸ **noun** a putative encounter with a UFO or with aliens: *Taylor said he is now an official MUFON (Mutual UFO Network) investigator and would be interested in speaking to individuals who feel they have experienced a UFO sighting or perhaps a close encounter of some sort.* [11 Dec. 1996 *Bloomington (Indiana) Herald-Times*]
–PHRASES **close encounter of the first** (or **second**, etc.) **kind** used to describe encounters involving increasing degrees of complexity and apparent exposure of the witness to aliens, with the

first kind being a mere sighting and the fourth kind being abduction.

clo•sure /ˈklōzHər/ ▸ **noun** a feeling that an emotional or traumatic experience has been resolved: *the memorial was intended to provide "closure" in the officers' minds.* [**9 May** 1993 *Fort Collins Coloradoan*]
USAGE: Despite more than two decades of usage, this sense of closure has not lost a jargony connotation, perhaps because its most avid users profess a relationship with feelings with which many people cannot identify.

club-sand•wich gen•er•a•tion /ˈkləb ˈsan(d)wiCH ˌjenəˌrāsHən/ ▸ **noun** a generation of people responsible for the care of their children, grandchildren, and parents or other aging relatives: *typically members of the club-sandwich generation also have busy careers.*
-ORIGIN from *club sandwich,* a sandwich using three slices of bread, on the pattern of *sandwich generation,* a generation responsible for the care of their children and parents.

clue•ful /ˈklo͞ofəl/ ▸ **adjective** slang well-informed; competently intelligent: *the point is that clueful implementors are aware of the issues and are looking out for you; it's not just some accident that things work.* [**16 Jan.** 2001 Usenet: comp.programming.threads]

coast•eer•ing /ˈkōst,i(ə)riNG/ ▸ **noun** chiefly British the sport of exploring a shoreline that does not have a continuous pedestrian route: *coasteering is like taking a gentle ramble along coastal cliff paths except that, when the path runs out, you jump into the sea and swim and scramble over rocks to where the trail starts again.* [**15 June** 2003 *Observer (UK)*]

COB ▸ **abbreviation** close of business: *you have until COB today to show us why you should not be disconnected.* [**11 Aug.** 2003 Usenet: news.admin.net-abuse.email]

co•bot /ˈkō,bät/ ▸ **noun** a computer-controlled robotic device designed to assist a person: *when a cobot and a UAW member work together to install a large truck instrument panel, the human being does the lifting (see how smart the machines really are) while the cobot provides guidance and direction.* [**2001** Faith Popcorn and Adam Hanft, *Dictionary of the Future*]
-ORIGIN blend of *collaborative* and *robot.*

co-brand /ˈkō ,brand/ ▸ **verb** [trans.] designate (a product or service) with the brands of joint manufacturers or sponsors: *E-Truck Leasing co-brands services with Truck Wash Guys.*

▸**noun** a product or service jointly offered by two manufacturers or sponsors: [as modifier] *We can easily set up a co-brand version of Small Business IS Here with your logo in the top right hand corner of every page with a link back to your web site.*
–DERIVATIVES **co-brand•ing noun**

code mon•key /ˈkōd ˌməNGkē/ ▸**noun** slang a computer programmer, especially an inexperienced or plodding one: *a code monkey in the trenches who needs a job to pay the bills isn't necessarily an enemy of open source.* [11 Sept. 2003 *Slashdot*]

cod•er /ˈkōdər/ ▸**noun** a computer programmer: *the flaws could be used by malicious coders to create new worms or "Trojan horse" attacks, but Microsoft said it doesn't believe any hackers have taken advantage of the security flaws.* [19 Oct. 2003 *Washington Post*]

code•share /ˈkōdˌsHe(ə)r/ **noun** ▸ a marketing arrangement in which two airlines sell seats on a flight that one of them operates: [as modifier] *Qantas is a codeshare partner with both American Airlines and Alaska Airlines in North America.*
■ a flight or aircraft in which such an arrangement is in effect.

cog•ni•tive pros•the•sis /ˈkägnitiv präsˈTHēsis/ ▸**noun** an electronic computational device that extends the capability of human cognition or sense perception: *a cognitive prosthesis is a computational tool that amplifies or extends a person's thought and perception, much as eyeglasses are prostheses that improve vision.* [30 Aug. 2003 *Science News*]

co•gon grass /kōˈgōn ˌgras/ ▸**noun** a perennial, rhizomatous grass of Asian origin, used for thatching and as a packing material; identified as a noxious weed in much of the southeastern U.S.
•*Imperata cylindrica*, family Poaceae.

coked /kōkt/ ▸**adjective** informal having taken a large amount of cocaine: *it could have been a druggie coked so far out of his mind that he'd torn the furniture apart looking for money.* [1988 Sara Paretsky, *Toxic Shock*]

col•lat•er•al dam•age /kəˈlatərəl ˈdamij/ ▸**noun** unintended damage to property or persons who are in the vicinity of a military target: *M60 GPMGs will punch through most interior floors without excessive collateral damage.* [Dec. 1991 *Soldier of Fortune*]
■ any unintentional damage resulting from an aggressive action:

New York City was right to mount an aggressive spraying campaign against encephalitis-bearing mosquitoes (news article, Sept. 14), but every aggressive campaign inevitably inflicts collateral damage. [20 **Sept. 1999** *New York Times*]

col•or ther•a•py /ˈkələr ˌTHerəpē/ ▸ noun a system of alternative medicine based on the use of color, especially projected colored light: *In the past, chromotherapists have been imprisoned for practicing—or for even just implying that there is such a practice as—color therapy or healing with color.* [**1991** M. Walker, *The Power of Color*]

col•tan /ˈkältan/ ▸ noun a dull metallic mineral composed of columbite and tantalite, and refined to produce tantalum: *most of the world's coltan comes from Australia, but Congo is also rich in the mineral, which is being mined in several World Heritage Sites designated as vital nature preserves.* [**25 June 2001** *New York Magazine*] -ORIGIN early 21st cent.: from *col(umbite)* + *tan(talite)*.

com•bi•na•tion ther•a•py /ˌkämbəˈnāSHən ˌTHerəpē/ ▸ noun treatment in which a patient is given two or more drugs (or other therapeutic agents) for a single disease: *in mice the combination therapy is more effective than interleukin-2 alone.* [**May 1990** *Scientific American*]

com•bin•er[1] /kəmˈbīnər/ ▸ noun any of various electronic devices that combine signals, in particular:
■ a device that couples different frequencies to a single antenna.
■ a component of a cipher that combines two data sources to encrypt text. ■ an electrical transformer comprising several smaller ones.

com•bin•er[2] /ˈkämˌbīnər/ ▸ noun an operator of a combine harvester: *Louis Jenkins has worked as a farm hand, ranch hand, custom combiner, oil field worker, truck driver, bookmobile driver, construction laborer, library assistant, house painter, carpenter, shoe salesman, janitor, surveyor's helper, and printer, among other things.* [**Jan. 1995** *Minnesota Monthly*]

comb•o•ver /ˈkōmˌōvər/ (also **comb-o•ver**) ▸ noun hair that is combed over a bald spot in an attempt to cover it: *asking them about the turning point of the race while they're heaving is as inconsiderate as asking Rudolph Giuliani how he's feeling before he cements his combover onto his head.* [**7 Nov. 1993** *New York Times*]

com•man•do ▸ verb phrase see GO COMMANDO.

com•men•tar•i•at /ˌkämən'te(ə)rēət/ ▸ noun members of the news media considered as a class: *like boxing cornermen disappointed that their fighter had to settle for a draw, the U.S. commentariat exuded recriminations when American air attacks on Iraq were called off.* [1 Dec. 1998 *Village Voice*]
-ORIGIN late 20th cent.: blend of *commentary* and *proletariat*.

com•mu•ni•ty bank /kə'myo͞onitē ˌbaNGk/ ▸ noun a commercial bank that derives funds from and lends to the community where it operates, and is not affiliated with a multibank holding company.

com•mu•ni•ver•si•ty /kə,myo͞onə'vərsitē/ ▸ noun an organization representing a liaison between a university and the community where it is located: [often as modifier] *a communiversity theater.*
-ORIGIN 1990s: blend of *community* and *university*.

co•mor•bid•i•ty /ˌkōmôr'biditē/ ▸ noun the simultaneous presence of two chronic diseases or conditions in a patient: *Preliminary examination of the comorbidity of anxiety and depression in Parkinson's disease.* [1995 *title in Parkinson.org archive*]

com•plete game /kəm'plēt 'gām/ ▸ noun Baseball a statistic credited to a pitcher who pitches from start to finish in a regulation game.

com•pli•ance /kəm'plīəns/ ▸ adjective undertaken or existing mainly in order to comply with an earlier treaty, order, or law: *Liberals' WTO compliance legislation ignores skyrocketing drug costs.* [Feb. 2001 *Canada Newswire*]

con•cha /'käNGkə/ ▸ noun (plural **con•chae** /-kē; -ˌkī/) a round or oval hammered metal disk used as decoration on jewelry, belts, harnesses, etc.
-ORIGIN late 20th cent.: from Spanish, via Latin, 'mussel shell'.

con•cho belt /'käNGkō ˌbelt/ ▸ noun a belt decorated with conchas.

con•densed tan•nin /kən'denst 'tanin/ ▸ noun any of various tannins with antioxidant properties occuring naturally in plants, comprising polymers of flavonoids linked by a carbon-to-carbon bond: *cranberries were found to be rich in special compounds called condensed tannins, known to keep bacteria from attaching itself to the bladder and urinary tract.* [July 2000 *Marie Claire (UK)*]

con•joined twin /kən'joind 'twin/ ▸ noun either of a pair of congenitally fused twins: [usually plural] *Conjoined twins, which result from the incomplete separation of identical twins early in fetal development, occur just once in every 100,000 births.* [**8 Sept. 1993** *Baltimore Sun*]
USAGE: This more accurate and correct term has supplanted the older *Siamese twin* in all contexts other than informal conversation.

con•jun•to /kän'hŏōntō; -'həntō/ ▸ noun (plural **con•jun•tos**) (in Latin America or Hispanic communities) a small musical group or band: [often attrib.] *San Antonio's Eva Ybarra ranks today as Texas' leading female conjunto accordionist.* [**Jan 1992** *Texas Monthly*]
-ORIGIN Spanish, literally 'an ensemble, group.'

con•sign•ment shop /kən'sīnmənt ˌSHäp/ (or **con•sign•ment store** /kən'sīnmənt ˌstôr/) ▸ noun a store that sells secondhand items (typically clothing and accessories) on behalf of the original owner, who receives a percentage of the selling price: *his Tulsa home, strewn with relics lugged home from his consignment shop, is testimony to his being first-rate at secondhand salvation.* [**Fall 1991** *Do It Yourself*]

con•sil•i•ence /kən'silēəns/ ▸ noun agreement between the approaches to a topic of different academic subjects, especially science and the humanities: *If this view of universal consilience is correct, the central question of the social sciences is, in my opinion, the nature of the linkage between genetic evolution and cultural evolution.* [**27 Mar. 1998** *Science*]
-DERIVATIVES **con•sil•i•ent** adjective
-ORIGIN mid 19th cent.: from *con(current)* + Latin *-silient-, -siliens* 'jumping' (as in *resilience*).
USAGE: Though first attested in the 19th century, this word has been largely ignored by smaller dictionaries. The publication in 1998 of Edward O. Wilson's *Consilience* has given it a new life.

con•tact cen•ter /'käntakt ˌsentər/ ▸ noun an integrated and usually automated communications system that coordinates all telephone and electronic contacts between an organization and the public: [typically as modifier] *a global provider of products and services focused on maximizing contact center effectiveness.* [**7 Oct. 2003** *Business Wire (press release)*]

con•tent /'käntent/ ▸ noun information made available by a Web site or other electronic medium: [as modifier] *online content providers.*

-ORIGIN late Middle English: from medieval Latin *contentum* (plural *contenta* 'things contained').

con•trol freak /kən'trōl ˌfrēk/ ▸ noun informal a person who feels an obsessive need to exercise control over themselves and others and to take command of any situation: *still another Bush vice is a high tolerance of loose management. Baker, a control freak, is bound to change this.* [**10 Aug.** 1992 *New Republic*]
-DERIVATIVES **con•trol freak•er•y** noun

con•ver•sion van /kən'vərzHən ˌvan/ ▸ noun a van in which the cargo space has been converted to a special purpose, such as a living space: *the first Arlington Heights bookmobile was a $5,000 conversion van.* [**10 May 1998** *Chicago Tribune*]

Cool•Max /'kōōlˌmaks/ ▸ noun trademark a polyester fabric that draws perspiration along its fibers away from the skin, used chiefly in sportswear.
-ORIGIN 1980s: an invented name, probably from *cool* + *max(imum)*.

co•op•e•ti•tion /kōˌäpi'tisHən/ ▸ noun collaboration between business competitors, in the hope of mutually beneficial results: *I think it's important that Apple be seen now not as a pure competitor with Microsoft but in "coopetition": competing in some areas, cooperating in others.* [**2 June 1998** *PC Week (UK)*]
-ORIGIN 1980s: blend of *cooperative* and *competition*.

cop•y•left /'käpēˌleft/ ▸ noun an arrangement whereby software or artistic work may be used, modified, and distributed freely on condition that anything derived from it is bound by the same conditions: [as modifier] *please note also that the code in this book is protected by copyright. It has not been placed in the public domain. Nor is it shareware. It is not protected by a "copyleft" agreement, like code distributed by the Free Software Foundation.* [**1992** P.J. Plauger, *Standard C Library*]
-DERIVATIVES **cop•y•left•ed** adjective
-ORIGIN 1980s: on the pattern of *copyright*.

co•qui /'kōkē/ noun ▸ a singing tree frog (*Eleutherodactylus coqui*), native to Puerto Rico, that has become an invasive pest in Hawaii.

cord blood /'kôrd ˌbləd/ ▸ noun blood from the human umbilical cord, a source of stem cells: *cord blood has already been used* *successfully to reconstitute the bone marrow of critically ill patients.* [**May 1994** *Scientific American*]

core asset /'kôr 'aset/ ▸ **noun** an asset of an enterprise considered to be essential to its success: *Soo Line and Chicago & North Western sharply raised their bids for the core assets of Milwaukee Road, which is in bankruptcy-law proceedings.* [**10 Apr. 1984** *Wall Street Journal*]

core com•pe•ten•cy /'kôr 'kämpitǝnsē/ ▸ **noun** a defining capability or advantage that distinguishes an enterprise from its competitors: *the industry is becoming a loosely structured network of service enterprises built around specialized core competencies and joined together . . . for one undertaking.* [**Mar. 1990** *Harvard Business Review*] ▪ a defined level of competence in a particular job or academic program.

co•ro•na•vi•rus /kǝ'rōnǝˌvīrǝs/ ▸ **noun** any of a class of viruses that cause colds, pneumonia, and some other infections in humans. In electron micrographs the viruses appear to have a halo that is caused by an array of surface projections on the viral envelope: *until SARS struck in Asia last year, coronavirus was never more than a pesky source of the sniffles in humans.* [**8 Oct. 2003** *Knoxville (TN) News Sentinel*]

co•ro•ni•al /kǝ'rōnēǝl/ ▸ **adjective** Australian relating to a coroner: *a spokesman for the police told the 7:30 Report that it was not possible to comment before a coronial hearing takes place.* [**17 Sept. 2003** *ABC Online (Australia)*]

cor•po•rat•ize /'kôrp(ǝ)rǝˌtīz/ ▸ **verb** [trans.] convert (a government organization) into an independent commercial company: *the report's recommendations support an outrageously undemocratic proposal to "corporatize" the national labs.* [**June 1995** *Mother Jones*] –DERIVATIVES **cor•por•a•ti•za•tion** noun

co-sign /'kō ˌsīn/ ▸ **verb** [trans.] designate with two different labels on a sign: *original interchange numbers will be co-signed with new numbers for two years after the conversion* [**2003** *Rand McNally Atlas*] | *US 400 is co-signed with US 166 for about 8 miles and the two routes share the same eastern terminus.* [**2003** Geocities.com]

co-sleep•ing /'kō 'slēpiNG/ ▸ **noun** the practice of sleeping in the same bed with one's infant or young child: *co-sleeping often facilitates a good breastfeeding relationship.* [**2003** iparenting.com]

-DERIVATIVES **co-sleep** verb (**co-slept**): *a more contemporary approach would be to teach parents who choose to co-sleep to do it safely.*

cos•me•ceu•ti•cal /ˌkäzməˈsōōtikəl/ ▸ noun a cosmetic that has or is claimed to have medicinal properties, especially anti-aging ones: *the possibility that these products have the biological effect manufacturers claim raises questions of whether these products are best classified—and therefore regulated—as drugs, as cosmetics or as a hybrid with the newly minted name of "cosmeceuticals."* [12 June 1990 *Washington Post*]
-ORIGIN 1980s: blend of *cosmetic* and *pharmaceutical.*

cos•mo•pol•i•tan /ˌkäzməˈpälitn/ ▸ noun a citrusy vodka cocktail, commonly made with Cointreau, cranberry juice, and lime juice.

cost cen•ter /ˈkôst ˌsentər/ ▸ noun a department or other unit within an organization to which costs may be charged for accounting purposes: *the most serious issue is the philosophical shift from a recreation/programming-based Indy Parks to a profit-making Indy Parks. It is the difference between viewing our resources as recreation centers or as cost centers.* [20 Aug. 1998 *Indianapolis Star*]

coul•ro•pho•bi•a /ˌkōlrəˈfōbēə/ ▸ noun extreme or irrational fear of clowns.
-ORIGIN from Greek *kolon*, 'limb' taken from *Kolobathristes* 'stilt walker,' + phobia.

coun•ter•sto•ry /ˈkountərˌstôrē/ ▸ noun an alternative or opposing narrative or explanation: *the counterstory does not take the form of a judicial dissent (since there was none); it's provided instead by Crenshaw.* [Spring 1999 *Newsletter on Philosophy, Law, and the Black Experience*]

coun•ter•ter•ror•ism /ˌkountərˈterəˌrizəm/ ▸ noun political or military activities designed to prevent or thwart terrorism: *counterterrorism is used to describe both a government's use of terrorism to oppose terrorism from a challenger and any official response, legal or otherwise, to terrorism.* [1995 M. Crenshaw, *Terrorism Reader*]
-DERIVATIVES **coun•ter•ter•ror•ist** /ˌkountərˈterərist/ noun

coun•try•pol•i•tan /ˌkəntriˈpälitn/ (also **Coun•try•pol•i•tan**) ▸ noun a type of country music that resembles pop music, usually characterized by orchestrated arrangements: [as modifier] *A slick "countrypolitan" ballad, the song is all orchestrated melodrama and high dynamics.* [25 Jan. 1993 *Newsweek*]

▸**adjective** relating to or denoting an architectural style that combines country charm with sophistication.
-ORIGIN on the pattern of *cosmopolitan.*

cov•er sheet /'kəvər ˌSHēt/ ▸ **noun** a page placed before a document giving information about its content, distribution, or the like, such as:
■ one prefacing a manuscript or report, typically with the name of the author, title of the book or report, and date.
■ a page sent as the first page of a fax transmission, identifying the sender, number of pages, etc.
■ a page naming the intended recipients of a circulating document: *a memo with a distribution cover sheet that had fifty names on it* [**1988** N. Baker, *Mezzanine*]

co•vert cou•ture /'kōvərt ko͞o'to͞or; kō'vərt; 'kəvərt/ ▸ **noun** the design and manufacture of subtly customized versions of fashionable clothing and accessories: *covert couture is perfect for these slightly less flush times: people still have money but flaunting your wealth as a war looms and the stock market wobbles won't impress anybody.* [**15 Dec. 2002** *New York Times Magazine*]

cow•boy /'kouˌboi/ ▸ **verb 1** work as a cowboy: *Hadley was looking off into Sonora, Mexico, where he learned to cowboy.* [**May 1993** *Albuquerque*]
2 (**cowboy up**) mount a brave effort to overcome a formidable obstacle: *Millar cowboyed up, but couldn't he have hit a bloop off Mo or flipped the Enrique grounder to Pedro?* [**16 Oct. 2003** Usenet: alt.sports.baseball.bos-redsox]

COX-2 in•hib•i•tor /'käks 'to͞o inˌhibitər/ ▸ **noun** a painkiller that works by inhibiting the enzyme Cyclooxygenase-2 (COX-2), which triggers the release of prostaglandins: *COX-2 inhibitors (the first of which, called Celebrex, is already on the market) ease pain about as well as aspirin, ibuprofen or other non-steroidal anti-inflammatory drugs (NSAIDs).* [**Aug. 1999** *More*]

cram•ming /'kramiNG/ ▸ **noun** the practice of charging a customer for telephone services that were not requested, authorized, or used: *the bill also deals with "cramming," the newest scam in telecommunications, in which companies cram services, such as voice mail, onto a customer's bill without authorization.* [**25 June 1998** *Indianapolis Star*]
-DERIVATIVES **cram•mer noun**

cra•ni•o•pa•gus /ˌkrānēˈäpəgəs/ ▸ noun conjoined twins with a fused skull: [as modifier] *this was the first time that surgeons had tried to separate adult craniopagus twins.* [8 July 2003 *Times (UK)*]

CRC ▸ abbreviation Computing cyclic redundancy check; a data code that detects errors during transmission, storage, or retrieval.

cre•den•tialed /krəˈdensHəld/ ▸ adjective awarded or in possession of credentials: *There would surely be streams of phone calls from impeccably credentialed professionals giving us first crack at the very best deals, all with a decade or more of carefully audited financial statements.* [30 July 1990 *Wall Street Journal*]

cringe•wor•thy /ˈkrinjˌwərTHē/ ▸ adjective informal causing feelings of deep shock, embarrassment, or awkwardness: *I've seen some pretty cringeworthy stuff, but nobody's hands ever got toasted.* [1996 dialog in *Buffy, the Vampire Slayer*]

crip•ple•ware /ˈkripəlˌwe(ə)r/ ▸ noun informal software distributed with reduced functionality with a view to attracting payment for a fully functional version: *if the software blocks crucial functions such as saving files, it's sneered at as "crippleware," but if it's only missing high-end options, it may provide everything you need.* [21 Mar. 2003 *Chicago Tribune*]

CRM ▸ abbreviation customer relationship management, denoting strategies and software that enable a company to organize and optimize its customer relations.

cron•ing /ˈkrōniNG/ ▸ noun (especially among feminists in the U.S. and Australasia) a celebration or ceremony to honor older women: *croning is becoming so popular with older women, there's even a nationwide crone festival scheduled for Oct. 22–25 in Salt Lake City.* [20 Mar. 1998 *Indianapolis Star*]
-ORIGIN 1990s: blend of *crone* + *crowning.*

cross-con•tam•i•na•tion /ˈkrôs kəˌtaməˈnāsHən/ ▸ noun the process by which bacteria or other microorganisms are unintentionally transferred from one substance or object to another, with harmful effect: *his speed in analyzing samples may have resulted in cross-contamination.* [Aug. 1995 *Vanity Fair*]
-DERIVATIVES **cross-con•tam•i•nate** /ˌkrôs kənˈtaməˌnāt/ verb

cross-par•ty /ˈkrôs ˌpärtē/ ▸ adjective involving or relating to two or more political parties: *unique cross-party (and largely cross-bench)* *defeat on a provision to curb alleged political teaching in primary schools.* [**1988** *Parliamentary Affairs (UK)*]

USAGE: Though appearing occasionally in American writing to denote cooperation between the two main political parties, this term does not compete very effectively with *bipartisan,* the default term. *Cross-party* is far more common in other English dialects, and in American English to describe political cooperation in other countries.

cross-post /'krôs ˌpōst/ (also **cross•post** /'krôsˌpōst/) ▸ **verb** post a single message to multiple Internet newsgroups or readings lists: [intrans.] *if you cross-post to both lists, several hundred people will receive two copies of your message.* [**2003** Biglist.com]
■ repost a message appearing on one list or newsgroup to another: [trans.] *please do not cross-post this vacancy.*
▸**noun** a message posted to more than one newsgroup or reading list: *please note that while we do not have any explicit policy about crossposting to other newsgroups, we do strongly recommend that the crossposts be to relevent newsgroups only.* [**2003** Hindunet.org]

crowd-pleas•er /'kroud ˌplēzər/ ▸ **noun** a person or thing with great popular appeal: *One of his crowd-pleasers is a novelty song called "Guitar Jamboree."* [**21 Oct. 1991** *New Yorker*]
–DERIVATIVES **crowd-pleas•ing** adjective

crowd-surf•ing /'kroud ˌsərfiNG/ ▸ **noun** the activity of being passed in a prone position over the heads of the audience at a rock concert, typically after having jumped from the stage: *a month later, 14-year-old Chris King suffered fatal injuries when he was dropped on his head while crowd-surfing at the Masterdome.* [**20 Sept. 2003** *Riverside (CA) Press Enterprise*]
–DERIVATIVES **crowd-surf** verb

crown mold•ing /'kroun 'mōldiNG/ ▸ **noun** ornamental molding that forms the topmost feature of a wall, cabinet, or furniture: *the crown molding trim on the top mimics the trim on the original mantel around the fireplace but does not block the double-hung windows in the room.* [**18 Sept. 2003** *Santa Cruz Sentinel*]

cru•ci•ver•bal•ist /ˌkrōōsi'vərbəlist/ ▸ **noun** a person who enjoys or is skilled at solving crossword puzzles: *this trove includes 100 puzzles by the master cruciverbalists Cox and Rathvon from the first decade of The Puzzler.* [**July 1992** *Atlantic Monthly*]
–ORIGIN 1970s: from Latin *crux, cruci-* 'cross' and *verbalist.*

crush space /'krəsH ˌspās/ **noun** ▶ **1** space in a motor vehicle between occupants and a point of impact that can absorb some of the shock of collision: *they are also not safe in a crash, mostly because they are so small to provide no adequate "crush space."* [**July 1993** *Garbage*]
2 space in the common area of a performance venue that can accommodate the largest crowd expected: *changes in scope from the original building program were introduced which included items such as the addition of crush space for lecture halls* [**2002** University of Toronto Web site]

cryp•to•spo•rid•i•o•sis /ˌkriptōspəˌridē'ōsis/ ▶ **noun** an intestinal disease caused by infection with cryptosporidium (a parasitic intestinal protozoan), causing diarrhea and vomiting.

crys•tal heal•ing /'kristl ˌhēliNG/ (also **crys•tal ther•a•py** /'kristl ˌtherəpē/) ▶ **noun** in alternative medicine, the use of crystals for their professed healing properties: *somebody got cold feet about releasing a crazed mishmash of pseudoscience, eco-erotica, and crystal healing over the airwaves.* [**20 Nov. 1990** *Village Voice*]

C2C ▶ **abbreviation** consumer-to-consumer, denoting transactions conducted via the Internet between consumers.

cube farm /'kyōōb ˌfärm/ ▶ **noun** a large open-plan office divided into cubicles for individual workers: *"It's not a cube farm," says Bedford, whose office boasts a real window and actual solid walls that rise all the way to the ceiling.* [**9 Nov. 1998** *Newsweek*]

cud•dle pud•dle /'kədl ˌpədl/ ▶ **noun** informal **1** a whirlpool or hot tub: [as modifier] *the charming cottage at El Nobo sleeps 2, has own TV and cuddle-puddle pool.* [**2003** spain-holiday.ws]
2 a group of people in intimate physical contact: *the whole time me, Brian, Stephanie, and James were all in a sort of cuddle puddle on one of the couches, just watching.* [**14 Aug. 2002** Weblog: anth.hey-pretty.net]

cued speech /'kyōōd 'spēCH/ ▶ **noun** a type of sign language that uses hand movements combined with mouth shapes to communicate to the hearing impaired: *I have learnt English through cued speech, which is a system that uses eight hand shapes in four positions to clarify the lip patterns of normal speech.* [**11 Nov. 2002** *Daily Telegraph (UK)*]

cul•tu•ra•ti /ˌkəlCHə'rätē/ ▶ **plural noun** well-educated people who appreciate the arts: *avant-garde enough to please the culturati but*

not there long enough to scare the old guard. [**6 Sept. 2003** *New York Times*]
-ORIGIN 1980s: blend of *culture* and *literati.*

cul•ture war /ˈkəlCHər ˌwôr/ ▸ noun a conflict between groups with different ideals, beliefs, philosophies, etc.: *the demonstration underscored a persisting culture war between religious and nonobservant Jews.* [**4 July 1993** *Fort Collins Coloradoan*]

cu•mec /ˈkyo͞oˌmek/ ▸ noun a unit of flow equal to one cubic meter of water per second: *the minimum flows proposed would vary seasonally between 80 cumecs in winter and 140 cumecs in summer.* [**2003** Meridian Energy Web site (NZ)]
-ORIGIN on the model of *cusec*, a traditional unit of flow equal to one cubic foot per second.

cup•ping /ˈkəpiNG/ ▸ noun (in Chinese medicine) a therapy in which heated glass cups are applied to the skin along the meridians of the body, creating suction as a way of stimulating the flow of energy.

cu•pro /ˈk(y)o͞oprō/ ▸ noun a type of rayon made by dissolving cotton cellulose with cuprammonium salts and spinning the resulting solution into filaments.
-ORIGIN 1980s: an invented word, probably from *cuprammonium* (an ion formed from copper salts and ammonia).

cush•ty /ˈko͞oSHtē/ ▸ adjective British informal very good or pleasing: *Jamie Oliver has shot to culinary fame with almost indecent speed, but not everyone is a fan of his "cushty" cuisine.* [**4 Apr. 2001** *Daily Telegraph (UK)*]
-ORIGIN 1920s: from Romany *kushto, kushti* 'good,' perhaps influenced by *cushy.*

cusp•ing /ˈkəspiNG/ ▸ noun 1 formation of a cusp or cusps: *the claim is that Ford tire spec is based on the OEM tire only, and that if you use the same pressure with the tires that I got, there will be serious cusping and uneven wear on the tire, and void any form or warantee with the tire.* [**19 Nov 1998** Usenet: rec.autos.makers.ford.explorer]
2 Architecture a decorative feature consisting of cusps.

cy•ber•at•tack /ˈsībərəˌtak/ ▸ noun Computing an effort by hackers to damage or destroy a computer network or system: *warning that America is increasingly vulnerable to cyberattacks, President Clinton ordered the strengthening of defenses against terrorists, germ warfare* *and other unconventional security threats of the 21st century.* [**3 May 1998** *Bloomington (IN) Herald-Times*]

-DERIVATIVES **cy•ber•at•tack•er** noun

cy•ber•cash /'sībər‚kasʜ/ ▸ noun **1** funds used in electronic financial transactions, especially over the Internet: *there's a form of cybercash that cannot be linked to an owner or spender.* [**July 1995** *Popular Science*]
2 money stored on an electronic smart card or in an online credit account: *but we can have something delivered over the Net, as long as we've got a walletful of CyberCash.* [**24 June 1996** *Time*]

cy•ber•chon•dri•ac /‚sībər'kändrē‚ak/ ▸ noun a person who reads health or medical information on the Internet and develops imaginary physical symptoms and ailments: [as modifier] *because online drug stores bypass doctors to deliver drugs, medical professionals are beginning to take alarm at cyberchondriac behavior.* [**4 May 2001** *Edupage*]
-DERIVATIVES **cy•ber•chon•dri•a** /‚sībər'kändrēə/ noun

cy•ber•crime /'sībər‚krīm/ ▸ noun crime conducted via the Internet or some other computer network: *in terms of lost sales and productivity, the bureau estimates cybercrime costs Americans more than $10 billion a year.* [**June 2000** *Vanity Fair*]

cy•ber•law /'sībər‚lô/ ▸ noun laws, or a specific law, relating to Internet and computer offenses, especially fraud, copyright infringement, etc.: *cyberlaw encompasses the regulations that govern cyberspace, and it's such a cutting-edge field that the search of the legal database Westlaw brings up no federal cases using the term.* [**19 Mar. 1994** *CompuServe Magazine*]

cy•ber•mall /'sībər‚môl/ ▸ noun a commercial Web site through which a range of goods may be purchased; a virtual shopping mall on the Internet: *a typical example would be shopping in a cybermall, where a user might move from store to store and acquire various merchandise along the way.* [**Aug. 1995** *Internet World*]

cy•ber•naut /'sībər‚nôt; -‚nät/ ▸ noun Computing a person who wears sensory devices in order to experience virtual reality: *a "cybernaut" can step through walls and wander at will.* [**4 Jan. 1992** *Science News*]
■ a person who uses the Internet.

-ORIGIN 1990s: from *cyber-*, on the pattern of *astronaut* and *aeronaut*.

cy•ber•pet /ˈsībərˌpet/ ▶ **noun** an electronic toy that simulates a real pet and with which human interaction is possible. (Also called **dig•i•pet** or **vir•tu•al pet**.)

cy•ber•pho•bi•a /ˌsībərˈfōbēə/ ▶ **noun** fear of or anxiety about computing or information technology; reluctance to use computers, especially the Internet.
-DERIVATIVES **cy•ber•phobe** /ˈsībərˌfōb/ noun; **cy•ber•pho•bic** adjective

cy•ber•porn /ˈsībərˌpôrn/ ▶ **noun** pornography viewable on a computer screen, especially accessed on the Internet: *my topic is cyberporn, that is, computerized pornography.* [**Sept. 1995** *Harper's Magazine*]

cy•ber•shop /ˈsībərˌSHäp/ ▶ **verb** [intrans.] (**cy•ber•shopped, cy•ber•shop•ping**) [often as noun] (**cybershopping**) purchase or shop for goods and services on a Web site: *research commissioned by Elron Software found that more than half of American workers cybershop on company time.* [**29 Nov. 1999** *Newsweek*]
▶ **noun** (also **cy•ber•store** /ˈsībərˌstôr/) a Web site that sells or provides information about retail goods or services: *the retailer's cybershop sometimes has different prices than in its mail-order catalog.*
-DERIVATIVES **cy•ber•shop•per** noun

cy•ber•slack•er /ˈsībərˌslakər/ ▶ **noun** informal a person who uses their employer's Internet and e-mail facilities for personal activities during working hours: *cyberslackers that download and distribute pornography waste productive time, consume expensive bandwidth and could be in breach of sexual harassment laws.* [**Nov. 2000** *APC (Australia)*]
-DERIVATIVES **cy•ber•slack•ing** noun

cy•ber•squat•ting /ˈsībərˌskwätiNG/ ▶ **noun** the practice of registering names, especially well-known company or brand names, as Internet domains, in the hope of reselling them at a profit: *a United Nations panel late last week issued a set of proposed rules that seek to end so-called cybersquatting—registering popular corporate or product names as Internet addresses in order to sell them back to the trademark holders or to divert Internet traffic from those companies.* [**4 May 1999** *Wall Street Journal*]
-DERIVATIVES **cy•ber•squat•ter** noun

cy•ber•stalk•ing /'sībər‚stôkiNG/ ▸ noun the repeated use of electronic communications to harass or frighten someone, for example by sending threatening e-mails: *fewer than one-third of states currently have anti-stalking laws that explicitly cover cyberstalking.* [**16 Sept. 1999** *NewsScan Daily*]
-DERIVATIVES **cy•ber•stalk•er** noun

cy•ber•surf•er /'sībər‚sərfər/ ▸ noun a person who habitually uses or browses the Internet.
-DERIVATIVES **cy•ber•surf•ing** noun

cy•ber•ter•ror•ism /‚sībər'terə‚rizəm/ ▸ noun the politically motivated use of computers and information technology to cause severe disruption or widespread fear in society: *a spending bill to finance the Justice Department that would make it easier for law enforcement to wiretap computers and combat cyberterrorism.* [**14 Sept. 2001** *New York Times*]
-DERIVATIVES **cy•ber•ter•ror•ist** noun

cy•ber•war /'sībər‚wôr/ ▸ noun acts of hostility carried out on the Internet against national interests or ethnic groups: *but this exploit took cyberwar a step further: the attacker stole some 3,500 e-mail addresses and 700 credit card numbers, sent anti-Israeli diatribes to the addresses and published the credit card data on the Internet.* [**12 Nov. 2000** *New York Times*]

cy•brar•i•an /sī'bre(ə)rēən/ ▸ noun a librarian or researcher who uses the Internet as an information resource: *find out what cybrarians involved in electronic information services think about these and other questions related to libraries and the national information infrastructure.* [**13 Jan. 1995** *Alawon*]
-ORIGIN blend of *cyber-* and *librarian.*

cy•cli•cals /'sīklikəlz; 'sik-/ ▸ plural noun stocks in cyclical companies (those whose success varies with the seasonal or economic cycle): *He's positive about prospects for health care, gold and consumer cyclicals—home building and retailing.* [**10 May 1998** *Chicago Tribune*]

Dd

da /də/ ▸ **adjective** nonstandard spelling of *the,* used in representing informal speech.

DAB ▸ **abbreviation** digital audio broadcasting.

dae•mon /'dēmən; 'dā-/ ▸ **noun** Computers a memory-resident computer program that is idle except when invoked to perform a routine task: *a background-only application (daemon) that allows you to control the resolutions of all your displays.* [**6 Nov.** 2003 *Mac News Network*]

dag /dag/ ▸ **noun** Australian/NZ informal an unfashionable or socially conservative person: *five stylists flounced around what Australians would call a Big Dag and transformed him, via a series of product placements, into an icon of casual elegance.* [**6 Oct.** 2003 *The Age (Australia)*]

dag•ger•board /'dagər,bôrd/ ▸ **noun** a board that slides vertically through the keel of a sailboat to reduce sideways movement: *it is most exhilarating to experience a 30-foot vessel, displacing 2,700 lbs and carrying a fully submerged daggerboard.* [**Oct. 1992** *Canadian Yachting*]

dai•sy-cut•ter /'dāzē ˌkətər/ ▸ **noun** informal an immensely powerful aerial bomb that derives its destructive power from the mixture of ammonium nitrate and aluminum powder with air: *fuel-air mixture (FAM) weapons, or "daisy-cutters," are used to clear (and, indeed, create) helicopter landing zones by the simple expedient of flattening everything in a huge, dispersed blast.* [**16 Jan. 1993** *New Scientist*]
‑ORIGIN early 20th cent.: so named because the bomb explodes just above ground level.

dam•i•an•a /ˌdamēˈanə/ ▸ **noun** a small shrub native to Mexico whose leaves are used in herbal medicine and in the production of a liqueur. It is reputed to possess aphrodisiac qualities.
•*Turnera diffusa,* family Turneraceae.

D&X ▸ **abbreviation** dilation and extraction; see PARTIAL-BIRTH ABORTION.

dark bi•ol•o•gy /'därk bīˈäləjē/ ▸ **noun** scientific research related to biological weapons: *unlike nuclear physics, where it is relatively easy* *to gauge the intent of research programs, the only way you can tell the difference between good biology and dark biology is in the application.* [22 **January** 2002 *Government Executive*]

dark en•er•gy /'därk 'enərjē/ ▸ **noun** Physics a theoretical repulsive force that counteracts gravity and causes the universe to expand at an accelerating rate: *Einstein's theories allow for the possible existence of dark energy.*

DARPA /'därpə/ ▸ **abbreviation** Defense Advanced Research Projects Agency, the central research and development organization for the U.S. Department of Defense.

da•shi /'däsHē/ ▸ **noun** stock made from fish and kelp, used in Japanese cooking.

da•ta•link /'datə‚liNGk; 'dātə-/ ▸ **noun** an electronic connection for the exchange of information: *NASA is working on a datalink system that would allow aircraft controllers and pilots to exchange electronic messages that could be viewed on video displays.* [18 **Feb.** 1990 *New York Times*]

da•ta•point /'datə‚point; 'dātə-/ ▸ **noun** an identifiable element in a data set: *software that can quickly process tens of thousands of datapoints.*

da•ta set /'datə ‚set; 'dātə/ ▸ **noun** a collection of related sets of information that is composed of separate elements but can be manipulated as a unit by a computer.

da•ta smog /'datə ‚smäg; 'dātə/ ▸ **noun** informal an overwhelming excess of information, especially from the Internet: *nowadays, people need help getting their intellectual bearings because cable has become a torrent of ideology, dueling experts and data smog.* [19 **Mar.** 2003 *Los Angeles Times*]

date-rape drug /'dāt ‚rāp ‚drəg/ ▸ noun a drug that causes temporary loss of memory or inhibition, surreptitiously given to a girl or a woman so that her date may sexually abuse or rape her: *police said the group drank alcohol and smoked pot and that Greenberg gave one of the girls the date rape drug GHB.* [13 **Oct.** 2003 *NBC4 (OH)*]

daugh•ter•card /'dôtər‚kärd/ (also **daugh•ter•board** /-‚bôrd/) ▸ **noun** an expansion circuit card affixed to a motherboard that accesses memory and the CPU directly rather than through a bus.

day trad•ing /'dā ˌtrādiNG/ ▸ **noun** a form of securities trading in which individuals buy and sell shares (usually over the Internet) frequently, with the intention of profiting from small price fluctuations.
-DERIVATIVES **day trad•er** noun

DDoS (also **DDOS**) ▸ **abbreviation** distributed denial of service, the intentional paralyzing of a computer network by flooding it with data sent simultaneously from many individual computers: [as modifier] *automation of so-called zombies, which are then used to stage DDOS attacks, has made it a lot easier to launch an attack from a single terminal.* [12 **July** 2001 *Newsbytes*]

dead-ball line /'ded 'bôl ˌlīn/ ▸ **noun** Soccer the part of the goal line to either side of the goal.

dead white Eu•ro•pe•an male /'ded '(h)wīt ˌyərə'pēən 'māl; ˌyo͞orə-/ (also **dead white male**) ▸ **noun** informal a writer, philosopher, or other significant figure whose importance and talents are considered to have been exaggerated by virtue of his belonging to a historically dominant gender and ethnic group: [as modifier] *classical music once was the exclusive realm of dead white European male composers.* [30 **Sept.** 2003 *Cleveland Plain Dealer*]

death met•al /'deTH ˌmetl/ ▸ **noun** a form of heavy metal music using lyrics preoccupied with death, suffering, and destruction: *Tannenbaum describes death metal this way: "The sound a corpse hears when the coffin slams shut."* [23 **Aug.** 1992 *Buffalo News*]

de Cle•ram•bault's syn•drome /də ˌklerəm'bōz ˌsindrōm/ ▸ **noun** Psychiatry another term for erotomania (excessive sexual desire).
-ORIGIN from the name of Gatin *de Clérambault* (1872–1934), French psychiatrist, who first described it.

de•com•pile /ˌdēkəm'pīl/ ▸ **verb** [trans.] Computing produce source code from (compiled code).
-DERIVATIVES **de•com•pi•la•tion** /dēˌkämpə'lāsHən; ˌdēkäm-/ noun; **de•com•pil•er** noun

de•con•di•tion•ing /ˌdēkən'disHəniNG/ ▸ **noun** Psychiatry the reform or reversal of previously conditioned behavior, especially in the treatment of phobia and other anxiety disorders in which the fear response to certain stimuli is brought under control.

de•con•flict /ˌdēkən'flikt/ ▸ **verb** resolve the conflicts or contradictions in (something): [trans.] *the spreadsheet is used to show approved*

events and to deconflict unit participation | [intrans.] *why the United States should deconflict.*
-DERIVATIVES **de•con•flic•tion** noun /-'fliksHən/

deep brain stim•u•la•tion /'dēp 'brān ˌstimyəˌlāsHən/ ▶ noun a non-surgical treatment to reduce tremor and to block involuntary movements in patients with motion disorders. Small electric shocks are delivered to the thalamus (especially in the treatment of multiple sclerosis) or the globus pallidus (especially in the treatment of Parkinson's disease), rendering these parts of the brain inactive without surgically destroying them.

deep e•col•o•gy /'dēp i'käləjē/ ▶ noun an environmental movement and philosophy that regards human life as just one of many equal components of a global ecosystem: *deep ecology stands firmly on one essential point, namely, a systematic resistance against the rationalist mind-set and commercial attitude of contemporary industrial life.* [**June 2002** *Organization & Environment*]

deep•en /'dēpən/ ▶ verb (of a weather system) decrease in barometric pressure. Compare with FILL. [as adjective] (**deepening**) *a deepening depression.*

deep mag•ic /'dēp 'majik/ ▶ noun any of the techniques used in the development of software or computer systems that require the programmer to have esoteric theoretical knowledge: *some hackers use deep magic to tweak existing software.*
-ORIGIN probably from C.S. Lewis's *Narnia* books.

deep-vein throm•bo•sis /'dēp ˌvān THräm'bōsis/ ▶ noun thrombosis in a vein lying deep below the skin, especially in the legs. It is a particular hazard of long-haul flying.

de•flesh /dē'flesH/ ▶ verb [trans.] remove the flesh from: *if you deflesh a rhino, there is an enormous amount of meat.* [**14 Sept. 1995** *Guardian (UK)*]

de•frag /dē'frag/ ▶ verb [trans.] (**de•fragged, de•frag•ging**) Computing reduce the fragmentation of files (on a disk) by concatenating the parts stored in separate locations: *we defragged the disk drives and did some more tweaking.* [**Nov. 1997** *Byte*]
▶noun an instance of defragging a disk, or the utility that does this: *maybe you leave it running to collect e-mails or carry out a defrag.* [**27 Aug. 2002** *Daily Telegraph (UK)*]
-ORIGIN shortened from *defragment.*

de•fund /dē'fənd/ ▸ verb [trans.] prevent from continuing to receive funds: *the California legislature has defunded the Industrial Welfare Commission.*

de•hy•dro•ep•i•an•dro•ste•rone /dēhīdrō,epēan'drästə,rōn/ ▸ noun see **DHEA**.

de-ink /dē'iNGk/ (also **de•ink**) ▸ verb [trans.] remove ink from (paper being recycled): *Ms. Shaw also says that 40 tons of "sludge" are created when 100 tons of paper are deinked, and that this sludge will probably end up in landfills.* [**23 Sept.** 1991 *Ad Age*]

de•in•stall /ˌdē-in'stôl/ (*British* also **de•in•stal**) ▸ verb (**de•in•stalls** also **de•in•stals, de•in•stalled, de•in•stall•ing,** also **de•in•stal• ling**) [trans.] remove (an application or file) from a computer; uninstall.■ humorous dismiss from employment: *I worked there for three months but then the company lost funding and I was deinstalled.*
-DERIVATIVES **de•in•stal•la•tion** /ˌdē-instə'lāsHən/ noun; **de•in• stall•er** noun

de•junk /dē'jəNGk/ ▸ verb [trans.] informal clear (a room or other space) by disposing of clutter and unwanted possessions: *dejunk the house before you move.* | figurative *how to dejunk your life.*

de•li•cense /dē'līsəns/ ▸ verb [trans.] deprive of a license or authority to operate: *physicians are being threatened, impoverished, delicensed, and imprisoned for prescribing in good faith with the intention of relieving pain.* [**10 Oct.** 2003 *U.S. Newswire (press release)*]

de•link /dē'liNGk/ ▸ verb [often as noun] (**delinking**) break the connection between (something) and something else: *the possibility of delinking from the international economic system.*

Del•phi tech•nique /'delfī tek,nēk/ ▸ noun a method of group decision-making and forecasting that involves successively collating the judgments of experts.
-ORIGIN in allusion to the ancient Greek oracle at *Delphi.*

de•mine /dē'mīn/ ▸ verb [trans.] remove explosive mines from: *the money will be used to demine a field in Afghanistan.*
-DERIVATIVES **de•min•er** noun

de•mu•tu•al•ize /dē'myo͞oCHo͞oə,līz/ [intrans.] ▸ verb (of a mutual insurance company) convert to a publicly held corporation: *the* *measure will be especially helpful to smaller insurers that want to demutualize.*

-DERIVATIVES **de•mu•tu•al•i•za•tion** noun

de•na•zi•fy /dē'nätsə‚fī/ ▸ verb (**de•na•zi•fies, de•na•zi•fied, de•na•zi•fy•ing**) [trans.] remove the Nazi (or figuratively, the fascist or repressive) influence from: *if Albania was a nato country, which it is not, this would be clear justification for a ground war, a war launched for the purpose of denazifying Serbia.* [**10 Apr. 1999** Usenet: alt.society.anarchy]
-DERIVATIVES **de•na•zi•fi•ca•tion** noun

den•dri•mer /'dendrəmər/ ▸ noun a synthetic polymer with a branching, treelike structure.
-ORIGIN 1990s: from Greek *dendron* 'tree' + *-i-* + *-mer.*

den•tex /'den‚teks/ ▸ noun (plural same or **den•tex•es**) any of various sea breams of the genus *Dentex*, especially *D. dentex* of the Mediterranean and the North African Atlantic coast. Many are important food fishes.
-ORIGIN modern Latin (genus name), from Latin.

de•pub•li•ca•tion /dē‚pəbli'kāsHən/ ▸ noun the act of depublishing: *Forty-four other cities had joined in an amicus brief supporting Long Beach in the Court of Appeal, and the League of California cities had requested depublication of the Div. Seven ruling.* [**2 Oct.** 2003 *Metropolitan News-Enterprise (CA)*]

de•pub•lish /dēpəblisH/ ▸ verb mainly Law remove from an official record or publication: *the Supreme Court may also elect to depublish a case on its own motion or upon the request of third parties.* [**July 1997** *California Lawyer*]

de•queue /dē'kyoō/ ▸ verb [trans.] (**de•queued, de•queu•ing** or **de•queue•ing**) Computing remove (an item) from a queue.

de•re•cho /də'rāCHō/ ▸ noun (plural **de•re•chos**) Meteorology a storm system that moves a long distance rapidly and brings winds that can devastate an area several miles wide: *the derecho produced convective wind gusts up to 100 mph across Michigan as well as isolated tornadoes.* [**1999** WRGB.com Weather]
-ORIGIN late 19th cent.: Spanish, literally 'direct, straight.'

DES ▸ abbreviation Computing data encryption standard.

des•ig•nat•ed driv•er /'dezig‚nātid 'drīvər/ ▸ **noun** a person who abstains from alcohol at a social gathering so as to be fit to drive others home.

de•sign•er stub•ble /di'zīnər ‚stəbəl/ ▸ **noun** beard stubble that is deliberately groomed to look fashionable or trendy: *Hoffman had gone as far as raising his media profile and shaving off his designer stubble: beards being generally unwelcome in City boardrooms.* [**9 Oct. 2003** *Financial Times (UK)*]

desk din•ing /'desk ‚dīniNG/ (also **desk-din•ing**) ▸ **noun** the eating of a meal at one's desk in an office.
-DERIVATIVES **desk din•er** noun

desk jock•ey /'desk ‚jäkē/ ▸ **noun** the holder of a desk job, especially an unimportant one: *I don't want to be a desk jockey answering phones and working on paperwork.* [**29 July 2003** *Billings (MT) Gazette*]

de•sol•der /dē'sädər/ ▸ **verb** [trans.] remove the solder from (electrical components), usually to effect separation: *just cut the pins one by one on the component side, desolder the halves of the pins still on the board, then throw the chip out.* [**18 Apr. 1999** Usenet: sci.electronics.basics]

des•ti•na•tion /‚destə'nāsHən/ ▸ **adjective** being a place that people will make a special trip to visit: *a destination restaurant.*

des•ti•na•tion charge /‚destə'nāsHən ‚CHärj/ ▸ **noun** a fee added to the price of a new car to cover the cost of shipping the vehicle from the manufacturer to the dealer.

de•ter•ri•to•ri•al•i•za•tion /dē‚teri‚tôrēələ'zāsHən/ ▸ **noun** the severance of social, political, or cultural practices from their native places and populations: *Christian deterritorialization of identity is powerfully present in one of my favorite moments from St. Augustine's great Confessions.* [**26 Aug. 2003** *Harvard Divinity Bulletin*]
-DERIVATIVES **de•ter•ri•to•ri•al•ize** verb

de•vel•op•men•tal de•lay /di‚veləp'mentl di'lā/ ▸ **noun** the condition of a child being less developed mentally or physically than is normal for its age: *mercury contributes to many known health problems, including neurological injury, developmental delay and cerebral palsy.* [**16 Sept. 2003** *Journal Times (WI)*]

de•vo•ré /də'vôrā/ (also **de•vo•re**) ▶ noun a velvet fabric with a pattern formed by burning the pile away with acid: [as modifier] *a devoré top.*
-ORIGIN 1990s: from French *dévoré,* lit. 'devoured,' past participle of *dévorer.*

DHEA ▶ abbreviation dehydroepiandrosterone; a naturally occurring weak androgenic steroid hormone produced by the adrenal glands. It is also prepared synthetically and sold as a food supplement with the intended benefits of improved of sexual function, enhancement of athletic performance, and the amelioration of osteoporosis.

dhikr /'THikər/ (also **zikr** /'zikər/) ▶ noun Islam a form of devotion, associated chiefly with Sufism, in which the worshipper is absorbed in the rhythmic repetition of the name of God or his attributes.
■ a Sufi ceremony in which this is practiced.
-ORIGIN from Arabic *d̲ikr* 'remembrance.'

DHTML ▶ abbreviation Computing dynamic HTML; a collection of web browser enhancements that enable dynamic and interactive features on web pages.

di•al-a•round /'dīl ə,round/ ▶ adjective used to describe a telephone service that requires callers to dial a special access code that enables them to bypass (or 'dial around') their chosen long-distance carrier in order to obtain a better rate.

dick•wad /'dik,wäd/ ▶ noun vulgar slang a contemptible person: *this little dickwad, this stupid stupid little sucker, he stood there this whole time shaking, half naked in the snow, and really believed somebody could even promise something so impossible.* [2001 Chuck Palahniuk, *Choke*]
-ORIGIN 1980s: from *dick* in the sense 'penis' + *wad.*

dic•tion•ar•y at•tack /'dikSHə,nerē ə,tak/ ▶ noun an attempted illegal entry to a computer system that uses a dictionary headword list to generate possible passwords: *it's going to be pretty hard to argue that someone doing a dictionary attack on a hotmail or an AOL or a Yahoo has actually been using personal information, although that could end up with a lot of silk in a very expensive courtroom working that one through.* [15 Sept. 2003 *ZDNet (UK)*]

diff ▶ verb [trans.] Computing compare (files) in order to determine how or whether they differ: *I diffed my new XF86config file with the old* *one and found the only diffs were that I had uncommented the lines refering to linear addressing.* [**8 May 1997** Usenet: comp.os.linux.x]

dig•i•cam /'diji,kam/ ▸ **noun** a digital camera.

dig•i•pet /'diji,pet/ ▸ noun see CYBERPET.

dig•it•al cam•er•a /'dijitl 'kam(ə)rə/ ▸ **noun** a camera that records and stores digital images.

dig•it•al com•pact cas•sette /'dijitl 'kämpakt kə'set/ (abbreviation: **DCC**) ▸ **noun** a format for tape cassettes similar to ordinary audio-cassettes but with digital rather than analog recording.

dig•it•al com•pres•sion /'dijitl kəm'presHən/ ▸ **noun** a method of reducing the number of bits (zeros and ones) in a digital signal by using mathematical algorithms to eliminate redundant information.

dig•it•al di•vide /'dijitl di'vīd/ ▸ **noun** the gulf between those who have ready access to computers and the Internet, and those who do not: *these results, if confirmed by other studies, point to a worrying "digital divide" based on race, gender, educational attainment and income.* [**1997** *Internet Research*]

dig•it•al lock•er /'dijitl 'läkər/ ▸ **noun** Computing an Internet service that allows registered users to access data stored by other users or by vendors via a web browser.

dig•it•al sig•na•ture /'dijitl 'signəCHər; -,CHŏŏr/ ▸ **noun** Computing a digital code (generated and authenticated by public key encryption) that is attached to an electronically transmitted document to verify its contents and the sender's identity.

dig•it•al tel•e•vi•sion /'dijitl 'telə,vizHən/ ▸ **noun** television broadcasting in which the pictures are transmitted as digital signals that are decoded by a device in or attached to the receiving television set.

dig•i•tal vid•e•o re•cord•er /'dijitl 'vidēō ri,kôrdər/ ▸ **noun** (abbreviation **DVR**) a programmable electronic device that writes audio and video input, typically from a television signal, to a rewritable hard disk.

di•rect deb•it /di'rekt 'debit; dī'rekt/ ▸ **noun** a payment system whereby creditors are authorized to debit a customer's bank account directly at regular intervals.

dirt•y /'dərtē/ ▸ adjective (**dirt•i•er, dirt•i•est**) slang using or carrying illegal drugs: *why didn't you tell me you was dirty? You know I'm on probation, man. I'll get a bid 'cause your fat ass traveling dirty.* [2000 P. Beatty, *Tuff*]

dirt•y bomb /'dərtē 'bäm/ ▸ noun an improvised nuclear weapon from radioactive nuclear waste material and conventional explosives: *radiation from a dirty bomb would increase the risk of getting cancer in the long term, but the primary concern might actually be the psychological impact and the potential for economic damage.* [4 Mar. 2003 *Insight*]

dirt•y rice /'dərtē 'rīs/ ▸ noun a Cajun dish consisting of white rice cooked with onions, peppers, chicken livers, and herbs.

dis•ap•pear /ˌdisə'pi(ə)r/ ▸ verb [trans.] cause to disappear, as by consumption: *statistics show that the community disappears about 200 pounds of cabbage a year.*

dis•cern•ment /di'sərnmənt/ ▸ noun (in Christian contexts) perception in the absence of judgment with a view to obtaining spiritual direction and understanding: *without providing for a time of healing and discernment, there will be no hope of living through this present moment without a shattering of our common life.* [12 Oct. 2003 *Sarasota Herald-Tribune*]

dis•con•nect /ˌdiskə'nekt/ ▸ noun a discrepancy or lack of connection: *there can be a disconnect between boardrooms and IT departments when it comes to technology.*

di•sease man•age•ment /di'zēz ˌmanijmənt/ ▸ noun a system that seeks to manage the chronic conditions of high-risk, high-cost patients as a group.

dish•pan hands /'disH,pan 'handz/ ▸ plural noun red, rough, or chapped hands caused by sensitivity to or excessive use of household detergents or other cleaning agents.

Dis•ney•land /'diznē,land/ ▸ noun a place of fantasy or make-believe: *their own think tank, their own Disneyland of future ideas* | [as modifier] *Disneyland conceptions of defense which have no genuine relevance.* -ORIGIN after the amusement park in Anaheim, California, of this name, opened in 1955.

dis•play ad /dis'plā ˌad/ ▸ **noun** a large advertisement, especially in a newspaper or magazine, that features eye-catching type or illustrations.

dis•tant ear•ly warn•ing /'distənt 'ərlē 'wôrniNG/ (abbreviation: **DEW**) ▸ **noun** a radar system in North America for the early detection of a missile attack.

dis•trib•ut•ed /di'stribyo͞otid/ ▸ **adjective** Computing (of a computer system) spread over several machines, especially over a network: *the Wi-Fi IDS would package two new features from IBM Research, including the capability to do security auditing in a distributed environment.* [**9 Oct. 2003** *InternetNews.com*]

dis•tro /'distrō/ ▸ **noun** a distributor, especially of Linux software or of web-based zines: *I've been working on this project for a little while and decided to post this here in case anyone who runs a distro is interested.*
■ a particular distributable or distributed version of Linux software: *I was excited enough about this distro that I forked over the cash to buy it.*

Dix•ie Cup /'diksē ˌkəp/ ▸ **noun** trademark a brand of disposable paper cup; used generically and variously capitalized for any small disposable cup: *These days, the public-school principals . . . can, on . . . short notice, distribute Dixie cups and send their charges to the lavatories. Once, only athletes faced these random drug tests.* [**14 Apr. 2002** *New York Times*]

djem•be /'jembə; -bā/, ▸ **noun** a kind of goblet-shaped hand drum originating in West Africa.
-ORIGIN French *djembé*, from Mande *jembe*.

DLL ▸ **abbreviation** dynamic link library; a collection of small programs for common use by larger programs or software suites.
■ a particular file containing such a program, and carrying the extension .DLL: *a program that has been corrupted by a DLL.*

DMCA ▸ **abbreviation** the Digital Millennium Copyright Act; a 1998 U.S. law that was intended to update copyright law for electronic commerce and electronic content providers. It criminalizes the circumvention of electronic and digital copyright protection systems: *this is a classic fair-use right protected under the copyright act, but it is a right that is extinguishable under the DMCA.* [**11 Oct. 2003** *Wired News*]

DNR ▸ **abbreviation 1** Department of Natural Resources.
2 do not resuscitate; a code used in hospitals and nursing homes
with reference to particular patients, indicating that no extraordinary measures should be implemented to prevent imminent
death.

DNS ▸ **abbreviation** Computing domain name system; the system by which
Internet domain names and addresses are tracked and regulated.

Dob•son u•nit /ˈdäbsən ˌyo͞onit/ (abbreviation: **DU**) ▸ **noun** a unit of
measurement for the total amount of ozone in the atmosphere
above a point on the earth's surface, one Dobson unit being equivalent to a layer of pure ozone 0.01 mm thick at standard temperature and pressure.
-ORIGIN 1980s: from the name of G. M. B. *Dobson* (1889–1976),
British meteorologist.

doc•u•soap /ˈdäkyəˌsōp/ ▸ **noun** a documentary, usually produced
for television and having elements of soap opera, following people in a particular occupation or location over a period of time:
*the speaker, Betty Boothroyd, is set to end the tradition of secrecy by
approving the filming of a Channel 4 "docusoap" which will show politicians at work and play throughout the House of Commons.* [**24 Mar.**
1998 *Daily Telegraph*]
-ORIGIN 1990s: blend of *documentary* and *soap (opera)*.

dog•gy style /ˈdôgē ˌstīl/ (also **dog•gy fash•ion** /ˈdôgē ˌfasHən/)
▸ **noun and adverb** vulgar slang (in) a position for human sexual intercourse modeled on that of dogs.

DOHC ▸ **abbreviation** dual overhead cam (engine).

DOI ▸ **abbreviation** Computing digital object identifier, a unique identifying number allocated to a Web site.

dol•phin-safe /ˈdälfin ˌsāf; ˈdôl-/ ▸ **adjective** (on canned tuna labels)
indicating that the tuna has been harvested using fishing methods that are not harmful to dolphins.

do•main name /dōˈmān ˌnām/ ▸ **noun** Computing a series of alphanu-
meric strings separated by periods, such as *www.oup-usa.org*, serving as an address for a computer network connection and identifying the owner of the address. The last three letters in a domain
name indicate what type of organization owns the address: for

instance, .com stands for commercial, .edu for educational, and .org for nonprofit.

dong quai /'dôNG 'kwā; 'kwī/, ▸ **noun** an aromatic herb native to China and Japan, the root of which is used by herbalists to treat premenstrual syndrome and menopausal symptoms.
•*Angelica sinensis*, family Umbelliferae.
-ORIGIN from Chinese *dāngguī*.

do•nor fa•tigue /'dōnər fə‚tēg/ ▸ **noun** an unwillingness to contribute to a charitable cause, typically because of repeated appeals or the perception that previous donations have addressed the problem: *donor fatigue suggests the West's increasing frustration over trying to assist the Third World with problems that, instead of diminishing over time, simply grow more massive year by year.* [13 **July 1991** *New Scientist (UK)*]

door•bust•er /'dôr‚bəstər/ ▸ **noun** 1 (in retailing) a special discount price available for a limited period, typically during special early-opening hours: [as modifier] *is it sad when you realize that the main reason you're out there standing in line is not so you can take advantage of the doorbuster deals but rather so you can talk about the social phenomenon later?* [**29 Nov. 2000** Weblog at Mindspillage.net]
2 a firearm with special attachments for forcing entry through a door.

do•pa•min•er•gic /‚dōpəmi'nərjik/ ▸ **adjective** Biochemistry releasing or involving dopamine as a neurotransmitter. Drugs with this effect are used in the treatment of Parkinson's disease and some psychiatric disorders; some are subject to abuse.
-ORIGIN 1960s: from *dopamine* + Greek *ergon* 'work' + -*ic*.

do-rag /'dōō ‚rag/ ▸ **noun** black slang a scarf or cloth worn to protect one's hairstyle: *13 year old kids in big pants, "wife beater" T-shirts, and do-rags dancing to the sound of 50 Cent and calling each other "G."* [**2003** Patrick Shea]
-ORIGIN 1990s: from *hairdo* and *rag*.

DoS ▸ **abbreviation** denial of service, an interruption in an authorized user's access to a computer network, typically one caused with malicious intent.

DOT ▸ **abbreviation** directly observed therapy, a method of supervising patients to ensure that they take medication as directed.

dot-bomb /'dät 'bäm/ (also **dot bomb** or **dot.bomb**) ▸ **noun** informal an unsuccessful dot-com: *many promising Internet start-ups ended up as dot-bombs.*
-DERIVATIVES **dot-bomb verb** [intrans.]

dot-com /'dät 'käm/ (also **dot.com**) ▸ **noun** a company that conducts its business on the Internet.
▸**adjective** of or relating to business conducted on the Internet.
-DERIVATIVES **dot-com•er** /'kämər/ **noun**
-ORIGIN 1990s: from '.com' in an Internet address, indicating a commercial site.

007 /'ō'ō'sevən; 'dəbəl ˌō-/ ▸ **noun** the fictional British secret agent James Bond, or someone based on, inspired by, or reminiscent of him: *When the wife of Bond's buddy is wiped out in "License to Kill," 007 goes berserk and seeks revenge.* [**26 June 1989** *U.S. News and World Report*]
▸**adjective** reminiscent of or inspired by features of the James Bond films: *"This is not 007 territory," said Julian Murfitt, Managing Director of document tracking and management firm Mekon. "It can be achieved with the tools that are available already."* [**3 July** 2003 *BBC News Online*]

dou•la /'dōōlə/ ▸ **noun** a woman giving support, help, and advice to another woman during pregnancy and during and after the birth: *for the better part of a year, I have been serving as doula to a mother guinea pig named Lucy.* [**June** 2002 *Ladies Home Journal*]
-ORIGIN 1960s: modern Greek, from Greek *doulē* 'female slave.'

down•burst /'doun,bərst/ ▸ **noun** a strong downward current of air from a cumulonimbus cloud, which is usually accompanied by intense rain or a thunderstorm.

down•code /'doun,kōd/ ▸ **verb** **1** designate (a medical procedure or insurance claim) with a lower value: [trans.] *I was surprised to learn only recently that Pennsylvania Blue Shield systematically downcodes professional charge submissions for critical care services.* [**2003** *Physician's News Digest*] | [intrans.] *we cannot turn to Medicaid to pay if Medicare downcodes since, when acting as a secondary payer, Medicaid only pays the 20% co-insurance.* [**2003** Wata.org]
2 rewrite or convert (programs or software) into a lower level language: [trans.] *some of the libraries written into C were also downcoded into assembly primarily for compactness but with the side effect of speeding them up.* [**18 Nov. 1996** Usenet: comp.sys.amiga.programmer]
-DERIVATIVES **down•cod•ing noun**

down•lev•el /'doun₁levəl/ ▸ **adjective** using an earlier version of software, hardware, or an operating system: *even if all the vulnerabilities were fixed tomorrow morning in all of the products, there's still 600 million computers, many of them downlevel, many of them on funny versions that wouldn't have all of these vulnerabilities patched, fixed and up to date.* [**9 Oct.** 2003 *InternetNews*]

down•tem•po /'doun₁tempō/ ▸ **adjective** (of music) having a relatively slower beat: *they'd rock at ferocious velocity, spitting slogan lyrics about eating the bourgeoisie, then stop and play a downtempo reggae song as religiously numbed out as it gets.* [**7 Aug.** 1999 *New York Times*]
▸ **noun** a genre of electronic dance music with influences from jazz, bossa nova, and dub reggae: *although downtempo has a growing following in club capitals like New York City, London, Tokyo and Berlin, its epicenters are in Vienna and Washington D.C.* [**11 Oct.** 2002 *Wall Street Journal*]

down•wind•er /'doun'windər/ ▸ **noun** a person living downwind of a nuclear test site or reactor, where the risk from fallout or radiation leaks is greatest.

draft pick /'draft ₁pik/ ▸ **noun** a professional athlete who becomes a member of a team through the draft system: *North Carlolina's top draft pick is ready to play ball.*
■ the activity or an instance of choosing such an athlete: *Steelers make history with worst draft pick ever.*

drag-and-drop /'drag ən 'dräp/ ▸ **verb** Computing [trans.] move (an icon or other screen element) to another part of the screen using a mouse or similar device, typically in order to perform some operation on a file or document.
▸ **adjective** of, relating to, or permitting the movement of data in this way.

dress-down Fri•day /'dres₁doun 'frī₁dā; 'frīdē/ ▸ **noun** another term for CASUAL FRIDAY.

drill /dril/ ▸ **verb** [intrans.] (**drill down**) Computing access data that is in a lower level of a hierarchically structured database: *just as the department can view a single screen showing the IT infrastructure, and drill down to any faulty component, so a single screen shows the entire electricity distribution infrastructure, and can drill down to the source of any fault.* [**14 Nov.** 1996 *Computer Weekly*]

drop /dräp/ ▸ verb (**dropped, drop•ping**) [trans.] British informal (of a DJ) select and play (a record): *various guest DJs drop quality tunes both old and new.*

drop box /'dräp ˌbäks/ ▸ noun a secured receptacle into which items such as returned books or videotapes, payments, keys, or donated clothing can be deposited.

drop-ship /'dräp ˌSHip/ ▸ verb (**drop-shipped, drop-ship•ping**) [trans.] move (goods) from the manufacturer directly to the retailer or consumer without going through the usual distribution channels: *television shopping network ShopNBC, looking to improve its fulfillment process, has begun drop-shipping orders taken by telephone or over the Internet.* [**30 Sept.** 2003 *DM News (NY)*]
-DERIVATIVES **drop ship•ment** noun

drug mule /'drəg ˌmyo͞ol/ ▸ noun a person who transports illegal drugs by swallowing them or concealing them in a body cavity.

dry•er sheet /'drīər ˌSHēt/ ▸ noun a fabric softener sheet.

dry mount•ing /'drī ˌmountiNG/ ▸ noun Photography a process in which a print is bonded to a mount using a layer of adhesive in a hot press.
-DERIVATIVES **dry-mount** /'drī ˌmount/ verb; **dry-mount•ed** adjective

DSL ▸ abbreviation digital subscriber line, a technology for the high-speed transmission of digital information over telephone lines within a certain radius of an exchange.

DTD ▸ abbreviation document type definition; a template that sets out the format and tag structure of an SGML-compliant document.

DTV ▸ abbreviation digital television.

DU ▸ abbreviation 1 depleted uranium.
2 Dobson unit(s).

dub-dub-dub /'dəb 'dəb 'dəb/ ▸ noun Computing, informal short form used instead of pronouncing the three letters in the abbreviation WWW (World Wide Web).

dub reg•gae /'dəb ˌregā; ˌrägā/ ▸ noun a genre of popular dance music made from remixing reggae recordings: *Phase Selector Sound's inventive dub reggae recordings transcend their Music City origins.*

dul•ce de le•che /'dōōl,sā də 'läcHä/ ▸ **noun** a traditional Argentinian dessert made by caramelizing sugar in milk.
-ORIGIN Spanish, 'sweetness of milk.'

dumb•size /'dəm,sīz/ ▸ **verb** [intrans.] (of a company) reduce staff numbers to levels so low that work can no longer be carried out effectively.
-ORIGIN 1990s: humorously, on the pattern of *downsize*.

dump•ster div•ing /'dəmpstər ,dīviNG/ ▸ **noun** the practice of raiding dumpsters to find discarded items that are still useful, recyclable, or edible.

Dun•geons and Drag•ons /'dənjənz ən 'dragənz/ ▸ **noun** trademark a fantasy role-playing game set in an imaginary world based loosely on medieval myth.

Dust•bust•er /'dəst,bəstər/ ▸ **trademark** a hand-held vacuum cleaner.

DVR ▸ **abbreviation** DIGITAL VIDEO RECORDER.

dwell time /'dwel ,tīm/ ▸ **noun** technical time spent in the same position, area, stage of a process, etc.: *overall, average "dwell time" at U.S. airports has reached a new high—almost 70 minutes, says the firm, Air Marketing Services.* [21 **Apr.** 2000 *Wall Street Journal*]

DWEM ▸ **abbreviation** DEAD WHITE EUROPEAN MALE.

DWM ▸ **abbreviation 1** dead white male; used to describe a writer, philosopher, or other significant figure whose importance and talents may have been exaggerated by virtue of his belonging to a historically dominant gender.
2 (in personal ads) divorced white male.

dy•nam•ic link li•brar•y /dī'namik 'liNGk ,lībrerē; -brərē/ (abbreviation: **DLL**) ▸ **noun** see **DLL**.

dy•nam•ic pric•ing /dī'namik 'prīsiNG/ ▸ **noun** the practice of pricing items at a level determined by a particular customer's perceived ability to pay.

dys•mor•phi•a /dis'môrfēə/ ▸ **noun** Medicine deformity or abnormality in the shape or size of a specified part of the body: *muscle dysmorphia.*
-DERIVATIVES **dys•mor•phic** adjective

-ORIGIN late 19th cent.: from Greek *dusmorphia* 'misshapenness, ugliness,' from *dus- dis- + morphē* 'form.'

dys•prax•i•a /dis'praksēə/ ▸ **noun** an inability to plan, coordinate, or execute coordinated movements, especially as a developmental syndrome in children.
-DERIVATIVES **dys•prax•ic, adjective:** *is my toddler dyspraxic?*

Ee

e¹ ▸ (€) **symbol for** euro(s).

e² /ē/ ▸ **noun** (plural **e's**) an e-mail system, message, or messages: *On your next business trip, you might want to go surfing, or you may want to do an "e." An e-mail that is.* [23 Nov 1996 *Independent (UK)*] ▸**verb** (**e'd, e'•ing**) [trans.] **1** send an e-mail to (someone): *Anime Vids FOR SALE (E-me to make offer)* [1 Nov. 1996 Usenet: rec.-arts.anime.marketplace] **2** send (a message) by e-mail.

ear can•dy /'i(ə)r ˌkandē/ ▸ **noun** informal light music that is pleasant and entertaining but intellectually undemanding: *the faint incense is as mellow as the background music—New Age chords and reverberations sometimes called "ear candy," with titles such as "Inside The Great Pyramid" or "Life on the Double Planet."* [13 Nov. 1987 *Washington Post*]

ear•ly doors /'ərlē 'dôrz/ ▸ **adverbial phrase** British informal early on, especially in a game or contest: *this little rabbit's warren has played a major role in the Edinburgh scene for some time and early doors I could tell my feet were going to slip and slide all over the small dance floor within those low arches.* [4 Nov. 2000 www.soul-a-go-go-demon.co.uk] -ORIGIN apparently originally with reference to admission to a music hall some time before the start of the performance.

ear•ly a•dopt•er /'ərlē ə'däptər/ ▸ **noun** a person who starts using a product or technology as soon as it becomes available: *Sony's product is still too costly and too flawed to be ready for mainstream business users, in my view. It is likelier to be embraced by "early adopters," people willing to pay for new technology, despite its high price and rough edges.* [6 Oct. 1994 *Wall Street Journal*]

ear•ly warn•ing sys•tem /'ərlē 'wôrnɪNG ˌsistəm/ ▸ **noun** a network of radar stations established at the boundary of a defended region to provide advanced warning of an aircraft or missile attack. ■ a condition, system, or series of procedures indicating a potential development or impending problem: *the Colorado Department of Transportation is designing an early-warning system intended to alert motorists to accidents or slow-moving vehicles in or near the tunnel.* [30 July 2003 *Grand Junction (CO) Sentinel*]

e-book /'ē ˌbo͝ok/ ▸ noun an electronic version of a printed book that can be read on a personal computer or hand-held device designed specifically for this purpose: *the arrival of the e-book could change the way many books are read, written and published—a shakeup under way thanks to the Internet.* [5 **Oct 1998** *Baltimore Sun*] ▪ a dedicated device for reading electronic versions of printed books.

e-busi•ness /'ē ˌbiznis/ ▸ noun another term for E-COMMERCE.

ec•o•cen•trism /ˌekō'senˌtrizəm; ˌēkō-/ ▸ noun a point of view that recognizes the ecosphere, rather than the biosphere, as central in importance, and attempts to redress the imbalance created by anthropocentrism: *Max Oelschlaeger, in his much more scholarly and thorough book,* The Idea of Wilderness, *clearly distinguishes between preservationism and ecocentrism.* [10 **Feb. 1997** Bill Deval] –DERIVATIVES **ec•o•cen•tric** /-'sentrik/ adjective

ec•o•con•sum•er /'ekōkənˌso͞omər; 'ēkō-/ ▸ noun a consumer who makes purchasing decisions partly or largely on the basis of ecological issues: *a large number of sophisticated ecoconsumers are descending upon some destinations that are not capable of delivering the expected services.* [(**undated**) *Understanding the Market for Sustainable Tourism*]

ec•o•lodge /'ekōˌläj; 'ēkō-/ ▸ noun a type of tourist accommodation designed to have the minimum possible impact on the natural environment in which it is situated: *Mayor Bob Ornelas mentioned an ecolodge or ecohostel as potential uses for the site.* [19 **July 2003** *(CA) Times Standard*]

ec•o•log•i•cal cas•cade /ˌekə'läjikəl kas'kād/ ▸ noun a shift in the balance of populations in an ecosystem occasioned by marked depletion in one species, usually as a result of human action: *once those prey dwindled, orcas would settle for the smaller fur seals and aggressive sea lions. Finally, killer whales would snack on otters. In what may be a further iteration of this ecological cascade, sea urchins—a favorite food for otters—have thrived.* [27 **Sept. 2003** *Science News*]

ec•o•log•i•cal foot•print /ˌekə'läjikəl 'fo͝otˌprint/ ▸ noun the sum of an individual's or other entity's impact on the enviornment, based on consumption and pollution: *the company is working to reduce its ecological footprint by using organic ingredients, supporting a wind farm to offset its CO2 emissions, purchasing certified organic cotton for its promotional T-shirts, and incorporating "green" office practices.* [13 **Aug. 2003** *Daily Peloton*]

e-com•merce /'ē ˌkämərs/ (also **E-commerce**) ▸ noun commercial transactions conducted electronically on the Internet: *it is also a major problem for ground carriers, all of which acknowledge they are ill-equipped to handle the onslaught if E-commerce really catches on.* [**30 Mar.** 1998 *New York Times*]

e•con•o•box /i'känəˌbäks/ ▸ noun informal a car that is small and economical rather than luxurious or stylish: *VW hopes to distance the Golf from the econobox image of the Rabbit, which also was hurt by mechanical problems and competition from a flood of look-a-like cars from Japan.* [**7 Sept.** 1984 *Wall Street Journal*]

ec•o•nom•ic mi•grant /'ekəˌnämik 'mīgrənt; 'ēkə-/ ▸ noun a person who travels from one country or area to another in order to improve their standard of living: *the US and Vietnam oppose a drive by Britain and most Southeast Asian nations to set up a UN-run program to force Vietnam's "economic migrants," or boat people, to return home.* [**22 June** 1989 *Christian Science Monitor*]

e•con•o•my-class syn•drome /i'känəmē ˌklas ˌsindrōm/ ▸ noun deep-vein thrombosis said to be caused by periods of prolonged immobility on long-haul flights: *in-Flight Yoga in my opinion presents an excellent preventive with respect to the economy class syndrome.* [**(undated)** stretch.com]

e•con•tent /'ē ˌkäntent/ (also **e-con•tent, eContent**) ▸ noun text and images designed for display on web pages: [often as modifier] *Visit our eContent call pages for more details of the multilingual and multicultural content action line.* [**17 Sept.** 2003 HLTCentral.org]

ec•o•re•gion /'ekōˌrējən; 'ēkō-/ ▸ noun a major ecosystem defined by distinctive geography and receiving uniform solar radiation and moisture: *from a conservation standpoint, the Hanford Site is a vital . . . link in preserving and sustaining the diverse plants and animals of the Columbia Basin Ecoregion.* [**20 Aug.** 1998 *Christian Science Monitor*]

ec•o-war•ri•or /'ekō ˌwôrēər; 'ēkō-/ ▸ noun a person actively involved in preventing damage to the environment: *a year after retiring from Greenpeace, a British lord-cum-ecowarrior has joined the other side.* [**11 Jan.** 2002 *Wall Street Journal*]

ECOWAS ▸ abbreviation Economic Community of West African States.

ed•a•ma•me /ˌedə'mämä/ ▶ noun a Japanese dish of salted green soybeans boiled or steamed in their pods.
– ORIGIN Japanese, literally 'beans on a branch.'

ed•u•crat /'ejəˌkrat/ ▶ noun disparaging an education administrator: *it won't be long before the educrat dim-bulbs, idiots and imbeciles of the National Education Association and their brainless humanoid "teachers" and administrators start punishing little boys for the egregious simulated criminal activity identified as "shredding."* [**8 July 2002** conservativetruth.org]

EEA ▶ abbreviation European Economic Area, a free-trade zone created in 1994, composed of the states of the European Union together with Iceland, Norway, and Liechtenstein: [as modifier] *if you are an EEA national you can come and go freely from the country.*

Ee•yor•ish /'ēyôrisн; 'ēôr-/ (also **Ee•yore•ish**) ▶ adjective pessimistic or gloomy: *However, none of the delegates were remotely as glum as Douglas Hurd who made one of the most Eeyorish speeches a Tory conference can have heard.* [**26 Mar. 1994** *Guardian (UK)*]
– ORIGIN 1990s: from *Eeyore*, the name of a donkey in A. A. Milne's *Winnie-the-Pooh* (1926), characterized by his gloomy outlook on life.

ef•fing /'efiNG/ ▶ adjective informal a euphemistic substitute for the word *fucking*.

E-fit /'ē ˌfit/ ▶ noun an electronic picture of a person's face made from composite photographs of facial features, created by a computer program: *the suspects were identified to police from computer-enhanced photofits, or E-Fits, of the two men.* [**14 Aug. 1995** *Daily Telegraph (UK)*]
– ORIGIN 1980s: from *e-* 'electronic' and *fit*, on the pattern of *Photofit* (trademark method of creating a composite picture of a crime suspect's face).

EFM ▶ abbreviation electronic fetal monitor.

EGD ▶ noun a technology or system that integrates a computer display with a pair of eyeglasses, using a lens or mirror to reflect images into the eyes: *some EGDs are designed to clip right on to your eyeglasses.*
– ORIGIN abbreviation of 'eyeglass display.'

e•go•surf /'ēgōˌsərf/ ▶ verb [intrans.] informal search the Internet for instances of one's own name or links to one's own Web site: *I*

egosurfed a bit to see what the DSS would find if they searched the Web to find out about me. [11 **May** 2001 posting on the FoRK mailing list]
-DERIVATIVES **e•go•surf•ing** noun

el•der•care /'eldər₁ke(ə)r/ ▸ noun care of the elderly or infirm, provided by residential institutions, by paid daily help in the home, or by family members: *why do adult daughters provide 72 percent of eldercare outside of institutions?* [28 **Mar.** 1991 *New York Review of Books*]

e•lec•tro•fu•sion /i₁lektrō'fyo͞ozнən/ ▸ noun fusion (in cells or other materials) that is induced by the application of electric current: *the shell and centre are joined by electrofusion, with the reconstructed embryo retaining most of the mother's DNA.* [13 **Oct.** 2003 News.com.au]

e•lec•tron•i•ca /ilek'tronikə; ₁ēlek-/ ▸ noun 1 a popular style of music deriving from techno and rave and having a more ambient, esoteric, or cerebral quality: *downstairs, the likes of Original Rocker DJ Dick and Nathan Gregory spin dustbeats, underground electronica and other assorted stoned grooves for the ultimate chill-out experience.* [Oct. 1994 *i-D*]
2 electronic devices or technology considered collectively.
-ORIGIN 1990s: from *electronic* + *-a* Greek and Latin plural ending of neuter nouns.

e•lec•tron•ic mu•sic /ilek'tränik 'myo͞ozik; ₁ēlek-/ ▸ noun music created using synthesizers and other electronic instruments: *one of the clichés of ambient and electronic music criticism is the non-existence of stars and "exciting," sweat-drenched, sexually bulging performers.* [**Jan.** 1998 *Face (UK)*]

e•lec•tron•ic or•gan•iz•er /ilek₁tränik 'ôrgə₁nīzər; ₁ēlek-/ ▸ noun a pocket-sized computer used for storing and retrieving information such as addresses and appointments: *that's right, I don't believe in Filofaxes or electronic organizers or datebooks or any of those other sissy devices for making a list.* [28 **Apr.** 1996 *Daily Yomiuri (Japan)*]

e•lec•tro•so•mat•ic /i₁lektrōsə'matik; -sō-/ ▸ adjective 1 pertaining to electronic devices implanted in an organism: *intriguing as the electrosomatic devices are, it is the psychic and behavioural functions of the brain that are the most spectacularly controlled by ESB.* [1973 David Rorvik, *As Man Becomes Machine*]

2 (sometimes in pseudoscientific use) pertaining to electrical fields within an organism: *oh, that's right, there is still this nagging matter of the curative properties of certain plants, and electrosomatic healing energy, which endangers the livelihood of slash-and-burn medicine* [**13 Apr. 1998** Usenet: misc.activism.militia]

el•e•va•tor talk /'elə‚vātər ‚tôk/ ▸ **noun** brief and superficial talk that is suitable for an elevator ride: *We made some small talk on the way up—we talked about the weather and he said how cute my daughter was—just that kind of "doctor elevator talk".* [**16 May 2000** Usenet: alt.support.single-parents]
■ an example of this that summarizes an idea: *The first few sentences of their statements would constitute an "elevator talk" a brief response to the question "So, what is your research about?" that could be offered in an elevator ride between several floors.* [**17 Jan.** 2000 *Speaking of Computers*]

e•lim•i•na•tion di•et /i‚limə'nāsHən ‚dī-it/ ▸ **noun** a diet that eliminates foods that are suspected of causing disease symptoms in an individual: *if you suspect an allergy, your therapist might suggest an elimination diet, which will allow her to pinpoint which foods are causing your symptoms.* [**1996** *Hamlyn Encyclopedia of Complementary Health*]

el•lip•ti•cal gal•ax•y /i'liptikəl 'galəksē / ▸ **noun** a galaxy in the shape of a spheroid or ellipsoid, thought to be formed by the merger of two spiral galaxies: *with some practice, you can learn to visually tell what type of elliptical galaxy you are observing.* [**(undated)** Sloan Digital Sky Survey Web site]

ELSS ▸ **abbreviation** Aerospace extravehicular life support system.

ELT ▸ **abbreviation** English language teaching.

em•bed /em'bed/ (also **imbed** /im-/) ▸ **verb** (**em•bed•ded, em•bed•ding**) [trans.] **1** Computing incorporate (a text or code) within the body of a file or document: *You don't just paste objects like data, text, graphics or pictures anymore. You embed them. Into one unified working environment.* [**Dec. 1993** *MacWorld*]
■ design and build (a microprocessor) as an integral part of a system or device.
2 permit (a journalist) to travel with a military unit: *Air Force brass are crying the blues because their guys aren't getting a headline role in the Afghan campaign. It's mostly Go Navy, which has reporters "embedded" on carriers.* [**29 Oct. 2001** *U.S. News and World Report*]

▸**noun** /'em͵bed/ an embedded journalist: *no fewer than 500 "embeds" are now eating and sleeping with the soldiers.* [**30 Mar.** 2003 *Sunday Times (UK)*]
–DERIVATIVES **em•bed•ment** noun

em•bry•ec•to•my /͵embrē'ektəmē/ ▸ noun (plural **em•bry•ec•to•mies**) the surgical removal of an embryo, especially one implanted outside the uterus in an ectopic pregnancy.

em•bry•op•a•thy /͵embrē'äpəTHē/ ▸ noun (plural **em•bry•op•a•thies**) a developmental defect in an embryo or fetus.

e•mer•gent /i'mərjənt/ ▸ **adjective** arising and existing only as a phenomenon of independent parts working together, and not predictable on the basis of their properties: *one such emergent property is the ability, already described, of an established ecosystem to repel an invading species even if it is competitively superior to its potential rival within the community.* [**29 Nov.** 1997 *New Scientist (UK)*]
▸**noun** an emergent object or phenomenon: *the mind may be an emergent—that is, unpredictable and irreducible—property of the brain's complex behavior, just as James Joyce's* Ulysses *is a surprising outcome of applying the rules of spelling and grammar to the alphabet.* [**July** 1994 *Scientific American*]

e•merg•ing mar•ket /i'mərjiNG 'märkit/ ▸ noun a market, typically in a developing economy, that is expected to become profitable soon: *their eyes—and wallets—quickly alighted on the world's so-called emerging markets.* [**15 Feb.** 1999 *Time*]

e•mo /'ē͵mō/ (also **e•mo•core** /'ēmō͵kôr/) ▸ noun a style of rock music resembling punk but having lyrics that deal with more emotional subjects: *Dashboard Confessional lifts the genre known as emocore out of the elitist indie rock gutter and delivers it straight-faced to the MTV generation.* [**14 Oct.** 2002 *New Yorker*]
–ORIGIN 1990s: short for *emotional hardcore.*

em•press tree /'empris ͵trē/ ▸ noun a fast-growing Paulownia widely grown as an ornamental in the U.S. and lately considered an ecological threat, in light of its prolific growth and reproductive capacity.
•*Paulownia tomentosa,* family Scrophulariaceae.

en•a•bled /en'ābəld/ ▸ **adjective** [in combination] adapted for use with the specified application or system: *Java-enabled push technology* *which aims to make the Internet a simple, yet media-rich, plug 'n' play environment.* [27 **May 1997** *Independent (UK)*]

en•clave /'en‚klāv; 'äNG-/ ▸ **noun** a secured area within another secured area: *the cost of a security service is going to be proportional to the size of the enclave that you must secure.* [**July 1995** *Network Security (on Navy Web site)*]

end•i•an /'endēən/ ▸ **adjective** Computing denoting or relating to a system of ordering data in a computer's memory whereby the most significant (**big endian**) or least significant (**little endian**) byte is put first: *Microsoft recently confirmed that Virtual PC does not work on G5 processors, because processor support for a little endian mode does not exist on the G5.* [**4 Sept. 2003** *Macworld (UK) Daily News*]
-ORIGIN 1980s: a reference to Swift's *Gulliver's Travels*, in which the Lilliputians were divided into two camps, those who ate their eggs by opening the 'big' end and those who ate them by opening the 'little' end.

end use /'end ‚yo͞os/ ▸ **noun** the application or function for which something is designed or for which it is ultimately used: *bankers say it is difficult to monitor the end use of funds.* [**14 Sept. 2003** *Economic Times (India)*] | [as modifier] *policy encouraging increase of prices for end-use commodities* [**9 Sept. 2003** *Pravda*]

en•ne•a•gram /'enēə‚gram/ ▸ **noun** a nine-sided figure used in a particular system of analysis to represent the spectrum of possible personality types: *the enneagram, a little-known personality test, is part psychology, part numerology.* [**24 Apr. 2003** *Time Out New York*]
-ORIGIN from Greek *ennea* 'nine' + *-gram* 'something written or recorded.'

e•no•ki /i'nōkē/ (also **e•no•ki mush•room** /i'nōkē 'məsH‚ro͞om; -‚ro͞om/) ▸ **noun** an edible Japanese mushroom (*Flammulina velutipes*, family Agaricaceae), growing in clusters, with slender stems and small caps.
-ORIGIN 1980s: from Japanese *enoki-take*, from *enoki* 'nettle-tree' + *take* 'mushroom.'

en•queue /en'kyo͞o/ ▸ **verb** [trans.] (**en•queued, en•queu•ing** or **en•queue•ing**) Computing add (an item) to a queue: *your message has been enqueued and undeliverable for 1 day(s) to the following recipients.* [**14 June 1999** Usenet: news.admin.net-abuse.email]

en•the•o•gen /en'thēə‚jen; -jən/ ▸ **noun** a chemical substance, typically of plant origin, that is ingested to produce a nonordinary

state of consciousness for religious or spiritual purposes: *the purpose of the Entheogen Project is to systematically gather knowledge about the immediate and long-term effects of entheogen use.* [2003 Council on Spiritual Practices Web site]
-DERIVATIVES **en•the•o•gen•ic** adjective
-ORIGIN 1970s; from Greek, literally 'becoming divine within'; coined by an informal commitee studying the inebriants of shamans.

en•ti•tle•ment pro•gram /en'tītlmənt ˌprōgram; ˌprōgrəm/ ▸ noun a government program that guarantees certain benefits to a particular group or segment of the population: *"Let's not just throw more money at it," said Sen. Rick Santorum, R-Pa., who said the government should not make child care an entitlement program.* [10 **Sept.** 2003 *Newsday*]

en•try in•hib•itor /'entrē inˌhibitər/ ▸ noun a class of anti-HIV drugs that work by blocking the entry of the virus into a host cell: *entry inhibitors have arisen, in part, from a better understanding of how HIV gets inside lymphocytes and the other blood cells that are the microbe's principal targets.* [3 **Feb.** 2000 *Washington Post*]

en•vi•ro /en'vīrō/ ▸ noun (plural **en•vi•ros**) informal an environmentalist: *he tends to favor market incentives over the kind of command-and-control solutions demanded by the more radical enviros.* [18 **Jan.** 1993 *Forbes*]
▸ adjective environmental: *the League of Conservation Voters, an enviro group that combats the committee's advocates for Western ranching, mining and energy interests.* [21 **Mar.** 1993 *New Republic*]

en•vi•ron•men•tal au•dit /en'vīrən'mentl 'ôdit; en'vī(ə)rn-/ ▸ noun an assessment of the extent to which an organization is observing practices that seek to minimize harm to the environment: *it was the first instance where a major environmental group partnered with McDonald's on an environmental audit.* [11 **Sept.** 2003 *Forbes*]

en•vi•ron•men•tal med•i•cine /en'vīrən'mentl 'medisən; en'vī(ə)rn-/ ▸ noun a branch of medicine that studies environmental inputs and the individual's physical, mental, and emotional responses to them: *Dr. Betts will illustrate this approach with a case study that will use industrial hygiene, toxicology and occupational and environmental medicine tools to ferret out the causes of an IAQ problem and health-related symptoms and offer a sound solution.* [9 **Sept.** 2003 *Press Release from Aerias, LLC*]

EQ ▸ abbreviation equalizer, specifically a graphic equalizer (often as **graphic EQ**).

e•qual time /ˈēkwəl ˈtīm/ ▸ noun (in broadcasting) a principle of allowing equal air time to opposing points of view, especially to political candidates for two or more parties: *Stern had booked California gubernatorial candidate Arnold Schwarzenegger for an August appearance but was forced to cancel over concerns about equal time.* [**10 Sept.** 2003 *MSNBC*]

e•rec•tile dys•func•tion /iˈrektl disˈfəNGSHən; iˈrekˌtīl/ ▸ noun inability of a man to maintain an erection sufficient for satisfying sexual activity: *now there's a simple new pill for the treatment of erectile dysfunction (a common medical problem also called impotence).* [**25 Aug. 1998** *Popular Science (advertisement)*] | [as modifier] *an erectile dysfunction clinic.*

ESV ▸ abbreviation earth satellite vehicle.

e-tail•er /ˈē ˌtālər/ ▸ noun a retailer selling goods via electronic transactions on the Internet: *a November study by the Boston Consulting Group of 127 Internet retailers found that e-tailers spend about $26 to generate each on-line order.* [**22 Feb. 1999** *Chicago Tribune*] -ORIGIN 1990s: blend of *e-* 'electronic' and *retailer*.

ETV ▸ abbreviation educational television.

eu•ro•creep (also **Eu•ro•creep**) /ˈyərōˌkrēp; ˈyo͞orō-/ ▸ noun informal the gradual acceptance of the euro in European Union countries that have not yet officially adopted it as their national currency: *his decision to fight the next election on a clear ticket is as courageously right as the Government's reliance on eurocreep is dangerously wrong.* [**25 June 1998** *Times (UK)*]

Eu•ro•land /ˈyərōˌland; ˈyo͞orō-/ (also **eu•ro•land**) ▸ noun the economic region formed by those member countries of the European Union that have adopted the euro: *the damage done to the Euro by the Swedish referendum decision not to join Euroland.* [**17 Sept. 2003** *Gulf News (UAE)*]

Eu•ro•pe•an kitch•en /ˈyərəˈpēən ˈkiCHən; ˈyo͞orə-/ ▸ noun a compact kitchen with fitted cabinets and appliances, usually white: *description: All-brick townhouse under construction—you get to put the first scratch in the wide-plank cherry flooring. European kitchen and baths* *(bidet optional), wine cellar, hydraulic closet rods.* [**24 Oct.** 2002 *Wall Street Journal*]

Eu•ro•skep•tic /ˌyərō'skeptik; ˌyo͝orō-/ (also **eu•ro•skep•tic**, British **eu•ro•scep•tic**) ▶ noun one who is skeptical about the benefits of membership in the European Union or of adopting the Euro: *one school of thought, embodied by trenchant euroskeptic and former prime minister Margaret Thatcher, sees Europe as essentially alien to the Anglo-Saxon way.* [**16 Sept.** 2003 *Christian Science Monitor*]
-DERIVATIVES **Eur•o•skep•ti•cal** adjective

Eur•o•zone /'yərə,zōn; 'yo͝orə-/ (also **eur•o•zone**) ▶ noun another term for EUROLAND.

eu•stress /'yo͞o,stres/ ▶ noun moderate or normal psychological stress interpreted as being beneficial for the experiencer: [as modifier] *limited data exist describing the resultant neuroendocrine and immunomodulatory effects of positive emotional interventions that promote eustress states such as mirthful laughter.* [**Mar.** 2001 *Alternative Therapies in Health and Medicine*]
-ORIGIN late 20th cent.: EU-+ STRESS, on the pattern of *distress.*

Eve hy•poth•e•sis /'ēv hī,päTHəsis/ (also **Af•ri•can Eve hy•poth•e•sis**) ▶ noun the hypothesis (based on study of mitochondrial DNA) that modern humans have a common female ancestor who lived in Africa around 200,000 years ago: *according to the out-of-Africa theory—also called the Eve hypothesis and Noah's Ark—these ancestors were replaced by a later wave of* H. sapiens. [**May 1994** *Scientific American*]

e•vent cre•a•tion /i'vent krē,āsHən/ ▶ noun 1 the activity of planning, organizing, and staging public events: *in time we hope to be able to grow and develop our presence in the UK market, notably in the areas of event creation and professional congress organisation.* [2003 Incon Group Web site]
2 (in computer programming) the activity of or facility for creating an event that will unfold in real-time when conditions for it have been met: *I have tried using the createEventProc method for event creation but my latest effort has been using the insertLine method of the codeModule of interest.* [**22 Jan** 2002 Usenet: microsoft.public.excel.programming]

ev•i•dence-based /'evidəns ,bāst/ ▶ adjective Medicine denoting disciplines of health care that proceed empirically with regard to the patient and reject more traditional protocols: *reformers have struggled since the 1970s to promote a more consistent, "evidence-based"* *model of care, but managing the relevant data has proved a daunting challenge.* [**20 Sept. 1999** *Newsweek*]

ex•cus•al /ik'skyōōzəl/ ▸ **noun** (typically in legal contexts) the action or fact of excusing or being excused: *based upon the responses . . . set forth in the record, however, we conclude that there is not substantial evidence to support a determination that [he] harbored views that would prevent or substantially impair the performance of his duties so as to support his excusal for cause.* [**29 Aug. 2003** *Metropolitan News-Enterprise (CA)*]

ex•o•plan•et /'eksō‚planit/ ▸ **noun** a planet that orbits a star outside the solar system: *this new harvest, which brings the total number of known extrasolar planets to 90, includes an exoplanet that orbits farther from its star than Jupiter orbits the sun—the greatest known star-planet distance of any exoplanet.* [**14 June 2002** *Science*]

ex•pan•sion team /ik'spansHən ‚tēm/ ▸ **noun** a new team added to an established professional league: *baseball commissioner Fay Vincent is expected to announce which two cities will be awarded franchises as the two expansion teams that will join the National League in the 1993 season.* [**10 June 1991** *Sports Illustrated*]

ex•pense /ik'spens/ ▸ **verb** [trans.] charge (something) to an expense account. ■ designate (an expenditure) as a business expense for tax purposes: *this means up to $17,500 in capital expenditures can be expensed in the year they were incurred—a much better deal than if you capitalize an asset and depreciate it over time.* [**Dec. 1994** *Entrepreneur*]

ex•press lane /ik'spres ‚lān/ ▸ **noun** (on a highway) a lane for through traffic, having fewer exits than the other lanes: *the $5.4 million project will deprive the toll plaza of three lanes in each direction through December, when two express lanes in each direction are to open.* [**9 Sept. 2003** *Newsday*]
■ (in a grocery store) a checkout aisle for shoppers buying only a few items: *Mr. Miskinis got stuck in line behind a couple with a full shopping cart, and since that D'Agostino's, like many of the chain's supermarkets, has no express lane, all he could do was wait.* [**6 Oct. 2002** *New York Times*]
■ any activity offering an accelerated alternative: *Express Lane Opens for People Shopping for Federal Jobs* [**4 Aug. 2003** *Washington Post (headline)*]

ex•ten•sion /ik'stensHən/ ▸ **noun 1** (**extensions**) lengths of artificial hair woven into a person's own hair to create a long hairstyle: *he*

usually tried to talk to this girl named Fran/the type of female with fly Gucci wear/with big trunk jewelry and extensions in her hair. [1992 A. Hardy, *rap lyric*]
2 Computing an optional suffix to a file name, typically consisting of a period followed by several characters, indicating the file's content or function: *extensions are up to three characters long and are optional, but help to identify whether the file is a basic program—.BAS.; a program stored on disk in a ready-to-use form—.COM. or .EXE.; a spreadsheet calculation file—.CAL.; or a word-processing document—.DOC.* [1993 R. J. Pond, *Introduction to Engineering Technology*]

ex•tra•net /'ekstrə͵net/ ▸ **noun** an intranet that can be partially accessed by authorized outside users, enabling businesses to exchange information over the Internet in a secure way: *this takes information from the SQL server and publishes it to an intranet for Allianz Indonesia staff, and to a secure extranet for brokers and agents.* [2 **Sept.** 2003 *CIO Asia (Singapore)*]
–ORIGIN 1990s: from *extra-* 'outside' + *net*, by analogy with *intranet.*

ex•tra•so•lar /͵ekstrə'sōlər/ ▸ **adjective** outside the solar system: *technology is on the brink of major advances that will allow scientists to determine over the next 10 to 30 years whether "extrasolar" planets with masses between those of Jupiter and Uranus are common or very rare.* [12 **Jan.** 1991 *Science News*]

ex•treme /ik'strēm/ ▸ **adjective 1** designating a sport or variety of sport requiring unusual stamina, daring, or strength: *I asked if extreme skiers were crazy, and he said, yeah, probably.* [14 **May** 2000 *NewYork Times Magazine*]
■ designating locales, equipment, or other features associated with this: *the mountain has five of the eight best "extreme" slopes in Colorado.* [30 **Apr.** 1995 *Denver Post Magazine*]
2 informal (used as an adjectival intensifier where an adverbial would be expected): *I just thought I'd tell you that you won't be meeting Coach Foster, the woman with chest hair, because gym has been cancelled due to the extreme dead guy in the locker.* [2000 *dialog in Buffy, the Vampire Slayer*]

Ex•tro•py /'ekstrəpē/ (also **ex•tro•py**) ▸ **noun** the pseudoscientific principle that life will expand indefinitely and in an orderly, progressive way throughout the entire universe by the means of human intelligence and technology; the antithesis of entropy: *in the*

*1990s, an embryonic subculture of technocrats thriving in the U.S. calls
the life force "extropy."* [**1994** K. Kelly, *Out of Control*]
-DERIVATIVES **Ex•tro•pi•an** /ekˈstrōpēən/ **adjective** & **noun**
-ORIGIN 1980s: from *ex-* 'out' + a shortened form of *entropy*.

eye track•ing /ˈī ˌtrakiNG/ (also **eye-track•ing**) ▸ **noun** a technology
that monitors eye movements as a means of detecting abnormalities or of studying how people interact with text or online documents: *a privately-held company that uses eye tracking to evaluate
visual products.* [**2003** San Diego State University Web site]

eye wall /ˈī ˌwôl/ ▸ **noun** Meteorology the area immediately outside the
eye of a hurricane or cyclone, associated with tall clouds, heavy
rainfall, and high winds: *the outer edge of Isabel's western eye wall,
harboring its highest winds, begins to edge onshore just south of Cape
Hatteras.* [**18 Sept. 2003** *Virginia Pilot*]

Ff

fab /fab/ ▸ **noun** Electronics a microchip fabrication plant: *with about 900 fabs now operating in the world and an attrition rate of 20 years, the industry ought to be replacing about 40 to 50 plants a year.* [5 June 1994 *Denver Post*]
■ a particular fabrication process in such a plant.
-ORIGIN late 20th cent.: abbreviation of *fabrication*.

fab•less /'fablis/ ▸ **adjective** denoting or relating to a company that designs microchips but contracts out their production rather than owning its own factory: *the newcomers' strategy was fabless production. . . . Let the Japanese make the stuff; we'll design it and reap most of the profit.* [18 Jan. 1993 *Forbes*]
-ORIGIN 1980s: from *fab* 'a microchip fabrication plant' + *-less*.

face•print /'fās,print/ ▸ **noun** a digital scan or photograph of a human face, used for identifying individuals from the unique characteristics of facial structure: *hidden cameras and faceprints are used to single out individuals in a crowd.*
-ORIGIN on the pattern of *fingerprint*.

face•print•ing /'fās,printiNG/ ▸ **noun** the process of creating a digital faceprint and using software to compare it with a database of photographs, especially to identify known criminals: *the "biometrics" industry, of which faceprinting is only a part, is now trying to find a few heart-warming "Good News Biometric Stories" to counteract opposition.* [Nov. 2001 *Bulletin of the Atomic Scientists*]
-ORIGIN on the pattern of *fingerprinting*.

fa•cial pro•fil•ing /'fāsHəl 'prōfīliNG/ ▸ **noun** the recording and analysis of a person's facial characteristics, especially to assist in identifying an individual: *the police have set up a system of facial profiling at major sporting events.*

fac•to•ry farm /'fakt(ə)rē ,färm/ ▸ **noun** a livestock farm that uses mass production methods: *factory farms, processing plants and retail outlets are silent partners with the USDA in the annual ritual of the turkey slaughter.* [22 Nov. 1987 *Washington Post*]
-DERIVATIVES **fac•to•ry farm•ing noun**

fail•o•ver /'fāl,ōvər/ ▸ **noun** Computing a method of protecting computer systems from failure, in which standby equipment automatically takes over when the main system fails: *automatic failovers can be handled in one of two ways—either via mirroring software or through shared-disk clustering.* [**Oct.** **1996** *Data Communications International*]

fair•ness doc•trine /'fe(ə)rnis ˌdäktrin/ ▸ **noun** a former federal policy requiring television and radio broadcasters that presented one side of a controversy to provide the opportunity for opposing points of view to be expressed at no charge: *a push to reinstitute the fairness doctrine represents a bid to "shut down" talk radio, top rated host Rush Limbaugh warned on Friday.* [**15 Sept.** 2003 News-Max.com] See also EQUAL TIME.

fair-trade a•gree•ment /'fe(ə)r 'trād əˌgrēmənt/ ▸ **noun** an agreement, typically illegal, between a manufacturer of a trademarked item in the U.S. and its retail distributors to sell the item at a price at or above that designated by the manufacturer.

fair use /'fe(ə)r 'yo͞os/ ▸ **noun** (in U.S. copyright law) the doctrine that copyright material may be quoted verbatim without need for permission from or payment to the copyright holder, provided that attribution is clearly given and that the material quoted is reasonably brief in extent: *what should the average consumer understand about copyright law when it comes to file-swapping, and how does "fair use" come into play?* [**1 Oct.** 2003 *Washington Post*] -DERIVATIVES **fair-use adjective**

faith-based /'fāTH ˌbāst/ ▸ **adjective** affiliated with or based on religion or a religious group: *faith-based plan bilked investors out of millions.* [**2 Oct.** 2003 *AP (headline)*]

USAGE: The preponderance of usage for this term today connects it with institutions and programs that are affiliated with an organized religion, and with President George W. Bush's *faith-based initiative* which enables religious institutions doing social work to receive government funding.

fake bake /'fāk 'bāk/ (also **fake-bake**) ▸ **noun** informal the process of getting a sunless tan, as under sunlamps or by applying a sunless-tanning lotion: *a salon in my neighborhood is advertising reasonable prices for fake bakes.*
▸**verb** [intrans.] to get a sunless tan: *in the winter months, she likes to fake-bake about once a week.*

Fa•lun Gong /'fälo͞on 'go͞oNG; 'gäNG/ (also **Fa•lun Da•fa** /'fälo͞on 'däfä/) **noun** a spiritual exercise and meditation regime with similarities to t'ai chi ch'uan, practiced predominantly in China.

■ a Taoist-Buddhist sect practicing Falun Gong.
-ORIGIN 1990s: Chinese, literally 'wheel of law,' from *fǎ* 'law' + *lún* 'wheel' (+ *gōng* 'skill' or *dà fǎ* 'great method').

fam•i•ly hour /'fam(ə)lē ˌou(ə)r/ ▶ **noun** a period in the evening during which many children and their families are presumed to watch television together: *during the so-called "family hour," from 8-9 pm, foul language increased by 94.8 percent between 1998 and 2002, the study found.* [25 **Sept.** 2003 *Troy (NY) Record*]

fan•fic /'fanˌfik/ (also **FanFic**) ▶ **noun** another name for FAN FICTION.

fan fic•tion /'fan ˌfiksHən/ ▶ **noun** a genre of imaginative amateur writing that uses characters and events from mass entertainment or popular culture: *fan fiction developed within a decade of the debut of "Star Trek."*

far gone /'fär 'gôn/ ▶ **adjective** informal **1** very intoxicated or ill: *I'd like to work with children, teen-agers, not older people who are really far gone, terribly withdrawn, or psychotic.* [1970 R. Thorp and R. Blake, *The Music of Their Laughter*]
2 advanced or deteriorated to a stage from which return seems unlikely: *that Sharon and his advisers are even talking about such an act reveals how far gone they are.* [17 **Sept.** 2003 *Progressive*]

farm•ers' mar•ket /'färmərz 'märkit/ ▶ **noun** a market where local farmers and growers sell their produce directly to the public.

fas•ci•a /'fasH(ē)ə; 'fä-/ (also **fa•ci•a**) ▶ **noun** a covering, typically a detachable one, for the front part of a cellular phone.

fash•ion•is•ta /ˌfasHə'nēstə/ ▶ **noun** informal **1** a designer of haute couture.
2 a devoted follower of fashion: *Gucci's sexy but sleek designs still press all the fashionistas' buttons, but the firm has been buffeted by other ill winds.* [22 **June 1998** *Time*]
-ORIGIN 1990s: from *fashion* + Spanish suffix *-ista*, as in *Sandinista, turista.*

fat burn•er /'fat ˌbərnər/ ▶ **noun** an over-the-counter drug that claims to burn calories by increasing the rate of the body's metabolism: *capsules which were labeled as an "extremely effective fat burner, working especially well for conditions of obesity and reducing problematic areas of fat (cellulite)".* [21 **Nov.** 2000 *FDA Talk Paper*]

fa•toush /fa'toōsh/ ▸ noun a Middle Eastern salad consisting of tomatoes, cucumber, and other vegetables together with croutons made from toasted pita bread.
-ORIGIN Arabic.

feath•er /'feTHər/ ▸ verb [trans.] blend or smooth delicately: *feather the paint in, in a series of light strokes.*

fe•da•yeen /ˌfedä'yēn/ (also **fi•da•yeen** /ˌfidä'yēn/) ▸ plural noun Arab guerrillas operating especially against Israel.
■ a special militia organized by Saddam Hussein for internal security and largely disbanded after the Iraq War: [as modifier] *US soldiers Thursday captured two suspected senior Fedayeen members in an overnight raid here that also netted $12,000 in cash.* [25 Sept. 2003 *CNN International*]
-ORIGIN 1950s: from colloquial Arabic *fidā'iyīn*, plural of classical Arabic *fidā'ī* 'one who gives his life for another or for a cause,' from *fadā* 'to ransom someone.' The singular *fedai* (from Arabic and Persian *fidā'ī*) had previously been used (late 19th cent.) to denote an Ismaili Muslim assassin.

Fed•er•al O•pen Mar•ket Com•mit•tee /'fed(ə)rəl 'ōpən 'märkit kəˌmitē/ ▸ noun a committee of the Federal Reserve Board that meets regularly to set monetary policy, including the interest rates that are charged to banks.

Fed•er•al Reg•is•ter /'fed(ə)rəl 'rejəstər/ ▸ noun a daily publication of the U.S. government that issues proposed and final administrative regulations of federal agencies.

fee•bate /'fēˌbāt/ ▸ noun a system of charges and rebates whereby energy-efficient or environmentally friendly practices are rewarded while failure to adhere to such practices is penalized: *consideration is . . . being given to using such fees to pay rebates ("feebates") for the most energy efficient buildings.* [Sept. 1990 *Scientific American*]
-ORIGIN 1990s: blend of *fee* and *rebate.*

feed /fēd/ ▸ noun a broadcast distributed by a satellite or network from a central source to a large number of radio or television stations: *a satellite feed from Washington.*

feel-good fac•tor /'fēl ˌgood ˌfaktər/ ▸ noun originally British a widespread feeling of well-being and financial security, viewed as a factor in increased consumer spending: *Chancellor of the Exchequer Kenneth Clarke unveiled an annual budget with modest tax cuts and a longer-term strategy of steadily fueling the "feel-good factor" among voters.* [1 **Dec.** 1995 *Christian Science Monitor*]

feet first /ˈfēt ˈfərst/ ▸ **adverb phrase 1** after death; as a corpse: *"When I left I had worked on every piece of equipment in the plant," he said. "Everyone told me that they were going to carry me out feet first.".* [1 **Oct.** 2003 *Bellevue (NE) Leader*] **2** without hesitation or preparation: *It's like a big puzzle. . . . The audience has to jump in feet first because it's already warm. . . . You jump right into the complications.* [2 **Oct.** 2003 *Baltimore Sun*]

feh /fe/ ▸ **exclamation** conveying disapproval, displeasure, or disgust: *The greatest writer in the English language? Feh!* –ORIGIN Yiddish.

fen•flu•ra•mine /fenˈflo͝orəˌmēn/ ▸ **noun** Medicine a prescription drug once prescribed for obesity, withdrawn from the U.S. market in 1997 because of its implication in causing heart disease. It is a component of fen-phen.

fen-phen /ˈfen ˌfen/ ▸ **noun** a drug combination of fenfluramine and phentermine, used to treat obesity and later withdrawn before becoming the subject of a massive class-action lawsuit and settlement. –ORIGIN 1996: from the initial syllables of its components.

fen•ta•nyl /ˈfentənil; ˈfentn-il/ ▸ **noun** a fast-acting narcotic analgesic and sedative that is sometimes abused for its heroin-like effect: *the man, who had not been identified by late Thursday, died after they illegally ingested fentanyl, a synthetic opiate up to 100 times more powerful than morphine.* [12 **Sept.** 2003 *WAVE (KY)*]

fi•bro•my•al•gia /ˌfībrōmīˈalj(ē)ə/ ▸ **noun** a chronic disorder characterized by widespread musculoskeletal pain, fatigue, and tenderness in localized areas.

fi•da•yeen /ˌfidäˈyēn/ ▸ **plural noun** variant of FEDAYEEN.

fig•ure-hug•ging /ˈfigyər ˌhəgiNG/ ▸ **adjective** (of a garment) fitting closely to the contours of a woman's body: *a low-cut, figure-hugging dress.*

file-shar•ing /ˈfīl ˌSHe(ə)riNG/ ▸ **noun** the transmission of files from one computer to another over a network or the Internet: [often as modifier] *millions of people who downloaded . . . file-sharing software suddenly and simultaneously imagined a thousand ways to conjure with music's liquidity.* [**17 Mar. 2002** *New York Times Magazine*]

fill /fil/ ▸ **verb** [trans.] (of a weather system) increase in barometric pressure. Compare with DEEPEN.

fil•ter /'filtər/ ▸ **noun** Computing a routine or program that processes text, for example to remove unwanted spaces or to format it for use in another application.
▸ **verb** [trans.] Computing process or treat with a filter.

fi•nan•cials /fə'nansHəlz/ ▸ **plural noun** shares in financial companies.
■ financial data about a company: *take a look at their financials.*

fin•ger•pick /'fiNGgər,pik/ ▸ **verb** play (a tune) on a guitar or banjo by using the fingernails or small plectrums on the fingertips to pluck the strings.

fin•ish•er /'finisHər/ ▸ **noun** British (in soccer) a player who scores a goal: *he is one of the best finishers at the club.*

fire•wall /'fī(ə)r,wôl/ ▸ **noun** a system of software features that prevent unauthorized access to a computer via a network: *all requests from inside the firewall first go to the proxy server, which then makes the request to the external Internet. The proxy server retrieves the data and returns it to the computer that made the original request inside the firewall.* [**Apr. 1996** *Internet World*]
▸ **verb** protect with a firewall: *the ability to firewall broadcast frames is the switch's most important feature.* [**Jan. 1995** *Data Communications International*]

first-line /'fərst ,līn/ ▸ **adjective** of first resort: *first-line drugs for HIV exposure.*

First Na•tion /'fərst 'nāsHən/ ▸ **noun** (in Canada) an indigenous American Indian community officially recognized as an administrative unit by the federal government or functioning as such without official status.

first re•spond•er /'fərst ri'spändər/ ▸ **noun** someone designated or trained to respond to an emergency: *the department is expanding its smallpox vaccination program to first responders.*

fit /fit/ ▸ verb (**fit•ted** or **fit, fit•ting**) [intrans.] have an epileptic seizure: *he started fitting uncontrollably.*

Fitz•roy /'fits,roi/ a shipping forecast area covering part of the Atlantic off of northwestern Spain, west of the Bay of Biscay. Formerly (until 2002) called *Finisterre.*

flang•er /'flanjər/ ▸ noun 1 an electronic device that alters by varying a slight delay between two identical audio signals; used in popular music.
2 (also **flanger car**) a railroad car with a movable blade attached to the front, used for removing snow from the line.

flan•nel pan•el /'flanl ,panl/ ▸ noun informal a section in a magazine, newspaper, or other publication that lists the contributors or advertises the contents.

flash•mob /'flasH,mäb/ ▸ noun a sudden mass gathering, unanticipated except by participants who communicate electronically: *you'll also need an internet link and a text-capable cellphone because the flashmob is the idiot child of our instant-communication age.* [19 Sept. 2003 *Northland Age (New Zealand)*]
▸verb hold or subject to a flashmob.

fla•vi•vi•rus /'flāvə,vīrəs/ ▸ noun a virus whose genome consists of positive RNA, that is capable of reproducing in its arthropod vector, and that causes a number of serious human diseases including yellow fever, dengue, Japanese encephalitis, and West Nile encephalitis.
• family *Flaviviridae,* three genera.

fla•vor en•hanc•er /'flāvər en,hansər/ ▸ noun a chemical additive, e.g., monosodium glutamate, used to intensify the flavor of food.

flex•ec•u•tive /flek'sekyətiv/ (also **flex-exec** /'fleks ig,zek; eg,zek/) ▸ noun an executive or high-level employee who has flexible hours and can choose to work in any location: *flexecutives often work at home and come into the office only for important meetings.*
-ORIGIN blend of *flexible* and *executive.*

flex•wing /'fleks,wiNG/ ▸ noun a collapsible fabric delta wing, as used in hang gliders.

flight sim•u•la•tor /'flīt ,simyə,lātər/ ▸ noun a machine designed to resemble the cockpit of an aircraft, with computer-generated images that mimic the pilot's view and mechanisms that move the

entire structure in imitation of an aircraft's motion, used for training pilots.
■ a computer game incorporating many of the features of this.

flip /flip/ ▸ verb (**flipped, flip•ping**) [trans.] **1** buy and sell (a property) quickly and profitably using a fraudulent evaluation of its worth: *within one week of starting I flipped a property for a quick $3,000 profit.* **2** access the nonpublic parts of (a Web site): *if you want to learn who the main IT contact at a company is, just flip their Web site.*

flip-chip /'flip,CHip/ ▸ noun a computer chip that is installed on a circuit board facedown, with connections formed by solder bumps rather than wires: *flip chips offer the possibility of low cost electronic assembly for modern electronic products because interconnection on the chip can be made simultaneously in a single step.* [**Nov. 2002** global-technoscan.com]
–ORIGIN 1990s: from the fact the the chip is rotated 180 degrees from the traditional mode of attachment.

floor-through a•part•ment /'flôr ,THrōō ə'pärtmənt/ (also **floor-thru apartment**) ▸ noun an apartment that occupies an entire floor of a building.

flow•er es•sence /'flou(ə)r ,esəns/ ▸ noun a substance prepared from a flowering plant and used therapeutically for its alleged beneficial effects on mood, outlook, etc.

fluor•o•pol•y•mer /,flōōrō'päləmər; ,flôrō-/ ▸ noun any of a class of compounds that have a high melting point, low friction, high electrical resistance, and a relatively long service life. They have many uses, including nonstick cooking surfaces and electrical insulation.

fluor•o•quin•o•lone /,flōōrō'kwinl,ōn; ,flôrō-/ ▸ noun any of a class of therapeuatic antibiotics that are active against a range of bacteria associated with human and animal diseases; their use in livestock has sparked concerns about the spread of bacteria resistant to them in humans.

FOAF ▸ abbreviation friend of a friend: *investigations never do succeed in finding the FOAF who started any of these yarns.* [**1998** R.A. Wilson *Everything is Under Control*]
■ a story or urban legend attributed to one of these: *this detail—*

trivial to some and gruesome to others—may mean the difference between a "foaf" and a true story. [**Oct. 1994** *Fortean Times*]

foam par•ty /'fōm ˌpärtē/ ▸ **noun** a party, especially in a nightclub, at which guests dance and play in foam or soap suds.

fo•men•ta•tion /ˌfōmen'tāsHən; -mən-/ ▸ **noun** a herbal preparation for external use, typically made by soaking a cloth in a herbal decoction.

food bank /'fo͞od ˌbaNGk/ ▸ **noun** a place supplying food to poor or displaced people: *Hurricane Isabel only brushed the Shore, but the area's main food bank is feeling the storm's effects two weeks later.* [**1 Oct. 2003** *Chincoteague Beacon*]

foo fight•er /'fo͞o ˌfītər/ ▸ **noun** an unidentified flying object of a kind reported by U.S. pilots during World War II, usually described as a bright light or ball of fire.
-ORIGIN 1940s: from 'Where there's foo there's fire,' a nonsense catchphrase from the U.S. *Smoky Stover* cartoon strip.

foot•fall /'fo͝otˌfôl/ ▸ **noun** mainly British the number of people entering a store or shopping area in a given time: *while John Lewis stores lost footfall during sunny weekends, Waitrose benefited from strong demand for food.* [**19 Sept. 2003** *Liverpool Echo*]

foot-tap•ping /'fo͝ot ˌtapiNG/ ▸ **adjective** having or creating a strong rhythmical musical beat: *they nearly blow the roof off the church with one of their foot-tapping gospel hymns.* [**1990** J. Shields, *Chesapeake Bay Cookbook*]

foot•y /'fo͝otē/ (also **foot•ie** or **foot•er**) ▸ **noun** Australian/NZ informal term for football (Australian Rules).

Fore•man grill /'fôrmən 'gril/ (also **George Fore•man grill** /'jôrj ˌfôrmən 'gril/) ▸ **noun** a nonstick electric grill with a grooved heating surface that allows drainage of fat: *nonstick kitchen appliances such as waffle irons, Foreman grills, sandwich makers, and so forth have nonstick coatings and call for preheating prior to cooking.* [**2 Aug. 2003** *Science News (letter)*]
-ORIGIN 1990s: after former heavyweight boxer George *Foreman* (1949–), who promotes the product.

for•ward con•tract /'fôrwərd ˌkäntrakt/ ▸ **noun** Finance an informal agreement traded through a broker-dealer network to buy and sell specified assets, typically currency, at a specified price at a certain future date. Compare with FUTURES CONTRACT.

four-by-four /ˈfôr bī ˌfôr; -bə-/ (also **4X4**) ▸ **noun** a vehicle with four-wheel drive: *the county's commissioners authorized the county engineer's office to advertise for bids for a new 4x4 to be paid for from the MotorVehicle and Gas Tax Fund.* [**10 Sept.** 2003 *Marion (OH) Star*]

fowl•pox /ˈfoulˌpäks/ ▸ **noun** a slow-spreading viral disease of birds that produces wart-like nodules on the skin. Infestations sometimes threaten commercial poultry interests.
•*Avipoxvirus*, family Poxviridae.

frag•ile X syn•drome /ˈfrajəl ˈeks ˌsindrōm, ˈfrajˌīl/ ▸ **noun** a genetic condition mainly affecting males in which a mutation of a gene on the X chromosome typically causes learning disabilities, decreased attention span, and hyperactivity.

frag•ment re•ten•tion film /ˈfragmənt riˌtensʜən ˌfilm/ ▸ **noun** a polymer-based transparent film on a pane of glass that prevents fragments scattering in the event of breakage.

frame /frām/ ▸ **noun** Computing a graphic panel in a display window, especially in an Internet browser, that encloses a self-contained section of data and permits multiple independent document viewing: *frames can be a pain, however, in that viewers can no longer use the URL bar to see where they are, and they can't bookmark a frame.* [**Nov.** 1996 *Web Developer*]

Fran•ken•fish /ˈfraNGkənˌfiSH/ ▸ **noun** informal **1** a genetically modified fish: *Thresher insists the daughterless carp will not be a frankenfish.* [**Oct.** 2002 *Wired*]
2 the northern snakehead *(Channa argus)*, so dubbed for its voracious appetite and ability to survive adverse conditions: *the "Frankenfish," known for being able to walk short distances on land, was recently found in southern Wisconsin's Rock River.* [**24 Sept.** 2003 *WBAL News*]

Frank•en•food /ˈfraNGkənˌfo͞od/ ▸ **noun** informal, derogatory genetically modified food: *all the cool commodities in the world cannot compensate for a future that promises a massive extinction of plants and creatures, the devastating loss of topsoil and rain forest, a cornucopia of pesticide-laden monocrops and lab-engineered Frankenfoods, and the climatic instabilities of global warming.* [**1998** E. Davis *TechGnosis*]
–ORIGIN 1990s: from *Franken(stein)* + *food*.

free-to-air /'frē tōō 'e(ə)r/ ▶ adjective mainly non-U.S. denoting or relating to television programs broadcast on standard public or commercial networks, as opposed to subscription satellite or cable: *the ratings reflect the company's dominant position in free-to-air TV in the highly regulated French market, significant profitability, and conservative financial profile.* [2 Oct. 2003 *Reuters*]

French-cut /'french ˌkət/ ▶ adjective (of women's panties) cut so as to reveal much of the upper thigh.

friend of Dorothy /'frend əv 'dôrəTHē/ ▶ noun informal (plural **friends of Dorothy**) a gay man: *Bullough was AC/DC, offering male staff extra dosh if they wore the kilt. This has prompted Gary Otton, who edits the Scottish Media Monitor, to describe him as "a card-carrying Friend of Dorothy."* [20 Sept. 2003 *Sunday Herald (UK)*]
-ORIGIN from the name of *Dorothy*, a character played by the actress Judy Garland (a gay icon) in the movie *The Wizard of Oz* (1939).

front-and-center /'frənt ən 'sentər/ ▶ adjective prominent; at the forefront: *a list of society's front-and-center concerns. Obesity. Pollution. Food additives. Divorce. Soft porn.* [24 Dec. 2000 *New York Times*]
-DERIVATIVES **front and center** adverb *Arizona's Lute Olson stands front and center, making his presence known to every hopeful wearing a triple-digit number on his back.*

front bot•tom /'frənt 'bätəm/ ▶ noun mainly British informal used euphemistically to refer to the female genitalia: *These are women who insist on a "no front bottom" clause, and who line up on the sofa like naughty schoolgirls to apologise to the photographer, whom they have intimidated.* [25 Sept. 2003 *The Age (Australia)*]

fro-yo /'frō ˌyō/ ▶ noun informal frozen yogurt.

fro•zen smoke /'frōzən 'smōk/ ▶ noun another term for aerogel (a very low-density substance resulting when moisture is removed from a gel).

fruit ac•id /'frōōt ˌasid/ ▶ noun another term for alpha-hydroxy acid (an organic acid derived from fruit and milk sugars).

FSBO /'fizbō/ ▶ abbreviation for sale by owner; designating some aspect of sales of private homes by their owners: *sellers, especially FSBO sellers, may be tentative about making a commitment to you.* [18 Sept. 2003 *Realty Times*]

FTA ▸ **abbreviation** Free Trade Agreement, used to refer to that signed in 1988 between the U.S. and Canada.

FU•BU /ˈfoō͞,boō͞/ ▸ **trademark** a brand of designer and sports clothing marketed mainly at young consumers of hip-hop culture: [as modifier] *the suspect . . . was wearing a Fubu jersey with the number 5 on the back, a dark baseball hat, and a light-colored bandana around his face.* [**10 Oct.** 2003 *WXOW (WI)*]

FUD /fəd/ ▸ **noun** fear, uncertainty and doubt, usually evoked intentionally in order to put a competitor at a disadvantage: [as modifier] *IBM—once legendary for controlling its competitors by sowing what became known as FUD—for fear, uncertainty and doubt—is trying to avoid the FUD factor.* [**31 Mar.** 1992 *Baltimore Sun*]

Fu•ji•ta scale /foō͞ˈjētə ˌskāl/ (also **Fujita-Pearson scale** /foō͞ˈjētə ˈpi(ə)rsən/) ▸ **noun** Meteorology a scale of tornado severity with numbers from 0 to 6, based on the amount of observed damage: *the Fujita scale rating depends on a somewhat subjective assessment of property damage.*
–ORIGIN mid 20th cent.: named after Dr. Tetsuya Theodore *Fujita* (1920–1998), the meteorologist who chiefly devised it.

full-fig•ured /ˈfoō͞l ˈfigyərd/ ▸ **adjective 1** (of women's clothing) designed for larger women.
2 (of people, euphemistically) overweight: *we have created the perfect home for full-figured Americans who want to find an American partner.* [**3 Oct.** 2003 *PRNewswire (press release)*]

ful•vic ac•id /ˈfəlvik ˈasid/ ▸ **noun** a highly soluble organic phenol found in humus that chelates elemental mineral nutrients.

func•tion•al med•i•cine /ˈfəNGkSHənl ˈmedisən/ ▸ **noun** medical practice or treatments that focus on optimal functioning of the body and its organs, usually involving systems of holistic or alternative medicine: *you don't have to have a disease to benefit from functional medicine.*

fun•nel cake /ˈfənl ˌkāk/ ▸ **noun** a cake made of batter that is poured through a funnel into hot fat or oil, deep-fried until crisp, and served sprinkled with powdered sugar.

fun•nel neck /ˈfənl ˌnek/ ▸ **noun** a neck for a knit garment like a turtle-neck but shorter and without a fold.

fur•nish•ing /ˈfərniSHiNG/ ▸ **adjective** denoting fabrics used for curtains, upholstery, or floor coverings: *they create historic furnishing textiles for the finest museums.*

fu•sion /ˈfyo͞ozHən/ ▸ **adjective** referring to food or cooking that incorporates elements of diverse cuisines: *their fusion fare includes a sushi-like roll of gingery rice and eel wrapped in marinated Greek grape leaves.*

fu•tures con•tract /ˈfyo͞oCHərz ˌkäntrakt/ ▸ **noun** Finance an agreement traded on an organized exchange to buy or sell assets, especially commodities or shares, at a fixed price but to be delivered and paid for later. Compare with FORWARD CONTRACT.

Gg

gain•shar•ing /ˈgānˌSHe(ə)riNG/ ▸ **noun** an incentive plan in which employees or customers receive benefits directly as a result of cost-saving measures that they initiate or participate in: [as modifier] *the company's "gainsharing" program ties bonuses directly to team performance—specifically, sales per labor hour.* [**June 1996** *Fast Company*]

game face /ˈgām ˌfās/ ▸ **noun** a sports player's neutral or serious facial expression, displaying determination and concentration: *for both, the keynote was self-absorption, an unblinking android fixity. In money wars, this was called the Game Face, and it caught us unprepared.* [**1992** N. Cohn, *Heart of the World*]

gang•sta rap /ˈgaNGstə ˌrap/ ▸ **noun** rap music with lyrics about gangs, crime, and violence: *gangsta rap gets most of the publicity with its nasty, hard-core flaunting of sex and violence.* [**23 Aug. 1992** *Buffalo News*]
-ORIGIN 1980s: alteration of *gangster.*

gan•sey /ˈgänzē/ ▸ **noun** mainly British & W. Indian a sweater or T-shirt: *Bill's diamond pattern gansey unraveling at the cuffs.* [**1993** Annie Proulx, *Shipping News*]
-ORIGIN late 19th cent.: representing a pronunciation of *Guernsey.*

ganz•feld /ˈgänzˌfeld; ˈganz-/ (also **Ganz•feld**) ▸ **noun** a technique of controlled sensory input used in parapsychology with the aim of improving results in tests of telepathy and other paranormal phenomena.
-ORIGIN late 20th cent.: from German, literally 'whole field.'

GAPA ▸ **abbreviation** ground-to-air pilotless aircraft: *GAPA, a 16-foot needle-nose, solid-fuel supersonic rocket developed in response to German buzz bombs, laid the groundwork for mass production of the 45-foot Bomarc missiles.* [*Jets and Rockets Take Off* Boeing Web site]

gap year /ˈgap ˌyi(ə)r/ ▸ **noun** chiefly British a period, typically an academic year, taken by a student as a break between secondary school and higher education: *many opt for higher education and the* *increasingly popular "gap year" during which they travel.* [**8 Nov.** 1995 *Guardian (UK)*]

gar•lic mus•tard /'gärlik ˌməstərd/ ▸ **noun** a European mustard plant with medicinal and culinary uses that is also an aggressive woodland invader in most of the eastern U.S.
•*Alliaria petiolata,* family Brassicaceae: *the committee decided not to take action against an intrusive native plant, the wild grape, but it is working to eradicate another exotic from Europe, garlic mustard.* [**Mar** 1994 *Canada Geographic*]

gas•tro•porn /'gastrəˌpôrn/ (also **gas•tro•por•nog•ra•phy** /ˌgastrōpôr'nägrəfē/) ▸ **noun** videos, photographs, or descriptions of food that are intended to be sexually suggestive: *Miss Lawson's television series* Nigella Bites *has so far had mixed responses in America, where critics have called it "gastroporn" and her cooking "the prelude to an orgy."* [**22 Mar.** 2002 *Daily Telegraph (UK)*]
-ORIGIN blend of *gastronomy* and *pornography.*

gas•tro•pub /'gastrəˌpəb/ ▸ **noun** British a pub that specializes in serving high-quality food: *five or so years ago young chefs eager to go it alone invented the gastropub—London's version of the Paris bistro— as an inexpensive venue where they could serve a clientele happier without a restaurant's formality.* [**Oct.** 2002 *Departures*]
-ORIGIN 1990s: blend of *gastronomy* and *pub.*

gate•keep•ing /'gātˌkēpiNG/ ▸ **noun 1** the activity of controlling, and usually limiting, general access to something: *by most accounts, though, Wal-Mart's cultural gatekeeping has served to narrow the mainstream for entertainment offerings while imparting to it a rightward tilt.* [**29 Sept.** 2003 *InfoShop News*]
2 Computers a function or system that controls access or operations to files, computers, networks, or the like: [as modifier] *you will need to set up a gatekeeping mechanism that allows reads under some circumstances and blocks them under others.* [**18 Sept.** 1993 Usenet: comp.sys.mac.programmer]

gate•way drug /'gātˌwā ˌdrəg/ ▸ **noun** a drug that supposedly leads the user on to more addictive or dangerous drugs: *the study . . . rebutted the theory that marijuana acts as a so-called gateway drug to more harmful narcotics.* [**3 Dec.** 2002 *Washington Post*]

ga•tor /'gātər/ ▸ **verb** [usually **be gatored**] Computing cause a competitor's advertisement to appear on (a commercial Web site): *Gator came into the spotlight mid-2001 for its practice of selling pop-up ads*

that are delivered to customers visiting rival Web sites, what was then known as getting "Gatored." [**14 Jan.** 2003 *CNET*]
■ cause (a Web-site visitor) to view a competitor's advertisement: *he was gatored with an ad for a competitor while visiting his own company's site.*
-ORIGIN from *Gator*, the name of the software that creates this effect.

gay•dar /ˈgā,där/ ▸ **noun** informal the putative ability of gay people to recognize one another intuitively or by means of very slight indications: *gays and lesbians still maintain an edge when it comes to gaydar: Forty-two percent claim they can tell if someone is gay or lesbian just by looking at them, compared with 26 percent of straight New Yorkers.* [**5 Mar.** 2001 *New York Magazine*]
-ORIGIN 1990s: blend of *gay* and *radar*.

gaze track•ing /ˈgāz ,trakiNG/ ▸ **noun** another name for EYE TRACKING: *many gaze trackers use a small beam of infrared light reflected off the cornea, which has an outward curve.* [**12 Apr.** 2001 *New York Times*]

geas /gɛsH/ ▸ **noun** (plural **geas•a** /ˈgɛsHə/) (in Irish folklore) an obligation or prohibition magically imposed on a person: *actually I use an old Irish charm I'd learned in my travels—a tiny geas that compels the hearer to acts of senseless generosity.* [**Dec.** 1997 *Interzone*]
-ORIGIN Irish.

G8 ▸ **abbreviation** GROUP OF EIGHT: [often as modifier] *during protests at the G8 summit in the summer of 2002, members of the group acted as observers.* [**5 Oct.** 2003 *Ottawa Citizen (Canada)*]

gel•cap /ˈjel,kap/ ▸ **noun** a gelatin capsule containing liquid medication or other substances to be taken orally.

gel pen /ˈjel ,pen/ ▸ **noun** a pen that uses a gel-based ink, combining the permanence of oil-based ballpoint ink and the smooth glide of water-based ink: *gel pens—a pen that writes like a marker—are a hit with students this year.* [**7 Aug.** 2003 *Peoria Journal*]

ge•mel•li /jəˈmelē/ ▸ **noun** pasta in the form of two short rods twisted around each other.
-ORIGIN Italian, literally 'twins'.

gen•der bend•er /ˈjendər ,bendər/ ▸ **noun** a device for changing an electrical or electronic connector from male to female, or from female to male: *we found a nice looking gender bender, took a stand-*

ard universal Token-Ring workstation cable with a DB-9 male con-
nector and another Token-Ring media filter cable with a DB-9 male
connector on one end and twisted-pair RJ-45 jack on the other, used
the gender bender in the middle and that was it. [1 **July** 1995 *Network*
Computing]

gene-al•tered /ˈjēn ˌôltərd/ ▸ **adjective** (especially in journalism)
genetically modified: *the Flavr Savr—the much ballyhooed, vine-*
ripened, gene-altered, rot-resistant tomato—finally may roll onto pro-
duce stands this month. [18 **Oct.** 1993 *USA Today*]

Gen•er•a•tion D /ˈjenəˈrāSHən ˈdē/ ▸ **noun** the generation of people
with great interest or expertise in computers and other digital
devices: *their readers are generation D, the digital generation, which*
adapts very easily to new technology [9 **Aug.** 2000 Channel-
Seven.com]
-ORIGIN from an abbreviation of *digital generation.*

gen•er•a•tion-skip•ping tax /ˌjenəˈrāSHən ˌskipiNG ˌtaks/ (abbreviation **GST**) ▸ **noun** an estate tax imposed on beneficiaries who are
two or more generations removed from the testator: *a married*
couple has a total generation-skipping tax exemption of transfers of up
to $2,000,000.

ge•net•i•cal•ly mod•i•fied /jəˈnetik(ə)lē ˈmädəˌfīd/ (abbreviation:
GM) ▸ **adjective** (of an organism or crop) containing genetic material that has been artificially altered so as to produce a desired
characteristic: *Biosource's technology, on the other hand, uses geneti-*
cally modified viruses to insert new genes into growing plants. [28 **Dec.**
1989 *Wall Street Journal*]

ge•net•ic blue•print /jəˈnetik ˈblo͞oˌprint/ ▸ **noun** [not in technical
use] a gene map or genome map: *incorporating its genetic blueprint*
into the cell's chromosomes, the retrovirus hides inside the DNA, mak-
ing it difficult to detect. [**Dec.**1989 *Omni*]

ge•net•ic pol•lu•tion /jəˈnetik pəˈlo͞oSHən/ ▸ **noun** the spread of
altered genes from genetically engineered organisms to other,
nonengineered organisms, especially by cross-pollination: *escapes*
from Scotland's salmon farms have also contributed to the wild-salmon
population crash, with "genetic pollution" meaning farmed fish now
outnumber catches of wild salmon by seven to one. [29 **Sept.** 2003 *New*
Zealand Herald]

ge•net•ic test•ing /jəˈnetik ˈtestiNG/ ▸ **noun** the sequencing of human
DNA in order to discover genetic differences, anomalies, or muta-

tions that may prove pathological: *the doctors undertook genetic testing to identify HLA status in the foetuses of 49 couples considered at risk of having a baby with beta thalassaemia.* [2003 health-news.co.uk]

gen•lock /'jen‚läk/ ▶ noun a device for maintaining synchronization between two different video signals, or between a video signal and a computer or audio signal, enabling video images and computer graphics to be mixed: [as modifier] *if you've got the appropriate genlock device, you can transfer the text to a videotape machine.* [**Aug. 1989** *Byte*]
▶ verb [intrans.] maintain synchronization between two signals using the genlock technique: *perhaps the only serious criticism of the system regards its ability to genlock.* [**Winter 1993** *Videography*]
–ORIGIN 1960s: from *generator* + the verb *lock*.

ge•no•mics /jē'nōmiks; -'näm-/, ▶ plural noun [treated as singular] the branch of molecular biology concerned with the structure, function, evolution, and mapping of genomes: *an entirely new field is being born, one that takes as its study not individual genes, but sets of them: genomics, as opposed to genetics.* [**24 Oct. 1992** *Economist*]
–ORIGIN 1980s: from *genome* 'the complete set of genes present in an organism' + *-ics*.

gen•o•type /'jenə‚tīp; 'jē-/ ▶ verb Biology [trans.] investigate the genetic constitution of (an individual organism): *the person appointed will be responsible for maintaining and genotyping many different lines of zebrafish.* [**Mar. 2000** *New Scientist (advertisement)*]
–ORIGIN verbal usage of the noun *genotype*.

gen-X•er /'jen 'eksər/ (also **Xer**) ▶ noun a member of Generation X (born in the 1960s and 1970s): *I'm rooting for the gen-Xers to convince the bleating mass that espresso shops are the venue for personal statements in the coming millennium.* [**9 Dec. 1996** *High Country News*]

ge•o•cach•ing /'jēō‚kaSHiNG/ ▶ noun the recreational activity of hunting for and finding a hidden object by means of Global Positioning System (GPS) coordinates posted on a Web site: *this is the premise of a new sport called geocaching, a 21st-century treasure hunt with a digital spin.* [**13 Jan. 2001** *New Scientist*]
–ORIGIN blend of *geographical* and *cache* 'hide something in a safe place.'

ge•o•code /'jēə‚kōd/ ▶ noun the characterization of a region or neighborhood based on population statistics such as the average age or income of its inhabitants, used especially for marketing purposes.

■ encoded data obtained by this method: *the 2004 edition includes: full-color geographic maps to help users quickly find terminals at a glance within North America and overseas; valuable geocodes to easily import terminals into mapping software to research and analyze new markets.* [**2 Oct.** 2003 *Yahoo News (press release)*]

▸**verb** characterize an area in this way: [trans.] *geographic mapping software makes it possible to "geocode" the loss and exposure data used for ratemaking—in other words, to map it to specific longitude and latitude coordinates.* [**12 Oct. 1996** *National Underwriter*]

ge•o•mat•ics /ˌjēə'matiks/ ▸ **plural noun** [treated as singular] the application of computerization to information in geography and related fields: [as modifier] *a further advantage of geomatics technologies, remote sensing in particular, is that satellites are able to provide worldwide coverage on often a continuous basis from spatial resolutions of 1 kilometer down to a few meters.* [**Feb. 1997** *Canadian Mining Journal*]
– DERIVATIVES **ge•o•mat•ic** adjective
– ORIGIN 1980s: blend of *geography* and *informatics* 'the science of processing data for storage and retrieval.'

ge•o•spa•tial /ˌjēō'spāsHəl/ ▸ **adjective** Geography relating to or denoting data that is associated with a particular location: *geospatial information technologies, such as sensors and systems that analyze geographical information, can offer valuable information to firefighters in battle.* [**9 Sept.** 2003 *Washington Technology*]

GHB ▸ **abbreviation** gammahydroxybutyrate; a naturally occurring organic compound that is used synthetically to treat alcoholism, narcolepsy, and anxiety disorders. It is also used illicitly as a recreational drug: *detectives today confirmed they are considering the possibility she was knocked out with the date-rape drug Rohypnol or its similar counterpart, GHB.* [**16 Oct.** 2003 *Manchester Evening News (UK)*]

gi•ant reed /'jīənt 'rēd/ ▸ **noun** a fast-growing perennial grass native to India that is a principal source for reeds used in musical instruments. In the U.S. it threatens some native plant habitats because of its spreading and dispersal habits.
•*Arundo donax*, family Poaceae: *a year later, after the Arundo was cleared and the bridge rebuilt at a cost of $700,000, the giant reed grew back.* [**16 Oct.** 2002 *Wall Street Journal*]

gi•nor•mous /ji'nôrməs; jī-/ ▸ adjective informal, humorous extremely large; enormous: *a ginormous five volume treatment of Greek and Arabic medicine by Avicenna, called the* Canon of Medicine, *was released.* [**1994** *Suspiciously Simple Hist. Sci. &. Invention (UK)*] -ORIGIN blend of *gigantic* and *enormous.*

Git•mo /'git‚mō/ ▸ noun informal the U.S. naval base or detention facility at Guantánamo Bay, Cuba: *Gitmo—the base's nickname—is separated from Cuba by ideology and a fence.* [**18 Mar. 1988** *USA Today*]

GLA ▸ abbreviation gamma linolenic acid; an essential fatty acid, manufactured by the body and also taken in the diet for its beneficial effects on a number of ailments.

glam•a•zon /'glamə‚zän; -zən/ ▸ noun informal a glamorous, powerfully assertive woman: *George Wayne of Vanity Fair phones Jerry Hall to ask the Texan glamazon about her marriage to Mick and how she intends to tame him.* [**15 Apr. 1997** *Guardian (UK)*] -ORIGIN 1990s: from *glam* + *Amazon.*

GLBT ▸ abbreviation gay, lesbian, bisexual, and transgendered: [mainly as modifier] *the Cheney family dynamic is yet another example of what the Bush administration would represent—that GLBT people, even if seen, should not be heard.* [**16 Oct. 2000** *Advocate*]

glo•bal com•mon /'glōbəl 'kämən/ ▸ noun any of the earth's ubiquitous and unowned natural resources, such as the oceans, the atmosphere, and space: [usually plural] *one quarter of global weapons spending together with some of the international taxes on speculators and other abusers of our global commons could provide the world with needed public goods.* [**21 Sept. 2003** *Sunday Times (Manila)*]

glurge /glərj/ ▸ noun informal inspirational but overly sentimental stories, poems, etc., that are circulated on the Internet: *they're urban legends, of course, also known as modern myths, folk tales, or by the relatively new Internet-age term of "glurge."* [**23 Sept. 2001** *Boston Globe*] ▸ verb [trans.] [usually **be glurged**] send glurge to (someone): *when I've been glurged I sometimes forward the e-mail to friends.* -ORIGIN origin uncertain.

glu•te•al /'glo͞otēəl/ ▸ noun (usually **gluteals**) a gluteus muscle in the buttocks: *once you're at your target weight, reshaping the gluteals isn't a matter of doing 25 more leg lifts.* [**Feb. 1991** *Elle*]

gly•co•bi•ol•o•gy /ˌglīkōbī'äləjē/ ▸ **noun** the scientific study of carbohydrates and their role in biology.
■ this field limited to the study of sugars: [as modifier] *this glycobiology renaissance springs from newly developed tools and techniques that have enabled investigators to more quickly decipher the complex structures of sugars and to synthesize the molecules in more-efficient ways.* [**13 Apr.** 2002 *Science News*]

GM ▸ **abbreviation** GENETICALLY MODIFIED: *in November 2001, scientists reported finding genes from GM corn in Mexican "criollo maize," a source of modern corn varieties.* [**21 Jan.** 2002 *U.S. News and World Report*]

goal•hang•er /'gōl,haNGər/ ▸ **noun** Soccer derogatory a player who spends much of the game near the opposing team's goal in the hope of scoring easy goals: *Rooney isn't a goalhanger, nor a jinking winger, nor a midfield scrapper, but he can occupy those positions when required.* [**9 Oct.** 2003 *Guardian (UK)*]

go com•man•do /ˌgō kə'mandō/ ▸ **verb phrase** informal wear no underpants: *go commando once in a while: it's not good for the twins to be stuffed into tight briefs all the time, as it stops them producing quality product.* [**July** 2002 *Loaded*]

God•zil•la /gäd'zilə/ ▸ **noun** informal a particularly enormous example (of something): *a Godzilla of a condominium tower.*
-ORIGIN from the name of a huge prehistoric monster featured in a series of Japanese films from 1955.

gold•en hour /'gōldən ˌou(ə)r/ ▸ **noun** [in singular] Medicine the first hour after a traumatic injury, when emergency treatment is most likely to be successful: *anything we can do in the golden hour to improve oxygen levels is bound to have an effect on survival.* [**Aug.** 2002 *Wired*]

gold•en rai•sin /'gōldən 'rāzən/ ▸ **noun** a raisin made from a white grape.

gold•en rice /'gōldən 'rīs/ ▸ **noun** a genetically modified variety of rice containing large amounts of the orange or red plant pigment betacarotene, a substance important in the human diet as a precursor of vitamin A.

go•mer /'gōmər/ ▸ **noun 1** military slang an inept or stupid colleague, especially a trainee.
2 informal (used by doctors) a troublesome patient, especially an elderly or homeless one: *as pressure to curtail medical costs increases*

and as the number of inner-city physicians diminishes, more ailing old people are likely to struggle to get to hospital emergency rooms, and more attendants are apt to think, if not say, Gomer. [5 **Aug.** 1990 *New York Times Magazine*]
-ORIGIN 1960s: origin uncertain; sense 1 perhaps from the television character *Gomer* Pyle, a bungling Marine Corps enlistee; sense 2 perhaps an acronym from *get out of my emergency room.*

goo•ber /'go͞obər/ ▶ noun informal often offensive a person from the southeastern U.S., especially Georgia or Arkansas.
■ derogatory an unsophisticated person: *folks around here think of him as an Arkansas "goober" and a no-class "rube."* [**Oct.** 1989 *Texas Monthly*]
-ORIGIN late 19th cent.: from an earlier sense 'peanut,' from Kikongo *nguba.*

good oil /'go͝od 'oil/ ▶ Australian/NZ informal reliable information: *Keeling and Rich were great believers in importing Feng Shui masters from Hong Kong . . . to give them the good oil, or good incense, on office design.* [30 **June** 2001 *News Weekly (Aus.)*]
-ORIGIN figurative use referring to lubricating oil and the successful running of a machine.

goof•us /'go͞ofəs/ ▶ noun informal a foolish or stupid person (often used as a term of abuse): *even now, years after Vince McMahon himself openly admitted pro wrestling is choreographed, there's still the odd goofus who acts like this is still a revelation.* [24 **Sept.** 2003 *Toronto Eye Weekly*]
-ORIGIN 1920s: based on *goof.*

goo•gle /'go͞ogəl/ ▶ verb informal [intrans.] use an Internet search engine, particularly Google.com: *she spent the afternoon googling aimlessly.*
■ [trans.] search for the name of (someone) on the Internet to find out information about them: *you meet someone, swap numbers, fix a date, then Google them through 1,346,966,000 web pages.* [12 **July** 2001 *Guardian (UK)*]
-ORIGIN from *Google,* the proprietary name of a popular Internet search engine.

gosht /go͞sHt/ ▶ noun Indian red meat (beef, lamb, or mutton): [as adj.] *gosht biryani.*
-ORIGIN from Hindi *gośt.*

go south /'go͞'soUTH/ ▶ verb phrase (**goes south, going south;** past **went south** /'went 'soUTH;/ past part **gone south** /'gôn 'soUTH/)

informal fall in value, deteriorate, or fail: *my stock portfolio hasn't exactly gone south, but it's seen better days* | *don't drink that milk—it went south a few days ago.*

go-team /ˈgō ˌtēm/ ▶ **noun** a group of investigators who can be dispatched immediately to investigate accidents, attacks, and the like: *a go-team from the National Transportation Safety Board is en route to the scene.*

go-to guy /ˈgō ˈto͞o ˌgī/ ▶ **noun** informal a person who can be relied upon for help or support: *a relentlessly hands-on manager who is the go-to guy for any issues related to the 17-day festival.* [**17 Oct.** 2003 *Shreveport (LA) Times*]
■ Sports a member of a sports team who can be relied on to score points if given the opportunity: *Greene was the go-to guy when it came to keeping things running.* [**5 May** 2002 *Mercury News*]

gov•ern•ess•y /ˈgəvərnisē/ ▶ **adjective** having or showing characteristics considered to be characteristic of a governess, especially primness or strictness: *I know this sounds governessy, but looking grown-up is something you can't borrow from anyone else.* [**14 Nov.** 1999 *New York Times Magazine*]

gov•ern•ment•wide /ˈgəvər(n)məntˌwīd/ ▶ **adjective and adverb** affecting or involving all areas and departments of government: *a governmentwide program to determine if work in the nation's forests could be done better by private contractors.* [**5 Oct.** 2003 *Billings (MT) Gazette*]

GPRS ▶ **abbreviation** general packet radio services, a technology for radio transmission of small packets of data, especially between cellular phones and the Internet.

grab /grab/ ▶ **noun** [usually with modifier] Computing a frame of video or television footage, digitized and stored as a still image in a computer memory for subsequent display, printing, or editing: *a screen grab from Wednesday's program.*

gran•u•lar /ˈgranyələr/ ▶ **adjective** technical characterized by a high level of granularity: *a granular database.*

gran•u•lar•i•ty /ˌgranyəˈlaritē/ ▶ **noun** technical the scale or level of detail present in a set of data or other phenomenon: *the granularity of this war is not the sand that covers most of the country, but these details that have proved so elusive.* [**26 Mar.** 2003 *Guardian (UK)*]

grass•cy•ling /ˈgrasˌsīkliNG/ ▸ noun the leaving of chopped grass clippings on a mowed lawn as a fertilizer: *grasscycling is the easiest, most environmentally beneficial method of dealing with grass clippings.*
–DERIVATIVES **grass•cy•cle** /ˈgrasˌsīkəl/ verb

gray /grā/ (British **grey**) ▸verb [trans.] (**gray something out**) Computing display a menu option in a light font to indicate that it is not available: [usually passive] *when I right-click on the icons, all the property fields on the Shortcut tab are either missing or grayed out.* [**29 Nov. 1999** Usenet: microsoft.public.office.misc]

gray goods /ˈgrā ˌgo͞odz/ ▸ plural noun **1** newly manufactured fabrics that have not been subjected to whitening processes: *these "gray goods" go through a rigorous process of chemical bleaching, cleaning and finally bluing to make them appear sparkling white in color.* [**2003** *Mrs. Stewart's On-Line Home Washing Guide*]
2 goods traded in a gray market (one not operating strictly according to laws and regulations): *material differences have been found based on seemingly slight variations, including the use of a foreign language on the gray goods or the use of one or two different ingredients in the production of the foreign goods as opposed to the production of the U.S. goods.* [**2003** Web site of Vincenti & Vincenti, P.C.]

green crab /ˈgrēn ˌkrab/ (also **European green crab**) ▸ noun a name for the common shore crab in its capacity as an invasive species in the U.S.

green jer•sey /ˈgrēn ˈjərzē/ ▸ noun (in a cycling race involving stages) a green knit shirt worn each day by the rider accumulating the highest number of points, and presented at the end of the race to the rider with the highest overall points total.

green•tail•ing /ˈgrēnˌtāliNG/ ▸ noun the sale of goods that are not harmful to the environment or were produced in conformity with environmental standards: *organic gardening is part of our commitment to greentailing.*
–ORIGIN blend of *green* 'not ecologically harmful' and *retailing.*

green•wash /ˈgrēnˌwäSH; -ˌwôSH/ ▸ noun disinformation disseminated by an organization so as to present an environmentally responsible public image: *the recycling bins in the cafeteria are just feeble examples of their corporate greenwash.*
–DERIVATIVES **green•wash•ing** noun
–ORIGIN 1980s: from *green* 'not ecologically harmful,' on the pattern of *whitewash.*

grid /grid/ ▸ noun Computing a number of computers linked together via the Internet so that their combined power may be harnessed to work on difficult problems.

G-ride /ˈjē ˌrīd/ ▸ noun slang a stolen car: *if I jack for a car it's only for somethin' we can use for like shootings, or g-rides, you know?* [**1991** L. Bing, *Do or Die*]
-ORIGIN perhaps from the name *Grand Theft Auto,* a video game.

grom•met /ˈgrämit/ ▸ noun slang a young or inexperienced skier, snowboarder, surfer, or skateboarder: *you just see the pros getting their insane air and hitting the mega moves that make gods out of grommets.* [**Aug. 1996** *Wake Boarding Magazine*]
-ORIGIN of uncertain origin.

ground clut•ter /ˈground ˌklətər/ ▸ noun noise in a radar echo caused by untargeted built or natural landscape features.

ground•ed /ˈgroundid/ ▸ adjective well balanced and sensible: *the kids have money and a rock-star dad, but they seem grounded.* [**4 Mar. 2002** *Time*]

Ground Ze•ro /ˈground ˈzi(ə)rō/ ▸ noun [in singular] the site of the former World Trade Center in New York, destroyed by terrorists on September 11, 2001.

Group of Eight /ˈgro͞op əv ˈāt/ (abbreviation: **G8**) the eight leading industrial nations (U.S., Japan, Germany, France, UK, Italy, Canada, and Russia), whose heads of government meet regularly.

grrrl /grrl/ (also **grrl**) ▸ noun a young woman perceived as independent and strong or aggressive, especially in her attitude to men or in her sexuality: [as modifier] *today . . . we have both chololate martinis and women's suffrage, "grrrl power" and a variety of tasty wine.* [**1 April 2002** *Time*]
-ORIGIN 1990s: a variant of *girl,* as in *riot grrrl,* with the *grrr* representing the sound of an animal growling.

grudge match /ˈgrəj ˌmaCH/ ▸ noun a contest or other competitive situation involving personal antipathy between the participants: *the change became apparent when the Bulls swept the aging bullies from Detroit in last year's playoff grudge match.* [**17 May 1992** *New York Times*]

guai•fen•e•sin /gwī'fenəsin/ ▸ **noun** an expectorant used in cough syrups and sometimes for pain relief from fibromyalgia.

gua•ra•na /gwə'ränə/ ▸ **noun 1** a substance prepared from the seeds of a Brazilian shrub, used as a tonic or stimulant.
2 the shrub (*Paullinia cupana*) of the soapberry family that yields guarana.
-ORIGIN mid 19th cent.: from Tupi.

guay•a•ber•a /ˌgīə'berə/ ▸ **noun** a lightweight open-necked Cuban or Mexican shirt with two breast pockets and two pockets over the hips, typically having short sleeves and worn untucked.
-ORIGIN 1970s: Cuban Spanish, apparently originally from the name of the *Yayabo* river, influenced by Spanish *guayaba* 'guava.'

guer•ril•la mar•ket•ing /gə'rilə ˌmärkitiNG/ ▸ **noun** innovative, unconventional, and low-cost marketing techniques aimed at obtaining maximum exposure for a product: [as modifier] *a print and guerrilla marketing campaign will launch in the third quarter for Rivella Red, a whey-based beverage.* [25 **Sept.** 2003 *AdWeek*]

guest•book /'gest,bo͝ok/ ▸ **noun** a blank book in which visitors to a museum, hotel, or event may sign their names and leave comments.
■ a web page where visitors to a site may leave their names and comments: *the site also has a guestbook where notes of encouragement can be left.* [2 **Oct.** 2003 *St. Paul (MN) Pioneer Press*]

gug•gul /'go͞ogəl/ ▸ **noun** a herbal preparation made from the sticky gum of various myrrh trees that has been alleged to aid in lowering serum cholesterol.
•The trees providing the main source are *Commiphora mukul* and *Commiphora wightii*, family Burseraceae: [as modifier] *recent laboratory studies in the United States and research on obese people in India had led some scientists to expect a beneficial effect from guggul extract, which is derived from the resin of the mukul myrrh tree.* [23 **Aug.** 2003 *Science News*]

guid•ed im•age•ry /'gīdid 'imijrē/ ▸ **noun** the use of words and music to evoke positive imaginary scenarios in a subject with a view to bringing about some beneficial effect: *guided imagery has been rejected by almost every school district in America due to protests by parents.* [**Mar.** 1994 *Harper's*]
■ particular images used in this exercise.

guilt /gilt/ ▸ **verb** [trans.] informal make (someone) feel guilty, especially in order to induce them to do something: *Celeste had been guilted into going by her parents.*

gun•a /ˈgo͞onə/ ▸ **noun** (in Vedanta) any of the three interdependent modes or qualities of prakriti: sattva, rajas, or tamas.

gut•kha /ˈgo͞otkə/ ▸ **noun** a sweetened mixture of chewing tobacco, betel nut, and palm nut, originating in India as a breath freshener.
-ORIGIN 1990s: from Hindi 'a shred; small piece.'

gut-wrench•ing /ˈgət ˌrenCHiNG/ ▸ **adjective** informal extremely unpleasant or upsetting: *the film is a gut-wrenching portrait of domestic violence.*

gym /jim/ ▸ **noun** informal a membership organization that provides a range of facilities designed to improve and maintain physical fitness and health.

gyo•za /ˈgyōzə/ ▸ **noun** a Japanese dish consisting of wonton wrappers stuffed with pork and cabbage.
-ORIGIN Japanese, from Chinese *jiaozi.*

gy•ro•sta•bi•lized /ˌjīrōˈstābəˌlīzd/ ▸ **adjective 1** (of a vessel) stabilized by a gyrostabilizer.
2 (of cameras, binoculars, and other optical devices) capable of securing a steady view by means of an electronic device that corrects for movement: *the specialized gyrostabilized optics allow the helicopter to deliver steady, detailed pictures while maintaining a safe altitude and "stand-off" distance from a news scene.* [2003 KXTV Web site]

Hh

hair•cut /'he(ə)r͵kət/ ▸ **noun** 1 a reduction in the stated value of an asset in order to determine the collateral or market value.
2 the amount, usually a percentage, by which an asset is reduced: *what is the haircut on Foreign Denominated Securities Positions for the Euro?* [**March 1999** Nasdr.com]
■ any ad hoc reduction in value: *if you paid in dollars, you were going to pay more; they were going to give you a haircut of about 20 percent.* [**10 July 2003** Edmund Andrews, speaking on *Fresh Air*]

hal•lou•mi /hä'lo͞omē/ ▸ **noun** a mild, firm, white Cypriot cheese made from goats' or ewes' milk, used especially in cooked dishes.
-ORIGIN 1990s: from Egyptian Arabic *ḥalūm*, probably from Arabic *ḥaluma* 'to be mild.'

ha•ma•chi /hə'mäCHē/ ▸ **noun** the Japanese name for Pacific yellowtail, especially when used in sushi and sashimi: *his hamachi sashimi dish is a single slice of yellowtail brushed with a bit of olive oil and white soy sauce and sprinkled with chives and sesame seeds.* [**19 Nov. 1997** *New York Times*]

ham-and-egg•er /͵ham ən 'egər; ənd/ ▸ **noun** informal an ordinary person of little consequence: *I was able to, through the courtesy of other people, do some things that were extraordinary for a ham-and-egger of my background.* [**6 Sept. 2003** *Sebastian (FL) Sun*]

han•cock /'han͵käk/ ▸ **verb** informal put one's signature to (a document): *on December 10, 1998 Secretary Richardson hancocked a memorandum written to managers across the weapons-complex with the Department's goal spelled out.* [**Feb. 1999** *Envirowatch*]
-ORIGIN from *John Hancock*, 'autograph signature'.

hand•phone /'hand͵fōn/ ▸ **noun** SE Asia a cordless or cellular phone.

hands-free /'handz 'frē/ ▸ **adjective** (of a telephone or other electronic device) designed to be operated without using the hands: *the two-line capability permits conference calling, and a speakerphone facilitates hands-free operation.* [**1991** *Fax Buyer's Guide*]

hand•span /'hand͵span/ ▸ **noun** the width of a person's hand, as measured when the fingers and thumb are spread out: *he freed the* *sails and trimmed them back, ducking as wind filled them and the boom sliced through the air a handspan away.* [**1997** Elizabeth Hand, *Glimmering*]

hand-wav•ing /'hand ,wāviNG/ ▸ **noun** the use of gestures and insubstantial language meant to impress or convince: *there's a lot of handwaving going on as to the physics of Byrne's convoluted time travel plot.* [**17 Sept.** 2003 *review of Superman/Batman: Generations III #9*]

hap•ki•do /häp'kēdō/ ▸ **noun** a comprehensive Korean martial art that stresses domination of one's opponent through the eclectic use of joint-locks, throws, choking, tackling, kicking, and punching.
–ORIGIN Korean: 'way of gathered strength'

hard•bod•y /'härd,bädē/ ▸ **noun** (plural **hard•bod•ies**) informal a person with very toned or well-developed muscles: *you're in the cockpit of a ragtop Testarossa with a tanned, blond hardbody at your side.* [**Sept.** 1989 *Car & Driver*]
–DERIVATIVES **hard•bod•ied** adjective

hard•core /'härd 'kôr/ ▸ **noun** the most active, committed, or doctrinaire members of a group or movement: *nearly everyone had left that bar in the middle of winter except the hardcore.* [**1990** Joy Harjo, *In Mad Love and War*]
■ popular music that is experimental in nature and typically characterized by high volume and aggressive presentation: *a hardcore band from New Jersey re-introducing hardcore as it should be.* [musicmoz.org]

hard•gain•er /'härd'gānər/ ▸ **noun** (in bodybuilding) a person who does not find it easy to gain muscle through exercise: [as modifier] *the hardgainer crowd scoff at creatine for novices.* [www.tim-richardson.net]

hard•scape /'härd,skāp/ ▸ **noun** the nonliving or manmade fixtures of a planned outdoor area: *before you begin to implement your plan, consider the "hardscape" of your ornamental vegetable garden.* [**Apr.** 1998 *National Gardening*]

hard•scap•ing /'härd,skāpiNG/ ▸ **noun** the placement of nonplant elements such as fences, walkways, paving, and lighting in a planned outdoor area: *LANDSCAPE DESIGN and installation, hardscaping, paver walks, patios, retaining walls, ICPI certified installers, ponds, mowing, complete property care, old landscape renovations, free estimates.* [**16 Sept.** 2003 *Merchandiser (PA; advertisement)*]

hard•wir•ing /'härd'wī(ə)riNG/ ▸ **noun 1** electronic connection by means of wires: *to achieve effective automation of a line of this type, Eurobend would have had to use numerous handshaked PLC units and extensive hardwiring, as well as spending many hours on system programming.* [engineertalk.com]
2 a predisposition for a particular kind of learning on behavior, thought to be based on structures within the brain or nervous system: *there might be a subtle abnormality in the brain stem, or your hardwiring somewhere makes it impossible.* [**21 Sept.** 1990 *Wall Street Journal*]

Har•ring•ton /'hariNGtən/ ▸ **noun** a man's short lightweight jacket with a collar and a zipped front: *Harringtons, DMs, Fred Perrys were the normal street fashion of the time, so that's how I started my skinhead collection.* [1995 Jayne Miller, *Voxpop*]
-ORIGIN from the name of Rodney *Harrington*, a character in the 1960s television series *Peyton Place*, who was associated with the garment.

ha•wa•la /hə'wälə; -'välə/ ▸ **noun** a system or agency for transferring money traditionally used in the Muslim world, whereby the money is paid to an agent who then instructs a remote associate to pay the final recipient: *the new list of suspect organizations, under review by a group of officials led by Treasury Department representatives, includes charities in Saudi Arabia and Chicago, an Arab bank and at least three hawalas, the informal money-lending networks common in the Arab world.* [**1 Oct.** 2001 *New York Times*]
-ORIGIN from Arabic, literally 'change, transform.'

head•shot /'hed₁sHät/ ▸ **noun 1** a photograph of a person's head: *he claimed to be a fashion photographer looking to shoot headshots and put together portfolios.* [**Jan.** 1992 *Crime Beat*]
■ a frame, or a sequence of frames, of videotape or motion-picture film that captures a close-up of a person's head: [as modifier] *there is a really cool headshot scene, which was cut from some previous versions of the film.* [**6 Aug.** 2002 *Pasquale Festa Campanile's "Hitch-Hike" on DVD*]
2 a bullet or gunshot aimed at the head.

head•space /'hed₁spās/ ▸ **noun** informal the notional space occupied by a person's mind: *to play, you enter the headspace of female bounty hunter Samus Aran on her mission to waste evil mutant Space Pirate Mother Brain.* [**Oct.** 1994 *i-D*]

health tour•ism /'helTH ₁to͞orizəm/ ▸ **noun** travel to a tourist destination with the main purpose of receiving some therapeutic treat-

ment: *the government is mulling over this move as part of efforts to boost health tourism by allowing more foreigners to tap into Malaysia's medical facilities.* [**2003** Asia One Careers Web site]
-DERIVATIVES **health tour•ist** noun

heart•sink pa•tient /'härt͵siNGk ͵pāsHənt/ (also **heart•sink**) ▸ noun British informal (among doctors) a patient who makes frequent visits to a doctor's office, complaining of persistent but unidentifiable ailments: *we call them heartsink patients, for obvious reasons, and someone once reckoned that most partners in a practice have about fifty heartsinks on their books. They come in, and sit down, and they look at me, and both of us know it's hopeless.* [**2001** Nick Hornby, *How to be Good*]
-ORIGIN early 21st cent.: from the notion that the appearance of the patient makes the doctor's heart sink.

heav•y hit•ter /'hevē 'hitər/ (also **big hit•ter**) ▸ noun informal **1** an important or powerful person: *what started as a local conflict has erupted into a high-profile national issue pitting heavy hitters in the Senate against the Department of Agriculture.* [**18 Feb. 1993** *Fort Collins (CO) Triangle Review*]
2 a high-scoring athlete: *Utah hoopster is now a heavy hitter in hoops.* [**2003** ihigh.com]

height•ism /'hītizəm/ ▸ noun prejudice or discrimination against someone on the basis of their (usually short) height: *will they practice prenatal heightism, aborting some male fetuses because they will not grow tall enough?* [**Spring 1992** *Wilson Quarterly*]
-DERIVATIVES **height•ist** adjective & noun

Hel•ler•work /'helər͵wərk/ ▸ noun a type of bodywork that combines some techniques of Rolfing with verbal dialogue and movement exercises.
-ORIGIN 1970s: after Joseph *Heller* (born 1940), its inventor.

help desk /'help ͵desk/ ▸ noun a service providing information and support to the users of a computer network or product: *a 36-year-old computer technician who worked on the school's IT help desk, Perry had received a message the previous Friday that Samuels thought his computer had a virus.* [**23 June 2003** *New York Magazine*]

her•biv•o•ry /(h)ə'bivərē/ ▸ noun the eating of plants, especially ones that are still alive: *in response to herbivory, plants defend themselves with arrays of structural and chemical weapons.* [**1997** *Effects of Herbivory and Plant Parasites*]

herd im•mu•ni•ty /'hərd i͵myo͞onitē/ ▶ **noun** general immunity to a pathogen in a population based on the acquired immunity to it by a high proportion of members over time: *the World Health Organisation says that 95 per cent of children need to be vaccinated to ensure "herd immunity" protection for the whole population.* [27 **Sept.** 2003 *Belfast Telegraph (UK)*]

high-band /'hī 'band/ ▶ **adjective** relating to or denoting a video system using a relatively high carrier frequency, which allows more bandwidth for the signal: *AHi8 model priced at $850, far surpassed the other 10 camcorders we tested, thanks to its high-band picture quality.* [**Oct. 1996** *Consumer Reports*]

high con•cept /'hī 'kän͵sept/ ▶ **noun** (especially in a movie or television plot) emphasis on a striking and easily communicable idea: *for mainstream media companies, the focus has shifted from high concept to hard cash: "show me the money" is the new mantra heard in corporate corridors.* [2003 *Online Journalism Review*] –DERIVATIVES **high-con•cept** adjective

high-main•te•nance /'hī 'mānt(ə)nəns; 'māntn-əns/ ▶ **adjective** needing a lot of work to keep in good condition.
■ informal (of a person or relationship) demanding a lot of attention: *"Look, Ted is a very high-maintenance guy," says a long-term girlfriend of Fonda's from Los Angeles.* [**Apr. 1997** *Vanity Fair*]

hi•jab /hi'jäb/ ▶ **noun** a head covering worn in public by some Muslim women: *for many Algerian women, the veil (hijab) represents a rejection of Western influence, liberation from unwanted male advances, and the right to promote their own social status through education and self-appointed professions.* [**Mar. 1992** *Utne Reader*]
■ the religious code that governs the wearing of such clothing: *women must cover their hair, a requirement called* hijab. [**Mar. 2001** *National Geographic*]
–ORIGIN from Persian, from Arabic *ḥajaba* 'to veil.'

him•bo /'him͵bō/ ▶ **noun** informal a man who has no estimable qualities other than good looks: *how did Austen trick audiences conditioned to drool over himbos into falling for a middle-aged guy with a slight case of rheumatism?* [12 **Apr. 1996** *Entertainment Weekly*]
–ORIGIN late 1980s: blend of *him* and *bimbo*.

hink•y /'hiNGkē/ ▶ **adjective** (**hink•i•er, hink•i•est**) informal (of a person) dishonest or suspect: *Hass didn't know who he was or where he came from but he knew the guy was hinky.* [**June 1992** *Police*]

▪ (of an object) unreliable: *the dishwasher had to go hinky, flooding the kitchen floor.* [**1992** Eileen Goudge, *Such Devoted Sisters*] -ORIGIN 1950s: of obscure origin.

hired gun /'hī(ə)rd 'gən/ ▸ **noun** informal **1** an expert brought in to resolve complex problems or to lobby for a cause: *it is a chance for an insurance company hired gun to find some excuse to deny your benefits.* [**1997** Gordon S. Johnson, Jr.]
2 a hired bodyguard, mercenary, or assassin.

hit /hit/ ▸ **noun** Computing **1** an instance of a particular Web site being accessed by a user: *the site gets an average 350,000 hits a day—that's a staggering four per second* [**20 Feb. 1998** *London Evening Standard*]
2 a single instance of finding a search target, on the Internet or in a database: *It's not fancy, and sometimes browsing gets you more relevant hits, but it is easy.* [**2003** AIRS Human Capital Solutions Web site]

hol•i•day sea•son /'hälidā ˌsēzən/ ▸ **noun** the period of time from Thanksgiving until New Year, including such festivals as Christmas, Hanukkah, and Kwanzaa: *what was once an annual custom at the holiday season has turned into a year-round appeal.* [**12 Mar. 2003** *Christian Science Monitor*]

hol•low at•om /'hälō 'atəm/ ▸ **noun** an atom in which inner-shell electrons are missing, usually as a result of electrical excitation: *the result is a neutral atom in which most or all of the electrons are at large distances from the nucleus—a hollow atom.* [**3 June 1995** *New Scientist*]

Hol•o•caust de•ni•al /'hälə,kôst diˌnīəl; 'hōlə-/ ▸ **noun** the belief or assertion that the Holocaust did not happen or was greatly exaggerated: [as modifier] *the Atlantic Monthly and other mainstream media reported uncritically on Fred Leuchter, a self-styled death-penalty expert, even after he appeared in a much-publicized Holocaust denial trial that demolished his claims to know his subjects.* [**23 Aug. 1993** *Baltimore Sun*]
-DERIVATIVES **Hol•o•caust de•ni•er** /'hälə,kôst diˌnīər; 'hōlə-/ **noun**

home•port /'hōm,pôrt/ ▸ **verb** [trans.] assign (a vessel) to a particular port as its home: *Guam's strategic location as the western-most U.S. deepwater port in the Pacific makes it the logical place to homeport an aircraft carrier.* [**6 Oct. 2003** *Pacific Daily News (Guam)*]

home stud•y /'hōm ˌstədē/ ▸ **noun** an assessment of prospective adoptive parents to see if they are suitable for adopting a child: *you worry: What if you spend $1,200 on a home study for an adoption?* [**16 Aug.** 1990 *Los Angeles Times*]

ho•mog•e•ny /hə'mäjənē/ ▸ **noun** Biology a variant, with growing currency in journalism, of the word homogeneity: *as we witnessed from the fans of Ohio State, there is a homogeny that exists in Columbus that doesn't exist here anymore.* [**15 Sept.** 2003 Dawgman.com]

hon•ey•trap /'hənēˌtrap/ ▸ **noun** a stratagem in which irresistable bait is used to lure a victim.
■ the bait so used: *the house was a honey trap, fitted out with a gaming machine, a sauna, plenty of videos and drink and drugs and anything else that might persuade a wandering boy to come in off the streets.* [**25 Nov.** 2000 *Guardian (UK)*]

hood•i•a /'ho͞odēə/ ▸ **noun** a southern African cactus that contains a highly effective appetite suppressant.
•Genus *Hoodia*, family Asclepiadaceae; about 20 species: *visitors to the Kalahari Desert cluster gingerly around a hoodia plant, a spiny cactus that produces a chemical being developed as a drug by Pfizer.* [**1 Apr.** 2003 *New York Times*]

hood•ie /'ho͞odē/ (also **hood•y**) ▸ **noun** [plural **hood•ies**] informal a hooded sweatshirt or jacket: *a phalanx of boys from Naughty's East Orange, N.J. neighborhood lines the stage, suited in NBN hoodies, baseball caps, and T-shirts.* [**Fall** 1992 *Vibe*]

hoop-head /'ho͞op ˌhed/ ▸ **noun** informal a basketball player or devoted fan: *since Sunday, McDaniel College's Gill Center has been home to hoop-heads of all ages who gathered for the McDaniel Basketball Camp.* [**26 June** 2003 *Carroll County (MD) Times*]

hô•tel de ville /hō'tel də 'vil; ô'tel də 'vēl/ ▸ **noun** (in France) a city hall or town hall.

ho•tel•ing /hō'teliNG/ ▸ **noun** the short-term provision of office space to a temporary worker: *in a modest way, hoteling has been around for a while, but it's specific to each company.* [**17 Jan.** 2000 *Newark (NJ) Star-Ledger*]
■ the short-term letting of surplus office space to employees from other companies.

hot•tie /'hätē/ (also **hot•ty**) ▸ **noun** (plural **hot•ties**) informal a sexually attractive person: *"I used to beat the crap out of that guy," a garage* *mechanic in the town tells his wife, a former high school hottie who never would have noticed Dennis before.* [**18 Sept. 1998** *Indianapolis Star*]

HR ▸ abbreviation human resources (the department of an organization that handles employee affairs, payroll, and the like): [usually as adj.] *the report concludes that the happiest employees are those where positive HR practices are in place.* [**28 Oct. 1999** *Daily Telegraph (UK)*]

hryv•na /ˈ(h)rivnyə; -nēə; həˈriv-/ (also **hryv•nia**) ▸ noun the basic monetary unit of Ukraine, equal to 100 kopiykas.
-ORIGIN from Ukrainian *gryvnya* '3-kopek coin of pre-independent Ukraine,' from Old Russian *grivina* 'necklace, ring, coin.'

HSGT ▸ abbreviation high speed ground transit: a designation for high-speed, relatively short-haul trains in heavily populated areas: *HSGT can offer such social, economic, and environmental benefits as energy savings, emission reductions, and maximized use of existing facilities.* [**2003** Federal Railroad Administration Web site]

hue•vos ran•che•ros /ˌ(h)wevōs ränˈCHerōs/ ▸ plural noun a dish of fried or poached eggs served on a tortilla with a spicy tomato sauce, originating in Mexico.
-ORIGIN 1960s: Spanish 'ranch eggs.'

huff /həf/ ▸ verb [trans.] informal sniff fumes from (gasoline or solvents) for a euphoric effect, the consequences of which may be lethal: *we get kids that are huffing spray paint like crazy.* [**16 Jan. 1994** *Coloradoan*]
-DERIVATIVES **huff•er** noun

hum•mer /ˈhəmər/ ▸ noun a Humvee: *I was driving along in my hummer [the new version of the jeep], and I saw this T-55 that everyone had passed.* [**11 Mar. 1991** *Newsweek*]

Hum•vee /ˈhəmˌvē/ ▸ noun a large-wheeled vehicle used by the military and designed to improve on the Jeep: *Humvee is lightweight deathtrap in Iraq.* [**18 Sept. 2003** *Minneapolis Star Tribune (headline)*]
-ORIGIN late 1980s: stylized initialism from 'high-mobility, multipurpose wheeled vehicle. '

hy•brid car /ˈhībrid ˈkär/ ▸ noun a car with a gasoline engine and an electric motor, each of which can propel it: *the decision to offer a* *relatively hefty tax credit for "hybrid" cars, which use a combination of gas and battery power, is bound to help both Detroit and two Japanese automakers.* [**17 May 2001** *New York Times*]

hy•dro•fluor•o•car•bon /ˌhīdrōˈflo͝orəˌkärbən; -ˈflôr-/ (abbreviation: **HFC**) ▸ noun Chemistry any of a class of partly chlorinated and fluorinated hydrocarbons, used as an alternative to chlorofluorocarbons.

hy•per•fli•er /ˈhīpərˌflīər/ ▸ noun a person who travels a great deal, especially for business: *Orensten is a "hyperflier," a relatively new species whose members spend more time aloft than aground.* [**Aug 1999** *Wired*]
–ORIGIN 1990s: from *hyper-* 'excessively, above normal' + *flier* 'a person or thing that flies, especially in a particular way.'

hy•per•i•cin /hīˈperəsin/ ▸ noun a substance found in St. John's wort, credited with chemical and pharmacological properties similar to those of antidepressants.
•A polycyclic quinone; chem. formula: $C_{30}H_{14}O_8$.
–ORIGIN early 20th cent.: from *hypericum* 'a yellow-flowered plant' + *-in*, chemical suffix.

hy•per•sphere /ˈhīpərˌsfi(ə)r/ ▸ noun a sphere that exhibits more than three dimensions: *a formula to determine the volume of an n-dimensional hypersphere.* [**(undated)** A E Lawrence]

hy•po•cen•ter /ˈhīpəˌsentər/ ▸ noun the point on the earth's surface directly above or below an exploding nuclear bomb: *fifty-four years ago, half a mile from the hypocenter of the blast of a big bomb named Little Boy, Michiko was burned terribly.* [**20 July 1999** *Christian Science Monitor*]

hy•po•spray /ˈhīpəˌsprā/ ▸ noun (chiefly in science fiction) a device used to introduce a drug or other substance into the body through the skin without puncturing it: *corpsmen with red M symbols on their jackets scurried among them, sorting them for triage and slapping on hyposprays of anesthetic.* [**1993** Jerry Pournelle and SM Stirling, *Prince of Sparta*]

hy•pox•i•a /hīˈpäksēə/ ▸ noun Medicine deficiency in the amount of oxygen reaching the tissues.
■ oxygen deficiency in a biotic environment leading to this: *the waterway's most serious ecological problem has been hypoxia.* [**Autumn 1994** *Origins (Canada)*]

-DERIVATIVES **hy•pox•ic** /-sik/ **adjective**
-ORIGIN 1940s: from HYPO- (denoting an element in a low valency)
+ OXYGEN + -IA.

hys•ter•i•cal re•al•ism /hi'sterikəl 'rēə,lizəm/ ▶ **noun** realistic fiction
that is characterized by overblown prose and intellectual digres-
sions: [as modifier] *this March in Newsday, Adam Kirsch smashed Viken
Berberian's novel* The Cyclist *with the hysterical-realism hammer.* [15
Dec. 2002 *New York Times Magazine*]

Ii

IAQ ▸ abbreviation indoor air quality.

IBS ▸ abbreviation irritable bowel syndrome.

ICANN ▸ abbreviation Internet Committee for Assigned Names and Numbers, the nonprofit organization that oversees the use of Internet domains.

ICC ▸ abbreviation International Criminal Court.

ice wine /ˈīs ˌwīn/ ▸ noun a sweet, concentrated wine made from grapes that froze on the vine: *V.Q.A. standards specify that ice wine can only be made after temperatures have fallen below 12 degrees and the grapes have been naturally frozen on the vine.* [**19 July 1998** *New York Times*]

ich•thus /ˈikTHəs/ ▸ noun an image of a fish used as a symbol of Christianity: *a Federal judge in Missouri has ordered the City of Republic to remove a fish symbol, known as an ichthus, from its seal because the symbol unconstitutionally depicts Christianity as the city's official religion.* [**14 July 1999** *New York Times*]
–ORIGIN from Greek *ikhthus* 'fish' : the initial letters of the word are sometimes taken as short for Iesous Christos, Theou Uios, Soter (Jesus Christ, Son of God, Savior).

i•con•ize /ˈīkəˌnīz/ ▸ verb [trans.] **1** Computing reduce (a window on a video display terminal) to a small symbol or graphic: *unlike Windows, which right out of the box iconizes background programs and puts them in a line across the bottom of the screen.* [**Dec. 1993** *Byte*] **2** treat as an icon: *SIMI has integral and demonstrable links both to the ISI and a number of Pakistan-based terrorist groups, and substantially derives its inspiration from Osama bin Laden—who it iconizes as an outstanding example of a "true mujahid"'(holy warrior) and a "champion and true savior of Islam."* [**1 Sept. 2003** Outlook-India.com]

ICT ▸ abbreviation information and computing technology.

i•den•ti•ty pol•i•tics /īˈdentitē ˌpälitiks/ ▸ plural noun [treated as singular] a tendency for people of a particular religion, race, social background, etc., to form exclusive political alliances, moving away from traditional broad-based party politics: *it is very important for historians to remember their responsibility, which is, above all, to stand aside from the passions of identity politics—even if they also feel them.* [**16 Dec.** 1993 *New York Review of Books*]

i•den•ti•ty theft /ī'dentitē ˌTHeft/ ▸ noun the fraudulent acquistion and use of a person's private identifying information, usually for financial gain.

IM ▸ abbreviation Computing ■ instant message. ■ instant messaging.
▸verb [trans.] (IM's, IM'd, IM'•ing) send a message to (someone) by using an instant messaging system: *by now I was being IM'd (instant messaged) by a tireless horde of hot-blooded all-American testosterone-crazed males.* [**Jan.** 1995 *Wired*]

IMAP /'ī,map/ ▸ abbreviation Computing Internet Mail Access Protocol.

im•mu•no•blot•ting /ˌimyənō'blätiNG; iˌmyōō-/, ▸ noun a technique for analyzing or identifying proteins in a mixture, involving separation by electrophoresis followed by staining with antibodies: *protein immunoblotting has been performed to assess specificity.* [1995 *Clinical Infectious Diseases*]

i-Mode /'ī ˌmōd/ ▸ trademark a technology that allows data to be transferred to and from Internet sites via cell phones: *i-mode is the internet-on-your-mobile service you see kids in Tokyo using on those funky flip-tops with the palm-size screens.* [**21 Sept.** 2001 *Evening Standard Magazine (UK)*]
-ORIGIN early 21st cent.: from *I* (referring to the user's ability to interact directly with the Internet) + *mode*.

im•plant•able /im'plantəbəl/ ▸ adjective capable of or designed for being implanted in living tissue: *the implantable defibrillator allows Claude Larreur, 53, of Silver Spring, to continue a career that takes him throughout South and Central America and the Caribbean.* [**30 May** 1989 *Washington Post*]

im•pres•sion /im'presHən/ ▸ noun an instance of a pop-up or other Web advertisement being seen on computer users' monitors: *in July, Nielsen/NetRatings reported Web publishers served 7.3 billion pop-up ad impressions.* [**11 Sept.** 2003 InternetNews.com]

in-box /'in ˌbäks/ ▸ noun Computing the window in which an individual user's received e-mail messages and similar electronic communications are displayed: *another version from Puma uses Orchestrate, a Web-based universal in-box for faxes, E-mail and voice mail.* [**9 July 1998** *New York Times*]

in•cen•tiv•ize /in'sentə‚vīz/ ▸ **verb** [trans.] provide incentives for: *to incentivize managers more efficiently, Pepsi said there will be a "greater differentiation in the amount of grants, bonus and compensation, based on performance."* [**2 Dec. 2003** *TheStreet.com*]

in•clu•sion•a•ry /in'klo͞oZHə‚nerē/ ▸ **adjective** designed or intended to accommodate diversity in age, income, race, or some other category: *the St. Louis Country Club, Annandale Golf Club in Pasadena, Calif., and Merion Golf Club in Ardmore, Pa., decided they preferred not to hold USGA events rather than adhere to the new, inclusionary policies.* [**6 Aug. 1991** *Washington Post*]

in•clu•siv•i•ty /‚inklo͞o'sivitē/ ▸ **noun** an intention or policy of including people who might otherwise be excluded or marginalized, such as the handicapped, learning-disabled, or racial and sexual minorities: *the Venice lineup conjured a fuzzy global inclusivity, with numerous protagonists displaced across borders, gamely leapfrogging cultural, political, and linguistic hurdles.* [**10 Sept. 2003** *Village Voice*]

in•flect /in'flekt/ ▸ **verb** influence pervasively, so as to affect the character of: [usually as participle] *she still treats a painting as a flat surface to be acted upon . . . by sketching the outlines of people and objects inflected by her own graphic sensibility.* [**14 Nov. 2003** *Baltimore Sun*] | [as combining form] *Scott may . . . grill her own Asian, Southern and California-inflected entrees by herself.* [**Mar. 1993** *Albuquerque Journal*]

in•fo•dem•ic /‚infō'demik/ ▸ **noun** a surfeit of information about a problem that is viewed as being a detriment to its solution: *evidence of the current infodemic's potency came last week with the news that the Chinese government had detained four people for spreading rumors about SARS.* [**11 May 2003** *Washington Post*]
-ORIGIN early 21st cent.: blend of *information* and *epidemic*.

in•fo•me•di•ar•y /‚infō'mēdē‚erē/ ▸ **noun** an Internet company that gathers and links information on particular subjects on behalf of commercial organizations and their potential customers: *"Infomediaries sit between buyers and sellers," says the managing director for an investment bank. "They market everything from blueberries to backhoes."* [**15 Dec. 1998** *Edupage*]

-ORIGIN 1980s: from *info(rmation)* + *-mediary,* on the pattern of *intermediary.*

in•forma•tion scent /ˌinfərˈmāsHən ˌsent/ ▸ noun visual or textual cues provided on a Web site to suggest what information it or its links may contain: *not unlike an animal's foraging behavior users use "information scent" to optimize their efforts to find what they want.* [5 **Dec.** 2002 *review of Human Factors and Web Development*]
■ the perceived usefulness of a page based on such information.

in•for•ma•vore /inˈfôrmə͵vôr/ ▸ noun a consumer of information: *we're all informavores now, hunting down and consuming data as our ancestors once sought woolly mammoths and witchetty grubs.* [11 **Nov.** 2000 *New Scientist (UK)*]
-ORIGIN from *informa(tion)* + *-vore* 'one who consumes or devours,' on the pattern of *carnivore, herbivore.*

in•fo•war /ˈinfō͵wôr/ ▸ noun 1 hostile actions against an enemy's information infrastructure: *Yugoslav hackers are waging infowar against NATO's computer network, but the fighters appear to be poorly armed.* [1 **Apr.** 1999 *Washington Post*]
2 a propaganda war waged via electronic media.

in•nit /ˈinit/ chiefly British informal ▸ contraction isn't it (often used in conversation when seeking confirmation or as a general filler): *well, it's a hoax of a hoax, innit?* [**Nov.** 1991 *New Age*]
USAGE: The word **innit** arose as an informal way of saying "isn't it," especially in questions in spoken English where the speaker is seeking confirmation of a statement, as in *weird that, innit?* More recently, however, **innit** has developed into a general-purpose tag question both to seek confirmation or merely for emphasis.

in•sight med•i•ta•tion /ˈinsīt medi͵tāsHən/ ▸ noun a form of Buddhist mediation that employs concentration sharply focused on bodily sensations and mental events, practiced with the intention of gaining insight into reality: *feeling is one of the objects of immediate introspection recommended in insight meditation, and it is also one of the "aspects of experience in the mind and body."* [1983 M. Carrithers, *Founders of Faith*]

in•sourc•ing /ˈin͵sôrsiNG/ ▸ noun the practice of using an organization's own personnel or other resources to accomplish a task: *Procter & Gamble gained recognition for sidestepping automation through its offshore insourcing of expense reporting processing.* [8 **Sept.** 2003 *Business Travel News*]

■ the practice whereby an organization provides its own personnel to accomplish specialized tasks for a client, at the client's place of business: *insourcing is likely to work best for companies that occupy small niches, sell high-margin products and compete on quality rather than price.* [2 **Mar.** 1996 *Economist (UK)*]
-DERIVATIVES **in•source** verb

in•stant mes•sag•ing /'instənt 'mesijiNG/ (abbreviation: **IM**) ▸ noun Computing the exchange of typed messages between computer users in real time via the Internet: *AOL heavily promotes its features such as chat room, instant messaging, and (filtered) Web access* [**Aug.** 2000 *Genre*]
-DERIVATIVES **in•stant mes•sage** noun

in•te•gra•tive /'inti,grātiv/ ▸ adjective serving or intending to unify separate things: *the editor might have gone further in seeking some integrative papers, or in writing a more comprehensive introduction.* [1991 *Review of Anthropology*]
■ Medicine combining allopathic and complementary therapies: *it includes lots of information on integrative medicine, regularly offering herbal and homeopathic suggestions for common concerns of pregnancy.* [**19 Sept.** 2003 *Mercola Newsletter*]

in•tel /'in,tel/ ▸ noun [often as modifier] informal military intelligence; information: *the assessment came out via a just-released parliamentary report, which also formally cleared Blair's government of charges that they falsified—or as the Brits seem to put it, sexed up—prewar intel.* [**12 Sept.** 2003 *Slate*]
-ORIGIN 1980s: abbreviation.

in•tel•li•gent de•sign /in'telijənt di'zīn/ ▸ noun Computers the theory that life, or the universe, cannot have arisen by chance and was designed and created by some intelligent entity: *he offers an explanation he calls "intelligent design," which seems like a scientist's name for God.* [**Jan.** 1997 *Psychology Today*]

in•ter•op•er•a•bil•i•ty /,intər,äp(ə)rə'bilitē/ ▸ noun Computers the ability of two or more systems with different architecture, platforms, or the like to share information: *in many buildings, interoperability means that the front-end controls for the various systems in the building all terminate in the same room.* [2003 Stephen R. Ferree, Buildings.com]

in•tra•der•mal pig•men•ta•tion /,intrə'dərməl ,pigmən'tāsHən/ ▸ noun a tattooing method in which pigment is injected within the layers of the skin with a very small needle: *the Intradermal Pigmentation procedure for lip color is beautiful. It can change the size and shape of the lips as well as the color.* [2002 Web site of Dermagraphix, LLC]

in•tra•net /'intrə,net/ (also **In•tra•net**) ▸ **noun** Computing a local or restricted communications network, especially a private network accessible via ordinary Internet connectivity software: *intranets may be used entirely in isolation from the outside world . . . or, as is more likely given the benefits of doing so, they may be hooked up to the global Internet.* [15 Feb. 1996 *Computer Weekly (UK)*]

in•tra•pre•neur /,intrəprə'nōōr; -'nər/ ▸ **noun** an entrepreneur operating within an organization and developing its capabilities or resources: *you don't have to leave a corporation to become an entrepreneur. You can become an "intrapreneur": a person who creates innovation within an organization.* [23 May 1996 *Wall Street Journal*]
-DERIVATIVES **in•tra•pre•neur•ship noun**

in•vac•u•ate /in'vakyōō,āt/ ▸ **verb** [trans.] confine (people) to a space in an emergency: *these buildings can now "invacuate" tenants to safe havens within the building and evacuate to agreed locations that are a safe distance from the building.* [2001 *Impact and Implications for Corporate Real Estate Occupiers*]
-DERIVATIVES **in•vac•u•a•tion** /in,vakyōō'āsHən/ **noun**
-ORIGIN on the pattern of *evacuate*.

IP ad•dress /'ī'pē ə,dres/ ▸ **noun** Computing a unique string of numbers separated by periods that identifies each computer attached to the Internet: *web server logs use host names or IP addresses to tell where users are coming from.* [Apr. 1996 *Internet World*]

Is•lam•o•pho•bi•a /is,lämə'fōbēə; iz-/ ▸ **noun** a hatred or fear of Islam or Muslims, especially as a political force: *Islamophobia also accounts for Moscow's reluctance to relinquish its position in Afghanistan, despite the estimated $300 million a month it takes to keep the Kabul regime going.* [Feb. 1991 *Insight*]

Is•mail Sa•ma•ni Peak /'ismīl sə'mänē 'pēk/ one of the principal peaks in the Pamir Mountains of Tajikistan, rising to 24,590 feet (7,495 m). It was the highest mountain in the former Soviet Union. Former names: **Mount Garmo** (until 1933), **Stalin Peak** (1933–62), **Communism Peak** (1962–98).
-ORIGIN named after the 9th-century founder of the Tajik nation.

i•so•thi•o•cy•a•nate /ˌīsō͵THī-ō'sīənāt; -nit/ ▸ **noun** a family of organic compounds found in tangy herbs such as horseradish, mustard, and onions. They have several patented applications including use as a pesticide, and their presence in the diet is thought to help prevent cancer in humans.

ISP ▸ **abbreviation** Internet service provider: *the fear is that ISPs will not be able to keep up with the rate of growth in traffic on their respective networks or will not be able to muster sufficient revenues and profit margins to justify further investment to expand their capacity.* [**Aug.** 1995 *Internet World*]

is•sues /'isHᴏᴏz/ ▸ **plural noun** informal personal problems or difficulties: *Extremely Pretty and petite, very young-looking Jewish woman seeks professional, handsome, nice guy with great sense of humor and as few "issues" as possible* [**13 Dec. 1999** *New York Magazine*]
-DERIVATIVES **is•sue•less** adjective
USAGE: The objection to this usage by language purists seems to be based mainly on the idea that other words, which they prefer, exist to describe the phenomenon. The usage, while not particularly elegant, is a natural outgrowth of the meaning "a topic or problem for debate."

-ista ▸ **suffix** informal forming nouns denoting a person associated with a particular activity, often with a derogatory intent: *fashionista.*
-ORIGIN from the Spanish suffix *-ista*, as in *Sandinista.*

ISV ▸ **abbreviation** independent software vendor.

it girl /'it ͵gərl/ (also **It Girl**) ▸ **noun** a young woman who has achieved celebrity because of her socialite lifestyle: *and it was even more fortuitous that Jane Austen, this year's posthumous It Girl, has a 20th-century cosmic twin in Emma Thompson, who not only stars in* Sense and Sensibility *but also wrote the screenplay.* [**22 Dec. 1995** *Entertainment Weekly*]
-ORIGIN coined by American screenwriter Elinor Glyn (1864–1943) with reference to American actress and sex symbol Clara Bow (1905–65), who starred in Glyn's romantic comedy *It* (1927). The current usage dates from the 1960s.

ITV (also **iTV**) ▸ **abbreviation** interactive television.

I•vo•ri•an /ī'vôrēən/ ▸ **adjective** relating to the Ivory Coast or its people: *Ivorian protests cool, but damage takes toll* [**10 Feb. 2003** *Christian Science Monitor (headline)*]

▶**noun** a native or inhabitant of the Ivory Coast: *at a news conference in Abidjan, the Special UN Representative, Albert Tevoedjre, announced the plan, and called for all Ivorians to participate.* [17 **Sept.** 2003 *Voice of America*]

ix•nay /ˈiks,nā/ informal ▶ **exclamation** (**ixnay on/to**) used in rejecting something specified: *mental note: nice place to paddle, but* ixnay *on the swimming.* [**Mar. 1991** *Canoe*]
▶**verb** [trans.] cancel or stop: *if Lowenthal really wants to revive a society suffocating in its own decadence, he ought to* ixnay *with the moral exhibitionism and get into the entertainment biz.* [31 **Aug. 1999** *Newark Star-Ledger*]
-ORIGIN 1930s: Pig Latin for *nix.*

Jj

jack /jak/ ▸**verb** [trans.] informal take (something) illicitly; steal: *his MO in the studio remains the same—jack other people's tracks and present them in a new context.* [**14 Oct.** 1993 *Rolling Stone*]
■ rob (someone): *G.C. and I had jacked a civilian for his car one night.* [**1993** K. Scott, *Monster*]
-ORIGIN 1990s: from *hijack*.

jake brake /'jāk ˌbrāk/ ▸**noun** an engine brake for truck diesel engines that cuts off fuel flow and interrupts the transfer of mechanical energy to the drive mechanism: *another pulled in next to him and hit the jake brake—emitting the ratchet-down growl you hear trucks make on interstate off-ramps.* [**22 Jan.** 1996 *Washington Post*]
-ORIGIN 1980s: from the *Jacobs* Company, who invented the most common implementation of the technology that the brake is based on.

jal•fre•zi /jäl'frāzē/ ▸**noun** (plural **jal•fre•zis**) a medium-hot Indian dish consisting of chicken or lamb with fresh chili peppers, tomatoes, and onions.
-ORIGIN 1980s: Bengali.

Jap•a•nese stilt grass /'japə,nēz 'stilt ˌgras; -,nēs/ ▸**noun** an annual grass of Asian origin that is established as an invasive ecological threat in the eastern and southern U.S.
•*Microstegium vimineum*, family Poaceae.

jazz funk /'jaz ˌfəNGk/ ▸**noun** a style of popular dance music incorporating elements of jazz and funk: *a half-dozen new albums spread along the continuum of jazz funk and hip-hop have developed a new groove.* [**16 June 1994** *Rolling Stone*]

Jed•i /'jedī/ (also **Jed•i knight** /'jedī ˌnīt/) ▸**noun** (plural same or **Jed•is**) a member of the mystical knightly order in the *Star Wars* films, trained to guard peace and justice in the universe.
■ anyone with special privileges or supernormal powers reminiscent of a Jedi: *the dirty little secret of Washington is these guys hang out in places mere mortal lobbyists who were not Jedi warriors cannot go.* [**12 Sept. 2003** *Washington Post*]

jeet kune do /'jēt ˌkōōn 'dō/ ▸ noun a modern martial art incorporating elements of kung fu, fencing, and boxing, devised by the American actor Bruce Lee (1941–73).
-ORIGIN 1990s: from Cantonese, literally 'the way of the intercepting fist.'

je•fe /'hefā/ ▸ noun informal a boss or leader; a person in charge of something: *the drugs in Adams-Morgan are controlled by an organization of contra jefes. It's a Nicaraguan Cosa Nostra, and they run a tight ship.* [**1990** *Current Affairs*]
-ORIGIN late 19th cent.: Spanish from French *chef* 'chief.'

Jhar•kand /'jär ˌkand/ a state in northeastern India, formed in 2000 from the southern part of Bihar; capital, Ranchi.

jig•gy /'jigē/ ▸ adjective (**jig•gi•er, jig•gi•est**) informal **1** uninhibited, especially in a sexual manner: *the script required her to **get jiggy with** Leonardo.*
2 trembling or nervous, especially as the result of drug withdrawal.
-ORIGIN 1930s: from *jig* + *-y.*

ji•had•i /ji'hädē/ (also **je•had•i**) ▸ noun (plural **ji•had•is**) a person involved in a jihad (Islamic holy war); an Islamic militant.
-ORIGIN from Arabic *jihādi*, from *jihād.*

ji•had•ist /ji'hädist/ ▸ noun a jihadi: *the band of jihadists, or "holy warriors," has precious few friends.* [**29 Oct. 2001** *U.S. News and World Report*]
USAGE: There doesn't seem to be a pressing need for this English-friendly form since the Arabic term for a holy warrior, *mujahid*, had already made it into English in the plural form (*mujahedin*), along with *jihadi*, a form more in keeping with Arabic morphology. *Jihadist*, however, is the preferred form for all writers who are vehemently anti-Arab or anti-Islam.

jir•ga /'jərgə/ ▸ noun (in Afghanistan) a tribal council. A grand tribal council (**loya jirga**) presently has a legislative function in the country: *the village council, or jirga, decreed that the father could use his daughter as compensation for the loss of the animal.* [**11 Nov. 2002** *Daily Telegraph (UK)*]

jis•som /'jizəm/ ▸ noun vulgar slang variant of jism (semen).

job spill /'jäb ˌspil/ ▸ noun a situation in which job-related work or anxiety encroaches on one's leisure time: *your headaches may be related to job spill, so try to reduce your workload.*
-ORIGIN on the pattern of *oil spill.*

jock•ey shorts /'jäkē ,sʜôrts/ (also **Jock•ey shorts** or **Jock•eys**) ▸ plural noun trademark men's close-fitting underpants with a short leg.

jocks /jäks/ ▸ plural noun informal jockey shorts.

Joe Schmoe /'jō 'sʜmō/ (also **Schmo** /sʜmō/) ▸ noun (plural **Joe Schmoes**) informal (also **Joe Schmo** /'jō 'sʜmō/) a hypothetical ordinary man: *a lot of Joe Schmoes make it to the big leagues.* -ORIGIN 1940s: alteration of *schmuck.*

john•ny /'jänē/ (also **rub•ber john•ny** /'rəbər 'jänē/) ▸ noun (plural **john•nies**) mainly British slang a condom.

joined-up /'joind 'əp/ ▸ adjective mainly British (of handwriting) written with the characters joined; cursive: *every class starts a daily session of five to 10 minutes' instruction in joined-up handwriting.* [**16 Dec. 1991** *Independent*]
■ (especially of a policy) characterized by coordination and coherence of thought; integrated: *a joined-up approach to rural poverty, public services, and employment.*

Jor•dan•esque /ˌjôrdn'esk/ ▸ adjective resembling the basketball player Michael Jordan in skill or agility: *a brand of basketball that features no spectacular alley-oops, no Jordanesque jams, and no shot-swatting seven-footers.*

joy•pad /'joi,pad/ ▸ noun an input device for a computer game that uses buttons to control the motion of an image on the screen. -ORIGIN late 20th cent.: blend of *joystick* and *keypad.*

juice box /'jo͞os ,bäks/ ▸ noun a small disposable carton containing a single serving of fruit juice: *only juice boxes (no cans, no bottles) are allowed in the cafeteria.*

juke /jo͞ok/ informal ▸ noun (also **juke joint** /'jo͞ok ,joint/) **1** a roadhouse, nightclub, or bar, especially one providing food, drinks, and music for dancing: *Williamson and Wolf teamed up and toured the jukes of Tennessee, Arkansas, and Mississippi.* [**Nov. 1991** *Living Blues*]
2 a jukebox: *it was too early to be crowded, but there was music playing from a juke.* [**1987** M. Dorris, *Yellow Raft in Blue Water*]
▸ verb [intrans.] **1** dance, especially to the music of a jukebox: *a middle-aged couple juked to the music.*
2 move in a zigzag fashion: *I juked down an alley.*
-ORIGIN 1930s: from Gullah *juke* 'disorderly.'

jump the shark /'jəmp T͟Hə 'sHärk/ ▸ **verb phrase** informal pass the peak of creativity, excellence, or inspiration, as evidenced by a decline in quality or performance: *he's like "The Simpson's." He's never jumped the shark.* [**4 Oct.** 2003 *ESPN*]
-ORIGIN with allusion to an episode in 1977 of the television series *Happy Days*, in which a central character (the Fonz) jumps over a shark on water skis.

jump•sta•tion /'jəmp ˌstäsHən/ ▸ **noun** Computing a site on the World Wide Web containing a collection of hypertext links, usually to pages on a particular topic: *use the form below to search the GIS Jump Station.* [2003 Geographic Information Services Web site]

june•teenth /ˌjo͞on'tēnT͟H/ ▸ **noun** a festival held annually on the nineteenth of June by African Americans (especially in the southern states), to commemorate emancipation from slavery in Texas on that day in 1865: *rain came, but the parade went on yesterday at the 30th annual Juneteenth celebration.* [**16 June** 1996 *Denver Post*]
-ORIGIN 1930s: blend of *June* and *(nine)teenth.*

junk sci•ence /'jəNGk ˌsīəns/ ▸ **noun** untested or unproven theories when presented as scientific fact (especially in a court of law): *she concludes that until judges prevent unwarranted jury verdicts, "the Frankenstein monster of junk science will be a regular visitor to America's courtrooms."* [**Jan.** 1997 *Skeptical Inquirer*]

just war /'jəst 'wôr/ ▸ **noun** a war that is deemed to be morally or theologically justifiable: [as modifier] *Architects of an authentic new world order must . . . move beyond castles in the air—beyond imaginary truths that transcend politics—such as, for example, just war theory and the notion of the sovereign equality of states.* [**May** 2003 *Foreign Affairs*]
-ORIGIN translation of Latin 'bellum justum.'

Kk

ka-ching /kəˈCHiNG/ (also **ker-ching** /kə(r)ˈCHiNG/) ▸ **noun** used to represent the sound of a cash register, especially with reference to making money: *you're going to walk into the store and say, "Hi, I'm here. I have some Priceline prices." And they'll say, "Great." Ka-ching!* [**20 Sept. 1999** *Newsweek*]
–ORIGIN early 1990s: imitative.

kan•al /ˈkanl/ ▸ **noun** a land measure used in Pakistan, standardized under British rule to equal one-eighth acre: *petitioner Kalsoom Bibi alleged that 17 kanals of her agricultural land had been illegally occupied by the Qabza Group (land grabbers).* [**4 Sept. 2003** *Daily Times (Pakistan)*]

kan•ga•roo care /ˌkaNGgəˈro͞o ˌke(ə)r/ ▸ **noun** a method of caring for a premature baby in which the infant is held in skin-to-skin contact with a parent, typically the mother, for as long as possible each day: *skin to skin contact, also known as kangaroo care, began in Bogota, Columbia, where doctors advised mothers to hold and breastfeed their premature babies because of a shortage of incubators.* [**2 Oct. 1998** *Guardian (UK)*]

kar•el•a /ˈkärələ/ ▸ **noun** the Indian name for BITTER GOURD.

ka•ro•shi /kəˈrōSHē; ˈkär.ō-/ ▸ **noun** death by overwork: *said execs might note the recent news that in Japan karoshi—death from overwork—is now the second leading cause of death after cancer.* [**Oct. 1994** *Face (UK)*]
–ORIGIN Japanese.

kei•ret•su /kāˈretso͞o/ ▸ **noun** a form of conglomerate in Japan, formed by cross-holdings or close cooperation among different companies: *the industrial sector is largely organized into great families of companies—keiretsu—each of which consists of 20 to 40 big corporations.* [**Mar. 1990** *Harvard Business Review*]

Ken•tuck•y colo•nel /kənˈtəkē ˈkərnl/ ▸ **noun** an honorary commission given by the state of Kentucky to individuals noted for their public service and their work for the advancement of Kentucky: *for her dedication to shedding light on Appalachian history, Love was commissioned last week as a Kentucky Colonel in the Honorable*

Order of Kentucky Colonels. [**1 Sept.** 2003 *Huntington (WV) Herald Dispatch*]

ker•a•to•mi•leu•sis /ˌkerətōmī'lo͞osis/ ▸ **noun** the surgical reshaping of the cornea, carried out in order to correct a refractive error. -ORIGIN 1990s: from *kerato-* 'of the cornea' + Greek *smileusis* 'carving.'

key•pal /'kē͟ˌpal/ ▸ **noun** a person with whom one becomes friendly by exchanging e-mails; an e-mail pen pal: *one of the things on the Internet is e-mail. I mainly use it for sending e-mails to my keypals.* [**6 May 1995** *New Scientist (UK)*] -ORIGIN 1990s: from *key* + *pal*, by analogy with *pen pal.*

kha•bar /'kəbər/ ▸ **noun** Indian the latest information; news. -ORIGIN mid 19th cent.: from Urdu and Persian *k̲h̲abar*, from Arabic.

ki•a•su /'kēəˌso͞o/ SE Asian ▸ **noun** a grasping, selfish attitude. ▸ **adjective** (of a person) very anxious not to miss out on an opportunity; grasping: *Mr Khaw's action may be seen as 'kiasu' by some. But to the WHO, it was 'exemplary'.* [**10 Sept.** 2003 *Straits Times (Singapore)*] -ORIGIN from Chinese, 'scared to lose.'

kid•ult /ki'dəlt; 'kidˌəlt/ ▸ **noun** informal an adult with childish tastes: *toymakers now take aim at "kidults," defined by the Italian company Kidult Games as "adults who take care of their kid inside."* [**2 Sept.** 2003 *Taipei Times*]

kill•er app /'kilər 'ap/ ▸ **noun** informal a feature, function, or application of a new technology or product that is presented as virtually indispensable or much superior to rival products: *e-mail is clearly the "killer app" that entices people online.* [**2 Dec.** 1996 *Washington Post*]

kill•ing field /'kiliNG ˌfēld/ ▸ **noun** (usu. **killing fields**) a place where a heavy loss of life has occurred, typically as the result of massacre or genocide during a time of warfare or violent civil unrest: *Digging Up the Past in Iraq's Killing Fields* [**16 May** 2003 *New York Times (headline)*]

kink /kiNGk/ ▸ **noun** an unusual sexual preference: *now, I'm no prude. I've done my fair share of role-playing, and I've sampled all kinds of kink.* [**2000** M. Hamid, *Moth Smoke*]

ki•san /ki'sän/ ▸ noun Indian an agricultural worker; a peasant: *quoting Vajpayee's speech from the Red Fort on August 15, in which the prime minister said "education will be for all" and that "kisan is the heart of India," Sinha recalled that Jawaharlal Nehru had made similar promises on August 15, 1947.* [**14 Sept.** 2003 *People's Democracy (India)*] -ORIGIN 1930s: Hindi *kisān*, from Sanskrit *kṛṣāṇa* 'person who plows.'

kite•surf•ing /'kīt,sərfiNG/ (also **kite•board•ing** /'kīt,bôrdiNG/) ▸ noun the sport or pastime of riding on a modified surfboard while holding on to a specially designed kite, using the wind for propulsion. -DERIVATIVES **kite•surf•er** noun

kit•ten heel /'kitn ,hēl/ ▸ noun (on a shoe) a type of low curvy heel, typically between 1 and 2 inches in height.
■ [plural] a pair of shoes with such heels: *Theresa May has become famous for her shoes since her appearance last year on the Conservative conference platform in a pair of leopard-skin kitten heels.* [**14 Sept.** 2003 *Independent on Sunday (UK)*]

klep•to•crat /'kleptə,krat/ ▸ noun a ruler who uses political power to steal their country's resources: *that cynical ring of kleptocrats whose monopoly of the political process has kept them in office long enough to rack up the world's largest per capita debt.* [**28 Aug.** 1993 *Globe and Mail (Canada)*]
-DERIVATIVES **klep•toc•ra•cy** /klep'täkrəsē/ noun; **klep•to•crat•ic** /,kleptə'kratik/ adjective
-ORIGIN 1960s: from Greek *kleptēs* 'thief' + -crat.

Kling•on /'kliNGän/ ▸ noun 1 a member of a warlike humanoid alien species in the television series *Star Trek* and its derivatives and sequels.
2 the language of the Klingons: *the site is also available in synthetic languages like Esperanto and Klingon.* [**2 Sept.** 2003 *TechCentral (Malaysia)*]
-ORIGIN 1960s: invented name.

knock•out /'näk,out/ ▸ adjective designating a genetically modified organism in which a normally functioning gene has been deactivated or eliminated: *these so-called knockout mice invariably died about a week into their embryonic development.* [**21 June 1997** *Science News*]

knowl•edge /'nälij/ ▸ adjective relating to organized information stored electronically: *the need for accurate self-assessment is magnified in the knowledge economy.* [**1 Nov. 1999** *Newark Star-Ledger*]

knowl•edge base /'nälij ˌbās/ ▸ noun 1 a store of information or data that is available to draw on.
2 the underlying set of facts, assumptions, and rules that a computer system has available to solve a problem: *the knowledge base is a collection of facts and rules which relate to the subject of the expert system.* [**May 1989** *PC Magazine (UK)*]

knowl•edge man•age•ment /'nälij ˌmanijmənt/ ▸ noun efficient handling of information and resources within a commercial organization: *autonomy is one of a number of companies specializing in knowledge management, an industry growing as fast as the Internet itself.* [**Feb. 2000** *Wired*]

knowl•edge work•er /'nälij ˌwərkər/ ▸ noun a person whose job involves handling or using information: *another cause often cited for the decline in the appeal of unions is that they do not connect with a new generation of knowledge workers.* [**Mar. 1992** *Utne Reader*]

Kol•ka•ta /käl'kätə; -'kətə/ official name (since 2000) for Calcutta, India.

kom•bu•cha /kôm'boochə/ ▸ noun a food supplement prepared from a symbiotic colony of yeast and bacteria that is added to tea for its alleged health benefits.
–ORIGIN Japanese, 'tea sponge'.

ko•piy•ka /kô'pēkə/ ▸ noun a monetary unit of Ukraine, equal to one-hundredth of a hryvna.
–ORIGIN 1990s: Ukrainian from Russian *kopeĭka* 'kopek.'

Kraut•rock /'kroutˌräk/ ▸ noun an experimental style of rock music associated with German groups of the 1970s, characterized by improvisation and strong, hypnotic rhythms: [as modifier] *autumn is Krautrock season in the meat-packing district, as some fairly heavy hitters of seventies and eighties German experimental pop make their U.S. debuts.* [**14 Sept. 1998** *New York Magazine*]
–DERIVATIVES **Kraut•rock•er** noun

Krav Ma•ga /'kräv mə'gä/ ▸ noun a form of self-defense and physical training, first developed by the Israeli army in the 1940s, based on the use of reflexive responses to threatening situations.
–ORIGIN 1990s: from Hebrew, 'contact combat.'

Ku-band /'kā'yoo ˌband/ ▸ noun a microwave frequency band used for satellite communication and broadcasting, using frequencies

of about 12 gigahertz for terrestrial reception and 14 gigahertz for transmission.
-ORIGIN 1990s: from *Ku* (arbitrary serial designation) + *band.*

Kui•per belt /'kīpər ‚belt/ ▸ noun a region of the solar system beyond the orbit of Neptune, believed to contain many comets, asteroids, and other small bodies made largely of ice.
-ORIGIN 1990s: named after Gerard P. *Kuiper* (1905–73), Dutch-born U.S. astronomer.

Ku•rile Is•lands /'k(y)o͞or‚ēl 'īləndz; k(y)o͞o'rēl/ (also **Kuril Islands** or **the Kurils**) a chain of 56 islands between the Sea of Okhotsk and the North Pacific Ocean, stretching from the southern tip of the Kamchatka peninsula to the northeastern corner of the Japanese island of Hokkaido. They are the subject of dispute between Russia and Japan.

L1

-laced /lāst/ ▸ **adjective** [in combination] forming adjectives with nouns, indicating a substance (usually harmful or toxic) present in small amounts: *dioxin-laced sludge | anthrax-laced letters.*

lac•tiv•ist /ˈlaktəvist/ ▸ **noun** informal humorous an advocate for breast-feeding, especially one who promotes the right to breastfeed a child in public places: *I'm just saying that a lot of lactivists' initiatives are aimed at the right demographic but trying some of their reforms on a different social class would be horrifying.* [**20 Jan.** 2001 Usenet: alt.newlywed]
– ORIGIN a blend of *lactation* and *activist.*

lad•ette /laˈdet/ ▸ **noun** British informal a young woman who behaves in a boisterously assertive or crude manner and engages in heavy drinking sessions: *the only attempt to distinguish these ladettes from men is to allow them the occasional opportunity to gossip about boyfriends or pop stars.* [**26 Mar.** 1999 *Interzone*]
– ORIGIN 1990s: from *lad* + *-ette.*

la•dy•boy /ˈlādēˌboi/ ▸ **noun** (in Thailand) a transvestite: *I look like a Bangkok ladyboy.* [**June** 1999 *Cosmopolitan*]

lair•y /ˈle(ə)rē/ ▸ **adjective** (**lair•i•er, lair•i•est**) British informal **1** cunning or conceited.
2 ostentatiously attractive; flashy: *former Hollywood bad girl Shannen Doherty is putting her lairy tinseltown past behind her for a bash at TV comedy.* [**7 Oct.** 2003 *Megastar News (UK)*]
3 aggressive or rowdy: *a couple of lairy people pushed me around.*
– ORIGIN mid 19th cent. (originally Cockney slang): alteration of *leery.* Sense 2 was originally Australian slang and dates from the early 20th cent.

lake ef•fect snow /ˈlāk iˌfekt ˌsnō/ ▸ **noun** snow falling on the lee side of a lake, generated by cold dry air passing over warmer water, especially in the Great Lakes region.

lamp /lamp/ ▸ **verb** [trans.] British hit or beat (someone): *I punched her out of self-preservation, seeing as how she'd already lamped me five or six times and I was leaking more blood than you'd get with the average shrapnel wound.* [**1996** C. Bateman, *Of Wee Sweetie Mice and Men*]

-ORIGIN early 19th cent.: of uncertain origin; perhaps related to *lam*.

-land /land; lənd/ ▸ **combining form** forming nouns denoting a particular sphere of activity or group of people: *the blunt, charmless climate of technoland.*

land•fall /'land,fôl/ ▸ **noun** the contact of a hurricane with a landmass: *they forecast the storm's peak winds at between 110 and 130 miles an hour when it makes landfall on the E Gulf Coast, probably between 8 P.M. today and 2 A.M. Wednesday.* [**25 Aug. 1992** *New York Times*]
-DERIVATIVES **land•fall•ing** adjective

land•fill•ing /'land,filiNG/ ▸ **noun** the burying of waste in landfills: *even under a crisis atmosphere, the solution to our garbage problem is a mix of options: reduction, recycling, incineration and landfilling.* [**21 Dec. 1987** *Washington Post*] | [with obj.] *Eight of its 25 assembly plants are scheduled to eliminate the landfilling of packaging waste by early 1994.* [**15 Aug. 1993** *Coloradoan*]

lane /lān/ ▸ **noun** Astronomy a streak or band that shows up against its background, especially in a spiral galaxy: *look for the dark lane which gives this galaxy the common name Black Eye.* [**2002** *Twelve Month Tour of the Messier Catalog*]

lan•guage en•gi•neer•ing /'laNGgwij ,enjə,ni(ə)riNG/ ▸ **noun** any of a variety of computing procedures that use tools such as machine-readable dictionaries and sentence parsers in order to process natural languages for industrial applications such as speech recognition and speech synthesis.

La Ni•ña /lä 'nēnyə/ ▸ **noun** a cooling of the water in the equatorial Pacific, which occurs at irregular intervals and is associated with widespread changes in weather patterns complementary to those of El Niño, but less extensive and damaging in their effects.
-ORIGIN Spanish, literally 'the girl child,' after *El Niño*.

lap•dance /'lap,dans/ ▸ **noun** an erotic dance performed directly in front of a single, seated customer: *you can contemplate the club's pretty waterfall* and *get that drag-queen lap dance you've been craving.* [**July 1997** *Time Out New York*]

la•ser gun /'lāzər ,gən/ ▸ **noun** a hand-held device with a laser beam, such as one used to determine the speed of moving objects: *with*

a laser gun, officers can time vehicles up to a quarter-mile away. [**18 Sept. 2003** *Toledo (OH) Blade*]
■ (in science fiction and figuratively) a deadly weapon that uses a laser beam.

la•ser point•er /ˈlāzər ˌpointər/ ▸ noun a pen-shaped pointing device that contains a small diode laser that emits an intense beam of light, used to direct attention during presentations.

la•ser tweez•ers /ˈlāzər ˌtwēzərz/ ▸ plural noun another name for OPTICAL TWEEZERS.

lashed /lasHt/ ▸ adjective British informal very drunk: *both the Big Market and the Quayside are crammed full of bars, which are in turn crammed full of lads and lasses, dressed for a beach party (whatever the weather) and all eager to get lashed and obviously start their working week off with a hangover.* [**Aug. 1997** *Rugby World*]

LASIK /ˈlāzik; -sik/ ▸ noun corrective eye surgery in which a flap of the corneal surface is raised and a thin layer of underlying tissue is removed using a laser.
-ORIGIN 1990s: acronym from *laser-assisted in situ keratomileusis*.

la•va tube /ˈlävə ˌt(y)o͞ob; ˈlavə/ (also **la•va tun•nel** /ˈlävə ˌtənl; ˈlavə/) ▸ noun a natural tunnel within a solidified lava flow, formerly occupied by flowing molten lava.

leaf•y spurge /ˈlēfē ˈspərj/ ▸ noun a perennial Eurasian herb that produces a flat-topped cluster of yellow bracts bearing small flowers. It is a noxious weed in prairie and grassland areas of the U.S., where it aggressively displaces native plants.
•*Euphorbia esula*, family Euphorbiaceae.

learn•fare /ˈlərnˌfe(ə)r/ ▸ noun a welfare system in which attendance at school, college, or a training program is necessary in order to receive benefits.
-ORIGIN 1990s: from *learn*, on the pattern of *workfare*.

left-brained /ˈleft ˌbrānd/ ▸ adjective having the left part of the brain as the dominant or more efficient part, often said to indicate abilities in language, mathematics, and logical reasoning: *Savage Beast is even more left-brained. Eschewing public opinion, the service employs a roomful of musicology PhDs to assess songs using a proprietary list of 180-plus aspects of harmonic structure, dynamics, meter, melody, and instrumentation.* [**Feb. 2001** *Wired*]

left coast /'left 'kōst/ ▸ **noun** the West Coast of the United States, especially California: *America's left coast should be on everyone's vacation list.*

leg-rope /'leg ˌrōp/ ▸ **noun 1** (in surfing) a rope attached to a surfboard and tied to the surfer's ankle to prevent the board being washed away by the surf: *he was unable to hang in there with his leg rope breaking and a long swim back to shore.* [1 Oct. 2003 *Victor Harbor Times (Australia)*]
2 a rope secured to a horse's leg, used to prepare the horse for a rider: *the first couple of mountings are usually done with the trainer controlling that front leg with a leg rope and a rider simply getting on.* [5 Sept. 1996 Usenet: rec.equestrian]

leop•ard lil•y /'lepərd ˌlilē/ ▸ **noun** a lily resembling a tiger lily, native to the southwestern U.S.
•*Lilium pardalinum*, family Liliaceae.

life coach /'līf ˌkōCH/ ▸ **noun** a person who counsels and advises clients on matters having to do with careers or personal challenges: *according to life coach Suzy Greaves it's all about aligning yourself with the right kind of energy forces.* [19 Sept. 2003 *News24 (South Africa)*]
–DERIVATIVES **life coach•ing noun**

life•style drug /'līfˌstīl ˌdrəg/ ▸ **noun** a drug used to improve the quality of life rather than alleviating or curing disease: *there has been concern in the medical community that Provigil could become a lifestyle drug, used as a substitute for sleep by those who want to work or play longer.* [25 Sept. 2003 *New York Times*]

like /līk/ ▸ **adverb** informal used to convey a person's reported attitude or feelings in the form of direct speech (whether or not representing an actual quotation): *so she comes into the room and she's like "Where is everybody?"*
USAGE: This usage of *like* predominates in speech. In the writing of anyone to whom it is not a natural locution, it is usually intended to suggest the lack of education or sophistication of its users.

lime•scale /'līmˌskāl/ ▸ **noun** mainly British a whitish deposit on the inside of pipes, pots, etc., caused by minerals leeched from the water.

lin•guis•tic pro•fil•ing /liNG'gwistik 'prōˌfīliNG/ ▸ **noun** the analysis of a person's speech or writing, especially to assist in identifying or characterizing an individual or particular subgroup: *linguistic profiling revealed that the bomber was probably an uneducated southerner.*

Lin•ux /'linəks/ ▸ **trademark** Computing an operating system modeled on Unix, whose source code is publicly available at no charge.
–ORIGIN 1990s: from the name of *Linus* Benedict Torvalds (b. 1969), a Finnish software engineer who wrote the first version of the system, + -*x*, as in *Unix.*

li•po•dys•tro•phy syn•drome /ˌlīpə'distrəfē ˌsindrōm; ˌlipə-/ ▸ **noun** a metabolic disease in which fat distribution in the body becomes abnormal, often as a result of taking protease inhibitor drugs. Fat is lost from the face, arms, and legs, and is built up in other places, especially the breasts, abdomen, and back of the neck.

-lish /lish/ ▸ **combining form** forming nouns denoting a blend of a particular language with English, as used by native speakers of the first language: *Japlish.*

li•so•fyl•line /ˌlīsō'fil,ēn; -in/ ▸ **noun** an anti-inflammatory drug that shows some promise in being able to prevent the development of diabetes: *the trial . . . is a Phase II/III study of lisofylline among patients who require mechanical ventilation for acute lung injury and acute respiratory distress syndrome.* [1 **June 1999** *Wall Street Journal*]

lock•box /'läk ˌbäks/ ▸ **noun 1** a service provided by a bank, whereby the bank receives, processes, and deposits all of a company's receivables.
2 any of various computerized devices or services intended to prevent the unauthorized distribution or copying of digitally stored or transmitted data: *IBM prepares lockbox for home networks* [**16 Sept. 2003** *BusinessWeek (headline)*]

lo•gis•tics /lə'jistiks; lō-/ ▸ **plural noun** the commercial activity of transporting goods to customers: [as modifier] *Trinks is Germany's largest beverage logistics organization and already realizes nearly 50 percent of its sales in the beer sector.* [**10 Oct. 2003** *Pressi.com (press release)*]

LOL ▸ **abbreviation** laughing out loud; used in e-mail, chatrooms, etc., as an indication that the writer is highly amused.

lo•ma•ti•um /lō'māsH(ē)əm/ ▸ **noun** a perennial herb of the parsley family, found throughout western North America It has various

folk-medicine applications (mainly antibiotic) and is eaten as a survival food.
•(genus *Lomatium*; numerous species).

look•ism /'lŏok,izəm/ ▸ **noun** prejudice or discrimination on the grounds of a person's appearance: *Etcoff describes the extent to which "lookism" dominates our transactions with each other, albeit often unconsciously.* [7 **Oct.** 1999 *New York Review of Books*]
–DERIVATIVES **look•ist** noun & adjective

USAGE: The persistence of writers to use quotation marks around this word now more than ten years after its first appearance suggests that it still has some way to go before most people take it seriously.

look•up /'lŏok,əp/ ▸ **noun** [usually as modifier] the action of or a facility for systematic electronic information retrieval: *you need an online dictionary with fast phonetic lookup.*

loon•ey tunes (also **loon•y-tunes**) /'lŏonē ,t(y)ŏonz/ informal ▸ **adjective** (variously capitalized) crazy; deranged: *I think it's an embarrassing thing for the city and county of Denver when you have a Looney Tunes initiative like this around.* [15 **Sept.** 2003 *Christian Science Monitor*]
▸ **plural noun** crazy or deranged people.
–ORIGIN 1980s: from *Looney Tunes,* the name of an animated cartoon series that began in the 1930s, featuring Bugs Bunny and other characters.

loos•ey-goos•ey /'lŏosē 'gŏosē/ ▸ **adjective** informal undesirably lacking in definition, care, or precision: *"From now on, it can't be loosey-goosey anymore,"* Bodiford said. *"We're not going to deviate two centimeters."* [9 **Oct.** 2003 *Atlanta Journal Constitution*]
–ORIGIN 1980s: fanciful formation from *loose* + *goosey.*

USAGE: While retaining its original meaning (mainly in sports contexts) of being relaxed and unconstrained, *loosey-goosey* is now increasingly used disparagingly.

los•ing•est /'lŏoziNGist/ ▸ **adjective** informal losing more often than others of its kind; least successful: *the losingest club in baseball history.*

lounge•core /'lounj,kôr/ ▸ **noun** songs from the 1960s and 1970s, including easy listening music, orchestral verions of rock songs, and television or movie theme songs.
–ORIGIN 1990s: blend of *lounge* and (hard) core.

love•ware /'ləv,we(ə)r/ ▸ noun informal Computing computer software that is distributed freely, with the developer asking for the users to think kindly of the developer or of a dedicatee in lieu of payment.

low-hang•ing fruit /'lō ,haNGiNG 'fro͞ot/ ▸ noun informal a thing or person that can be won, obtained, or persuaded with little effort: *the ads went after financial advisers by urging consumers to "Fire your broker" ("an easy target—the brokers were the low-hanging fruit", says Silverstein).* [**Feb. 2000** *Wired*]

low-main•te•nance /'lō 'mānt(ə)nəns; 'māntn-əns/ ▸ adjective requiring little work to keep in good condition: *low-maintenance lawns.*
■ informal (of living and abstract things) desirably trouble-free and undemanding: *changes in society can be considered responsible for the shift towards the low maintenance small companion dog.* [**8 Oct. 2003** *K9 Online (UK)*]

low post /'lō ,pōst/ ▸ noun Basketball an offensive position on the court close to the basket.

loy•a jir•ga /'loiə 'jərgə/ ▸ noun see JIRGA

LRD ▸ abbreviation (plural **LRDs** or **LRD's**) living related donor; an organ donor who is genetically related to the recipient: *brothers and sisters commonly volunteer to be LRDs.*

LTR ▸ abbreviation long-term relationship: *WESTCHESTER DWM: Communicative, Ivy-education . . . seeks LTR with upbeat, free-spirited woman.* [**1 Dec. 1994** *New York Review of Books (advertisement)*]

lunch box /'lənCH ,bäks/ ▸ noun slang a fool; an inept person.

LURD /lərd/ ▸ abbreviation (plural **LURDs** or **LURD's**) living unrelated donor; an organ donor who is genetically unrelated to or has no prior relationship with the recipient: *they were the first hospital in the region to do transplants with LURDs.*

lurk•er /'lərkər/ ▸ noun a user of an Internet chat room or newsgroup who does not participate: *Mr. Rickard, of Boardwatch Magazine, estimates that there are five or six lurkers for each poster on a bulletin board.* [**1 Dec. 1992** *New York Times*]

ly•o•cell /'līə,sel/ ▸ noun a strong synthetic fiber made from reconstituted cellulose, used in carpets and in apparel when blended with other fibers.

Mm

M ▶ **abbreviation** money, when used with a following numeral in measures of money supply: *broad money, M3, grew by an annualized 9.7%.*

mac•chi•a•to /ˌmäkēˈätō/ ▶ **noun** espresso coffee with a dash of frothy steamed milk.
–ORIGIN 1970s: from Italian, literally 'stained, marked.'

mac•ro•lide /ˈmakrəˌlīd/ ▶ **noun** any of a class of antibiotics containing a lactone ring, of which the first and best known is erythromycin.

mag•ne•tar /ˈmagniˌtär/ ▶ **noun** Astronomy a neutron star with an extremely strong magnetic field.
–ORIGIN 1990s: from *magnetic* + *-ar* on the pattern of *pulsar* and *quasar.*

mag•no•lia vine /magˈnōlyə ˌvīn/ ▶ **noun** another name for SCHIZANDRA.

ma•hal /məˈhäl/ ▶ **noun** Indian **1** a mansion or palace: [in names] *the Taj Mahal.*
2 living quarters set aside for a particular group of people: *the whole servant mahal has been buzzing with the gossip.*
–ORIGIN early 17th cent.: from Urdu and Persian *maḥal(l)*, from Arabic *maḥall*, from *ḥall*, 'stopping-place, abode.'

main man /ˈmān ˈman/ ▶ **noun** informal **1** a close and trusted friend.
2 the most important person in a team, organization or situation: *now their main man can give his loving fans a big present by helping his team go all the way.*

ma•ki /ˈmäkē/ (also **ma•ki zu•shi** /ˈmäkē ˈzōōsHē/) ▶ **noun** a Japanese dish consisting of sushi and raw vegetables wrapped in seaweed.
–ORIGIN 1970s: Japanese, from *maki-* (combining form of *maku* 'roll up') + *-zushi, sushi.*

mal•fat•ti /mälˈfätē/ ▶ **plural noun** dumplings or gnocchi made with spinach and ricotta.
–ORIGIN 1980s: Italian, from *malfatto*, 'badly made' (because they resemble ravioli without their pasta envelopes).

mal•ware /ˈmalˌwe(ə)r/ ▸ **noun** Computing software that is intended to damage or disable computers and computer systems: *protect your computer against viruses and other malware.*
–ORIGIN blend of *malicious* and *software.*

man•age•ment in•for•ma•tion sys•tem /ˈmanijmənt infərˌmāsHən ˌsistəm/ ▸ **noun** (abbreviation **MIS**) a computerized information-processing system designed to support the activities of company or organizational management.

man•ny /ˈmanē/ ▸ **noun** (plural **man•nies**) a male nanny: *my husband would like us to hire a manny for our two boys.*
–ORIGIN 1990s: blend of *man* and *nanny.*

man•u•fac•tured home /ˈmanyəˈfakCHərd ˈhōm/ ▸ **noun** (mainly in advertising) a mobile home.

MAOI ▸ **noun** Medicine monamine oxidase inhibitor, a type of antidepressant drug.

March Mad•ness /ˈmärCH ˈmadnis/ ▸ **trademark** informal the time of the annual NCAA college basketball tournament, generally coinciding with the month of March.
USAGE: Though the phrase predates its association with college Basketball, an August 2003 court ruling stated that *March Madness* was a trademark rightfully owned by the NCAA and the Illinois High School Association. Its usage in contexts unrelated to basketball or college sports is probably not litigable.

mar•go•sa /märˈgōsə/ ▸ **noun** a tropical Old World tree that yields mahoganylike timber, oil, medicinal products, and insecticide. Also called *neem.*
•*Azadirachta indica*, family Meliaceae.
–ORIGIN Portuguese *amargosa*, feminine of *amargoso* 'bitter.'

mark•er /ˈmärkər/ ▸ **noun** a distinctive feature or characteristic indicative of a particular quality or condition: *identification with one's own language has always been a marker of nationalism* | *using gene expression, one can simultaneously track multiple markers associated with potency, specificity and toxicology.*

mar•ket•space /ˈmärkitˌspās/ ▸ **noun** a share or sector of a market, especially one represented on the Internet: *the successful market-space will be one that makes shopping a transaction not just involving* *goods and services but also communal experience.* [20 **Mar.** 1995 *New York Times*]

Mar•sanne /mär'sän/ ▸ **noun** a variety of white wine grape originating in the northern Rhône area of France: *the white is a blend of Riesling (64%), Sauvignon Blanc (24%) and Marsanne (12%). Very pale gold in color, it shows a light, pleasant floral perfume.* [19 **Sept.** 2003 *Wine Lover's Page*]
- ORIGIN from *Marsanne,* the name of a town in southern France.

Mar•y Jane /'me(ə)rē 'jān/ ▸ **noun** a flat, round-toed shoe for women and girls, with a single strap across the top: *Sarah Jessica Parker is hailing a cab on "Sex and the City" wearing "the big boys"—a pair of Manolo Blahnik Mary Janes.* [6 **Oct.** 2003 *Fort Wayne News Sentinel*]
- ORIGIN 1920s: from the female given name *Mary Jane.*

mash-up /'maSH ˌəp/ ▸ **noun** informal a recording created by digitally combining and synchronizing instrumental tracks with vocal tracks from two or more different songs: *we all compete to make the craziest mash-ups.*

mas•sive•ly par•al•lel /'masivlē 'parəˌlel/ ▸ **adjective** (of a computer) consisting of many individual processing units, and thus able to carry out simultaneous calculations on a substantial scale: *a massively parallel computer with 168 processors.*

MAT /mat/ ▸ **noun** a technology that uses chemicals (usually petrolatum, dimethicone, and polyquaternium) to reduce the ability of bacteria to adhere to the skin: *the company is developing MAT-containing soaps.*
- ORIGIN abbreviation of *Microbial Anti-attachment Technology.*

ma•tu•ri•ty /mə'CHo͞oritē, -'t(y)o͞ori-/ ▸ **noun** (plural **ma•tu•ri•ties**) an insurance policy, security, etc. having a fixed maturity date.

Mc•Man•sion /mək'mansHən/ ▸ **noun** a large modern house that is considered ostentatious and lacking in architectural integrity: *let's hope it happens before David Geffen erects cyclone fences on either side of his Malibu McMansion to keep away the riff-raff.* [17 **Jan.** 2003 *San Francisco Examiner*]

m-com•merce /'em ˌkämərs/ ▸ **noun** electronic commerce conducted on cellular phones.

Mc•Tim•o•ney /mək'timənē/ ▸ **noun** [as modifier] denoting a gentle form of chiropractic treatment involving very light and swift movements of the practioner's hands.
-ORIGIN 1970s: named after John *McTimoney* (1914–80), its British inventor.

ME ▸ **abbreviation 1** Medical Examiner.
2 myalgic encephalitis, another name for chronic fatigue syndrome.

meat•space /'mēt͵spās/ ▸ **noun** informal the physical world, as opposed to cyberspace or a virtual environment: *I'd like to know a little more before we talk about a get-together in meatspace.*

me•da•ka /mə'däkə/ (also **me•da•ka•fish** /mə'däkə ͵fiSH/) ▸ **noun** a small Japanese freshwater fish of variable color that is bred for aquariums and also extensively studied in the sciences: *freshwater Japanese medaka may soon replace lab mice in chemical screening, toxicity testing.*

med•al /'medl/ ▸ **verb** (**med•aled, med•al•ing**; British **med•alled, med•al•ling**) [intrans.] win a medal in a sporting event: *Larsen medaled in 4th place in the 3,200 meter run.*

me•di•a mail /'mēdēə ͵māl/ ▸ **noun** a class of mail for sending books, recordings, and computer media. It is cheaper and slower than first-class mail.

me•di•a•scape /'mēdēə͵skāp/ ▸ **noun 1** communications media as a whole: *the rapidly changing mediascape in Belgium.*
2 [in singular] the world as presented through, or perceived by, the mass media: *the vast, ubiquitous mediascape we inhabit today.*

me•di•a stud•ies /'mēdēə ͵stədēz/ ▸ **plural noun** [usually treated as singular] the study of the mass media, especially as an academic subject.

me•di•um /'mēdēəm/ ▸ **noun** (plural **me•di•a** /'mēdēə/ or **me•di•ums**) a particular form of storage material for digitized information, such as magnetic tape or discs: *it provides seamless integration between different storage mediums by moving or copying backed-up data through a hierarchy of different storage mediums.* [**18 Sept. 2003** Byteandswitch.com]

Meg•a•loc•er•os /͵megə'läsərəs/ ▸ **noun** a very large extinct deer of the Pleistocene epoch, of which the Irish elk was the main example.

-ORIGIN modern Latin, from Greek *megas, megalo-* 'great' + *keras* 'horn.'

meg•a•pix•el /'megə,piksəl/ ▸ **noun** one million pixels; used as a measure of the resolution in digital cameras: [in comb.] *a 3.2-megapixel camera*

mem•an•tine /'memən'tēn/ ▸ **noun** a prescription drug for the treatment of Alzheimer's disease. It protects the brain's nerve cells against glutamate, which is released in excess by Alzheimer's-damaged braincells.

mem•o•ry leak /'memərē ,lēk/ ▸ **noun** a failure in a computer program to deallocate discarded memory, causing impaired performance or failure: *repeatedly deleting toolbars using scripting impairs the performance of XMetaL Author because of a "memory leak."* [2003 *Release Notes to Corel XMetaL Service Pack 1*]

men in black /'men in 'blak/ ▸ **plural noun** informal anonymous government agents who carry out top-secret missions: *even getting close to the prez will be tough for bad guys because the men in black are also producing facial recognition devices.* [18 June 2001 *U.S. News and World Report*]

men's move•ment /'menz ,mo͞ovmənt/ ▸ **noun** a movement aimed at liberating men from their traditional roles in society.

mer•chant ac•count /'mərCHənt ə,kount/ ▸ **noun** a bank account that enables the holder to accept credit cards for payment: *companies also have the option of establishing a merchant account that lets customers pay with a credit card at a cost of $0.08 per transaction.* [28 Sept. 2003 *EMediawire (press release)*]

merge /mərj/ ▸ **verb** [trans.] Computers **1** incorporate revisions to a document to supersede the original: *if you answer "no" your changes will not be merged.*
2 combine (data or files) to produce a single entity: *The files were merged using the Patient Identification Code . . . as the common variable.* [1997 *Journal of the American Dental Association*]

mes•o•cy•clone /,mezə'sī,klōn; ,mē-/ ▸ **noun** Meteorology a cyclonic airmass associated with a supercell; its presence is a condition for a tornado warning.
-ORIGIN late 20th cent.

met•a /'metə/ ▸ noun short for META KEY.
▸ adjective (of a creative work) referring to itself or to the conventions of its genre; self-referential.
-ORIGIN 1980s: from *meta* in the sense 'beyond'.

met•a•da•ta /'metə,datə; -,dātə/ ▸ noun a set of data that describes and gives information about other data: *finally, they can search so-called metadata—extra information stored with the picture, including captions, the name of the photographer, the date of a picture, and so on.* [**June 1997** *Scientific American*]

met•a key /'metə ,kē/ ▸ noun Computing a function key on a keyboard that is activated by simultaneously holding down a control key.

met•a•rule /'metə,rōol/ ▸ noun a rule governing the content, form, or application of of other rules: *the rest of a legal system depends for its vitality and coherence on the strength of its metarules, and three particular metarules of international law provide especially weak support.* [**Autumn 2003** *Wilson Quarterly*]

me•thaq•ua•lone /mə'THakwə,lōn/ ▸ noun trademark a sedative and sleep-inducing drug. Also called QUAALUDE (trademark).
-ORIGIN 1960s: from elements of its chemical name *meth-* + *-a-* + *qu(inine* + *a(zo-* + *-o)l* + *-one.*

met•ro•sex•ual /,metrō'seksHōōəl/ ▸ noun a young, urban, heterosexual male with liberal political views, an interest in fashion, and and a refined if not prissy sense of taste: *maybe we should pity President Bush, stranded in his 50's world of hypermasculinity as his country goes gay and metrosexual (straight men with femme tastes like facials).* [**3 Aug.** 2003 *New York Times*]
-DERIVATIVES **met•ro•sex•u•al•i•ty** /-,seksHōō'alitē/ noun

mez•za•lu•na /,metsə'lōōnə/ ▸ noun a utensil for chopping herbs, vegetables, etc., with a semi-circular blade and a handle at each end.
-ORIGIN 1950s: from Italian, literally 'half moon.'

mi•asm /'mī,azəm; 'mē-/ ▸ noun (in homeopathy) any of the three underlying chronic diseases that afflict humankind: sycosis, syphilis, and psora.
-ORIGIN 19th cent.: from Greek *miasma*, 'stain'.

mi•cro•ar•ray /'mīkrō-ə,rā/ ▸ noun a grid of DNA segments of known sequence that is used to test and map DNA fragments, antibodies, or proteins: *many researchers are incorporating microarrays and*

DNA chips into efforts to learn when and where genes are turned on.
[**5 Oct.** 2001 *Science*]

mi•cro•brows•er /'mīkrō,brouzər/ ▸ **noun** Computing a small Internet browser for use with cellular phones and other handheld devices.

mi•cro•chip /'mīkrō,CHip/ ▸ **verb** (**mi•cro•chipped**, **mi•cro•chip•ping**) [trans.] implant a microchip under the skin of (a domestic animal) as a means of identification: *now, when you adopt, the animal is spayed/neutered, tested, vaccinated, microchipped and ready to go beforehand.* [**1 Oct.** 2003 *Ukiah (CA) Daily Journal*]

mi•cro•cin•e•ma /'mīkrō,sinəmə/ ▸ **noun** a genre consisting of low-budget alternative or independent films and videos: *she took a course in microcinema at the state college.*
■ a small room or theater used to show such films and videos: *the campus has three microcinemas.*

mi•cro•cred•it /'mīkrō,kredit/ ▸ **noun** the lending of small amounts of money at low interest to new businesses in the developing world.
■ such a loan considered individually: *microcredits should not be considered a substitute for long-term investment in infrastructure.*

mi•cro•derm•a•bra•sion /,mīkrō,dərmə'brāzHən/ ▸ **noun** surgical removal of skin imperfections, especially wrinkles, by means of a vacuum containing mineral crystals: *ever since crystal clearing, or microdermabrasion, was introduced a year ago at Bliss, a day spa in SoHo, the staff can barely keep up with the demand for power sloughing.* [**31 Oct.** 1999 *New York Times*]

mi•cro•e•lec•tro•me•chan•i•cal /,mīkrō-i,lektrōmə'kanikəl/ ▸ **adjective** denoting systems or compenents relating to microscopic electronic machines that are typically built on computer chips: *optical true-time delay devices with microelectromechanical mirror arrays.*
–DERIVATIVES **mi•cro•e•lec•tro•me•chan•ics** noun

mi•cro•pay•ment /'mīkrō,pāmənt/ ▸ **noun** a payment, typically via credit card, for a small amount of money: *the availability of "micropayments" is a critical component in allowing publishers to charge for online information, say industry observers.* [**1 Oct.** 1996 *Edupage*]

mi•cro•RNA /'mīkrō,ären'ā/ ▸ **noun** a cellular RNA fragment that prevents the production of a particular protein by binding to and destroying the messenger RNA that would have produced the protein.

mi•cro•scoot•er /'mīkrō‚skōōtər/ ▶ noun a small two-wheeled foldable aluminium scooter, used by children and adults.

mi•cro•site /'mīkrə‚sīt/ ▶ noun 1 an auxiliary Web site with independent links and address that is accessed mainly from a larger site: *to find out more about the winners and losers and where key industry figures rate Sulston, visit our Agenda Setters microsite.* [3 Oct. 2003 Silicon.com]
2 a small part of an ecosystem that differs markedly from its immediate surroundings.

mi•cro•suede /'mīkrə‚swād/ ▶ noun a polyester microfiber fabric with a suedelike, water-repellent finished surface.

mid•dl•es•cent /‚midl'esənt/ ▶ adjective 1 middle-aged, but typically still maintaining the interests and activities of younger people.
2 (in technical use) people of age forty to sixty
-DERIVATIVES **mid•dl•es•cence** /‚midl'esəns/ noun
-ORIGIN 1960s: blend of *middle* + *adolescent.*

mid•dle•ware /'midl‚we(ə)r/ ▶ noun Computing software constituting the interface between a database and a client: *we can help your organization achieve business process integration through the use of customized middleware.*

mid•ses•sion /'mid‚seSHən; ‚mid'seSH-/ ▶ noun the middle of a session, particularly:
■ a period of active trading on a securities exchange: *the Mexico peso regained some lost ground to the US dollar toward midsession Friday.* [10 Oct. 2003 *El Financiero México*]
■ a period of instruction: *the self-policing style of e-learning allows for intrusions from the day-to-day business tasks—both students and instructors can be called away in midsession to cope with emergencies.* [18 Feb. 2003 *ZDNet (UK)*]
■ a legislative session: *the bill, re-introduced in midsession by Senate Majority Leader Truman Chafin.* [23 Sept. 2003 *Beckley (WV) Register-Herald*]

mile-high club /'mīl 'hī ‚kləb/ ▶ phrase humorous used in reference to having sex on an aircraft: *she joined the mile-high club by making love on a flight between New York and LA.*

mile-a-min•ute weed /'mīl ə 'minit ‚wēd/ ▶ noun an invasive and noxious vine, native to Asia, that has downward-pointing barbs on

the stem and the underside of leaves; considered an ecological threat in the eastern U.S.
•*Polygonum perfoliatum*, family Polygonaceae.

mi•lieu ther•a•py /mil'yōō ˌTHerəpē; mēl'yœ/ ▸ **noun** psychotherapy in which the patient's social environment is controlled or manipulated with a view to preventing self-destructive behavior.

milk•y spore /'milkē 'spôr/ ▸ **noun** a bacterial disease of beetle larvae, including the Japanese beetle; the bacterium has been isolated and used in a commercial pesticide sold under the same name.
•*Bacillus popilliae*, family Bacillaceae.

Mil•len•nial /mi'lenēəl/ ▸ **noun** a member of the generation born from about 1980 onwards: *in short, it seems as though Millennials—the post-Gen X cohort born after 1981—are leaning to the right, with a strong libertarian streak.* [**29 Sept.** 2003 *Reason Online*]

mind•er /'mīndər/ ▸ **noun** chiefly British a person whose job it is to look after someone or something: [in combination] *their baby-minder is getting married.*
■ informal a bodyguard employed to protect a celebrity or criminal: *he was accompanied by his personal minder.* ■ an official whose job is to restrain access or the free flow of information, especially with an implied threat of force: *their dispatches were censored, delayed and sometimes blocked by military minders.*

mind•share /'mīnd‚sHe(ə)r/ ▸ **noun** relative public awareness of a phenomenon: *blogs do a pretty good job of fact checking the news. That's a useful antidote to a problem universal to all news: the need to compete for mindshare from an audience with a short attention span.* [**22 June** 2002 Webword.com]

ming•er /'miNGər/ ▸ **noun** British informal, derogatory an unattractive or unpleasant person or thing. *Why can't anyone see that Spencer is a complete minger?*
-ORIGIN 1990s: from MINGING.

ming•ing /'miNGiNG/ ▸ **adjective** British informal foul-smelling.
■ very bad or unpleasant: *what I'd really like to do is burn that minging beige jacket he has glued to him all the time.*
-ORIGIN 1970s: perhaps from Scots dialect *ming* 'excrement.'

min•i•camp /'minē‚kamp/ ▸ **noun** a session run by a professional sports team to train particular players, or to test potential new players, before the main preseason training: *Glanville is running most of his players through voluntary workouts in a minicamp.* [**9 July 1990** *Sports Illustrated*]

min•i•stroke /ˈminēˌstrōk/ ▸ noun a temporary blockage of the blood supply to the brain, lasting only a few minutes and leaving no noticeable symptoms or deficits. Also called TRANSIENT ISCHEMIC ATTACK.

mis•con•fig•ure /ˌmiskənˈfigyər/ ▸ verb [trans.] [often as adj.] (**misconfigured**) Computing configure (a system or part of it) incorrectly: *misconfigured Windows systems.*
-DERIVATIVES **mis•con•fig•u•ra•tion** /ˌmiskənˌfigyəˈrāSHən/ noun

mis•er•a•bi•lism /ˈmiz(ə)rəbəˌlizəm/ ▸ noun gloomy pessimism or negativity: *the duo spent much of the eighties exploring the lonely outer reaches of miserabilism.*
-DERIVATIVES **mis•er•a•bi•list** noun & adjective

mis•sion creep /ˈmiSHən ˌkrēp/ ▸ noun a gradual shift in objectives during the course of a military campaign, often resulting in an unplanned long-term commitment.
■ such a development in a nonmilitary context, resulting in undesirable policies or consequences: *the IMF's mission creep has been consistently endorsed by the Treasury Department as a way of furthering U.S. economic foreign policy.*

MLS ▸ abbreviation **1** Multiple Listing Service, an organization that holds computerized listings of U.S. real estate offered for sale. **2** Major League Soccer.

MMR (also **M.M.R.**) ▸ abbreviation measles, mumps, and rubella (usually denoting the combination vaccine for them)

mo•chac•ci•no /ˌmōkəˈCHēnō/ ▸ noun (plural **mo•chac•ci•nos**) a cappuccino containing chocolate syrup or chocolate flavoring.
-ORIGIN 1990s: blend of *mocha* and *cappucino.*

mock•u•men•ta•ry (also **moc•u•men•ta•ry**) /ˌmäkyəˈment(ə)rē/ ▸ noun a television program or film that takes the form of a serious documentary in order to satirize its subject: *a heavy metal mocumentary that lampoons rock excess but almost doesn't go far enough.* [**Mar. 2003** *Book*]
-DERIVATIVES **mock•u•men•tar•i•an** /ˌmäkyəmenˈte(ə)rēən/ noun
-ORIGIN 1960s: blend of *mock* and *(doc)umentary.*

mo•dal•i•ty /mōˈdalitē/ ▸ noun (plural **-ties**) a particular mode in which something exists or is experienced or expressed.
■ a particular method or procedure: *they addressed questions concerning the modalities of Soviet troop withdrawals.* ■ (in medicine, particularly homeopathy) a symptom or pattern that aids in diagnosis: *the modality of "worse with activity" is associated with Rhus Tox.*
-ORIGIN early 17th cent.: from medieval Latin *modalitas*, from *modalis* (see MODAL).

moe•ri•the•ri•um /ˌmirəˈTHi(ə)rēəm/ ▸ noun a medium-sized mammal of the late Eocene and Oligocene epochs with a long snout and short legs, related to modern elephants.
•*Moeritherium trigodon.*
-ORIGIN modern Latin, from the name of Lake *Moeris* in Egypt, where the first fossils were found + Greek *thērion* 'wild beast.'

moi /mwä/ ▸ exclamation (usually **moi?**) humorous me? (used especially when accused of something that one knows one is guilty of).
-ORIGIN French, 'me.'

mo•jo /ˈmōjō; -hō/, ▸ noun a Cuban sauce or marinade containing garlic, olive oil, and sour oranges.
-ORIGIN probably from Spanish *mojo* 'wet' from *mojar* 'make wet.'

mo•lec•u•lar e•lec•tron•ics /məˈlekyələr ilekˈträniks; ˌēlek-/ ▸ plural noun [treated as singular] a branch of electronics in which individual molecules perform the same function as microelectronic devices such as diodes.
-DERIVATIVES **mo•lec•u•lar e•lec•tron•ic** adjective *molecular electronic materials and inorganic particles*

mol•et•ron•ics /ˌmäliˈträniks/ ▸ plural noun [treated as singular] short for MOLECULAR ELECTRONICS.
-DERIVATIVES **mol•et•ron•ic** adjective

mom-and-pop /ˈmäm ən ˈpäp/ ▸ adjective denoting a small store or business of a type often run by a married couple: *most of the town relies on a local mom-and-pop ISP for their email.*

mom•my track /ˈmämē ˌtrak/ ▸ noun informal a career path for women who sacrifice some promotions and pay raises in order to devote more time to raising their children: *a three-and-a-half-hour discussion—part dialectic, part shouting match—in which the mommy track, female management styles, sexual tensions between men and women*

and even the significance of skirts were explored. [**Mar.** 1992 *Working Woman*]
-DERIVATIVES **mom•my track•er** noun; **mom•my track•ing** noun

mon•ey grab /'mənē ˌgrab/ ▸ noun an undignified or unprincipled acquisition of a large sum of money with little effort: *there is no conclusive evidence to support either global warming or a rise in the sea level, many scientists have used erroneous models and sensational media coverage to predict catastrophic scenarios. These scenarios have been used to threaten South Pacific island peoples and extort research funds from politicians. It is a conspiracy for a money grab.* [**16 Oct.** 1991 *Christian Science Monitor*]

mon•key•pox /'məNGkē ˌpäks/ ▸ noun a viral disease of African origin, related to smallpox and transmitted to humans through fluid exchange by rodents and primates: *a south Milwaukee pet distributor being treated for possible monkeypox.*

mon•o•brow /'mänə ˌbrou/ ▸ noun informal a pair of eyebrows that meet above the nose, giving the appearance of a single eyebrow.
-DERIVATIVES **mon•o•browed** adjective

mon•o•chrome /'mänə ˌkrōm/ ▸ adjective lacking variety and interest; insipid: *after years of whirring round the rather monochrome American circuit, Stevens could encounter no more extreme an insight than Epsom into the infinite variety of British tracks.* [**28 May** 1999 *Time*]
-ORIGIN mid 17th cent.: based on Greek *monokhrōmatos* 'of a single color.'

mon•o•pulse /'mänə ˌpəls/ ▸ adjective denoting a system of radar in which the angular location of a target is determined by comparison of two or more simultaneously received signals.
▸noun a monopulse radar system or installation.
-ORIGIN late 1950s: from *mono*, 'one' + *pulse*

mon•ster truck /'mänstər ˌtrək/ ▸ noun a pickup truck on an elevated chassis with oversized tires, especially one that competes in various motor sports.

mon•tu•no /män'tōōnō/ ▸ noun (plural **mon•tu•nos**) an improvised passage in a rumba: *the Afro-Cuban side than the jazz side, with rhythm-section montunos, articulated clave rhythms and an intermittently ferocious density.* [**30 Aug.** 2001 *New York Times*]

mon•ty /'mäntē/ ▸ noun (in phrase **the full monty**) British informal the full amount expected, desired, or possible: *they'll do the full monty for a few thousand each.*
–ORIGIN perhaps from *the full Montague Burton*, 'Sunday-best three-piece suit' (from the name of a tailor.)

moon•suit /'mōon,sōot/ (also **moon suit** /'mōon,sōot/) ▸ noun informal a protective coverall garment suitable for space travel.
■ a garment resembling this: *an emergency response team dressed in moonsuits.*

mo•tor vo•ter law /'mōtər ˌvōtər ˌlô/ ▸ noun another name for the National Voter Registration Act of 1993, designed to reverse declining voter registration by allowing voters to register at motor vehicle departments when they renew their driver's licenses.

moul•vi /'mōolvē/ (also **maul•vi, mol•vi**) ▸ noun (plural **moul•vis**) (especially in India) a Muslim doctor of the law: *the Hurriyat, led by its chairman Moulvi Abbas Ansari, has favoured talks with New Delhi.* [**15 Sept. 2003** *Reuters AlertNet*]
–ORIGIN from Urdu *maulvī*, from Arabic *mawlawī* 'judicial' (adjective used as a noun), from *mawlā* 'mullah.'

mouse /mous/ ▸ noun (plural **mice** /mīs/) a dull light brown color reminiscent of a mouse's fur; mousy: *her blonde hair dulled to mouse.*

mouse•trap /'mous,trap/ ▸ verb [trans.] Computing (often as **mouse•trap•ping**) to block (a user's) efforts to exit from a Web site, usually one to which he or she has been redirected: *mousetrapping is a tactic commonly used by pornographic Web sites.*

mouth•feel /'mouTH,fēl/ ▸ noun the physical sensations in the mouth produced by a particular food: *this Cabernet has a dense, tightly woven mouthfeel, with complex, chewy and velvety tannins.*

MPEG /'em,peg/ ▸ noun an international standard for encoding and compressing video images.
–ORIGIN 1990s: from *Motion Pictures Experts Group.*

MP3 ▸ noun a standard for compressing audio files, used especially as a way of downloading music from the Internet.
–ORIGIN 1990s: from **MPEG** + *Audio Layer-3.*

Mud•ville /'məd,vil/ ▸ noun the world of baseball: *but, as nemeses go, the Astros aren't exactly the Yankees and the unbridled joy here in Mudville South was short-lived.* [**25 Sept. 2003** *Houston Chronicle*]

-ORIGIN from the fictional locality in the 1888 poem *Casey at the Bat.*

mug•gle /'məgəl/ (also **Mug•gle**) ▸ **noun** informal an unimaginative or boring person: *this video game won't appeal to muggles.*
-ORIGIN used in the sense 'nonwizard' in J.K. Rowling's *Harry Potter* books, but of uncertain origin.

mul•let /'məlit/ ▸ **noun** a hairstyle in which the hair is cut short at the front and sides and left long in back: *the mullet's place in pop culture right now exists on two levels—at this elite, hipster top tier, and at the bottom of the barrel.* [**7 Oct. 2003** *Arizona Republic*]
-ORIGIN 1990s: of unknown origin.

mul•ti•cast /'məlti,kast; ,məlti'kast/ ▸ **verb** (past and past part. **mul•ti•cast**) [trans.] send data or transmit a signal to multiple selected recipients simultaneously: *during the day we'll multicast and during prime time, from probably 7-11 pm, we'll do our high-definition feed* [**28 Sept. 2003** *Southern Illinoisan*]
▸ **noun** a set of data or an audio/video signal that is multicasted.

mul•ti•cul•ti /,məltē'kəltē; ,məltī-/ informal ▸ **adjective** multicultural: *The author's multi-culti persona comes through—or sloppy editing: These girls live in London, where cookies are called biscuits, and chocolate chips are a nouveau American import.* [**16 Sept. 2003** *New York Daily News*]
▸ **noun 1** popular music incorporating ethnically disparate elements.
2 one who is literate or comfortable in more than one culture.
-ORIGIN 1990s: rhyming alteration of *multicultural.*

mul•ti•fe•tal /,məltē'fētl; ,məltī-/ ▸ **adjective** involving two or more fetuses: *coverage includes a detailed discussion of prenatal genetic diagnosis in multiple gestations and a review of the risks and benefits of multifetal pregnancy reduction and selective termination.* [**2003** website of Lippincott, Williams & Wilkins (publishers)]

mul•ti•pur•pose de•vice /,məltē'pərpəs di,vīs; ,məltī-/ (abbreviation: **MPD**) ▸ **noun** a device, especially an electronic device, that combines two or more functions or whose functionality can be altered: *a good choice for small offices is a multipurpose device for printing, faxing, scanning, and copying.*

mul•ti•slack•ing /,məltē'slakiNG; ,məltī-/ ▸ **noun** informal the practice of using a computer at work for tasks or activities that are not related to one's job: *most employers tolerate a certain amount of multislacking.* See also **CYBERSLACKER.**

-DERIVATIVES **mul•ti•slack•er** noun
-ORIGIN *multi-* + *slacking* 'working slowly or lazily,' on the pattern of *multitasking,* the simultaneous execution of multiple computer tasks by a single processor.

mul•ti-u•til•i•ty /ˌməltē yo͞o'tilitē; ˌməltī-/ ▸ noun a utility that has extended or combined its business to offer its customers additional services (especially those of another utility): *the July 2002 purchase of British power supplier Innogy by the Germany multi-utility RWE.* [**29 Sept.** 2003 *UK CommentWire*]

mul•ti•verse /'məlti,vərs/ ▸ noun the universe considered as lacking order or a single ruling and guiding power, instead comprising multiple entities with disparate governing laws: *this looks suspiciously flukey, but it can be readily explained by the multiverse. Most of the cosmic patches in the quilt will be sterile, their physics all wrong for making life. Only here and there, in rare patches where all the numbers come out right, will life arise and observers like us evolve to marvel at it all.* [**23 Sept.** 2003 *Guardian (UK)*]

Mum•bai /'məm,bī/ ▸ noun the official name, since 1997, for Bombay, India.

Mum•bai•kar /ˌməmbī'kär/ ▸ noun a native or resident of Mumbai: *even now, many Mumbaikars wonder how their city could have succumbed to a sectarian nationalism that is anathema to its traditional mercantile sophistication.* [**22 Apr. 1999** *New York Review of Books*]

mup•pet /'məpit/ ▸ noun British informal an incompetent or foolish person.
-ORIGIN 1990s: from *Muppet,* the generic name given to various puppets and marionettes created by Jim Henson (1936–90) for the children's television programs *Sesame Street* and *The Muppet Show.*

mus•cle dys•mor•phi•a /'məsəl dis,môrfēə/ ▸ noun a psychological disorder marked by a negative body image and an obsessive desire to have a muscular physique: *a large proportion of people with muscle dysmorphia are weightlifters or bodybuilders.*
-ORIGIN *muscle* + *dysmorphia* 'abnormality in the shape or size of a body part.'

must-have /'məst 'hav/ ▸ adjective essential or highly desirable: *the must-have blouse of the season.*
▸noun an essential or highly desirable item: *this season's must-have is an ostrich bowling bag.*

must-read /'məst 'rēd/ ▸ **noun** informal a piece of writing that should or must be read: *it's a must-read for anyone interested in the geologic history recorded in the landscape.*

must-see /'məst 'sē/ ▸ **noun** informal something that should or must be seen, especially a remarkable sight or entertainment: *this sassy and superior suspense thriller is a must-see.*

mys•ter•y shop•per /'mist(ə)rē ˌSHäpər/ ▸ **noun** a SECRET SHOPPER.

myth•i•fy /'miTHəˌfī/ ▸ **verb** mythicize: *as success mythified their reputation, the stormtroopers grew in distinctiveness.*
  –DERIVATIVES **myth•i•fi•ca•tion** /ˌmiTHəfi'kāSHən/ **noun**

Nn

nad ▸ **abbreviation** **1** nothing abnormal detected.
2 no appreciable response.

nads /nadz/ ▸ **plural noun** vulgar slang testicles: *on one particular rimshot, the butt of the stick did an upstroke right into my nads.* [24 **June 1998** Usenet: rec.music.makers.percussion]
-ORIGIN 1960s: shortening of *gonads.*

nag•ware /ˈnag͜weɪ(ə)r/ ▸ **noun** informal Computing computer software that is free for a trial period during which frequent reminders appear on screen asking the user to register and pay for the program in order to continue using it when the trial period is over: *my recent Weblog item about QuickBooks nagware elicited a number of comments from readers pointing out yet other shenanigans they've seen.* [30 **Sept. 2003** *Inforworld*]

nail wrap /ˈnāl ˈrap/ ▸ **noun** a beauty treatment in which a nail strengthener, usually containing fibers, is either brushed on or applied with adhesive.

nak•fa /ˈnäkfə/ ▸ **noun** (plural same or **nak•fas**) the basic monetary unit of Eritrea, equal to one hundred cents.
-ORIGIN 1990s: from *Nakfa,* the name of the town where the country's armed struggle against the Ethiopian regime was launched.

Na•men•da /nəˈmendə/ ▸ **trademark** a proprietary formulation of the Alzheimer's drug memantine.

na•na /ˈnanə; ˈnä-/ ▸ **noun** British a child's word for a grandmother.

nan•dro•lone /ˈnandrə͜lōn/ ▸ **noun** an anabolic steroid with tissue-building properties, used unlawfully to enhance performance in sports.
-ORIGIN 1950s: shortened form of its chemical name *norandrostenolone.*

nan•ny cam /ˈnanē ͜kam/ ▸ **noun** a webcam or CCTV camera in a private home for parents to monitor their childcarer: *so from a kitchen display, for example, you could monitor the baby's room—or* *you could create your own nannycam on your desktop computer at work.* [**Mar.** 2001 *Popular Science*]

nan•o- ▸ combining form submicroscopic; measurable only in nanometers (billionths of a meter): *nanotube.*

nan•o•bac•te•ri•um /ˌnanōbak'ti(ə)rēəm; ˌnā-/ ▸ noun (plural **nan•o• bac•te•ri•a**) a microorganism about a tenth the size of the smallest normal bacteria, claimed to have been discovered in living tissue and in rock: *nanobacteria are not alive, but instead are the result of enzymes that break down organic material, according to a new study published in the journal Geology.* [**17 Sept.** 2003 *Astrobiology Magazine*]

nan•obe /'nanōb; 'nā-/ ▸ noun another term for NANOBACTERIUM.

nan•o•ro•bot /'nanə,rōbät; 'nā-; -bət/ ▸ noun a machine made from individual atoms or molecules that is designed to perform a small and specific job: *adding a built-in ability to replicate would add unnecessary cost and complexity—unless one was trying to create a dangerous nanorobot as a weapon.* [**12 Sept.** 2000 *New York Times*]

nan•o•scale /'nanə,skāl, 'nā-/ ▸ adjective of a size measurable in nanometers or microns: *because the structures of the protein shells of many viruses are well understood even at atomic scales they can be particularly useful as nanoscale building tools.* [**5 July** 2003 *Science News*]

nan•o•struc•ture /'nanə,strəkCHər; 'nā-/ ▸ noun a nanoscale object: *the combination of the tightly bound micelle nanostructures and the microscale globules is what gives the silk its strength.* [**13 Sept.** 2003 *Science News*]

nan•o•wire /'nanə,wī(ə)r; 'nā-/ ▸ noun a nanoscale rod made of semiconducting material, used in miniature transistors and some laser applications: *this nanowire-based sensing scheme could have significant implications in chemical and biological warfare detection, national and global security, as well as medical detection applications.* [**15 Sept.** 2003 *Science Daily*]

NAS•CAR Dad (also **Nascar Dad**) /'nas,kär ,dad/ ▸ noun a representative of a demographic category: a blue-collar, highschool-educated father with relatively conservative values but without predictable political affiliation: *his administration's disregard for the severe understaffing of America's nursing homes means worse care for the elderly parents of the Nascar Dad.* [**8 Oct.** 2003 *Mother Jones*]

-ORIGIN early 21st cent.: from the popularity of stock car racing with white, working-class men.

Nas•sau /'nasô/ ▸ noun Golf an eighteen-hole match in which the players bet on the first nine holes, the second nine holes, and the entire round.

nas•ty•gram /'nastē₍gram/ ▸ noun Computing an offensive or threatening electronic communication: *late last year the company began sending out some nastygrams to subscribers they identified as being wireless broadband connection sharers.* [**16 Sept.** 2003 *DSLReports*]

nav•i•gate /'navi₍gāt/ ▸ verb Computing move around a Web site, file, the Internet, etc.: *we've added features that make our site much easier to navigate.*

need-blind /'nēd ₍blīnd/ ▸ adjective of or denoting a university admissions policy in which applicants are judged solely on their merits, irrespective of their ability to pay for tuition: *Yale's need-blind admissions and need-based financial aid ensures that these students have an equal academic footing at Yale.* [**9 Sept.** 2003 *Yale Daily News*]

net me•ter•ing /'net ₍mētəriNG/ ▸ noun a system in which solar panels or other renewable energy generators are connected to a public-utility power grid and surplus power is transferred onto the grid, allowing customers to offset the cost of power drawn from the utility: *when the wind turbine generates more power than we need, the net metering program gives us kilowatt credits for future use.*
-ORIGIN surplus energy, measured by an electric meter, is netted from the amount passing from the utility to the customer.

net•work ap•pli•ance /'net₍wərk ə₍plīəns/ ▸ noun a relatively low-cost computer designed chiefly to provide Internet access and without the full capabilities of a standard personal computer.

neu•ral com•pu•ter /'n(y)o͞orəl kəm'pyo͞otər/ ▸ noun a computer that uses neural networks based on the human brain: *the Ricoh machine might be the first complete neural computer, as opposed to a more general-purpose computer containing neural network chips or software.* [**20 June** 1992 *Baltimore Sun*]
-DERIVATIVES **neu•ral com•put•ing** noun

neu•ro•com•pu•ter /'n(y)o͞orōkəm₍pyo͞otər/ ▸ noun another term for NEURAL COMPUTER.

neu•tro•pe•ni•a /ˌn(y)ōōtrə'pēnēə/ ▸ **noun** Medicine the presence of abnormally few neutrophils in the blood, leading to increased susceptibility to infection. It is an undesirable side-effect of some cancer treatments.
-DERIVATIVES **neu•tro•pe•nic** /ˌn(y)ōōtrə'pēnik; -'penik/ **adjective**
-ORIGIN 1930s: from *neutral* + Greek *penia* 'poverty, lack.'

new•a•ter /'n(y)ōōˌwôtər; -ˌwä-/ ▸ **noun** purified domestic wastewater that is recycled for reuse: *government spin doctors who successfully sold Newater to the public and quelled fears during the Sars crisis have to tackle another national challenge now.* [22 **Aug.** 2003 *Straits Times (Singapore)*]

new e•con•o•my /'n(y)ōō i'känəmē/ ▸ **noun** new industries, such as biotechnology or the Internet, that are characterized by cutting-edge technology and high growth.

news•serv•er /n(y)ōōzˌsərvər/ (also **new•serv•er** /'n(y)ōōˌsərvər/) ▸ **noun** an Internet-connected server that receives and disseminates messages for a newsgroup.

news•feed /'n(y)ōōzˌfēd/ ▸ **noun** an electronic transmission of news, as from a broadcaster or an Internet newsgroup: *full Internet capabilities are available, such as Usenet newsfeeds for more than 7,000 newsgroups.* [**July** 1994 *Internet World*]

news•group /'n(y)ōōzˌgrōōp/ ▸ **noun** an Internet-based forum devoted to discussing a particular topic: *then I discovered 0.verizon.adsl newsgroup and there are about a dozen of serious users complaining about the problem all over Hampton Roads.* [28 **Sept.** 2003 *DSLReports*]
■ the subscribers to such a group.

news peg /'n(y)ōōz ˌpeg/ ▸ **noun** an aspect or angle of a story that makes it newsworthy: *Talese further expanded traditional journalistic practice by delaying a story's news peg until as late in a story as he could manage.* [1998 GayTalese.com]

New York min•ute /'n(y)ōō ˌyôrk 'minət/ ▸ **noun** informal a very short time; a moment: *you mention that price and she'll be out of here in a New York minute.*

NEX•RAD /'neksˌrad/ ▸ **noun** a system of Doppler radars across the U.S. that is used to track the location and movement of storm systems.
-ORIGIN 1990s: acronym from *NEXt generation weather RADar*

ni•gi•ri zu•shi /ˈnigərē ˈzo͞oSHē/ ▸**noun** sushi consisting of a small ball of rice, smeared with wasabi sauce and topped with raw fish or other seafood.
-ORIGIN 1990s: Japanese, from *nigiri-* (combining form of *nigiru* 'clasp, clench, roll in the hands') + *-zushi sushi.*

Ni•hang /niˈhäNG/ ▸**noun** (in India) a member of a militaristic sect of Sikhs.
-ORIGIN late 19th cent.: Persian *nihang,* literally 'crocodile.'

Ni•ña, La /lä ˈnēnyə/ ▸see **LA NIÑA.**

9/11 /ˈnīn iˈlevən/ (also **Sep•tem•ber 11th** /sepˈtembər iˈlevənTH/) September 11, 2001. On this date two hijacked commercial airliners were flown into the World Trade Center in lower Manhattan. Another airliner was crashed into the Pentagon, and one went down in a field in Pennsylvania: *his words after 9/11 were just what the nation and the world needed to hear.* [**6 May** 2002 *Time*] | [as modifier] *in Virginia Mark Warner posed with fire fighters but won on pre-9/11 issues.* [**19 Nov.** 2001 *Time*]

no•ce•bo /nəˈsēbō/ ▸**noun** a negative belief concerning a medical treatment or procedure that produces a detrimental effect on a person's health for purely psychological or psychosomatic reasons.
■ negative thinking generally as a detriment to good health and well-being: [as modifier] *a century before scientists researched the nocebo effect—the phenomenon of negative, fearful thoughts causing harm—Mary Baker Eddy investigated mental evil.* [**7 Sept.** 2003 *Christian Science Monitor*]
-ORIGIN 1960s: from Latin, literally 'I shall cause harm,' from *nocere* 'to harm,' on the pattern of *placebo.*

no-fly /ˈnō ˈflī/ ▸**adjective** designating a list, person, or category of persons prevented from flying for security reasons: *they criticize the no-fly list as being, at worst, a Big Brother campaign to muzzle dissent and, at best, a bureaucratic exercise that distracts airport security from looking for real bad guys.* [**27 Sept.** 2002 *San Francisco Chronicle*]

no-kill (also **no kill**) /ˈnō ˌkil/ ▸**noun** a policy or an animal shelter in which abandoned, neglected, or lost animals are not put to sleep even if no home can be found for them: *there are thousands of no-kills that rescue pets.*
▸**adjective** opposed to or not killing animals that live in shelters: *find out if the organization has a no-kill policy.*

no-mark /'nō ˌmärk/ ▸ **noun** British informal an unimportant, unsuccessful, or worthless person: *if that slippery no-mark comes up trumps, I'll kiss his fat head and that's the God's honest truth.* [**2001** K. Sampson, *Outlaws*]
-ORIGIN 1980s: perhaps from the idea of performing badly in school.

non•core /'nonˌkôr/ ▸ **adjective** not considered to be essential; expendable: *substantial expenditure cuts in noncore service areas.* [**7 Oct.** 2003 *Forbes*]

non•cus•to•di•al /ˌnänkəs'tōdēəl/ ▸ **adjective** Law **1** not having custody of one's children after a divorce: *the relationship between the children and their noncustodial father was virtually destroyed.*
2 not involving incarceration: *all offenders in the sample received a noncustodial sentence, and most of them received fines or probation.*

non•dig•i•tal /nän'dijitl/ ▸ **adjective 1** not represented by numbers, especially binary codes; not digitized: *nondigital items have only their location information (catalog records) in the digital library, as it happens in a traditional automated library situation.*
2 not using the Internet or computers: *nondigital submissions will be accepted only until February 1st.*

no•ni /'nōnē/ ▸ **noun** any of various evergreen trees or shrubs of the madder family (Genus *Morinda*) native to the South Pacific. Various preparations, mainly for the treatment of pain, are made from their leaves, root, and fruit.

non•ju•di•cial /ˌnänjoō'disHəl/ ▸ **adjective 1** not resulting from a court ruling or judgment: *nonjudicial punishment.*
2 not involving courts or judges: *nonjudicial appointments.*

non-net /'nän 'net/ ▸ **adjective** (of an amount) including tax and other sums in addition to the net amount.

non•struck /nän'strək/ ▸ **adjective 1** not having been the subject of a labor strike: *subsequent action by the nonstruck Association members, including the employer, to bar their employees from work was a direct reaction to the selective strike.* [**10 Oct.** 2003 *Unemployment Compensation Decision (WI)*]
2 not having been stricken: *occupants of the nonstruck side of the vehicle.*
3 not having been eliminated: *nonstruck jurors.*

noo•dle /'nōodl/ ▸ **verb** [intrans.] informal improvise or play casually on a musical instrument: *tapes of him noodling on his farfisa organ* | [as noun] (**noodling**) *ambient synthesizer noodling.*
-ORIGIN mid 19th cent.: of unknown origin.

no•pal /'nōpəl; nō'päl/ ▸ **noun** the Mexican-Spanish name for prickly pear; increasingly popular in the names of herbal preparations.
-ORIGIN Spanish, from Nahuatl *nopalli.*

No•ro•vi•rus /'nôrə‚vīrəs/ ▸ **noun** the Norwalk virus or one related to it: *just last week, more than 340 people were hit by norovirus on the Regal Princess—which is scheduled to stop in Norfolk on Nov.* [**6 Sept.** 2003 *Virginia Pilot*]

north•ern snake•head /'nôrTHərn 'snāk‚hed/ ▸ **noun** an Asian food fish of the carp family that is also a voracious predator. It is able to survive adverse conditions and has been inadvertently released into the wild in the U.S.
•*Channa Argus*, family Channidae.

Nor•walk vi•rus /'nôr‚wôk ‚vīrəs/ ▸ **noun** a virus that can cause epidemics of severe gastroenteritis.
-ORIGIN 1970s: from *Norwalk*, a town in Ohio where an outbreak of gastroenteritis occurred from which the virus was isolated.

nos•tal•gic /nä'staljik; nə-/ ▸ **noun** a nostalgic person: *it's basically a huge database where users identify themselves by name and school graduation date. To see classmates' E-mail addresses, nostalgics pay $36 a year.* [**22 April 2002** *U.S. News and World Report*]

no-till•age /'nō 'tilij/ (also **no-till** /'nō 'til/) ▸ **adjective** designating a method of planting in which soil is not tilled but instead is planted by insertion of seeds in small slits, weeds being controlled by other means: *a no-tillage tomato production system using hairy vetch and subterranean clover mulches.*

nought•ies /'nôtēz/ ▸ **plural noun** mainly British the decade from 2000 to 2009: [as modifier] *Magnum the movie has been given the go ahead and its eighties hero will be duly updated for a noughties incarnation.* [**26 Sept. 2003** *Empire Online*]
-ORIGIN 1990s: from *nought* 'zero,' on the pattern of *twenties, thirties,* etc.

no•vel•a /nō'velə/ ▸ **noun** another term for TELENOVELA.

no•wheres•ville /'nō(h)werz,vil/ ▸ noun informal a place or situation of no significance, promise, or interest: *an unhappy girl stuck in rural Nowheresville, KS.*

no wor•ries /'nō 'wərēz; 'wə-rēz/ ▸ phrase informal, chiefly Australian all right; fine.

NSAID /'en,sed/ ▸ abbreviation a non-steroidal anti-inflammatory drug, of which aspirin is the archetype.

NU ▸ abbreviation Nunavut (in official postal use).

nu- /n(y)o͞o/ ▸ combining form informal respelling of 'new,' used especially in names of new or revived genres of popular music: *nu-metal bands | nu-disco.*

nu•cle•ar thresh•old /'n(y)o͞oklēər 'THreSH(h)ōld/ ▸ noun a point in a conflict at which nuclear weapons are or would be brought into use.

num•ber one /'nəmbər 'wən/ ▸ noun informal (in the phrase **number one, number two, etc.**) the shortest, or next shortest, etc., men's haircut produced with electric hair clippers.

nump•ty /'nəm(p)tē/ ▸ noun (plural **nump•ties**) British informal a stupid or ineffectual person: *if we were playing Turkey with this numpty in the middle of the park we might not only be one down at half time.* [8 **Sept. 2003** *Football365.com*]
–ORIGIN 1990s: from obsolete *numps* 'a stupid person,' of unknown origin.

Nu•na•vut /'no͞onəvo͞ot/ ▸ noun a province of northern Canada, created in 1999 as an Inuit territory from a part of Northwest Territories.
–ORIGIN Inuktitut, 'our land'.

nu•tra•ceu•ti•cal /,n(y)o͞otrə'so͞otikəl/ ▸ noun foods or food-derived compounds and additives that have been demonstrated to offer health benefits: *the notion of food as elixir, hand-me-down from antiquity, has reemerged bearing a new set of names; among them are nutraceuticals, designer foods and functional foods.* [**Sept. 1994** *Scientific American*]

nu•tri•ge•no•mics /,n(y)o͞otrijē'nōmiks; -'näm-/ ▸ plural noun [treated as singular] the scientific study of the interaction of nutrition and

genes, especially the role of diet in causing disease: *nutrigenomics holds great promise in fighting obesity and cancer.*
-ORIGIN blend of *nutrition* and *genomics* 'analysis of an organism's complete set of genes.'

nvCJD ▸ **abbreviation** new variant Creutzfeldt–Jakob disease; see **vCJD**.

Oo

obsd. ▸ **abbreviation** observed: *Moreover, a relatively small difference was obsd. among the quinolones for the in vitro brain slice.* [1998 *NIH Abstracts*]

ob•ses•sive-com•pul•sive dis•or•der /əb'sesiv kəm'pəlsiv dis‚ôr-dər; äb-/ ▸ **noun** (abbreviation: **OCD**) a psychiatric disorder characterized by an inability to ward off disturbing thoughts and a compulsion to repeat ritualized behavior.

ob•ten•tion /əb'tensHən; äb-/ ▸ **noun** the action of obtaining something: *protests against the system by the pupils concerned serves no purpose and will only make their obtention of a diploma almost impossible.* [July 1998 *Strad*]
-ORIGIN early 17th cent.: French, or from late Latin *obtentio(n-)*, from *obtinere* 'obtain, gain.'

OCD ▸ **abbreviation** OBSESSIVE-COMPULSIVE DISORDER

och•loc•ra•cy /äk'läkrəsē/ ▸ **noun** government by a mob; mob rule. *the removal of the veil of secular government (for Mr. Bazargan has frequently admitted it to be little more) reveals the ochlocracy, mob-rule, beneath.* [17 Nov. 1979 *Globe & Mail*]
-DERIVATIVES **och•lo•crat** /'äklə‚krat/ noun; **och•lo•crat•ic** /‚äklə'kratik/ **adjective**
-ORIGIN late 16th cent.: via French from Greek *okhlokratia*, from *okhlos* 'mob' + *-kratia* 'power.'

of•fice park /'ôfis ‚pärk; 'äfis/ ▸ **noun** an area where a number of office buildings are built together on landscaped grounds: *he is disappointed with preliminary plans that call for an "American-style office park," based on the premise that most people will drive to work.* [5 Mar. 1994 *New Scientist*]

of•fice-park dad /'ôfis ‚pärk ‚dad; 'äf-/ (abbrev: **OPD**) ▸ **noun** a white middle-class father, aged 25 to 50, employed in a suburban white-collar job: *he reached the legal drinking age a long time ago, but is still far from the senior's discount. He commutes from the suburbs, works in a cubicle, likes his military strong and his stem-cell research legal. He is the Office Park Dad—the latest in demographic research, and the* *apparent successor to the Soccer Mom and the New Economy Voter.* [27 **May** 2002 *San Diego Union-Tribune*]

off-la•bel /'ôf 'lābəl; 'äf/ ▶ **adjective** (of a drug) prescribed in a way or for a condition not covered by the original FDA approval: [as adverb] *this drug is used off-label to help with seizures.* | [as adverb] *children with severe anxiety disorders are given antidepressants "off label"—in ways for which they were not specifically approved.* [7 **May** 2001 *Time*]

oh•no•sec•ond /'ō'nō,sekənd/ ▶ **noun** Computing, informal a moment in which one realizes that one has made an error, typically by pressing the wrong key: *you may have heard of the "ohnosecond" when you realise that the shit is about to hit the fan.* [**1999** *Watt's On*]

OIC ▶ **abbreviation** Organization of the Islamic Conference; a permanent delegation to the United Nations representing the interests of Muslims in several dozen countries.

oil /oil/ ▶ **noun** Australian/NZ informal information or facts: *the angel said "Stop looking like a bunch of stunned mullets. Let me give you the drum, the good oil, it's top news for the whole crew . . . today in that little town on the hill a rescuer has been born."* [**22 Aug.** 2003 *Hobart Mercury]*

old-growth /'ōld 'grōTH/ ▶ **adjective** (of a tree, forest, etc.) never felled; mature: *the desire to preserve primeval vegetation in the wake of European settlement led to the preservation of many excellent examples of* old growth *vegetation.* [**July–Aug.** 1983 *Explore*]

old-time /'ōld ,tīm/ ▶ **adjective** denoting ballroom dances in which a sequence of dance steps is repeated throughout, as opposed to modern dancing in which steps may be varied.

o•le•o•chem•i•cal /,ōlēō'kemikəl/, ▶ **noun** a chemical compound derived industrially from animal or vegetable oils or fats.

one-on-one /'wən än ,wən; ôn/ (also chiefly British **one-to-one** /'wən tə 'wən/) ▶ **noun** informal a face-to-face encounter: *Bush has adopted the McCain town-meeting format—Bush calls them "one on ones"—where he spends less time on his stump speech and more time answering questions.* [**21 Feb.** 2000 *U.S. News and World Report*]

one-trick po•ny /'wən ,trik 'pōnē/ ▶ **noun** a person or thing with only one special feature, talent, or area of expertise: *the Gear Daddies* *may musically be something of a one trick pony, but as the saying goes, it's a helluva good trick.* [**April-May 1991** *Creem*]

OPD ▸ abbreviation office-park dad.

o•pen class•room /'ōpən 'klas‚rōom; -‚rŏŏm/ ▸ noun an approach to elementary education that emphasizes spacious classrooms where learning is informally structured, flexible, and individualized.
■ a spacious instructional area shared by several groups of elementary students that facilitates such an approach and the movement of students from one activity to another: [as modifier] *under the open classroom plan, children and teachers were placed in a large, open space. Children with similar skills were grouped together for instruction.* [**13 July1983** *Oklahoma City Times*]

o•pen en•roll•ment /'ōpən en'rōlmənt/ ▸ noun a period during which a health insurance company or HMO is statutorily required to accept applicants without regard to health history.
■ such a period when employees can change insurance plans offered by their employer, without proof of insurability: *because the impasse came at the peak of open enrollment, which is the annual corporate ritual that allows workers to change benefit plans for the next year, some customers decided not to wait for the contract to be resolved.* [**16 Nov. 2002** *Chicago Tribune*]

op•er•a win•dow /'äp(ə)rə ‚windō/ ▸ noun a small fixed window usually behind the rear side window of an automobile: *picture yourself in a slick black convertible roadster with a metallic silver removable top and what NM calls "opera windows," or what anybody who rode around in the '50ish T-Birds called "porthole windows."* [**19 Nov. 2000** *Times-Picayune*]

op•ti•cal turn•stile /'äptikəl 'tərn‚stīl/ ▸ noun an access control system without barriers in which those attempting to enter are evaluated by CCTV or other visual means: *the final solution included optical turnstiles with glass barriers, electronic access control, digital CCTV, a visitor management system, and a package management system.* [**March 2003** *Security Distributing & Marketing*]

op•ti•cal tweez•ers /'äptikəl 'twēzərz/ ▸ plural noun a device that uses light from a low-wattage laser to manipulate individual molecules within cells. Also called (**laser tweezers**).

op•tion•aire /‚äpsHə'ne(ə)r; 'äpsHə‚ner/ ▸ noun a person whose great wealth is based on owning or exercising employee stock options:

millionaires on paper, a k a optionaires: high tech employees with stock options that total more than a million dollars, but with fewer liquid assets. [**July 2000** *Wired*]
-ORIGIN late 1990s: on the pattern of *millionaire*.

op•tion•ee /ˌäpSHə'nē/ ▸ **noun** a recipient or holder of stock options: *the optionee does not receive credit for dividends paid but does benefit if funds are used to buy back shares creating capital gains.* [**9 Jan. 2003** *Wall Street Journal*]

or•tho•ker•a•tol•o•gy /ˌôrTHōˌkerə'täləjē/ ▸ **noun** the temporary reshaping of the cornea (usually overnight) with specially-made rigid contact lenses, in order to correct myopia.

or•tho•mo•lec•u•lar /ˌôrTHōmə'lekyələr/ ▸ **adjective** pertaining to a theory that illness can be treated and health maximized by creating the optimal molecular environment for the cells of the body through the introduction of natural substances: *he ranks the impact of orthomolecular medicine, or "optimum nutrition," as one of the most significant medical coups in the past 200 years.* [**31 Mar. 2003** *Guardian (UK)*]
-ORIGIN 1968: coined by U.S. chemist Linus Pauling (1901–94).

or•tho•pox•vi•rus /'ôrTHōˌpäksˌvīrəs/ ▸ **noun** any of a set of viruses pathological in humans and animals that includes the cowpox, smallpox, and monkeypox viruses: *the Marshfield Clinic's lab looked at tissue samples from sick prairie dogs and sick people with an electron microscope and saw signs of an orthopoxvirus.* [**9 June 2003** *Milwaukee Journal Sentinel*]

or•tho•rex•i•a /ˌôrTHə'reksēə/ ▸ **noun** an obsession with eating foods that one considers healthy.
■ (also **or•tho•rex•i•a ner•vo•sa** /ôrTHə'reksēä nər'vōsə/) a medical condition in which the sufferer systematically avoids specific foods in the belief that they are harmful: *although orthorexia is not yet considered an official eating disorder like anorexia, it is a growing problem.* [**June 2002** *Ladies Home Journal*]
-DERIVATIVES **or•tho•rex•ic** adjective & noun
-ORIGIN 1990s: from *ortho-* + Greek *orexia* 'appetite,' after *anorexia*.

OST ▸ **abbreviation** original soundtrack: *Adam Sandler* Big Daddy *OST out now on Columbia Records.* [**26 Sept. 1999** *News of World*]

os•te•o•sper•mum /ˌästēō'spərməm/ ▸ **noun** a plant or shrub of the daisy family, native to Africa and the Middle East, some varieties of which are cultivated for their yellow or violet flowers.

•Genus *Osteospermum*, family *Compositae*.
-ORIGIN mid 19th cent.: modern Latin, from Greek *osteo-* 'bone' + Greek *sperma* 'seed.'

out•draw /ˌout'drô/ ▶ verb (past **out•drew** /ˌout'drōō/; past participle **out•drawn** /ˌout'drôn/) [trans.] (of a person or event) attract a larger crowd than (another person or event): *the stores in Paris outdraw both the Louvre and the Eiffel Tower.* [**Dec. 1998** *Icon*]

out•drink /ˌout'driNGk/ ▶ verb (past **out•drank** /ˌout'draNGk/; past participle **out•drunk** /ˌout'drəNGk/) [trans.] drink more than (another person): *to use his own words, he "could outrun, outwork, and outdrink any other human critter atop of dirt."* [**Jan. 1858** *Harper's*]

out•gross /ˌout'grōs/ ▶ verb [trans.] surpass in gross income or profit: *this is the first time since the mid-60s that Hollywood imports have outgrossed local hits.* [**Oct. 1994** *Sight & Sound (UK)*]

out•hit /ˌout'hit/ ▶ verb (past and past participle **out•hit; out•hit•ting**) [trans.] surpass (someone) in hitting; hit a higher score than: *we outscored them for the Series, 55–27, and outhit them, 91–60.* [**1991** Mickey Mantle, *My Favorite Summer: 1956*]

out•look /ˌout'lŏŏk; 'out͵lŏŏk/ ▶ verb predict on the basis of current information: [trans.] *streamflow for the upcoming runoff season is presently outlooked to be much below average for most of the upper Rio Grande basin.* [**1 Jan. 2003** NOAA Web site]
■ predict that certain conditions will prevail in (a region): *the Storm Prediction Center outlooked the northeast quarter of Iowa for a moderate risk of severe storms, while the rest of Iowa was outlooked with a slight risk.* [**30 May 1998** Stormproductions.com]

out•par•cel /'out͵pärsəl/ ▶ noun a building lot separated or separable from a commercial development, the selling of which provides liquidity for the developer: *the undeveloped outparcel is zoned B-1 and is available for sale or lease by DRE's Newport News, Virginia, office.* [**2003** Divaris Real Estate Web site]

out•punch /ˌout'pənCH/ ▶ verb [trans.] surpass (an opponent) in punching ability: *Matlala, much to the disappointment of the fans, was both outpunched and outboxed by Culshaw for most of their 12 rounds.* [**31 May 2000** *S. Afr. Times (UK)*]

out•sprint /ˌout'sprint/ ▶ verb [trans.] sprint faster than (someone): *I'll not be trying to outsprint an antelope.* [**5 Dec. 2002** *New York Review of Books*] o•ver•breed /ˌōvər'brēd/ ▸ verb (past and past participle o•ver•bred /ˌōvər 'bred/) breed or cause to breed to excess: *the husband and wife were not only breaking town codes but forcing the female dogs to overbreed and litters to grow up with several health problems.* [17 **May** 1999 *Newsday*]

o•ver•con•nect•ed•ness /ˌōvərkə'nektidnis/ ▸ noun a social malaise characterized by an obsessive need to keep in constant touch with people or events by means of cell phones, the Internet, and other communications technology: *overconnectedness is the disease of the Internet age.* [12 **Aug.** 1999 *San Franciso Chronicle*]

o•ver•dry /ˌōvər'drī/ ▸ verb (o•ver•dries, o•ver•dried, o•ver•dry•ing) cause to become too dry: [as gerund] *overdrying also causes shrinkage, generates static electricity, and shortens fabric life.*

o•ver•fund /ˌōvər'fənd/ ▸ verb [trans.] provide more funding for (something) than is necessary or permitted: *if they could prove that the pension fund was "overfunded," i.e. more than able to meet its future liabilities, they could take a pension holiday.* [**Jan.** 2000 *Personal Finance (UK)*]

o•ver•hit /ˌōvər'hit/ ▸ verb (past and past participle o•ver•hit; o•ver•hit• ting) [trans.] (in sporting contexts) hit (a ball) too strongly or too far: *Marat Safin was overhitting, mucking up volleys, but he won anyway.*

o•ver•hype ▸ verb /ˌōvər'hīp/ [trans.] make exaggerated claims about (a product, idea, or event); publicize or promote excessively: *there was so much built-in hype to this movie we didn't want to overhype it ourselves.* [19 **Jan.** 1992 *New York Times*]
▸noun /'ōvərˌhīp/ excessive publicity or promotion: *were the media more rational about it, the unmistakable taste of overhype would not be so strong.* [4 **Dec.** 1994 *Coloradoan (Fort Collins)*]

o•ver•keen /ˌōvər'kēn/ ▸ adjective excessively keen or enthusiastic: *don't leave your valuables lying around in your room; otherwise the overkeen security staff will remove them for safekeeping.* [*BBCi (UK)*]

o•ver•lay•er /'ōvərˌlā-ər/ ▸ noun a top or covering layer: *conservators faced the difficult task of removing overlayers of paint, oil gilding and varnish which had been added to the tables in later years.* [19 **Oct.** 1999 *DailyTelegraph (UK)*]

o•ver•loud /ˌōvər'loud/ ▸ adjective excessively noisy or loud: *the announcer's overloud phony-excited voice reading an ad . . . was distracting.* [**1996** Joyce Carol Oates, *We Were the Mulvaneys*]

o•ver•pack /ˌōvərˈpak/ ▸ verb [trans.] **1** pack too many items into (a container): *to help the process along in frost-free freezer sections, don't overpack, because air needs to circulate.* [**Apr. 2002** *Which? (UK)*] **2** add a protective layer to items or material packed in a container: *we always overpack, with the usual 2" of packaging material all the way around.* [**25 June 2001** Usenet: rec.crafts.glass]

o•ver•spin /ˈōvərˌspin/ ▸ noun a rotating motion given to a ball when throwing or hitting it, used to give it extra speed or distance or to make it bounce awkwardly: *his googly, because of the overspin, was inclined both to dip and to bounce higher than expected.* [**6 June 2002** *Guardian (UK)*]

o•ver•stored /ˌōvərˈstôrd/ ▸ adjective **1** stored for too long a period: *he looked down at a face round and crumpled like an overstored apple.* [**1986** P. D. James, *Taste for Death*] **2** supplied with more retail stores than the market demands: *the mall . . . is going to be so big, just at a time when the country and this area is already overstored.* [**30 June 1991** *Washington Post*]

o•ver•stud•y ▸ noun /ˈōvərˌstədē/ excessive study.
▸ verb /ˌōvərˈstədē/ study too long or too intensely: *if your child is a high achiever, but overstudies for fear of not receiving an A+, help her to gradually study a little less.*

o•ver•sweet /ˌōvərˈswēt/ ▸ adjective **1** excessively sweet in taste: *you must not use the ready-diced, bitter and oversweet at the same time, vile stuff in tubs.* [**1998** Nigella Lawson, *How to Eat*] **2** excessively sentimental or maudlin: *if oversweet metaphors like this are your bag, then you're really going to like Bagger Vance.*

o•ver•tip /ˌōvərˈtip/ ▸ verb (**o•ver•tipped, o•ver•tip•ping**) [trans.] give (someone) an excessively generous tip: *people who undertip always maintain that waiters, taxi-drivers and porters despise those who overtip.* [**1991** F. King, *Ant Colony*]

o•ver•wear /ˈōvərˌwe(ə)r/ ▸ noun outer clothing: *with effective perversity she wore her underwear as overwear: floppy pink knickers over the black cycling-pants; tight white bra emblazoning the black T-shirt.* [**1995** Martin Amis, *Information*]

ox•a•zo•lid•i•none /ˌäksəzōˈlidnˌōn/ ▸ noun any of a class of synthetic antibiotics that inhibit protein synthesis, used against gram-positive bacteria.

Ox•y•Con•tin /ˌäksē'käntin/ ▸ **trademark** a synthetic analgesic drug that is similar to morphine in its effects and subject to abuse and addiction.

ox•y•gen bar /'äksijən ˌbär/ ▸ **noun** an establishment where people pay to inhale pure oxygen for its reputedly therapeutic effects: *inhaling oxygen at an "oxygen bar" would not be much use because the effects would not last more than a few seconds.* [2 **Apr.** 2001 *Times (UK)*]

oys•ter bar /'oistər ˌbär/ ▸ **noun 1** a hotel bar, small restaurant, or other place where oysters are served.
2 (especially in the southeastern U.S.) an oyster bed.

oys•ter sauce /'oistər ˌsôs/ ▸ **noun** a sweet and salty sauce made with oyster extracts, used especially in Asian cooking.

Pp

pad site /'pad ˌsīt/ ▸ noun a building lot adjacent to a shopping center or mall: *Chili's is building a new restaurant on a pad site previously occupied by a freestanding diner.* [**26 Jan.** 2000 *Real Estate Weekly*]

paint•ball /'pānt͵bôl/ ▸ noun a game or sport in which participants fire paint capsules at each other with guns designed for this: *with all the sports you listed in your Olympics issue . . ., you still missed paintball, a fast-paced sport that is gaining popularity in leaps and bounds.* [**Nov.** 1996 *Internet World*]
▪ a projectile used in this sport: *the consequences of a 200 m.p.h. paintball in the eye are explained in gory detail.* [**Aug.** 1990 *Egg*]

Pakh•tun /pək'to͞on/ ▸ noun a variant form of *Pashtun*, used especially in Asia: *he said that Pakhtun was not a nationality but a nation and should be given its due place in the federation.* [**5 Oct.** 2003 *Hi Pakistan*]

pal•am•pore /'paləm͵pôr/ ▸ noun Indian a type of chintz cloth, used especially for bedspreads.
▪ a palampore bedspread: *the palampore, a hand-painted, printed and dyed fabric, in rich permanent colours, depicting a tree in the field of the fabric, enclosed by a border filled in with flowing floral patterns became immensely popular in the West.* [**July** 2001 *Informer (Italy)*]
-ORIGIN late 17th cent.: origin uncertain; perhaps from Portuguese *palangapuz(es)* plural, from Urdu, Persian *palangpoš* 'bedcover,' or perhaps from *Pālanpur*, a town in Gujarat, India.

pa•le•o•fe•ces /͵pālēō'fēsēz/ ▸ noun [with plural verb] dessicated prehistoric fecal matter, especially from humans: *sunflower-seed shells found in the paleofeces provide evidence that early American Indians in that region farmed the plants.* [**June** 2003 *University of Chicago Magazine*]
-DERIVATIVES **pa•le•o•fe•cal** /͵pālēō'fēkəl/ adjective

Palm Pi•lot /'päm 'pīlət/ ▸ noun trademark a hand-held computer.

Pa•loo•ka•ville /pə'lo͞okə͵vil/ ▸ noun informal 1 a state of obscurity: *this bum Wilson he gets the title shot—outdoors in the ball park!—and what*

do I get—a couple of bucks and a one-way ticket to Palookaville. [1954 *On the Waterfront*]
2 an economically depressed, working-class community: *there was, in effect, always a little voice inside you wondering why you didn't just give it up for that sporting-goods store in Palookaville.* [20 **Sept.** 1999 *New Yorker*]

pan•cha•kar•ma /ˌpənCHə'kärmə/ ▸ **noun** (in Ayurvedic medicine) a fivefold detoxification treatment involving massage, herbal therapy, and other procedures: *he gets four-handed* panchakarma *massages . . . and, by means of warm sesame oil dripped onto his forehead, attains a zone of ineffable bliss.* [**Oct.** 1995 *Esquire*]
-ORIGIN 1980s: from Sanskrit *panca* 'five' + *karman* 'action.'

pan•en•the•ism /pa'nenTHē,izəm/ ▸ **noun** a philosophy based on the notion that all things are in God and that God is manifest in all things: *. . . panentheism in which it is God that is seen to reside in nature, to be revealed through every twist and turn of evolution.* [22 **May 2000** *Guardian (UK)*]
-DERIVATIVES **pan•en•the•ist** adjective and noun

pan•gram /'pan,gram/ ▸ **noun** a sentence or verse that contains all the letters of the alphabet.

pan•ic dis•or•der /'panik dis,ôrdər/ ▸ **noun** a psychiatric disorder characterized by recurrent or unexpected panic attacks with no rational origin: *an international study shows that panic disorder—in essence, recurring panic attacks—occurs throughout the world and involves several universal symptoms.* [26 **May 1990** *Science News*]

pan•ic room /'panik ,rōom; ,rŏŏm/ ▸ **noun** another name for a **SAFE ROOM**.

pa•ni•no /pə'nēnō/ ▸ **noun** (plural **pa•ni•ni** /pə'nēnē/) a sandwich, usually toasted, made with a baguette or with Italian bread.
-ORIGIN 1950s: from Italian, literally 'bread roll.'

pants /pants/ ▸ **plural noun** British slang rubbish; nonsense: *he thought we were going to be absolute pants.*

par•a•chute /'parə,SHŏŏt/ ▸ **verb** appoint or be appointed in an emergency or from outside the existing hierarchy: *an old crony of the CEO was controversially* **parachuted into** *the job.*

par•al•lel port /'parəlel 'pôrt/ ▸ **noun** Computing a connector for a device that sends or receives several bits of data simultaneously on multiple wires.

Par•a•mo•tor /'parə,mōtər/ ▸ noun trademark a motorized steerable parachute, powered by a motor and propeller strapped to the pilot's back.
–DERIVATIVES **par•a•mo•tor•ing** noun

par•a•pto•sis /,parə'tōsis; ,parəp-/ ▸ noun a system of programmed cell death in which empty spaces form in the cell cytoplasm and the mitochondria swells, causing the cell to lose its vitality. It differs from aptosis in that the cell does not fragment.
–DERIVATIVES **par•a•ptot•ic** /,parə'tätik; ,parəp-; -'tōtik/ adjective

par•a•site store /'parə,sīt ,stôr/ ▸ noun a retail store that would not generate any significant traffic but for its location adjacent to a more successful store.

par•tial-birth a•bor•tion /'pärsHəl ,bərTH ə'bôrsHən/ ▸ noun a late-term abortion of a fetus that has already died, or that is killed before being completely removed from the mother.
USAGE: The term **partial-birth abortion** is used primarily in legislation and pro-life writing about this procedure. Pro-choice, scientific, and medical writing uses the term *D&X*, for *dilation and extraction*.

par•ti•cle beam /'pärtikəl ,bēm/ ▸ noun a concentrated stream of subatomic particles, generated to cause particle collisions that will shed new light on their nature and structure.
■ such a stream used in an antimissile defense weapon.

par•ty fa•vor /'pärtē ,fāvər/ ▸ noun a small inexpensive gift given to guests at a party: *inside, the host is wielding a syringe, giving Botox injections to female guests as a kind of party favor, while out by the pool an orgy is heating up.* [**28 Sept.** 2003 *Washington Post*]

Pas•sa•ma•quod•dy /,pasəmə'kwädē/ ▸ noun (plural same or **-dies**)
1 a member of a North American Indian people inhabiting parts of southeastern Maine and, formerly, southwestern New Brunswick.
2 the Algonquian language of this people.
▸ adjective of or relating to this people or their language.
–ORIGIN from Passamaquoddy *pest mokhatiy k*, 'place where pollack are plentiful,' referring to *Passamaquoddy* Bay.

Pass•face /'pas,fās/ ▸ noun trademark 1 a security system in which a user must recognize pictures of human faces in order to gain access to a computer or computer network: *their site uses Passface because it's less hackable than regular passwords.*

2 (**pass•face**) a digital photograph of a human face that is used for identification in a Passface system: *the company uses cameras and passfaces to make sure only authorized employees get through the door.*
-ORIGIN on the pattern of *password.*

Pat•a•go•ni•an tooth•fish /ˌpatəˈgōnēən ˈto͞oTH͟ˌfisH/ ▸ **noun** a demersal food fish of Antarctic waters, marketed as Chilean sea bass and recently overfished.
•*Dissostichus eleginoides,* family Nototheniidae.

pat•er•a /ˈpatərə/ ▸ **noun** (plural **pat•er•ae** /ˈpatərē/) a broad, shallow bowl-shaped feature on a planet's surface: *craters and volcanic calderas, called "paterae," on Venus are named for notable, actual women.* [**8 Mar. 1991** Usenet: sci.space]
-ORIGIN Latin, from *patere,* 'be or lie open'

pat•ter of ti•ny feet /ˈpatər əv ˈtīnē ˈfēt/ ▸ **noun phrase** humorous used in reference to the presence or imminent birth of a child: *I had long ago given up hope of ever **hearing the patter of tiny feet**.*

p-book /ˈpē ˌbo͝ok/ (**pbook** /ˈpēˌbo͝ok/) ▸ **noun** a book printed on paper, as distinguished from one in electronic form: *I prefer reading p-books, but I sometimes use the search capabilities of digitized text.*
-ORIGIN a retronym on the pattern of *e-book,* the p standing for *paper.*

peace or•der /ˈpēs ôrdər/ ▸ **noun** a court order offering protection to certain classes of person who are not eligible to petition for a protective order.

pearl tea /ˈpərl ˌtē/ ▸ **noun** another term for BUBBLE TEA.

peer-to-peer /ˈpi(ə)r tə ˈpi(ə)r/ ▸ **adjective, noun** see **P2P.**

pen•ta•quark /ˈpentəˌkwärk; -ˌkwôrk/ ▸ **noun** a baryon consisting of four quarks and an antiquark: *although it may be possible to interpret this particle as a combination of four quarks . . . and a strange anti-quark . . ., the challenge is to explain also why this "pentaquark" does not fall apart more quickly.* [**24 July 2003** *Nature (UK)*]

pep•per vine /ˈpepər ˌvīn/ ▸ **noun** a bushy vine of the grape family, originally cultivated but now established in much of the southeastern U.S. It bears blackish fruits sought after by wildlife.
•*Ampelopsis arborea,* family Vitaceae.

pep•per spray /'pepər ˌsprā/ ▸ noun an aerosol spray containing oils derived from cayenne pepper, irritating to the eyes and respiratory passages and used as a disabling weapon.

pe•ril•la /pə'rilə/ ▸ noun an annual Asian plant of the mint family with medicinal and culinary uses; regarded as an invasive weed in some areas.
•*Perilla frutescens*, family Labatiae.

per•ma•lanc•er /'pərməˌlansər/ (also **per•ma•temp** /'pərməˌtemp/) ▸ noun a long-term freelance, part-time, or temporary worker who does not have employee benefits: *the permalancers always have to park in the temporary spaces.*
-ORIGIN blend of *permanent* and *freelancer.*

per•ma•temp /'pərməˌtemp/ ▸ another term for PERMALANCER.
-ORIGIN a blend of *permanent* and *temporary.*

pes•ter pow•er /'pestər ˌpou-ər/ ▸ noun the ability of children to nag adults, especially to influence their parents to make certain purchases: *advertisers encourage the use of pester power, especially at Christmas.*

PETA /pētə/ ▸ abbreviation People for the Ethical Treatment of Animals.

pet•a•watt /'petəˌwät/ ▸ noun a quadrillion (10^{15}) watts: *each year warm-core eddies shed southward the equivalent of about 0.3 petawatt of power.* [14 June 2003 *Science News*]

pet sit•ting /'pet ˌsitiNG/ (also **pet•sit•ting** /'petˌsitiNG/) ▸ noun the activity of taking care of pets for absent owners: *an article on how to make money petsitting* | [as modifier] *a pet-sitting business.*
-DERIVATIVES **pet•sit** verb (**pet•sat, pet•sit•ting**); **pet•sit•ter** noun

phar•ma•co•ge•nom•ics /ˌfärməkōjē'nämiks; -ji-; -'nōmiks/ ▸ plural noun [treated as singular] the branch of genetics concerned with determining the likely response of a therapeutic drug, based on an individual's genome.
-DERIVATIVES **phar•ma•co•ge•nom•i•cist** /ˌfärməkōjē'näməsist; -ji-; -'nōməsist/ noun
-ORIGIN 1990s: from *pharmaco-* + *genomics.*

phar•ma•co•phore /'färməkəˌfôr/ ▸ noun a part of a molecular structure that is responsible for a particular biological or pharmacological interaction that it undergoes.

phen•ter•mine /'fentər,mēn/ ▸ noun an appetite suppressant that binds to receptors on the hypothalamus. It is a component of fenphen and also prescribed independently: *some doctors believe phentermine helps athletes by speeding up their metabolism. Others say it is of little or no use as a performance enhancer.* [13 **Dec.** 2000 *New York Times*]

phi•los•o•pause /fə'läsə,pôz/ ▸ noun a supposed period in a scientist's career during which they reflect on philosophical issues and explanations: *scientists in their later years sometimes enter a philosopause, characterized by armchair speculations and the writing of autobiographies.* [20 **Feb.** 2003 *Nature (UK)*]
-ORIGIN blend of *philosophical* and *pause*, on the pattern of *menopause.*

phish•ing /'fiSHiNG/ ▸ noun the activity of defrauding an online account holder of financial information by posing as a legitimate company: [as modifier] *a vigilant eye seems to be the best defence against internet "phishing" exercises in which criminals create replicas of commercial websites in an attempt to fool people into submitting personal information.* [4 **Nov.** 2003 *New Zealand Herald*]
-DERIVATIVES **phish verb**
-ORIGIN 1990s: inspired by *fishing*, perhaps borrowing the *ph* from *phony.*

phone it in /'fōn it 'in/ ▸ verb phrase informal work or perform in a desultory fashion: *I've learned a lot about being a Dad and I know for sure that you can't phone it in and you can't fax it in,"* he said. [18 **Sept.** 2003 *Chattanoogan*]

pho•ton•ic crys•tal /fō'tänik 'kristl/ ▸ noun a synthetic crystal that can manipulate or be sensitized to respond to specific wavelengths of light. Its development suggests the possibility of increased miniaturization and efficiency of computing components and other technologies: *it has taken over a decade to fabricate photonic crystals that work in the near-infrared (780-3000 nm) and visible (450-750 nm) regions of the spectrum.* [**Aug.** 2000 *PhysicsWeb*]

phys•i•cal the•a•ter /'fizikəl 'THēətər /* ▸ noun a form of theater that emphasizes the use of physical movement, as in dance and mime, for expression: *a talented ensemble, with roots in physical theater and mime, can't overcome the plethora of jejune jokes and lack of cohesion in the script.* [26 **Sept.** 1999 *Philadelphia Inquirer*]

phy•to•es•tro•gen /,fītō'estrəjən/ ▸ noun an estrogen occurring naturally in legumes, considered beneficial in some diets: *Asian* *women seem to have fewer menopausal symptoms than Western women, and some researchers believe one reason may be their diets, which are naturally high in phytoestrogens.* [**June 1996** *American Health*]

phy•to•san•i•tar•y /ˌfītō'saniterē/ ▸ **adjective** (of agricultural goods crossing borders) sanitary with regard to pests and pathogens: *a 20-year-old rule requiring that all seeds (as well as bulbs and living plants) entering the United States be accompanied by a point-of-origin phytosanitary certificate.* [**July 2002** *Horticulture*]

Pi•card /pi'kärd/, French ▸ **noun 1** a native or inhabitant of Picardy: *it was the task of the Alsatian Martin Bucer and the Picard John Calvin, through their long careers, to try to blend the insights of Luther and Zwingli into a spiritually satisfying whole.* [**24 Dec. 1999** *Church Times (UK)*]
2 the dialect of French spoken in Picardy.
▸ **adjective** relating to Picardy, its inhabitants, or their dialect.

pike /pīk/ ▸ **verb** [intrans.] Australian/NZ informal (**pike on**) **1** let (someone) down.
2 abandon: *Otto nearly piked on his first attempt to jump off Melbourne's tallest building.* [**July 2000** *Ralph (Australia)*]

pik•er /'pīkər/ ▸ **noun** informal Australian/NZ a person who withdraws from a plan, commitment, etc.

Pi•la•tes /pi'lätēz/ ▸ **noun** a system of exercises using special apparatus, designed to improve physical strength, flexibility, and posture, and enhance mental awareness: *this quest for better training has led many dancers to Pilates* | [as modifier] *the Pilates method.*
-ORIGIN 1960s: named after the German physical fitness specialist Joseph *Pilates* (1880–1967), who devised the system.

pill push•er /'pil ˌpooSHər/ ▸ **noun** informal **1** a doctor who resorts too readily to advocating the use of medication to cure illness rather than considering other treatments.
2 any seller of drugs for profit, such as a pharmaceutical company or a drug dealer: *June, Maybelle, and Ezra Carter moved into Johnny's house and slept in sleeping bags downstairs to keep the pill pushers away* [**12 Sept. 2003** *Christianity Today*] | *it's a cost effective way for women to share health information among themselves, it doesn't help feed the financial interests of the pill pushers and pro-menstrual suppression advocates and researchers.* [**26 Sept. 2003** *Infoshop News*]
-DERIVATIVES **pill-push•ing** noun & adjective

Pimm's /pimz/ ▸ trademark a gin-based alcoholic drink, served typically with lemonade or soda water and fresh mint: *memories of Pimms and heady summer evenings are a distant memory as the Firework Nursery opens Windsor's seven-race card today.* [**6 Oct.** 2003 *Glasgow Evening Times*]
-ORIGIN early 20th cent.: from the name of the proprietor of the restaurant where the drink was created.

pinch point /'pinCH ˌpoint/ ▸ noun British a place or point where congestion occurs or is likely to occur, especially on a road: *the planners have suggestions to ease traffic jams at ninety-two pinch points.*

pink /piNGk/ ▸ verb [intrans.] become pink; blush: *Phoebe, laughing, pinking with the strange attention she's attracted, tells them that she doesn't really know anything more, that she hadn't even known she knew what she'd just blurted out.* [1993 R. Goldstein, *Strange Attractors*]

pin•stripe /'pinˌstrīp/ ▸ adjective Sports of baseball: *shortstop Derek Jeter made a play that instantly became part of pinstripe legend, tracking down an errant throw from right field and somehow redirecting it to nail the base runner.* [**5 Nov.** 2001 *Time*]
-ORIGIN from the fact that most professional baseball players' uniforms have pinstripes.

pipe /pīp/ ▸ noun Computing **1** a command that causes the output from one routine to be the input for another: *you can use a pipe to send the output of the show command to the printer directly and then remove the messages after printing.* [**14 Jan.** 1991 Usenet: comp.newprod] **2** a connection to the Internet or to a Web site: *although many businesses have high-powered pipes, the vast majority of home users still have to dial up and wait a seeming eternity for Web pages to pop up.* [**24 Jan.** 2000 *U.S. News and World Report*]
-ORIGIN short for *pipeline*.

pi•rate fish•ing /'pīrit ˌfiSHiNG/ ▸ noun fishing on the high seas in contravention of national and international laws governing quotas, typically by ships under flags of convenience that are owned by dummy companies.

pit /pit/ ▸ noun informal a person's armpit: *does it bug you when girls don't shave their pits and legs?* [**Summer** 2000 *Twist*]

Pi•to•cin /pi'tōsin/ ▸ trademark a proprietary form of oxytocin, a drug used to expedite labor.

plan•o•gram /'planə,gram/ ▸ noun a diagram or model that indicates the placement of retail products on shelves in order to maximize sales: *Mr. Oldham spent a busy day inside a "planogram," a room set up with shelves and signs just like those found in a Target store.* [11 **Apr.** 2002 *Wall Street Journal*]

play date (also **play•date**) /'plā ,dāt/ ▸ noun 1 a date and time set by parents for children to play together: *she has play dates with two other childen on Wednesdays and Saturdays.*
2 mainly Asian the date on which a movie premieres: *the filmbio of former Ilocos Sur Governor Luis "Chavit" Singson, directed by Carlo J. Caparas, Jr., has been suffering a lot of delays lately—mostly due to the recent intermittent rains and typhoons—and so it wouldn't be able to meet its original September playdate.* [27 **Aug.** 2003 *Manila Bulletin*]
3 a day on which a sporting event takes place or is scheduled: *the Seminoles will only have one other play date where they will be on the road for two games in Massachusetts.* [26 **Sept.** 2003 Seminoles.com]

play•scape /'plā,skāp/ ▸ noun a designed and integrated set of playground equipment, often made of wood.

pleath•er /'pleTHər/ ▸ noun imitation leather made from polyurethane: *pleather is more shiny, but thanks to modern technology, some of the imitations run a close second to animal hide.* [6 **Jan.** 1997 *Daily Progress (VA)*]
–ORIGIN 1980s: blend of *polyurethane* and *leather.*

pluck /plək/ ▸ verb Geology (of glacier ice) break off (pieces of rock) by mechanical force.

plunge saw /'plənj ,sô/ ▸ noun an electric saw with a projecting blade that can make precision cuts by plunging into dense materials: *a plunge saw looks just like a portable circular saw but the blade assembly can be raised and lowered relative to the base plate, as well as the normal bevel and depth of cut functions.* [**Jan** 2001 *Practical Householder (UK)*]

plus-size /'pləs ,sīz/ ▸ adjective (of clothing or people) of a size larger than the normal range: *a new line of plus-size bathing suits.*

po•et•ry slam /'pōitrē ,slam/ ▸ noun a competetion using elimination rounds for the reading or performance of poetry: *he's held fundraisers for young professionals at bars and spoken with potential voters at a poetry slam.* [6 **Nov.** 2003 *WEEK TV (IL)*]

Poin•dex•ter /ˈpoinˌdekstər/ ▸ **noun** informal a boringly studious or socially inept person.
-ORIGIN 1980s: apparently from the name of one of the main characters in the comedy film *Revenge of the Nerds* (1984).

point set /ˈpoint ˌset/ ▸ **noun** (in acupuncture) a set of points stimulated simultaneously to treat a particular ailment or bring about a desired effect.

poi•son pill a•mend•ment /ˈpoizən ˈpil əˌmendmənt/ ▸ **noun** an amendment to a legislative bill that considerably weakens the bill's intended effect, or ruins the bill's chances of passing: *Republicans, led by Tom DeLay . . . offered a clever "poison pill" amendment that would have exempted gun-rights groups from the bill's limits on paid issues advertising.* [**18 Feb.** 2002 *CNN*]

Po•ke•mon /ˈpōkiˌmän/ ▸ **trademark** a video game, card game, or other toy featuring certain Japanese cartoon characters.
■ a colorful toy model of certain Japanese cartoon characters.
-ORIGIN from the name of the Japanese video game *Pokemon,* itself from the words 'pocket monster.'

po•lar•i•ty ther•a•py /pəˈlaritē ˌTHerəpē; pō-/ ▸ **noun** a system of treatment intended to restore a balanced distribution of the body's energy, and incorporating manipulation, exercise, and dietary restrictions.

pole build•ing /ˈpōl ˌbildiNG/ ▸ **noun** a quickly-constructed building in which vertical poles are secured in the ground to serve as both the foundation and framework: *the couple asked Burly Oak Builders of Dexter to construct a custom-designed pole building, replicating an old schoolhouse.* [**9 Oct.** 2003 *Chelsea (MI) Standard*]

pol•li•no•sis /ˌpäləˈnōsis/ ▸ **noun** a technical term for hay fever.

pol•y•am•o•ry /ˌpälēˈamərē/ ▸ **noun** the philosophy or state of being in love or romantically involved with more than one person at the same time: *more Americans . . . are practicing what is commonly known as polygamy but what adherents . . . call "polyamory": loving more than one person simultaneously.* [**15 Nov.** 1999 *Time*]
-DERIVATIVES **pol•y•am•o•rous** adjective; **pol•y•am•o•rist** noun
-ORIGIN on the pattern of *polygamy* and *polyandry.*

pol•y•crest /ˈpälēˌkrest/ ▸ **noun** (in homeopathy) a remedy that is frequently used, in general or for a particular condition: *the poison ivy polycrests.*
-ORIGIN 19th cent.: from Greek *polu-* 'many' + *khraosos* 'use.'

po•lyg•a•my /pə'ligəmē/ ▸ noun Botany the condition of bearing some male, some female, and sometimes some perfect flowers on the same plant.
  -DERIVATIVES **po•lyg•a•mous** adjective

pol•y•nos•ic /ˌpäli'näsik/ ▸ noun a long-fiber rayon-and-polyester blend with a soft finish, used mainly in clothing.

pol•y•pill /'pälē,pil/ ▸ noun a pill containing a number of medicines that all treat the same condition: *the benefits of the heart polypill would easily outweigh the risks because it would incorporate medicines proven to be generally safe.* [26 June 2003 *BBC News Online*]

pon•zu /'pän,zo͞o/ ▸ noun a Japanese dipping sauce made from soy sauce, lime juice, vinegar and fish flakes.
  -ORIGIN Japanese:'citrus vinegar.'

poor-mouth /'po͝or ˌmouTH; 'pôr/ ▸ adjective claiming to have no money; complaining of poverty: *but before we start swallowing Samtrans poor-mouth talk, we need to ask them why they continue to run bus service that competes with the new line.* [16 Sept. 2003 *Contra Costa (CA) Times*]

Poo•ter•ish /'po͞otərisH/ ▸ adjective self-important and mundane or narrow-minded: *Duran has a Pooterish way with an anecdote which makes his book often very funny.* [22 June 1995 *New York Review of Books*]
  -ORIGIN 1960s: from the name of Charles *Pooter*, the central character of *Diary of a Nobody* (1892) by George and Weedon Grossmith.

pop quiz /'päp 'kwiz/ ▸ noun a short test given to students without any prior warning.
  ■ any unexpected question or set of questions: *throwing out little pop quizzes will disarm him and totally get him to open up, renewing your lines of communication* [Dec. 2001 *Cosmopolitan*] | *McMullen's political goose was cooked by the dairy farmer, who gave the businessman a Vermont pop quiz on farming and geography.* [4 Oct. 2003 *Rutland (VT) Herald*]

pop-un•der /'päp ˌəndər/ ▸ adjective Computing of, relating to, or denoting an additional window, usually an advertisement, that is under a Web browser's main or current window and appears when a user tries to exit: *a plague of flashing pop-under ads.*

pop-up /ˈpäp ˌəp/ ▸ **adjective 1** denoting Internet advertisements in their own windows which appear adventitiously when visiting Web sites or following links: *a US district court judge has ruled that on-line advertising companies can launch pop-up ads on other parties' Web sites, the Wall Street Journal reported.* [15 **Sept.** 2003 *Canada.com*] **2** denoting a running program that is activated by one or more keystrokes: *users can control the buffer switch via pop-up memory-resident software and can thus direct their output to one of several printers.* [**Nov.** 1990 *Management Computing (UK)*] **3** denoting a collapsible camper: *pop-up campers are for the enthusiast who doesn't want to spend $80,000, but doesn't want to sleep on the ground, either.* [21 **Jan.** 1990 *Star-Ledger (NJ)*] ▸ **noun** a pop-up ad, window, program, or camper.

por•ce•lain•ber•ry /ˈpôrs(ə)lənˌberē/ ▸ **noun** a deciduous, woody perennial vine of Asian origin, first cultivated as an ornamental and now regarded as an aggressive invader in most of the eastern U.S. The attractive berries, in multiple colors from white to deep purple, appear in early autumn.
•*Ampelopsis brevipedunculata,* family Vitaceae.

porn /pôrn/ (also **por•no** /ˈpôrˌnō/) informal ▸ **noun** [with modifier] television programs, books, etc., regarded as catering to a voyeuristic or obsessive interest in a specified subject: *the movie, which opened May 10 to mixed reviews, nevertheless looks like a thrilling throwback to the golden age of disaster movies—weather porn of the highest order.* [22 **May** 1996 *City Paper (Baltimore)*]

por•tal /ˈpôrtl/ ▸ **noun** Computing an Internet site providing access or links other sites: *there is a name for this sort of Web service: a portal. The term signifies an Internet gateway, the shoreline from which Web surfers paddle out to sea.* [25 **May** 1998 *Newsweek*]

port•fo•li•o /pôrtˈfōlēˌō/ ▸ **noun** (plural **port•fo•li•os**) [as modifier] relating to, denoting, or engaged in an employment pattern which involves a succession of short-term contracts and part-time work, rather than the more traditional model of a single job for life: *portfolio careers allow women to balance work with family.*

pos•i•tive /ˈpäz(i)tiv/ ▸ **adjective** (of a person or their blood) having a specified substance or condition, especially HIV or a forbidden performance-enhancing drug: *Astrid Strauss, a former East German who won the 800 metres freestyle at the 1986 world championships in Madrid, was found positive following a random drug test.* [24 **July** 1992 *Daily Telegraph (UK)*]

post•ing /ˌpōstiNG/ ▸ **noun** a message sent to an Internet bulletin board or newsgroup: *tap into the postings in the Internet and you're swamped by a maelstrom of communicative debris.* [**6 Sept.** 1993 *Newsweek*]
■ the action of sending a message to an Internet bulletin board or newsgroup.

Post•Script /ˈpōstˌskript/ ▸ **noun** Computing, trademark a language used as a standard for formatting pages of text: [mainly as modifier] *Create your document and print to PostScript file. Then Distill your PostScript file to create your PDF document to be printed for public distribution.* [**14 Dec.** 2001 Usenet: usc.list.pdf-l]

pot /pät/ ▸ **noun** a shot aimed at someone or something; a potshot: *I certainly don't have to worry about being shot at by some idiot taking pots at random targets.* [**8 July** 2001 Usenet: rec.antiques]

POTUS (also **Po•tus**) /ˈpōtəs/ ▸ **abbreviation** President of the United States: *a nearby train would get us to Portsmouth by around four o'clock. I suggest to one of the Potus's aides that he should find a way to deliver us to the train station.* [**27 June** 1994 *New Republic*]
USAGE: A survey of citations suggests that when this term is not being used as argot by Washington or White House insiders, it is intended to be sarcastic or disrespectful.

pow•er•beads /ˈpou(-ə)rˌbēdz/ ▸ **noun** a bracelet or necklace of round beads that are purported to enhance the spiritual well-being of the wearer in different ways depending on the color or material of the beads.

pow•er•head /ˈpou(-ə)rˌhed/ ▸ **noun 1** informal a powerful egomaniac: *despite kick-ass demo tapes played for record-industry powerheads and support from music screenmakers . . . the star-maker machinery behind the popular song just couldn't be budged.* [**Dec.** 2000 *Out*]
2 any of various mechanical or electrical devices, including:
■ a submersible pump for an aquarium that creates current within a tank. ■ an attachment for a central vacuum system with beater bars. ■ the internal combustion engine of an outboard motor. ■ the power unit of a garage door opener.

pow•er rat•ing /ˈpou(-ə)r ˌrātiNG/ ▸ **noun 1** the amount of electrical power required for a particular device: *a continuous power rating of 150 watts.*

2 a numerical representation of a sports team's strength for betting purposes: *a 99 power rating and a home field edge of four points.*

pow•er us•er /ˈpou(-ə)r ˌyo͞ozər/ ▸ **noun** Computing an accomplished computer user who requires products having the most features and the fastest performance: *the Gateway 700XL's record-breaking performance packed into a stylish, easy-to-upgrade case is sure to please power users.* [**7 Oct.** 2003 *Computer Shopper*]

pow•er walk•ing /ˈpou(-ə)r ˌwôkiNG/ ▸ **noun** a form of cardiopulmonary exercise consisting of fast walking with rhythmic swinging of the arms.

PQ ▸ **abbreviation 1** Parti Québécois.
2 Province of Quebec.

prai•rie-dog•ging /ˈpre(ə)rē ˌdôgiNG/ (also **prai•rie dog•ging**) ▸ **noun** the practice of looking over the wall of an office cubicle to observe coworkers: *stop prairie-dogging and get back to work.*

pra•kri•ti /ˈprəkritē/ ▸ **noun** (in Vedanta) the prime material energy of which all matter is composed.

pre-Böt•zing•er com•plex /prē ˈbœtsiNGər ˌkämpleks/ ▸ **noun** a structure in the mammalian brain stem that controls respiration.

pre•but•tal /prēˈbətl/ ▸ **noun** (in politics) a response formulated in anticipation of a criticism; a preemptive rebuttal: *the White House political team and the lawyers . . . were debating whether to steal Starr's thunder by slamming his report in advance—a "prebuttal," in White House lingo.* [**Jan. 1999** *Vanity Fair*]
-ORIGIN 1990s: blend of *pre-* and *(re)buttal.*

pre•cau•tion•ar•y prin•ci•ple /priˈkôsHəˌnerē ˌprinsəpəl/ ▸ **noun** the principle that the introduction of a new product or process whose ultimate effects are disputed or unknown should be resisted. It has mainly been used to prohibit the importation of genetically modified organisms and food: *Brussels has flouted the ruling ever since, citing the "precautionary principle" and arguing that the meat may cause cancer and harm unborn babies.* [**15 Oct. 2003** *Guardian (UK)*]

pre•dawn /prēˈdôn/ ▸ **adjective** relating to or taking place before dawn: *Sunday's predawn raid by Israeli warplanes.*

pre•ex•ist•ing con•di•tion /ˈprē-igˈzistiNG kənˈdiSHən/ ▸ noun a medical condition existing at a time when new insurance is applied for; typically the cost of its treatment is not covered by the insurance.

pre•hos•pi•tal /prēhäspitl/ ▸ adjective prior to arrival at a hospital: *the bandage was developed . . . primarily for a prehospital setting, and to help the soldier control one of the biggest causes of death, which is hemorrhage.* [20 Sept. 2003 *Stars and Stripes*]

pre•hy•per•ten•sion /ˌprēhīpərˈtensHən/ ▸ noun the condition of having blood pressure between 120/80 mmHg and 139/89 mmHg, considered an indication of risk for hypertension.
 -DERIVATIVES **pre•hy•per•ten•sive** /ˌprēhīpərˈtensiv/ adjective
 -ORIGIN early 21st cent.

pre•kin•der•gar•ten /prēˈkindərˌgärtn; -ˌgärdn/ ▸ noun daycare with some educational content for children younger than five, provided by elementary schools or preschools. (abbreviation: **pre-K**)

pre•launch /prēˈlônCH; -ˈlänCH/ ▸ adjective concerning activities or conditions before the launch of a spacecraft, campaign, product, etc: *technology industry analysts who were shown prelaunch versions of the service applauded the results.* [1 Oct. 2003 *CNET News*]

pre•life /prēˈlīf/ ▸ adjective 1 prior to the appearance of life forms on earth: *prelife molecules.*
 2 (often in religious contexts) prior to a particular life or stage of life: *that spiritual decision, and prelife planning, have nothing to do with length of experience on earth.* [9 Feb. 2003 Usenet: talk.religion.course-miracle]

pre•loved /prēˈləvd/ (also **pre-loved**) ▸ adjective informal previously owned; secondhand: *preloved toys are just as appealing.*

pre•match /prēˈmaCH/ ▸ adjective in or relating to the period before a sports match: *his prematch press conference.*

pre•mod•ern /prēˈmädərn/ ▸ adjective anticipating the modern phase or period of something while not actually belonging to it: *our nostalgia for premodern times when natural bonds to kith and kin were unshakable continues to surface.*

pres•en•ta•tion graph•ics /ˌprezənˈtāSHən ˌgrafiks; ˌprēzen-/ ▸ noun another term for PRESENTATION SOFTWARE.

pres•en•ta•tion soft•ware /ˌprezən'tāsHən ˌsôftwe(ə)r; ˌprēzen-/ (also **pres•en•ta•tion graph•ics** /ˌprezən'tāsHən ˌgrafiks; ˌprēzen-/) ▸ **noun** software used to create a sequence of text and graphics, and often audio and video, to accompany a speech or public presentation: *the suite comes complete with a word-processor, spreadsheet, presentation software and various other components.*

pre•text•ing /'prēˌteksting/ ▸ **noun** the practice of using a pretext to obtain personal information from someone, usually over the telephone: *Docusearch had hired a woman who called Boyer and her family to get her work address without revealing why she was calling, a technique known as "pretexting."* [**30 Dec.** 2002 *Chicago Tribune*]

prime con•tract /'prīm 'känˌtrakt/ ▸ **noun** a contract whose requirements are partly fulfilled by the awarding of subcontracts: *Parsons has the prime contract with the Army to design, construct, operate, and close the chemical agent neutralization facility located at the Newport Chemical Depot in Indiana.* [**13 Oct.** 2003 *Yahoo News (press release)*] -DERIVATIVES **prime con•trac•tor noun**

print•er-friend•ly /'printər ˌfrendlē/ ▸ **adjective** formatted for output on a printer, with extraneous material deleted or suppressed: *users can also print printer-friendly sample ballots to take with them to their polling place.* [**19 Oct.** 2003 *Advertiser (CA)*]

pri•vate key /'prīvit 'kē/ ▸ **noun** see PUBLIC KEY.

pro•bi•ot•ic /ˌprōbī'ätik/ ▸ **adjective** denoting a substance that stimulates the growth of microorganisms, especially those with beneficial properties (such as those of the intestinal flora).
▸ **noun** a probiotic substance or preparation: *if you do have to go on antibiotics, take "probiotics," which help repopulate your gut with the healthy bacteria.* [**April 1999** *BBC Vegetarian Good Food*]
■ a microorganism introduced into the body for its beneficial qualities.

pro•gres•sive lens /prə'gresiv 'lenz/ ▸ **noun** (usually **progressive lenses**) an eyeglass lens having a smooth transition between parts with different focal lengths, correcting for vision at all distances.

pro•gres•sives /prə'gresivz/ ▸ **plural noun** a pair of eyeglasses having progressive lenses: *progressives for use when driving, reading, or using a computer.*

PROM /präm/ ▸ **noun** Computing a memory chip that can be programmed only once by the manufacturer or user.
-ORIGIN from *p(rogrammable) r(ead-)o(nly) m(emory)*.

proof-of-pur•chase /ˈpro͞of əv ˈpərcHəs/ ▸ **adjective** designating a feature or symbol on a product that can be removed by the buyer to prove that the product was purchased, in order to claim a rebate or refund.

pro•pel•ler-head /prəˈpelər ˌhed/ ▸ **noun** informal a person who has an obsessive interest in computers or technology.

pro•sum•er /prōˈso͞omər/ ▸ **noun 1** an amateur who purchases equipment with quality or features suitable for professional use: *the magazine is aimed at the prosumer who uses a $10,000 camera to make home movies of his dog.*
2 a prospective consumer who is involved in the design, manufacture, or development of a product or service: *a panel of prosumers weighed in on the plans for the new shampoo.*
■ a person who designs or produces a product for personal use or for sale: *she's a driven prosumer with one idea: to make a better-smelling toothpaste.* ■ a well-informed and proactive consumer: *prosumers read labels, sometimes obsessively.*
-ORIGIN blend of *professional* or *producer* or *proactive* and *consumer*.

pro•te•ase in•hib•i•tor /ˈprōtēˌās inˌhibitər/ ▸ **noun** a substance that breaks down protease, thereby inhibiting the replication of certain cells and viruses, including HIV.

pro•te•a•some /ˈprōtēəˌsōm/ ▸ **noun** a protein complex in cells containing proteases; it breaks down proteins that have been tagged by ubiquitin.

pro•tec•tive or•der /prəˈtektiv ˈôrdər/ ▸ **noun** a court order instructing a person to desist from abusing or harassing the petitioner (usually a related person) for a fixed period: *a protective order against the man accused of setting his wife on fire May 24 was dismissed Thursday.* [**18 Sept.** 2003 *Henderson (KY) Gleaner*]

pro•te•ome /ˈprōtēˌōm/ ▸ **noun** Genetics the entire complement of proteins that is or can be expressed by a cell, tissue, or organism: *now that the human genome has been deciphered, much of the fanfare surrounding it has transferred to the proteome, the full complement of proteins made from the genetic "blueprints" stored in our cells.* [**July 2002** *Scientific American*]
-ORIGIN 1990s: a blend of *protein* and *genome*.

pro•te•om•ics /ˌprōtēˈämiks/ ▸ **plural noun** [treated as singular] the branch of molecular biology concerned with determining the proteome.
–DERIVATIVES **pro•te•om•ic** adjective

prove /prōōv/ ▸ **verb** (past part. **proved** or **proven** /ˈprōōvən/) [trans.] (in homeopathy) demonstrate the action of (a remedy) by seeing what effect it produces in a healthy individual.

prov•ing /ˈprōōviNG/ ▸ **noun** (in homeopathy) the testing of a remedy: *many such provings are required to fully test the powers of a medicinal substance.*

psyched /sīkt/ ▸ **adjective** excited and full of anticipation: [rarely attributive] *we've told him you were coming—he's really psyched.*

P2P /ˈpētəˈpē/ ▸ **abbreviation** peer-to-peer; denoting a network or data communications in which no dedicated server is involved: [mainly as modifier] *what distinguishes the popular P2P programs such as Kazaa, Grokster and Gnutella from their now-crippled godfather Napster is the same thing that makes them more of a threat: the absence of central processing.* [2 **May** 2003 *Wall Street Journal*]

pub•cast•er /ˈpəbˌkastər/ ▸ **noun** a publically owned broadcaster: *a reality show developed for Norwegian pubcaster NRK.*

pub•lic key /ˈpəblik ˈkē/ ▸ **noun** a cryptographic key that can be obtained and used by anyone to encrypt messages intended for a particular recipient, such that the encrypted messages can be deciphered only by using a second key that is known only to the recipient (the **private key**).

Puf•fa /ˈpəfə/ (in full **Puf•fa jack•et** /ˈpəfə ˌjakit/) ▸ **noun** British trademark a type of thick padded jacket: *the understandably miffed man in the puffa jacket, David Diaz, took the Kat-Slater-alike rocker to court, seeking $75,000 in damages.* [10 **Sept.** 2003 *Megastar News (UK)*]
–ORIGIN 1990s: origin uncertain; perhaps respelling of *puffer.*

pull•back /ˈpōōlˌbak/ ▸ **noun** (of markets or prices) a retreat to a lower position after a higher one: *market watchers don't think Friday's modest pullback by the small-stock group means more losses loom.* [17 **Oct.** 1994 *Wall Street Journal*]

Pull•man kitch•en /ˈpōōlmən ˈkiCHən/ ▸ **noun** a kitchenette, especially one recessed and concealable behind doors: *it's a student apart-*

ment hotel in which every room is a studio unit with private bathroom and pullman kitchen. [20 **Apr.** 2000 Usenet: rec.travel.europe]

pull-quote /ˈpo͝ol ˌkwōt/ ▸ noun a brief, attention-getting quotation, typically in a distinctive typeface, taken from the main text of an article and used as a subheading or as a design element.

pump /pəmp/ ▸ verb [trans.] 1 (**pump something out**) produce or emit something in large quantities or amounts: *carnival bands pumping out music.*
2 (**pump something up**) informal turn up the volume of music.

pun•dit•oc•ra•cy /ˌpəndiˈtäkrəsē/ ▸ noun informal media commentators, viewed collectively: *the financial markets and the punditocracy continue to believe that Greenspan is the closest thing to God on Earth.*

pure-click /ˈpyo͝or ˌklik/ ▸ adjective denoting a company doing all of its business on the Internet: *in effect, 'pure click' Amazon picks up a 'brick' presence and thus can leverage brand identity and sales the way Barnes & Noble has been doing.* [21 **Apr.** 2001 *Washington Post*]

purse net /ˈpərs ˌnet/ ▸ noun a bag-shaped net with a mouth that can be drawn together with cords, for catching fish or rabbits.

push poll /ˈpo͝osH ˌpōl/ ▸ noun an ostensible opinion poll in which the true objective is to sway voters using loaded questions: *Mr. Morales also was visited by tobacco lobbyists bearing the results of a survey, known as a push poll, in which Texans were asked questions that cast the Attorney General in an unflattering light.* [22 **Apr.** 1997 *New York Times*]
−DERIVATIVES **push-poll•ing** noun

put•ta•nes•ca /ˌpo͞otəˈneskə; ˌpo͞otnˈeskə/ ▸ adjective [usually postpositive] denoting a pasta sauce typically including tomatoes, garlic, olives, and anchovies: *pasta puttanesca.*
−ORIGIN Italian, from *puttana* 'prostitute' (the sauce is said to have been devised by prostitutes as one that could be cooked quickly between clients' visits).

PVR ▸ abbreviation personal video recorder.

Qq

qaw•wal /kə'väl/ ▸ noun a performer of qawwali: *she could listen to recordings of ghazals for hours at a stretch, and was entranced, too, by the complex devotional music of the leading* qawwals. [**1999** Salman Rushdie, *Ground Beneath her Feet*]

qaw•wa•li /kə'välē/ ▸ noun a style of Muslim devotional music now associated particularly with Sufis in Pakistan: [as modifier] *here's a world-beat dilemma for you: Nusrat Fateh Ali Khan is one of the world's great singers, but his* qawwali *music is intended for Sufi Muslim religious ceremonies in Pakistan.* [**19 Apr. 1991** *Entertainment Weekly*] –ORIGIN from Arabic *qawwāli*, from *qawwāl* 'loquacious,' also 'singer.'

quak•ie /'kwākē/ ▸ noun informal **1** quaking aspen: *in places, the dirt road is very steep but the drama of the topography, the vistas, the quakies, pines and the pastel blue sky makes this ride an unforgettable.* [**2002** J. Martin Kohler, *The Cowboy Way*] **2** a frequent caller to an earthquake hotline: *some callers check in so often that operators fondly refer to them as "quakies."* [**27 Nov. 1992** *Baltimore Sun*]

quak•ing bog /'kwākiNG 'bäg/ ▸ noun a bog formed over water or soft mud, which shakes underfoot: *as the stagnant lakes become more oxygen-starved and acidic, only sphagnum moss can grow well. It finally takes over the lake as a thick mass of floating vegetation called a* quaking bog. [**1991** R. Krueger, *This Land of Ours*]

quan•tum com•put•er /'kwäntəm kəm,pyŌŌtər/ ▸ noun a computer that makes use of the quantum states of subatomic particles to store information: *in 1992 Deutsch and Richard Jozsa formulated a few problems that could be solved faster with a quantum computer than with a conventional Turing machine.* [**July 1995** *American Scientist*] –DERIVATIVES **quan•tum com•put•ing** noun

quan•tum dot /'kwäntəm ,dät/ ▸ noun Physics a nanoscale particle of semiconducting material that can be embedded in cells or organisms for various experimental purposes, such as labeling proteins.

quan•tum med•i•cine /'kwäntəm 'medəsin/ ▸ noun a branch of complementary medicine that uses uses low-dosage electromagnetic radiation in the treatment, diagnosis, and prevention of disease: *proponents of "quantum medicine" reject the idea of reductionism (that things can be understood in terms of their component parts), since everything is related.* [**1999** Thomas J. Wheeler, *Deepak Chopra & Ayurvedic medicine*]

quark-glu•on plas•ma /ˈkwärk ˈglo͞oän ˌplazmə; ˈkwôrk/ ▸ **noun** a hypothetical, highly-energized form of matter that contains unbound quarks and gluons, believed to have been present ten millionths of a second after the Big Bang: *can the Quark-Gluon Plasma in the early universe be supercooled?* [**2002** *Astrophysics Abstracts*]

que•so fres•co /ˈkäso͞ ˈfräsko͞; ˈfresko͞/ ▸ **noun** a semisoft fresh Mexican cheese, white in color, typically served shredded over hot foods: *Valerie Proctor and Eduardo Cardona will help fill your basket with peppers, black beans and* queso fresco, *and your head with tips on cooking Latin-style.* [**July 1993** *Canadian Living*]

quin•o•lone /ˈkwinə,lōn; ˈkwinl-,ōn/ ▸ **noun** any of a class of antibiotics used in treating a variety of mainly gram-negative infections, and thought to be responsible for antibiotic resistance in some microbes. Quinolones include the flurorquinolones, which were developed later and contain fluorine.

Rr

rac•er•back /'rāsər‚bak/ ▸ **noun** [as adjective] denoting an article of clothing with a T-shaped back behind the shoulder blades to allow ease of movement in sporting activities.

ra•cial pro•fil•ing /'rāsHəl 'prō‚fīliNG/ ▸ **noun** the practice of attributing criminal motives or intentions to people on the basis of their race: *to victims, racial profiling is millennial Jim Crow, creating "whites only" thoroughfares.* [16 July 2001 *Newsweek*]

Ra•el•i•an /rä'ēlēən/ ▸ **noun** a member of an atheistic cult based on the belief that humans originated from alien scientists who came to earth in UFOs.
▸**adjective** relating to the Raelians or their beliefs.
-ORIGIN 1990s: from *Rael*, assumed name of Claude Vorilhon, French singer and journalist, author of *The Message Given to Me by Extraterrestrials* (1974).

rage /rāj/ ▸ [with modifier] **noun** an instance of aggressive behavior or violent anger caused by a stressful or frustrating situation: *desk rage | sports rage | PC rage.*

rag•ged•y-ass /'ragidē ‚as/ (also **rag•gedy-assed**) ▸ **adjective** informal shabby; miserably inadequate: *the plaque is there, standing taller than the tallest weed, because this raggedy-ass lot was once the home of Stax Records.* [Dec. 1997 *Esquire*]
■ (of a person) new and inexperienced.

ra•jas /'rəjəs/ ▸ **noun** (in Vedanta) the element or mode of prakriti associated with passion, energy, and movement.

ra•jas•ic /rə'jasik/ ▸ **adjective** (in Ayurveda) denoting a class of foods that are bitter, sour, salty, pungent, hot, or dry, and are thought to promote sensuality, greed, jealousy, anger, delusion, and irreligious feelings. Compare SATTVIC, TAMASIC.

ran•che•ra /rän'CHe(ə)rə/ ▸ **noun** a type of Mexican country music typically played with guitars and horns.
■ a ranchera tune or song: *Santiago, Jr. has fashioned his most accessible album with this new release, full of sad corridas and rancheras of separated and jilted lovers.* [Oct. 1991 *Dirty Linen*]
-ORIGIN 1980s: from Spanish *cancion ranchera* 'farmers' songs.'

range•bound /'rānj,bound/ ▸ **adjective** (generally of market prices) not straying outside a particular range: *the euro remained range-bound, faltering again in its attempt to regain recent highs.* [17 **Jan.** 2001 *Wall Street Journal*]

Rap•id Ther•mal Ex•change /'rapid THərməl iks'CHānj/ (abbreviation: **RTX**) ▸ **noun** a system or device for cooling overheated muscles and organs by cooling blood in the palm of the hand, which then circulates throughout the body.

ra•toon crop /ra'tōon ,kräp/ ▸ **noun** a crop that grows from the stubble of one already harvested, especially of rice, bananas or sugarcane: *other producers are preparing for ratoon crops, or harvesting a second crop that grows from stubble after the main harvest.* [2 **Oct.** 2003 *Country World (TX)*]
–ORIGIN Spanish *retoño*, 'sprout.'

Ra•zor scoot•er /'rāzər ,skōōtər/ ▸ **noun** trademark a type of lightweight aluminum collapsible scooter.

RBE (also **rbe**) ▸ **abbreviation** relative biological effectiveness (with regard to therapeutic radiation): [as modifier] *the RBE factor can be found in tables and depends on the sort of radiation and the energy of the individual quanta.* [**Autumn 1997** Michigan State University Web site]

re•al•i•ty TV /rē'alitē ,tē'vē/ ▸ **noun** staged television programs about real people and situations, designed to be entertaining rather than informative.

rear pro•jec•tion /'rir prə'jeksHən/ (also **rear-pro•jec•tion**) ▸ **noun** the projection of a picture onto the back of a translucent screen for viewing or for use as a background in filming: [as modifier] *even though the biggest rear-projection televisions offer more expansive screens than even the largest plasmas, their bulky casings and limited viewing angles make them inconvenient.* [28 **Sept.** 2003 *Dallas Morning News*]
■ an image projected in this way.
–DERIVATIVES **rear-pro•ject•ed** adjective

rea•son•a•ble wom•an stand•ard /'rēz(ə)nəbəl 'wōomən ,standərd/ ▸ **noun** a guideline for determining what constitutes sexual harassment, based on suppositions about what a reasonable woman would find objectionable.

re•bal•ance /rē'baləns/ ▸ **verb** [trans.] balance again or restore the correct balance to: *consider rebalancing too, because with the long slide in stocks you may find that bonds make up a larger part of your asset mix than you like. If so, sell some bonds and buy stocks.* [**Oct. 2001** *Time*]

re•book /rē'bŏŏk/ ▸ **verb** [intrans.] book the same accommodations, seat, ticket, etc.: *a third of the tourists had rebooked for next year.*

re•com•bi•nase /ri'kämbə,nās; -,nāz/ ▸ **noun** Biochemistry an enzyme that promotes genetic recombination.

re•com•pile /,rēkəm'pīl/ ▸ **verb** [trans.] Computing compile (a program) again or differently.
▸ **noun** a recompilation of a computer program: *users should upgrade to SendMail version 8.12.10 or apply the provided patch. (This requires a recompile.).* [**29 Sept. 2003** *Tech Republic (KY)*]
– DERIVATIVES **re•com•pi•la•tion** /,rēkämpə'lāsʜən/ **noun**

rec•ord•set /'rekərd,set/ ▸ **noun** a set of records in a database that share an identifiable or isolatable characteristic.

re•count /ri'kount/ ▸ **noun** an act or instance of giving an account of an event or experience: *one woman's recount of a prolonged battle with "huge centipedes."* [**25 Sept. 2003** *Barbados Advocate*]

re•cut /rē'kət/ ▸ **verb** [trans.] remove further or different material from (a film or screenplay): *director Tony Scott is recutting several key scenes.*

red top /'red ,täp/ ▸ **noun** British a tabloid newspaper: [as modifier] *the U.K.'s populist "red top" newspapers pump up the pulse of British life, and they compete ferociously for every fleeting image of Beckham and Adams.* [**Sept. 1999** *Vanity Fair*]
– ORIGIN 1990s: from the red background on which the titles of certain British newspapers are printed.

re•fi /rē'fī/ ▸ **verb** (**re•fies, re•fied, re•fy•ing**) refinance (a mortgage): *still, a rush to refi could prove troublesome for short-handed lenders.* [**11 Jan. 1998** *Chicago Tribune*]
▸ **adjective** relating to refinancing and the refinancing market: *the refi boom is over and homeowners have larger mortgages and can no longer count on rapid appreciation to build equity.* [**18 Mar. 2002** *Time*]

re•flect•ed glo•ry /ri'flektid 'glôrē/ ▸ **noun** fame or approval achieved through association with someone else rather than through one's own efforts: *King made sure he had at his disposal some powerful friends like Franklin Delano Roosevelt and the Rockefellers to give him support and reflected glory.* [**11 Sept.** 2003 *CBC News (Canada)*]

re•frame /rē'frām/ ▸ verb [trans.] **1** place (a picture or photograph) in a new frame.
2 frame or express (words or a concept or plan) differently: *the death of her parents forces Molly to revisit difficult childhood experiences and to reframe them in a new context.* [**11 Sept.** 2003 *Emediawire (press release)*]

re•gen•er•a•tive brak•ing /ri'jenərətiv 'brākiNG; ri'jenə,rātiv/ ▸ noun a method of braking in which energy is extracted from the parts braked, to be stored and reused.

re•gift /rē'gift/ ▸ verb [trans.] give (a gift one has received) to someone else: *do you think she'll regift that horrendous vase?* | [intrans.] *the survey showed that 53% of consumers plan to regift this holiday.*
▸noun an item that has been regifted: *most of my regifts are more meaningful than the usual bouquet of flowers.*
–DERIVATIVES **re•gift•er** noun

re•gime change /ri'ZHēm ˌCHānj; rā'ZHēm/ ▸ noun a usually forcible change in leadership or management, as in a government or organization: *we knew that before the war, when they talked about regime change, they never inserted the word "democratic."* [**1 Oct.** 2003 *Daily Star (Lebanon)*]

re•hire /rē'hī(ə)r/ ▸ verb [trans.] hire (a former employee) again: *the company dismissed its workers and rehired them on a lower rate.*
▸noun a person rehired: *Miller said the company also plans to continue bringing back people on a limited basis, but he declined to give any specifics on the number of possible rehires.* [**17 Sept.** 2003 *Vero Beach Press-Journal*]

re•in•stall /ˌrē-in'stôl/ ▸ verb [trans.] install again (used especially with software).
▸noun a reinstallation of software: *if the preceding two tips don't help, try performing a "clean" reinstall of your system software.* [**Aug.** 1994 *MacUser*]
–DERIVATIVES **re•in•stal•la•tion** /ˌrē-instə'lāSHən/ noun

re•li•cens•ing /rē'līsənsiNG/ ▸ noun [trans.] the act or process of renewing a license or authority: *the state has no special requirements for relicensing the elderly.* [**16 Sept.** 2003 *WBAY (WI)*]

re•mail•er /'rē͵mālər/ ▸ **noun** a service that anonymously forwards email so as to disguise the original sender: *the need for anonymous remailers stems from the design of the Internet, which tags every packet of data with an electronic address so it can be returned or re-sent if something goes wrong in transit.* [**6 Mar.** 1995 *Time*]
■ a similar service for mail: *suppose that, because of cost or the quality of service, it is better to post a letter to Germany from Holland than from Britain. Remailers ship mail out of Britain in bulk and post it to Germany from Holland instead.* [7 **Jan.** 1995 *Economist*]

re•pet•i•tive-mo•tion dis•or•der /ri'petitiv 'mōsHən dis͵ôrdər/ ▸ **noun** work-related physical symptoms caused by excessive and repeated use of the upper extremities, especially when typing on a computer keyboard. Also called **repetitive injury**.

rep•li•cant /'replikənt/ ▸ **noun 1** (in science fiction) a genetically engineered or artifical being created as an exact replica of a particular human being.
2 a disparaging term for something that imitates or resembles another: *why American manufacturers chase some ill-defined image of exclusive European flavor in a price-sensitive class is the first mystery, but to create so plainly artificial a replicant is the deeper one.* [**Oct.** 1989 *Motor Trend*]
-ORIGIN from *replica* + *-ant*: first used in the movie *Blade Runner* (1982).

re•port /ri'pôrt/ ▸ **noun** an employee who is supervised by another employee: *all of his reports are twenty-somethings with no concept of proper attire for work.*

re•po•sa•do /͵repə'sädō/ ▸ **noun** (plural **re•po•sa•dos**) a type of tequila that has been aged in oak for between two months and a year.
-ORIGIN Spanish, literally 'rested.'

Re•pub•li•crat /ri'pəbli͵krat/ (also **re•pub•li•crat** or **Re•pub•lo•crat**) ▸ **noun** a Republican or Democrat whose political philosophy is a blend of policies and principles from both parties: *Republicrats are blurring the differences between our two parties* | [as modifier] *Republicat senators.* ■ a member of a political faction that includes both Republicans and Democrats. ■ a conservative Democrat with Republican sympathies.
-DERIVATIVES **Re•pub•li•crat•ic** /ri͵pəbli'kratik/ **adjective**
-ORIGIN blend of *Republican* and *Democrat*.

re•pur•pose /rē'pərpəs/ ▸ verb [trans.] adapt for use in a different purpose: *they've taken a product that was originally designed for a CD-ROM and repurposed it for the Microsoft Network.*

re•rate /rē'rāt/ ▸ verb [trans.] rate or assess (something, especially shares or a company) again: *Mr Smith said airline share prices globally had recovered as global growth prospects improved, and Qantas could be rerated as its share price had not rebounded* [23 **Sept.** 2003 *Daily Telegraph (Australia)*]

re•scale /rē'skāl/ ▸ verb [trans.] alter the scale of (something), typically to make it smaller or simpler: *his group recently submitted a report to the state Education Department urging that all the science exams be rescaled.* [12 **Sept.** 2003 *Buffalo News*]

re•shoot /rē'sнооt/ ▸ verb (past and past participle **re•shot** /rē'sнät/) [trans.] shoot (a scene of a film) again or differently: *they had to reshoot the whole thing with another actor* | [intrans.] *the insurance was enough to allow them to reshoot or finish with a double.*
▸noun an act of reshooting a scene of a film: *the reshoot is scheduled for Thursday.*

rest area /'rest ,e(ə)rēə/ ▸ noun an roadside area with restrooms and other facilities for the use of motorists.

re•state /rē'stāt/ ▸ verb [trans.] state (something) again or differently, esp. in order to correct or to make more clear or convincing: *he restated his opposition to abortion* | [as modifier] *restated earnings.*
-DERIVATIVES **re•state•ment noun**

re•struc•tur•ing /rē'strəkcнəriNG/ ▸ noun Commerce a reorganization of a company with a view to achieving greater efficiency and profit, or to adapt to a changing market: *why won't the economy grow faster? Two oft-mentioned culprits: brutal corporate restructurings and slowing federal spending.* [25 **Oct.** 1993 *Business Week*]

re•sus•pend /,rēsə'spend/ ▸ verb [trans.] place (cells or particles) in suspension in a fluid again: [as modifier] *East Carolina scientists will study nutrient contribution from resuspended sediments in Neuse and Pamlico estuaries* [2002 *Water Resources Research Institute of the University of North Carolina*]
-DERIVATIVES **re•sus•pen•sion** /,rēsə'spensнən/ **noun**

re•tail park /'rētāl ,pärk/ ▸ noun a shopping development situated outside a town or city, typically containing a number of large chain stores.

re•tail ther•a•py /'rētāl ˌᴛʜerəpē/ ▸ noun humorous shopping in order to make oneself feel happier.

re•test ▸ verb rē'test [trans.] test (someone or something) again. ▸ noun /'rēˌtest/ an act of retesting someone or something: *he was freed on bond days after the retest and now is seeking a pardon.* [7 **Sept.** 2003 *Fort Worth Star Telegram*]

Ret•in-A /'retn 'ā/ ▸ noun trademark a brand of tretinoin, used in the topical treatment of acne and to reduce wrinkles.

ret•i•nal scan•ner /'retn-əl 'skanər/ ▸ noun a biometric device that scans a person's or animal's retina in infrared for identification purposes: *when I worked at Winstar, someone from another department set up a mantrap with a retinal scanner to protect the tech center.* [6 **June** 2002 *Internet Security News*]

ret•i•no•ic ac•id /'retn'ō-ik 'asid/ ▸ noun a carboxylic acid, $C_{19}H_{27}COOH$, obtained from retinol by oxidation and used in ointments to treat acne.
-ORIGIN 1970s: from *retina*.

ret•ro•dict /'retrōˌdikt/ ▸ verb [trans.] state a fact about the past based on inference or deduction, rather than evidence: *the model must be able to retrodict a very large quantity of dark matter, and say something about its composition* | *Can tree ring records be used to retrodict paleofloods?*
-DERIVATIVES **ret•ro•dic•tion** noun
-ORIGIN late 20th cent.: on the pattern of *predict*.

re•verse split /ri'vərs 'split/ ▸ noun reduction in the number of a company's traded shares that results in an increase in the par value or earnings per share.

re•writ•able /rē'rītəbəl/ ▸ adjective (of digital storage media) capable of being written to and erased multiple times: *the subsidiary's first products are a 650-megabyte rewritable, removable optical drive and a 4mm DAT tape drive.* [**Dec.** 1991 *SunWorld*]

rhyth•mic gym•nas•tics /'riᴛʜmik jim'nastiks/ ▸ plural noun [usually treated as singular] a form of gymnastics emphasizing dancelike rhythmic routines, typically accentuated by the use of ribbons or hoops.
-DERIVATIVES **rhyth•mic gym•nast** /'riᴛʜmik 'jimˌnast; -nəst/ noun

rib•it /'ribit/ ▸ **noun** the sound that a frog makes: *he began to suspect that the power of the male's commanding "ribit" came not from the throat but from vibrations in ear membranes.* [**27 Sept.** 2003 *Science News*]
-ORIGIN imitative.

RICE /rīs/ ▸ **acronym** rest, ice, compression, and elevation (treatment method for bruises, strains, and sprains).

rice burn•er /'rīs ‚bərnər/ ▸ **noun** derogatory slang a Japanese motorcycle or other motor vehicle: *Ford trucks will always kick any rice burner.* [**17 Jan 1998** Usenet: rec.autos.4x4]

rid•gy-didge /'rijē ‚dij/ ▸ **adjective** Australian informal genuine, original, or good: *a true-blue ridgy-didge Aussie.*
-ORIGIN 1950s: from *ridge*, an old slang term meaning 'gold' or 'gold coin.'

right-brained /'rīt 'brānd/ ▸ **adjective** having the right part of the brain as the dominant or more efficient part, often said to indicate creative, imaginative, and intuitive abilities: *I'm much more right-brained now and depend almost exclusively on intuition when working with horses.* [**19 Sept.** 2003 *Bend (OR) Bulletin*]

right-click /'rīt 'klik/ ▸ **verb** [intrans.] Computing depress the right-hand button on a mouse.
▸ **noun** the action of right-clicking: [as modifier] *right-click features.*
■ [trans.] click on a link or other screen object in this way: *right-click a graphic and choose Resize.*

right stuff /'rīt 'stəf/ ▸ **noun phrase** (in full **the right stuff**) the necessary qualities for a given task or job: *he had the right stuff to enter this business.*

right-to-know /'rīt tə 'nō/ ▸ **adjective** of or pertaining to laws or policies that make certain government or company records available to any individual who can demonstrate a right or need to know their contents: *environmentalists and right-to-know advocates maintain that the data posted on the Net from the EPA have not been helpful to terrorists.* [**22 Oct.** 2001 *U.S. News and World Report*]

rip /rip/ ▸ **verb** (**ripped, rip•ping**) [trans.] Computing use a program to copy (a sound sequence on a compact disc) on to a computer's hard drive. *I have every Beatles song ever made (ripped from my boxed set of CDs at a bit-rate of 192 so they sound great, I might add).* [**26 Sept.** 2003 *Mac Observer*]

rip•per /ˈripər/ ▸ **adjective** informal, chiefly Australian particularly good; excellent: *everyone had a ripper time | this record still sounds ripper.*

road•map /ˈrōdˌmap/ ▸ **verb** (**road•mapped, road•map•ping**) schedule as part of a lengthy or complex program: *originally roadmapped for an early Q4 release, the next generation of the Pentium M processor will ship in the last few days of the year.* [3 **Sept.** 2003 *Register (UK)*]

road war•ri•or /ˈrōd ˌwôrēər/ ▸ **noun** informal a person who travels often as part of their job and does work at the same time.

roam•ing /ˈrōmiNG/ ▸ **noun** [usually as modifier] the use of a cell phone outside of its local area: *the roaming charges were too high.*

rogue trad•er /ˈrōg ˌtrādər/ ▸ **noun** a securities trader who attempts to hide tremendous losses suffered on speculative trading: *the Commodity Futures Trading Commission said . . . the exchange needs to pursue rogue traders more diligently and speed its investigations.* [10 **July** 1987 *Wall Street Journal*]

roll•ing /ˈrōliNG/ ▸ **adjective** steady and continuous: *a rolling program of reforms | a rolling news service.*

Rom /rōm/ ▸ **noun** (plural **Ro•ma** /ˈrōmə/) a gypsy, especially a man.
■ [as plural noun] (**Roma**) gypsy people collectively.
–ORIGIN mid 19th cent.: abbreviation of *Romany,* the gypsy language.

rom•com /ˈrämˌkäm/ ▸ **noun** informal (in movies or television) a romantic comedy: *Mel Gibson stars in his first romcom in 10 years as Nick Marshall, a rich sexist ad exec who suddenly gains the ability to hear women's thoughts after being electrocuted.* [11 **Apr.** 2001 Usenet: rec.arts.movies.reviews]

ROM•ve•lope /ˈrämvəˌlōp/ (also **rom•ve•lope**) ▸ **noun** Computing a protective envelope or sleeve, usually made of cardboard, used to package or mail a compact disc: *you can have one of these ROMvelopes to protect your CD.*
–ORIGIN blend of *(CD-)ROM* and *(en)velope.*

rort /rôrt/ ▸ **noun** informal Australian a fraudulent or dishonest practice: *the obscene fixed-to-mobile call price rort perpetrated by Telstra.* [1 **Oct.** 2003 *Australian IT*]
▸ **verb** [trans.] defraud while remaining nominally within the law: *Zimbabwe has been suspended from the Commonwealth since March*

2002, following general elections in the African country that Mr Howard said yesterday had been "rorted". [**16 Sept.** 2003 *Melbourne Herald Sun*]

rösti /'rôstē; 'rōōsHtē/ ▸ **noun** (plural same) a Swiss dish of grated potatoes formed into a small flat cake and fried: *place 4 of the rösti in the pan.*
-ORIGIN 1950s: from Swiss German.

Roth IRA /'rôTH ˌī-är'ā; 'īrə/ ▸ **noun** an individual retirement account on which taxes are paid at the time of deposit, yielding tax-free withdrawals.

ro•ti•ni /rō'tēnē/ ▸ **noun** pasta in short pieces with a helical shape.
-ORIGIN Italian, literally 'spirals.'

round go•by /'round 'gōbē/ ▸ **noun** a Eurasian freshwater goby that threatens native species of fish in the Great Lakes and Mississippi basin.
•*Neogobius melanostomus*, family Gobiidae.

rout•ing code /'rōōtiNG ˌkōd; 'routiNG/ ▸ **noun** any of various codes used to direct data, documents, or merchandise, including: ■ the magnetically encoded numbers on a check. ■ a numeric code that directs telephone calls or Internet traffic.

rox•ar•sone /räk'sär,sōn/ ▸ **noun** an arsenic-containing antibiotic drug that is widely used as a food additive in the poultry industry to promote growth and control intestinal parasites. It is considered a source of arsenic contamination in some ground and surface water systems near large poultry producers.

RTFM ▸ **abbreviation** Computing, vulgar slang read the fucking manual (used especially in e-mail in reply to a question whose answer is patently obvious).

RTX ▸ **abbreviation** RAPID THERMAL EXCHANGE.

run-time /'rən ˌtīm/ Computing ▸ **noun 1** the length of time a program takes to run. ■ the time at which the program is run: *web services provide referenceable, configurable programming code that can be integrated at run-time to seamlessly produce flexible, dynamic applications.* [**2 Oct.** 2003 *PRNewswire (press release)*]

2 a cut-down version of a program that can be run but not changed: *you can distribute the run-time to your colleagues.*
▸ **adjective** (of software) in a reduced version that can be run but not changed.

run-time li•cense /ˈrən ˌtīm ˌlīsəns/ ▸ **noun** a relatively broad software license enabling the holder to operate software on a network and in some cases to distribute it with other products.

ru•o•te /roōˈôtā; -ˈōtā/ ▸ **noun** pasta that resembles small wheels with five spokes radiating from a hub.
-ORIGIN Italian, literally 'wheels'.

RVer /ˈärˈvēər/ ▸ **noun** a user of a recreational vehicle.

Ss

safe haven /'sāf 'hāvən/ ▸ noun **1** temporary refuge given to asylum seekers. ■ a country or area within a country where this is provided: *if they merely hunker down in the six existing misnamed safe havens, it will become impossible for them to fulfill those missions.* [6 June 1995 *Time*]
2 any area of safety in threatening conditions: *this is a precautionary measure being taken to insure that Salem County residents have a safe haven to go to during this storm emergency.* [18 Sept. 2003 *Today's Sunbeam (NJ)*]
3 another term for SAFE ROOM.

safe house /'sāf ˌhous/ ▸ noun a temporary refuge for victims of domestic abuse: *all contact with residents of the safe house is through this office; no one is given the direct phone number.*

safe room /'sāf ˌro͞om; ˌro͞om/ ▸ noun a room in a house or other building that is invulnerable to attack or intrusion, from which security operations can be directed.

sal•vage ther•a•py /'salvij ˌтHerəpē/ ▸ noun a therapeutic regimen, normally based on drugs, that is resorted to when preferred therapies have failed: *in the clinical trials, 48 percent of seriously ill patients survived one month after completing salvage therapy with trimetrexate and leucovorin.* [21 Dec. 1993 *Washington Post*]

same-store sales /'sām 'stôr ˌsālz/ ▸ noun a figure used to determine what amount of sales growth is attributable to new store openings, based on sales made by stores that have been open more than one year: *same-store sales at Sam's Club warehouse club stores were on pace for a percentage increase in the high single digits.* [29 Sept. 2003 *Reuters*]

sao•la /'soulə/ ▸ noun a small two-horned mammal discovered in Vietnam in 1992, with similarities to both antelopes and oxen. •*Pseudoryx nghetinhensis.*
–ORIGIN 1990s: a local name, literally 'spindle horn.'

sar•co•pe•ni•a /ˌsärkə'pēnēə/ ▸ noun loss of muscle tissue as a natural part of the aging process: *resistance exercises or training (also*

referred to as strength or weight training and isotonics) is needed to prevent sarcopenia. [**25 Mar.** 1997 *Baltimore Sun*]
-ORIGIN 1990s; from Greek, literally 'lack of flesh'; coined by Irwin H. Rosenberg of the USDA.

SARS /särz/ ▸ **noun** a virulently infectious disease originating in China in 2002, caused by a corona virus.
-ORIGIN 2003: initialism from *Severe Acute Respiratory Syndrome.*

sat•el•lite tel•e•vi•sion /ˈsatl͵īt ˈtelə͵vizHən/ ▸ **noun** television broadcasting using a satellite to relay signals to appropriately equipped customers in a particular area.

satt•va /ˈsətvə/ ▸ **noun** (in Ayurveda) the element or mode of prakriti associated with purity, wholesomeness, and virtue.

satt•vic /ˈsətvik/ ▸ **adjective** (in Ayurveda) denoting a class of foods that are fresh, juicy, light, nourishing, and tasty, and thus give necessary energy to the body and help achieve balance. Compare RAJASIC, TAMASIC.

save /sāv/ ▸ **noun** Computing an act of saving data to a storage location, usually the hard drive: *creating a new editing context after each save helped; now it goes up to about 13,000 records before slowing down.* [**20 June 2003** Usenet: WebObjects-dev mailing list]

sca•mor•za /skəˈmôrtsə/ ▸ **noun** a mild white Italian cheese made from cow's or buffalo's milk, produced in small gourd-shaped balls.
-ORIGIN 1930s: Italian, from *scamozzare* 'cut off.'

scan•ty /ˈskantē/ ▸ **plural noun** (**scanties**) informal women's skimpy underwear: *it's not that I have anything against pictures of women clad in their scanties (not at all!), but why choose such girlie women?* [**Sept. 1997** *Total Film (UK)*]

Scheng•en a•gree•ment /ˈsHeNGən əˌgrēmənt/ **noun** an intergovernmental agreement on the relaxation of border controls between participating European countries. The ratified agreement was incorporated into the European Union in 1999 and the agreement was widened to include non-EU members of a similar Nordic union. Member countries now comprise Austria, Belgium, Denmark, France, Finland, Germany, Greece, Iceland, Italy, Luxembourg, the Netherlands, Norway, Portugal, Spain, and Sweden.

schiz•an•dra /skit'sandrə/ ▸ noun a Chinese herb whose berries are credited with various stimulant or medicinal properties. •*Schisandra chinensis*, family Magnoliaceae.
–ORIGIN mid 19th cent.: modern Latin *Schisandra*, formed as *schizo-* + Greek *andr-*, *anēr* man, on account of the divided stamens.

schli•ma•zel /sHlə'mäzəl/ (also **schle•ma•zel**) ▸ noun informal a consistently unlucky or accident-prone person.
–ORIGIN Yiddish, from Middle High German *slim* 'crooked' + Hebrew *mazzāl* 'luck.'

scis•sor•bill /'sizər,bil/ ▸ noun informal an incompetent or objectionable person: *we've had mixed success over in the eastern district, but they're a bunch of scissorbills anyway.* [1990 J. Welch, *Indian Lawyer*]

scrap•book /'skrap,bŏŏk/ ▸ verb [intrans.] [usually as noun] (**scrapbooking**) create scrapbooks as a hobby: *that site has all the supplies you need for scrapbooking.* | *I do all kinds of crafting and have scrapbooked for several years.*
–DERIVATIVES **scrap•book•er** noun

scrat•chi•ti /skra'cHētē/ ▸ plural noun [treated as singular or plural] graffiti that is scratched or etched onto a surface, usually glass: *names immortalized with scratchiti on the subway car window.*
–ORIGIN blend of *scratch* and *graffiti*.

screen•ag•er /'skrēn,ājər/ ▸ noun informal a person in their teens or twenties who has an aptitude for computers and the Internet: *today's "screenager"—the child born into a culture mediated by the television and computer—is interacting with his world in at least as dramatically altered a fashion from his grandfather as the first sighted creature did from his blind ancestors.* [1996 D. Rushkoff, *Playing the Future*]
–ORIGIN 1990s: blend of *screen* and *teenager*.

script kid•die /'skript ,kidē/ ▸ noun informal, derogatory a person who uses existing computer scripts or codes to hack into computers, lacking the expertise to write their own: *he threatened to strike others when they called him a "script kiddie," a know-nothing hacker.* [13 Sept. 2003 *Wired News*]

seal•coat•ing /'sēl,kōtiNG/ ▸ noun the application of a sealing coat to a paved surface in order to prolong its integrity: *the Commissioners voted to reject all bids for sealcoating the parking lots at the Gov-*

ernment Services Center. [23 **Sept.** 2003 *Holmes (PA) Media Town Talk News*]
–DERIVATIVES **seal•coat verb** *How soon can I sealcoat freshly laid asphalt?*

sec•ond growth /'sekənd 'grōTH/ ▸ **noun** woodland growth that replaces harvested or burned virgin forest.
▸ **adjective** denoting a wine considered to be the second-best in quality compared to the first growth (premier cru).

sec•ond•hand speech /'sekən(d),hand 'spēCH/ ▸ **noun** conversation on a cell phone that is overheard by people nearby: *I was alternately amused and annoyed by the secondhand speech in the waiting room.*

se•cret shop•per /'sēkrit 'SHäpər/ ▸ **noun** a person employed by a manufacturer or retailer to pose as a shopper in order to evaluate the quality of customer service. Also called MYSTERY SHOPPER: *every Kwik Trip store is also visited by a secret shopper 36 times a year.* [17 **Sept.** 2003 *Chetek (WI) Alert*]

se•cure serv•er /si'kyo͞or 'sərvər/ ▸ **noun** an Internet server that encrypts confidential information supplied by visitors to Web pages.

se•cu•ri•ty patch /si'kyo͝orite ,paCH/ ▸ **noun** a software or operating-system patch that is intended to correct a vulnerability to hacking or viral infection: *Swen (also known as Gibe-F or Gibe-C) traveled during September attached to an e-mail purporting to be a security patch from Microsoft support.* [8 **Oct.** 2003 *Search Security*]

Seg•way /'seg,wā/ ▸ **trademark** a two-wheeled motorized personal vehicle consisting of a platform for the feet mounted above an axle and an upright post surmounted by handles.

sei•tan /'sā,tan/ ▸ **noun** a high-protein vegetarian food made from processed wheat gluten: *a recipe for homemade seitan is included, but it seems too labor intensive for me.* [16 **Oct.** 2003 *Washington Post*]

se•lect /sə'lekt/ ▸ **verb** [mainly trans.] Computers highlight text or data on a screen, using the cursor or key combinations: *hold down the Ctrl key on your keyboard, and single-click on other entries you wish to select.* [27 **Apr.** 2001 *Printing Selected Records in CardScan*]

se•lec•tion /sə'leksHən/ ▸ **noun** Computers data highlighted on a computer screen that is a target for various manipulations: *the macro finds the text I told it to search for but it's not part of my original selection.* [**6 May 1999** Usenet: microsoft.public.vc.ide_general]
■ the activity or capability of selecting data in this way.

self-se•lect /ˌself sə'lekt/ ▸ **verb 1** choose for oneself: [trans.] *participants were asked to self select their titles which were divided into executive and non-executive.* [**25 Sept. 2003** *Globe and Mail (Canada)*] **2** [intrans.] determine one's own status with regard to membership in a group: *This isn't a place where tired traders should pitch up in pinstripes. The clientele is deeply stylish. "The crowd self-selects because this isn't a club for the passing trade," as Remzi puts it.* [**21 Aug. 1996** *Times (UK)*]
▸ **adjective** allowing users to select: *two years ago, Boots decided to move condoms from the pharmacy counter to self-select stands.* [**3 Aug. 1992** *Independent (UK)*]

self-stick /'self 'stik/ ▸ **adjective** coated with an adhesive on one side for ready application to a surface: *peel off the self-stick backing and attach to either side.*

sell•down /'selˌdoun/ ▸ **noun** widespread selling of futures, securities, or commodities, triggered by or resulting in falling prices: *that could provoke a selldown of banking stocks which, in turn, would further depress sentiment on a bourse that's dropped almost 20% over 2000.* [**8 Feb. 2001** *Far Eastern Economic Review*]

se•mes•ter•ly /sə'mestərlē/ ▸ **adjective** happening or appearing once per academic semester: *if students don't catch on through fliers and orientation, laws and fines may be added onto semesterly expenses.* [**24 Sept. 2003** *(CA State Univeristy) Orion*]

sen•si•tiv•i•ty train•ing /ˌsensi'tivitē ˌtrāniNG/ ▸ **noun** training intended to sensitize people to their attitudes and behaviors that may unwittingly cause offense to others, especially members of various minorities.

se•quence /'sēkwəns/ ▸ **verb** play or record (music) with a sequencer: *precocious Performer users were sequencing away on Macs two years earlier.* [**Apr. 1990** *Music Technology (UK)*]

se•quenc•ing /'sēkwənsiNG/ ▸ **noun 1** the practice of moving in and out of the workforce, especially in order to spend time caring for

one's young children: *more women than ever are sequencing, and companies are finding innovative ways to recruit them when they're ready to come back to work.*
2 the determination of the order of genes in a genome or on a chromosome: [as modifier] *J. Craig Venter, who gained fame when he shared credit in 2001 for "spelling out" the entire sequence of the human genome, led the dog sequencing effort.* [**5 Oct.** 2003 *Dallas Morning News*]

se•ri•al port /ˈsi(ə)rēəl ˈpôrt/ ▶ **noun** a connector for a peripheral device that sends bits sequentially, one at a time. Compare PARALLEL PORT.

se•ro•prev•a•lence /ˌsi(ə)rōˈprevələns/ ▶ **noun** the percentage of a population that tests positive for a particular infection: *17.7 percent seroprevalence* | [as modifier] *a history of sexually transmitted diseases and unsafe behaviors associated with enhanced sexual activity are the biggest risk factors for HIV infection, an eight-year seroprevalence and genetic surveillance program shows.* [**6 Oct.** 2003 *Doctor's Guide (press release)*]
–DERIVATIVES **se•ro•prev•a•lent** adjective

serv•ice e•con•o•my /ˈsərvis iˌkänəmē/ ▶ **noun** an economy or the sector of an economy that is based on trade in services: *the African deliveryman is one of the lowest-paid workers in New York's service economy, filling a niche that pampered city dwellers have come to depend on for their daily bread.* [**10 Nov.** 1999 *New York Times*]

serv•ice pack /ˈsərvis ˌpak/ ▶ **noun** (abbreviation **SP**) a periodically released update to software from a manufacturer, consisting of requested enhancements and fixes to known bugs: *I had to update XP to Service Pack 1 for WebInspect to run.* [**28 Sept.** 2003 *Australian Reseller News*]

serv•let /ˈsərvlit/ ▶ **noun** a small, server-resident program that typically runs automatically in response to user input: *students will learn to maximize Web application productivity by building servlets that generate Web pages, retrieve information, process data, communicate with applets, and communicate with other Java servers.*

set play /ˈset ˌplā/ ▶ **noun** Sports a prearranged maneuver carried out from a restart or after a time out by the team that has the advantage: *then the Germans scored the deciding goal on a set play, off a corner kick in the 15th minute.* [**6 Oct.** 2003 *New York Daily News*]

sew•age sludge /'sōōij ˌsləj/ ▸ noun semi-liquid waste obtained from the processing of municipal sewage, often used as a fertilizer: *nutrients are defined to include litter, compost, commercially manufactured chemical or organic fertilizers, sewage sludge, or combinations thereof.* [**15 Oct.** 2003 *Berryville (AR) Star Progress*]

sex•ile /'sekˌsīl/ ▸ verb [trans.] deny (a roommate) access in order to engage in private sexual activity: *there is a tie, sock, hat or some other article of clothing on the doorknob, meaning your roommate had a far more rewarding evening than you. You, my friend, have been "sexiled."* [**16 Sept.** 2003 *(University of Maryland) Diamondback*]

sex in•dus•try /'seks ˌindəstrē/ ▸ noun (**the sex industry**) prostitution, pornography, and other activities in which money is exchanged for sexual gratification: *the government has expressed concern that young textile factory workers who lost their jobs will be lured to work in the sex industry.* [**8 Oct.** 2003 *Bharat (India) Textile*]

sex work•er /'seks ˌwərkər/ ▸ noun one who earns income in the sex industry: *by decriminalizing prostitution . . . and treating sex workers more like hands-on sex therapists, the prostitute's spiritual status in society will be reclaimed, empowering not only whores but also women in general.* [**July 1991** *Utne Reader*]

shad•ow e•con•o•my /'sHadō iˌkänəmē/ ▸ noun illicit economic activity existing alongside a country's official economy, e.g., black market transactions and undeclared work.

shah•toosh /sHä'tōōsH/ ▸ noun high-quality wool from the neck hair of the Himalayan ibex. ■ a shawl made from this.
–ORIGIN Punjabi, ultimately from Persian.

shak•en ba•by syn•drome /'sHākən 'bābē ˌsindrōm/ ▸ noun injury to a baby caused by being shaken violently and repeatedly.

shape-mem•o•ry /'sHāp ˌmem(ə)rē/ ▸ noun the ability of a material to be deformed and then returned to its original shape when stimulated, as by heat.

shed•load /'sHedˌlōd/ ▸ noun British informal a large amount or number: *had she decided to show them by joining a rival, she would doubtless be causing them embarrassment today and earning a shedload of money.* [**1 Oct.** 2002 *Daily Telegraph (UK)*]
–ORIGIN 1990s: from *shed* + *load*; perhaps euphemistic after *shitload*.

shelf-sta•ble /'sHelf ˌstābəl/ ▸ **adjective** able to survive long periods on store or home shelves without spoiling: *a growing number of dairy-based beverages are shelf-stable and can be stored in the pantry rather than the refrigerator.*

shel•tered work•shop /'sHeltərd 'wərkˌsHäp/ ▸ **noun** a supervised workplace for physically disabled or mentally handicapped adults.

Shi•ga tox•in /'sHēgə ˌtäksin/ ▸ **noun** a toxin produced by certain strains of the bacterium *E. coli* that is pathogenic in humans: *during infection there are changes of cytokine levels that can be ascribed to an effect of Shiga toxin on different cell types.*
–ORIGIN about 2000: the name arose when it was discovered that the toxin was virtually indistinguishable in both structure and function from the toxin produced by *Shigella dysenteriae*, which was in turn named for Japanese scientist Kiyoshi *Shiga* (1870–1957).

shi•so /'sHēsō/ ▸ **noun** the Japanese name for the culinary herb PER-ILLA.

shit•can /'sHitˌkan/ ▸ **verb** (**shit•canned, shit•can•ning**) vulgar slang [trans.] throw (something) away: *rip up those pictures and shitcan the negatives.*
■ discard or reject (someone or something): *it's hard to shitcan someone who keeps winning writing awards.*

shit•load /'sHitˌlōd/ ▸ **noun** vulgar slang a large amount or number: *I have a shitload of work to do this week.*
–ORIGIN 1960s: from *shit* + *load*.

shock cord /'sHäk ˌkôrd/ ▸ **noun** a bungee cord or other elastic cord with hooks at either end: *balance the tension of the shock cords to set the tiller angle.* [**30 Oct. 1998** *San Juan 23 Technical Tips*]

shoot•ist /'sHo͞otist/ ▸ **noun** informal a person who shoots, especially a marksman: *a House of Representatives sworn to uphold the right of every "shootist" to fire at will.* [**27 Jan 1992** *Nation*]
–ORIGIN mid 19th cent.: from *shoot* + *-ist*.

shop•grift•ing /'sHäpˌgriftiNG/ ▸ **noun** the practice of buying an item, using it, and then returning it for a full refund.

short-hand•ed /'sHôrt 'handid/ ▸ **adjective** Ice Hockey (of a goal) scored by a team playing with fewer players on the ice than their opponent. ■ Ice Hockey (of a situation) occurring while or because a team has fewer than six players on the ice.

shrap•nel /'sHrapnǝl/ ▸ noun slang small change: *"What say we pick up a couple of beers?" "Sure. Want some shrapnel?"*

shrug /sHrǝg/ ▸ noun a woman's close-fitting cardigan or jacket, cut short at the front and back so that only the arms and shoulders are covered: *the shrug is, basically, two sleeves sewn together to make a cut-away cardigan with half a back and no front.* [**23 Apr. 1999** *Guardian (UK)*]

shu•mai /'sHōō,mī/ ▸ plural noun small steamed dumplings, typically stuffed with seafood and vegetables.
-ORIGIN Japanese, ultimately from Chinese.

sick /sik/ ▸ adjective slang excellent: *I'm listening to a sick new remix.*

sight•hound /'sīt,hound/ ▸ noun a hound originally bred to hunt independently from humans, such as a greyhound or a whippet.

sil•den•a•fil cit•rate /sil'denǝ,fil 'si,trāt/ ▸ noun the chemical name for Viagra; it is an off-white crystalline powder that works by inhibiting the breakdown of enzymes that lead to loss of erection.

si•lent com•merce /'sīlǝnt 'kämǝrs/ ▸ noun a group of technologies based on wireless communications and sensing devices that permit various business and marketing activities to proceed without direct human intervention, on the basis of communications between tagged products and controlling software.

silk tree /'silk ˌtrē/ ▸ noun an ornamental tree of the pea family with fernlike leaves and showy pink plumelike flowers that open in midsummer; naturalized in most of the eastern U.S.
•*Albizia julibrissin*, family Fabaceae.

SIM /sim/ (also **SIM card** /'sim ˌkärd/) ▸ noun a smart card inside a cell phone, carrying an identification number unique to the owner, storing personal data, and preventing operation if removed.
-ORIGIN 1980s: acronym from *subscriber identification module.*

si•mul•se•quel•ing /'sīmǝl,sēkwǝliNG/ ▸ noun the practice of writing or filming two or more sequels simultaneously: *the simulsequeling of popular movies usually pays off because of reduced production costs.*
-ORIGIN blend of *simultaneous* and *sequel.*

sin•gle cur•ren•cy /'siNGgəl 'kərənsē; 'kə-rənsē/ ▸ **noun** a currency used by all the members of an economic federation.

▪ (also **single European currency**) the currency (the euro) that replaced the national currencies of twelve member states of the European Union in 2002.

sin•gle nu•cle•o•tide pol•y•mor•phism /'siNGgəl 'n(y)o͞oklēə,tīd ˌpälē'môr,fizəm/ ▸ **noun** a variation in a single base pair in a DNA sequence.

sit•u•a•tion•ism /ˌsiCHo͞o'āSHə,nizəm/ ▸ **noun** a revolutionary political theory that regards modern industrial society as being inevitably oppressive and exploitative.
-DERIVATIVES **sit•u•a•tion•ist** noun & adjective

size•ism /'sīz,izəm/ ▸ **noun** prejudice or discrimination on the grounds of a person's size: *requiring large passengers to buy two seats is pure sizeism.*
-DERIVATIVES **size•ist** adjective

skank /skaNGk/ ▸ **verb** [trans.] slang swindle or deceive: *they made a tidy sum skanking the tourists.*
▪ obtain by deception or theft: *I skanked the poster off some wall.*
▸ **noun** a promiscuous woman: *After making out with coworker (and, as she finds out, junkie) Zach at the annual Peterman party, Elaine pretends to be his girlfriend to avoid the label of "office skank."* [4 **May 1998** *Entertainment Weekly*]

skell /skel/ ▸ **noun** informal (in New York) a tramp or homeless person: *someone noted that the number of skells who use the existing passageway, along the west side of the Herald Square station, is a pretty good reason why it would be unwise to reopen the 33rd Street one.* [4 **Mar. 1998** Usenet: nyc.transit]
-ORIGIN 1980s: perhaps a shortening of *skeleton.*

skim•ming /'skimiNG/ ▸ **noun** the fraudulent copying of credit or debit card details with a card swipe or other device.

skin /skin/ ▸ **noun** Computing a customized graphic user interface for an application or operating system: *the offerings here include music, reviews and attitude all wrapped up in the skin of a catalog.* [**Aug. 1996** *Internet Underground*]

SKU /sko͞o/ ▸ **abbreviation** stock-keeping unit; a bar-encoded number that uniquely identifies a retail product: [as modifier] *consumers also* *can enter a SKU number from the book in a Quick Shop box online and quickly buy the item.* [**25 Sept.** 2003 *DM News (NY)*]

slam /slam/ ▸ verb (**slammed, slam•ming**) [trans.] [usually as noun **slamming**] (of a telephone company) take over the account of (a telephone customer) without their permission.

sleep•er cell /ˈslēpər ˌsel/ ▸ noun a secretive group with suspected links to a terrorist organization that is planning or believed capable of carrying out an attack: *even as they work to understand how the arrested militants are connected, governments are frantically trying to uncover any other "sleeper" cells to prevent further attacks.* [**29 Oct.** 2001 *U.S. News and World Report*]

SLV ▸ abbreviation standard launch vehicle; and of a number of vehicles for launching rockets and weapons, typically distinguished by a number following the abbreviation.

smart card /ˈsmärt ˌkärd/ ▸ noun a plastic card with a built-in microprocessor, used typically to perform financial transactions: *you can use your smart card at any store on campus.*

smart dust /ˈsmärt ˌdəst/ ▸ noun a collection of microelectromechanical systems forming a simple computer in a container light enough to remain suspended in air, used mainly for information gathering in environments that are hostile to life: *cubic-millimeter specks of "smart dust" that, like slime molds, self-organize into amorphous, calculating swarms.* [**Jan.** 2000 *Wired*]

smart mob /ˈsmärt ˌmäb/ ▸ noun a group of people who assemble, move, or act collectively by using cell phones or other wireless devices to communicate: *smart mobs, moving from party to party with each new reported celebrity sighting.*

smart su•ture /ˈsmärt ˌsoōCHər/ ▸ noun a surgical suture made of biodegradable plastic that ties itself into a knot on the basis of its shape-memory.

smash-mouth /ˈsmasH ˌmouTH/ ▸ adjective & adverb Sports (of a style of play) aggressive and confrontational: *we're coming into this game ready to play smash-mouth because we know that's the type of game it's going to be.* [**9 Oct.** 2003 *Houston Chronicle*]

SME ▸ abbreviation small to medium-sized enterprise, a company with no more than 500 employees.

smoke•eas•y /'smōk,ēzē/ (also **smoke-eas•y**) ▸ noun (plural **-eas•ies**) a private club, bar, or other place where smokers gather to avoid anti-smoking laws: *after work we sometimes light up at a smokeeasy in the neighborhood.*
-ORIGIN on the pattern of *speakeasy.*

smok•ing /'smōkiNG/ ▸ adjective (often **smok•in'** /'smōkin/) informal lively and exciting: *he claimed the band would be smokin' but they were lame.*

SMPTE /'simtē/ ▸ abbreviation Society of Television and Motion Picture Engineers (used to denote a time coding system for synchronizing video and audiotapes).

SMS ▸ abbreviation Short Message (or Messaging) Service, a system that enables cell phone users to send and receive text messages.

snack•ette /sna'ket/ ▸ noun **1** a very small amount of food.
2 Caribbean English a roadside outlet for fast food.

snake•board /'snāk,bôrd/ ▸ noun trademark a type of skateboard consisting of two footplates joined by a bar, allowing for greater speed and maneuverability than with a standard skateboard.
-DERIVATIVES **snake•board•er** noun; **snake•board•ing** noun
-ORIGIN 1990s: blend of *snake* and *skateboard.*

snake•head /'snāk,hed/ ▸ noun **1** a member of a Chinese criminal network chiefly engaged in smuggling illegal immigrants. [ORIGIN: translation of Chinese *shetou*]
2 the NORTHERN SNAKEHEAD, or a closely related fish.

snert /snərt/ ▸ noun Computing informal a participant in an Internet chat room who acts in a rude, annoying, or juvenile manner: *I could tell he was a snert from his sarcastic comments.* ■ a person whose online posts or e-mails are annoying to others: *do you ever get unsolicited messages from snerts?*
-ORIGIN of uncertain origin, possibly an initialism from *snot-nosed egotistical rude twit* (or *teenager*).

SNP /snip/ ▸ abbreviation SINGLE NUCLEOTIDE POLYMORPHISM: *Altshuler and his colleagues first analyzed their 16 SNPs in 333 parent-offspring trios in which the offspring has type II diabetes—or impending signs of the disease—but the parents don't. The results suggested that just two of the SNPs influence diabetes risk.* [**9 Sept. 2000** *Science News*]

so /sō/ ▸ adverb informal used to emphasize a clause or negative statement: *that's so not fair* | *you are so going to regret this.*

so•ba /'sōbə/ ▶noun thin buckwheat noodles, used in Japanese cooking.
-ORIGIN Japanese.

soc•cer mom /'säkər ˌmäm/ ▶noun informal a middle-class suburban housewife, typically having children who play soccer.

so•cial pro•mo•tion /'sōSHəl prə'mōSHən/ ▶ noun the practice of promoting a child to the next grade level regardless of skill mastery in the belief that it will encourage self-esteem.

so•ci•o•ge•no•mics /ˌsōsēōjē'nämiks; -ji-; -'nōmiks/ ▶noun a scientific discipline that attempts to find the genetic basis of social behavior and its evolution: *Robinson's presentation on the genetic basis of behavior in honey bees and the new science of sociogenomics will review pioneering work, present exciting new discoveries, and provide a great introduction to one of our featured symposia.* [**July** 2003 *Entomological Society of America newsletter*]

soft-fo•cus /'sôft 'fōkəs/ ▶ adjective denoting a point of view or style of presentation that obscures or avoids sharp definition in order to be more widely acceptable: *a gig producing soft-focus, nonpolitical essays about American life.* [**27 Apr. 1998** *Time*]

soft land•ing /'sôft 'landiNG/ ▶noun a result that is the best that can be expected in the resolution of a fraught situation: [as modifier] *that certainly would be the perfect soft-landing scenario from a housing construction sector that's overheated.* [**29 Sept.** 2003 *ABC Online (Australia)*]

so•go•sho•sha /ˌsōgə'sōSHə/ ▶ noun (in Japan) a general trading company involved in import and export.
-ORIGIN Japanese 'integrated trading company.'

SOHO /'sōˌhō/ ▶ adjective relating to a market for relatively inexpensive consumer electronics used by individuals and small companies: *an all-in-one personal server designed to help consumers and SOHO professionals easily protect, remotely access and share their digital files.* [**7 Oct.** 2003 *PRNewswire (press release)*]
-ORIGIN 1990s: acronym from *small office home office.*

sor•ta•tion /sôr'tāSHən/ ▶ noun (especially in data processing) the process of sorting or its result.

south /souTH/ ▶ verb phrase see at GO SOUTH.

soy•bean meal /'soi‚bēn ‚mēl/ ▸ noun SOYMEAL.

soy•meal /'soi‚mēl/ (also **soy•bean meal** /'soi‚bēn ‚mēl/) ▸ noun a high-protein foodstuff made by cracking, heating, flaking, cooking, and grinding soybeans. It is used in livestock feeds and as a raw ingredient in some processed foods.

soy•milk /'soi‚milk/ ▸ noun a beverage with the approximate color and consistency of milk, made from cooked soybeans and used as a nondairy milk substitute.

SP ▸ abbreviation SERVICE PACK (usually followed by a number): *options within the code enable an attacker to specifically target either Windows 2000 SP3 and SP4.* [**2 Oct. 2003** *TechWeb News*]

spa•gy•ric /spə'ji(ə)rik/ ▸ adjective relating to alchemy: *the production of a spagyric tincture is the first and easiest of all operations.* [**29 Dec. 2002** Usenet: alt.drugs.salvia]
▸noun an alchemist.
–ORIGIN late 16th cent.: modern Latin *spagiricus*, used and probably invented by Paracelsus.

spawn /spôn/ ▸ verb [trans.] gencrate (a dependent or subordinate computer process): *from time to time it spawns two copies of the ip-up program, other times only one.* [**30 May 1997** Usenet: comp.os.-linux.networking]

speech rec•og•ni•tion /'spēCH ‚rekəg‚niSHən/ ▸ noun the process of enabling a computer to identify and respond to the sounds produced in human speech: [often as modifier] *a contact center automation solution using speech recognition technologies to streamline customer service.* [**30 Sept. 2003** *Destination CRM*]

speed bag /'spēd ‚bag/ ▸ noun a small punching bag used by boxers for practicing quick punches.

speed dat•ing /'spēd ‚dātiNG/ ▸ noun a social activity in which equal complements of potential partners spend a few minutes in short interviews with all other participants in order to determine whether there is mutual interest: [as modifier] *Dave, a welder, and Jamie, a medical assistant and model, were married in January after meeting on a radio station speed dating game.* [**3 Oct. 2003** *Arizona Republic*]

speed di•al /'spēd ‚dī(ə)l/ ▸ noun a function on some telephones that allows numbers to be entered into a memory and dialed using fewer buttons.

▸**verb** (**speed-dial**) [trans.] dial (a telephone number) by using the speed dial function.

spi•der /'spīdər/ ▸ **noun 1** a long-legged rest for a billiard cue that can be placed over a ball without touching it.
2 Computing a program that searches and indexes the World Wide Web.

spin•mei•ster /'spin,mīster/ ▸ **noun** informal an accomplished or politically powerful spin doctor: *not even the best political spinmeister could parse the president's meaning any other way.* [**8 Oct.** 2003 *Baltimore Sun*]
-ORIGIN 1990s: from *spin* + *-meister.*

spin•tron•ics /,spin'träniks/ ▸ **noun** [with a singular verb] a field of electronics in which electron spin is manipulated to yield a desired outcome: *most researchers in the field have the same distant goal: using spintronics to build computers that take advantage of the bizarre all-possibilities-at-once nature of quantum mechanics to perform divergent calculations simultaneously.* [**25 Apr.** 2002 Infosatellite.com]
-DERIVATIVES **spin•tron•ic** adjective: *a spintronic transistor that could play a major role in the quest for quantum computing.*

spi•ru•li•na /,spīrə'līnə/ ▸ **noun** any of various blue-green algae (mainly *Spirulina pratensis*), regarded as superfoods for their high content of amino acids, minerals, and vitamins.

spokes•mod•el /'spōks,mädl/ ▸ **noun** informal an attractive, elegant, and stylishly dressed person who appears in advertising: [as modifier] *with its spokesmodel anchors and stand-up weather comics, C-SPAN has had the visionary courage to opt out entirely and chuck the -tainment.* [**June 1991** *Mirabella*]

spoon /spo͞on/ ▸ **verb** [intrans.] (of two people) lie close together sideways and front to back with bent knees, so as to fit together like spoons.

spot•ted knap•weed /'spätid 'nap,wēd/ ▸ **noun** a biennial herb of European origin with pink flowers on prickly stems. It is established across most of N. America and is regarded as a noxious weed nearly everywhere.
•*Centaurea biebersteinii*, family Compositae.

SSL ▸ **abbreviation** Secure Sockets Layer, a computing protocol that ensures the security of data sent via the Internet by using encryption.

stab•bing /'stabiNG/ ▸ noun an act or instance of wounding or killing someone with a knife: *the fatal stabbings of four women.*

stage-div•ing /'stāj ˌdīviNG/ ▸ noun the practice (typically among audience members) of jumping from the stage at a rock concert or other event to be caught and carried aloft by the crowd below.
-DERIVATIVES **stage-dive** verb; **stage-div•er** noun

stained-glass ceil•ing /'stānd ˌglas 'sēliNG/ ▸ noun [usually in sing]
1 an unofficially acknowledged barrier faced by women who want to enter or be promoted within the clergy: *a stained-glass ceiling prevents more women from becoming rabbis.*
2 a discriminatory barrier that prevents a person from advancing in any field because of religious beliefs: *Roman-Catholic candidates are often at a disadvantage because of a stained-glass ceiling.*
-ORIGIN on the pattern of *glass ceiling.*

stair•climb•er /'ste(ə)r,klīmər/ ▸ noun an exercise machine on which the user simulates the action of climbing a staircase.

stake•hold•er /'stāk,hōldər / ▸ noun an interested party; one who holds a stake in something: *many companies . . . are responding innovatively to the changing demands of their customers, employees, stockholders, and other stakeholders.* [July 1991 *Utne Reader*]
USAGE: The traditional sense of stakeholder, "one who holds the stakes of bettors," has now been largely eclipsed by this more modern meaning.

stalk•er•az•zi /ˌstôkə'rätsē/ ▸ plural noun photojournalists who follow celebrities closely and persistently with the intention of obtaining sensational pictures.

stand•by /'stan(d),bī/ ▸ noun (plural **stand•bys**) an operational mode of an electrical appliance in which the power is switched on but the appliance is not actually functioning.

star•burst gal•ax•y /'stär,bərst ˌgaləksē/ ▸ noun a galaxy with very active star formation at its core that can dramatically alter the overall properties of the galaxy: *Chandra images also suggest that these black holes may be sinking to the center of one particular starburst galaxy, where they would merge with each other to create an engine that could illuminate a core millions of times brighter than the entire Milky Way galaxy.* [2003 NASA Web site]

stat•in /'statn/ ▸ noun Medicine any of a group of drugs that act to reduce levels of fats, including tryglicerides and cholesterol, in the blood.
–ORIGIN 1980s: from *stat-* + *in*.

sta•tus bar /'statəs ˌbär; 'stātəs/ ▸ noun Computing a horizontal bar, typically at the bottom of the screen or window, showing information about a document being edited or the currently active programs.

stench war•fare /'stenCH ˌwôrfe(ə)r/ ▸ noun the use of highly offensive odors to sicken, immobilize, or drive away an enemy: *they are hoping to win a big contract for their innovations in stench warfare.*

ste•roid /'sterˌoid; 'sti(ə)r-/ ▸ noun 1 short or informal for ANABOLIC STEROID
2 (**on sterioids**) used to suggest a highly exaggerated, enhanced, or accelerated version of something: *the dessert Avril serves when Hal's over is Mrs. Clarke's infamous high-protein-gelatin squares, available in bright red or bright green, sort of like Jell-O on steroids.* [1996 DJ.F. Wallace, *Infinite Jest*]

ste•vi•a /'stēvēə/ ▸ noun a composite herb native to Asia (Genus *Stevia*, especially *S. rebaudiana*) whose leaves are the source of a noncaloric sweetener.
■ a food supplement prepared from this, used as a sweetener.

stick•built (also **stick-built**) /'stikˌbilt/ ▸ adjective (of houses or other buildings) built piece-by-piece on the premises, rather than constructed from prefabricated units: *my guess is that 80% of the public would not even be able to tell if a home were modular or stickbuilt.* [19 June 2003 Usenet: alt.home.repair]

stick•y /'stikē/ ▸ adjective (**stick•i•er, stick•i•est**) informal (of a Web site) attracting a long visit or repeat visits from users: *experts measure the attractiveness of pages by how sticky they are.*

stock•feed /'stäkˌfēd/ ▸ noun food for livestock: *farmers are looking at industrial hemp as an opportunity to tap into a new industry, producing material, paper, rope, fuel, oil and stockfeed.* [22 Sept. 2003 *ABC (Australia) News Online*]

stock swap /'stäk ˌswäp/ ▸ noun 1 acquisition of a company in which payment consists of stock in the buying company: *Brands Corp. acquired the 15% of FTD.com Inc. it didn't already own in a stock swap.* [6 oct. 2003 *Smart Money*]

2 a means of exercising stock options in which shares already owned are traded for a greater number of shares at the exercise price.

sto•len gen•er•a•tion /ˈstōlən ˌjenəˈrāsHən/ ▸ **noun** Australian the Aboriginal people forcibly removed from their families as children between the 1900s and the 1960s, to be brought up by white foster families or in institutions.

storm•ing /ˈstôrmiNG/ ▸ **adjective** mainly British excellent: *my grades are absolutely storming at the moment, so I can get away with anything.* [**1997** H. H. Tan, *Foreign Bodies*]

sto•ry /ˈstôrē/ ▸ **noun** (plural **sto•ries**) the commercial prospects or circumstances of a particular company: *profitable businesses with solid stories.*

strange /strānj/ ▸ **adjective** Physics having a non-zero value for strangeness, one of the six values of quarks.

stream•ing /ˈstrēmiNG/ ▸ **noun** a method of relaying data (especially video and audio material) over a computer network as a steady continuous stream: *streaming means that the first part of the audio file is saved in memory, then played while the rest of the soundfile is simultaneously downloading.* [**May 1997** *Creative Technology (UK)*] ▸ **adjective** (of data) transmitted in a continuous stream: *adding streaming audio, video or data to a site is not brain surgery.* [**Nov. 1996** *Web Developer*]

street-leg•al /ˈstrēt ˌlēgəl/ ▸ **adjective** (of a vehicle) meeting all legal requirements for use on ordinary roads: *he was racing head-to-head with some of the fastest street legal cars in the Vortech Xtreme class.* [**9 Oct. 2003** *Oshkosh (WI) Northwestern*]

string•er /ˈstriNGər/ ▸ **noun** [in combination] a reserve sports player holding a specified position in an order of preference: *six of the team's 24 first-stringers are Canadian.*

struc•tured set•tle•ment /ˈstrəkCHərd ˈsetlmənt/ ▸ **noun** a legal settlement paid out as an annuity rather than in a lump sum, usually with certain tax advantages for the recipient and a savings for the payer.

stud•muf•fin /'stəd,məfin/ ▸ noun informal a man perceived as sexually attractive, typically one with well-developed muscles: *the courageous men had modeled for the first-ever "Studmuffins of Science" calendar.* [**Jan. 1996** *Scientific American*]

stut•ter tone /'stətər ,tōn/ ▸ noun a dialtone interrupted by several short gaps; it indicates the arrival of new voicemail messages to the user: *if you are unable to clear the stutter tone by retrieving your messages, try adding commas in front of the phone number you are dialing.*

sub•sense /'səb ,sens/ ▸ noun a subsidiary sense of a word defined in a dictionary.

sub•type /'səb,tīp/ ▸ noun a secondary or subordinate type.
■ a subdivision of a type of microorganism: *among United States military personnel, HIV-1 infections reflect a diverse range of non-B subtypes, a military study reveals.* [**6 Oct. 2003** *Doctor's Guide (press release)*]

sub•web /'səb,web/ ▸ noun an isolated part of a Web site, especially one that is password protected or that is not obviously accessible from the main page: *the hit counter will not work in a subweb on a Netscape Enterprise NT.* [**2000** Microsoft Support Knowledge Base]

su•i•cide gene /'sōōəsīd ,jēn/ ▸ noun an introduced gene that causes a tumor cell to produce an enzyme that will attract a lethal drug.

su•ma•trip•tan /,sōōmə'trip,tan/ ▸ noun a serotonin-agonist drug used for the acute treatment of migraine.

su•per•cell /'sōōpər,sel/ ▸ noun Meteorology a system producing severe thunderstorms and featuring rotating winds sustained by a prolonged updraft that may result in hail or tornadoes: [as modifier] *large, supercell thunderstorms in Nebraska and South Dakota formed a boundary of dry air to the west and wet air to the east.* [**10 Oct. 2003** *Casper (WY) Star Tribune*]

su•per•food /'sōōpər,fōōd/ ▸ noun (not in technical use) a natural food regarded as especially beneficial because of its nutrient profile or its health-protecting qualities: [as modifier] *blueberries have reached "superfood" status since US scientists discovered that they are a powerhouse of anthocyanins.* [**3 Mar. 1998** *Independent (UK)*]

su•per•fund /'so͞opər‚fənd/ ▸ noun a fund established to finance a long-term, expensive project.
■ **(Superfund)** a U.S. government program designed to fund the cleanup of toxic wastes: *billions have been spent on Superfund since 1980.*

su•per•hy•dro•pho•bic /‚so͞opər‚hīdrə'fōbik/ ▸ adjective repelling water to the degree that droplets do not flatten but roll off instead: *superhydrophobic butterfly wings*
–DERIVATIVES **su•per•hy•dro•pho•bi•a** noun

su•pe•ri•or plan•et /sə'pirēər ‚planit/ ▸ noun Astronomy any of the planets—Mars, Jupiter, Saturn, Uranus, Neptune, and Pluto—whose orbits are further from the sun than the Earth's.

su•per•size /'so͞opər‚sīz/ ▸ verb [trans.] produce or serve something in a larger size: *click here to supersize the picture.*
▸adjective larger than normal: *this supersize clock has black 2-inch numbers on white face in a simple lightweight black frame.*

su•per•soap /'so͞opər ‚sōp/ ▸ noun a soap that contains a bactericide.

su•per•sta•tion /'so͞opər‚stāsHən/ ▸ noun a television station that broadcasts widely via cable or satellite.

sup•port sys•tem /sə'pôrt ‚sistəm/ ▸ noun a group of people who are available to support one another emotionally, socially, and sometimes financially: *a support system for gay teens.*

sur•face bound•a•ry lay•er /'sərfis 'bound(ə)rē ‚lāər/ ▸ noun Meteorology the lowest layer of the earth's atmosphere extending to about one kilometer. Winds within it are affected by friction with the earth's surface.

swag /swag/ ▸ noun Australian/NZ informal a large number or amount: *the agricultural side to the show will see a swag of events including fleece competitions, poultry and water fowl competitions, and a tractor pull.* [**10 Oct. 2003** *Ararat Advertiser (Australia)*]

swap•file /'swäp,fīl/ ▸ **noun** Computing a file on a hard disk used to provide additional memory space for programs that have been transferred out of active memory.

swarm /swôrm/ ▸ **verb** [intrans.] to assemble, move, or act collectively, using cell phones or other wireless devices to communicate: [mainly as verbal noun] *the bartenders know to watch out for swarming when Leo walks in.*

SWAT team /'swät ˌtēm/ ▸ **noun** a group of elite police marksmen who specialize in high-risk tasks such as hostage rescue.
■ any group of specialists brought in to solve a difficult or urgent problem: *as members of Gov. Rod Blagojevich's economic SWAT team descend on Southern Illinois in the coming months they should take aim at bolstering the region's hunting and outdoor recreation industry.* [**30 Sept. 2003** *Southern Illinoisan*]
–ORIGIN 1980s: acronym from *Special Weapons and Tactics.*

SWF ▸ **abbreviation** single white female (used in personal ads).

swid•den ag•ri•cul•ture /'swidn ˌagrikəlCHər/ ▸ **noun** another name for slash-and-burn agriculture: *People and Forests:Yunnan Swidden Agriculture in Human-Ecological Perspective.* [**2003** *United Nations Development Programme (paper title)*]
USAGE: A survey of citations suggests that this term is used where the practice is viewed favorably. The gentle-sounding *swidden*, with its Middle English roots, is an excellent choice to replace the violent connotation of *slash-and-burn.*

swing•man /'swiNGmən; -ˌman/ ▸ **noun** (plural **swing•men** /'swiNGmən; -ˌmen/) Basketball a player who can play both guard and forward: *free-agent swingman Stephen Jackson signed with the Atlanta Hawks on Friday* [**3 Oct. 2003** *MSNBC*]

SWM ▸ **abbreviation** single white male (used in personal ads).

sym•pa•thet•ic smok•er /'simpə'THetik 'smōkər/ ▸ **noun** a person who smokes only in the company of another smoker: *sympathetic smokers are tempted the most in bars and at parties.*

symp•tom•ize /'simptə,mīz/ (also **symp•tom•ise**) ▸ **verb** [trans.] be a symptom or sign of: *hypothermia is symptomized by confusion, slurred speech, and stiff muscles.*

syn•tax er•ror /ˈsinˌtaks ˌerər/ ▸ **noun** Computers a character or string incorrectly placed in a command or instruction that causes a failure in execution: *I am trying to create a List implementation using templates, and am getting a syntax error.* [**11 June 1999** Usenet: comp.lang.c++]

syn•thes•pi•an /sinˈTHespēən/ ▸ **noun** a computer-generated actor appearing in a film with human actors and interacting with them or in a wholly animated film.

Tt

T-1 /'tē 'wən/ ▸ **noun** Computing a high-speed data line capable of transmitting at approximately 1.5 million bps: [as modifier] *on an intranet where everyone is connected at T1 rates or higher, you can achieve high video quality in quarter-screen windows.* [**Nov. 1996** *Internet World*]

tab•let PC /'tablit 'pē'sē/ ▸ **noun** a microcomputer that accepts input directly onto an LCD screen by means of a stylus, savable as image or text: *ever since Bill Gates started waving around a prototype of Microsoft's Tablet PC, consumers have been lusting after it: a notepad-sized digital slate that responds to voice commands, takes notes, is always wirelessly connected to the Internet, and can do anything a desktop computer can.* [**April 2001** *Popular Science*]

tab•loid•i•za•tion /'tab,loidə'zāsHən/ ▸ **noun** a change in emphasis from the factual to the sensational, especially in television news: *is it a grotesque invasion of privacy, a banal journalistic feeding frenzy, a new benchmark in the tabloidization of American politics?* [**24 Feb. 1992** *The Nation*]

Tac•tel /'tak,tel/ ▸ **noun** trademark a polyamide fabric or fiber with a soft, silky feel: [as adjective] *luxuriously soft, strong and easy to wear, its properties are so advanced that Tactel can be used in one form for the finest lingerie, and in another for the chunkiest outdoor wear.* [**3 Sept. 1995** *Independent on Sunday*]

tae-bo /'tī 'bō/ ▸ **noun** trademark an exercise system combining elements of aerobics and kick-boxing: *as I understand it, tae-bo is based on martial arts; the difference is that martial artists learn to defend themselves, whereas tae-bo people throw pretend punches and kicks strictly for fitness purposes.* [**22 Aug. 1999** *Star-Ledger (Newark, New Jersey)*]
-ORIGIN 1990s: from Korean *tae* 'leg' + *bo*, short for *boxing*).

tag wres•tling /'tag ,resliNG/ ▸ **noun** a form of wrestling involving tag teams: *the ever more exotic parade of giant moths, hydra-headed lizards and gleaming steel robo-monsters came to resemble the theatrical aspects of professional tag wrestling, whose very improbability and over-acted posturing is part of the fun.* [**31 July 1994** *Independent on Sunday*]

tai•ko•naut /'tīkə,nôt/ ▸ noun the English rendering of the Chinese word for astronaut: *China's first "taikonaut" Yang Liwei likewise boasted humble credentials to blaze his country's trail into space.* [**16 Oct. 2003** *Star*]
-ORIGIN early 21st cent.: from Chinese *taikong*, 'space' + *-naut*.

tail•gate /'tāl,gāt/ ▸ verb [trans.] gain unauthorized entry to a secured area by following on the heels of someone with authority to enter: *a Toyota pickup that tailgated the delivery vehicle into the prison.*
-DERIVATIVES **tail•gat•ing** noun

talk time /'tôk ,tīm/ ▸ noun the time during which a cell phone is used or can be used to handle calls: *the RSU queries the market server for talk time available to this account.* [**2003** *International Engineering Commission Web site*]

ta•mas /'təməs/ ▸ noun (in Vedanta) the element or mode of prakriti associated with lethargy, darkness, and ignorance.

ta•mas•ic /tə'masik/ ▸ adjective (in Ayurveda) denoting a class of foods that are dry, old, foul, or unpalatable, and are thought to promote pessimism, ignorance, laziness, criminal tendencies, and doubt. Compare RAJASIC, SATTVIC

tank /taNGk/ ▸ verb informal [intrans.] fail or drop spectacularly: *what really makes the company attractive for acquisition is that its stock has basically tanked.* [**29 Feb. 1996** *San Francisco Chronicle*]

tank•i•ni /taNG'kēnē/ ▸ noun a two-piece bathing suit consisting of a tank top and a bikini bottom.

tap•i•o•ca milk tea /,tapē'ōkə ,milk 'tē/ ▸ noun another term for BUBBLE TEA.

Tar•dis /'tärdis/ ▸ noun **1** a time machine.
2 a building or container that is larger inside than it appears to be from outside.
-ORIGIN the name (said to be an acronym of *time and relative dimensions in space*) of a time machine that had the exterior of a police telephone box in the British TV science-fiction series *Doctor Who*, first broadcast in 1963.

tax-and-spend /'taks ən 'spend/ ▸ noun a policy, usually associated with the political left, of increasing taxes in order to fund an increase in government spending, especially for social services.

■ relating to, denoting, or advocating a policy of tax-and-spend: [as modifier] *they remain committed to their tax and spend philosophy.* [**22 July 1999** Dennis Hastert] ▶**verb** [intrans.] implement a policy of raising taxes in order to increase spending: *you can't tax-and-spend your way to prosperity.* ‑DERIVATIVES **tax-and-spend•er** noun

tech•ni•cal sup•port /ˈteknikəl səˈpôrt/ (also **tech sup•port** /ˈtek sə ˌpôrt/) ▶ **noun** Computing a service provided by a hardware or software company that provides registered users with help and advice about their products. ■ a department within an organization that maintains and repairs computers and computer networks.

tech•no-thril•ler /ˈteknō ˌTHrilər/ ▶ **noun** a novel or movie in which the excitement of the plot depends in large part upon the workings of computers, weapons, software, military vehicles, or other machines: [as modifier] *Pierre Ouellette's* The Deus Machine *is a technothriller blockbuster kind of thing very much in the tradition of the best-selling technothriller blockbusters it hopes to emulate.* [**June 1994** *Interzone*]

teen•tail•er /ˈtēnˌtālər/ ▶ **noun** a retail store that caters to teenagers, especially teenage girls: *teentailers are the most recession-resistant facet of American retailing.* ‑ORIGIN blend of *teenager* and *retailer.*

Tef•lon /ˈtefˌlän/ ▶ **adjective** having an undamaged reputation, in spite of involvement in scandal or evidence of misjudgment: *the combination of being Irish Catholic, from south Boston, and a jock makes him a teflon candidate.* [**25 May 1993** *Boston Globe*]

tel•e-im•mer•sion /ˌtelə iˈmərzHən/ ▶ **noun** two-way remote communication in which each party gets an audio and three-dimensional visual representation of the other, via high-speed data exchange: *tele-immersion allows users to 'climb into a computer screen.'*

tel•e•no•vel•a /ˌtelənōˈvelə/ ▶ **noun** (in Latin America) a televised soap opera: [as modifier] *we were headed for the exclusive Barra da Tijuca district of Rio to have lunch with Lucélia Santos, a former* telenovela *(soap opera) star who had become a political activist.* [**Aug. 1990** *Vanity Fair*]

tel•e•pic /ˈteləˌpik/ ▶ **noun** a movie made for television: *the first one aired in late January to critical disdain and audience apathy and we're now told the series of telepics about forensic specialist Guy Hankes will*

be scrapped and converted into a weekly hourlong show for this fall.
[**Mar.** 1994 *Star-Ledger (Newark, NJ)*]

tel•e•scam /ˈtelə,skam/ ▸ **noun** a fraud conducted via telephone, especially one using telemarketing: *like other fraudulent telemarketing operations, investment telescams usually are carried out by boiler room operators, who may target those who have indicated an interest in other investments by responding to a newspaper ad or filling out an information request card.* [2003 Better Business Bureau Web site]

tel•e•sur•ger•y /ˈtelə,sərjərē/ ▸ **noun** surgery performed by a doctor considerably distant from the patient, using medical robotics and multimedia image communication: *while British patients might pale at the thought of intercontinental telesurgery, the Americans, following trials in Los Angeles, are already testing the radio-controlled equipment.* [9 **Oct.** 1995 *Daily Telegraph*]
-DERIVATIVES **tel•e•sur•geon** /ˈtelə,sərjən/ **noun**

tel•e•work /ˈtelə,wərk/ ▸ **noun** work done at home for one's employer via electronic connections to the workplace; telecommuting: [as modifier] *despite a mandate from Congress and more attention from the Office of Personnel Management and the General Services Administration, telework programs continue to grow slowly in the federal workplace, an OPM official says.* [6 **Oct.** 2003 GovExec.com]
▸**verb** work at home in this way.

te•lom•er•ase /təˈlämə,rās; -,rāz/ ▸ **noun** a reverse transcriptase enzyme that, when functioning normally, synthesizes telomeres and prevents their erosion: *scientists report that a new sensitive assay detected an enzyme called telomerase in nearly all of the cancer specimens tested, but the enzyme was not found in other types of cells.* [23 **Dec.** 1994 *Richmond Times-Despatch*]

ter•roir /terˈwär/ ▸ **noun** the complete natural environment in which a particular wine is produced, including factors such as the soil, topography, and climate: *terroir, to the semantic bafflement of at least one California grower engaged in perpetual argument with the growers of Bordeaux on the subject, is not translatable with the single word* soil: *It means soil and its environment taken together.* [1985 *Gourmet*]
■ (also **goût de ter•roir** /ˌgoo də terˈwär/) the characteristic taste and flavor imparted to a wine by the environment in which it is produced.
-ORIGIN 1970s: French, from medieval Latin *terratorium*.

text mes•sage /'tekst ˌmesij/ ▸ **noun** an electronic communication sent and received by cell phone.
–DERIVATIVES **text mes•sag•ing noun**

text•phone /'tekstˌfōn/ ▸ **noun** a telephone for use by the deaf or hard of hearing, having a small screen on which a message can be received and a keyboard on which an outoing message may be typed to another textphone.

-themed ▸ **adjective** [in combination] (mainly in journalism) characterized by a theme or pervasive influence: *a new £10 million golf-themed business park beside the first fairway of Loch Ness golf course.* [**21 Oct. 2003** *Scotsman (UK)*]

the•o•ter•ror•ism /ˌTHēō'terəˌrizəm/ ▸ **noun** terrorism that has a religious motive or purpose: *realistic worry about theoterrorism has caused a decline in tourism.*
–ORIGIN from *theo-* 'relating to God' + *terrorism.*

the•o•ther•a•py /ˌTHēō'THerəpē/ ▸**noun** another name for faith healing: *a major part of theotherapy is conflict resolution using the Biblical tools of Forgiveness, Acceptance, Surrender and Love.* [**1 Nov. 2002** Martin Stokeley]

ther•mal de•po•lym•er•i•za•tion /'THərməl ˌdēpəˌlimərə'aāSHən; -ˌpäləmərə-/ ▸ **noun** a process of breaking down complex hydrocarbons in an oxygen-deprived, heated, and pressurized environment to yield simpler compounds that can be used in turn to produce substances with the same properties as fossil fuels.

ther•mal im•ag•ing /'THərməl 'iməjiNG/ ▸ **noun** the formation of images based on heat in the objects represented, using infrared and other technologies: [as modifier] *more technology, too, like thermal imaging detectors that can help find indoor marijuana but are under constitutional challenge as illegal search devices.* [**28 Feb. 2001** *New York Times*]

ther•mo•pho•to•vol•ta•ic /ˌTHərmōˌfōtōväl'tāik; -vōl-; -vôl-/ ▸ **adjective** (abbreviation **TPV**) denoting or relating to the capacity to convert infrared radiation (i.e. radiant heat) into electricity: *thermophotovoltaic cells utilize heat and low energy photons and convert them into electrical potential using technology similar to solar cells.* [**1999** paper on Johns Hopkins University Web site]

THG ▸ **abbreviation** tetrahydrogestrinone; an artificial anabolic steroid taken for enhancement of athletic performance. It was until recently undetectable in the bloodstream using normal testing techniques: *THG is a "designer drug," one that is manipulated in the laboratory to make it difficult to detect.* [17 **Oct.** 2003 *Pittsburgh Tribune-Review*]

thought lead•er /'THôt ˌlēdər/ ▸ **noun** one whose views on a subject are taken to be authoritative and influential: *these thought leaders are independent experts who keep our thinking both broad and deep.* [2003 Satmetrix.com Web site]

thread•ing /'THrediNG/ ▸ **noun 1** a process in which unwanted facial hair is removed by using twisted cotton thread to pull the hair from the follicle: *she looks so refreshingly natural. Her eyebrows are like two huge hairy caterpillars, and she has clearly never heard of threading or been anywhere near a personal trainer.* [28 **Feb.** 2001 *New York Times*]

2 the system by which consecutive messages relating to a single subject on an electronic bulletin board or newsgroup or stored for retrieval: *users can append messages at any time, but there is no threading and no way to inform others when new messages are added.* [**Dec.** 1993 *MacWorld*]

three-par•ent /'THrē ˌpe(ə)rənt; ˌpar-/ ▸ **adjective 1** containing a chromosomal complement from a mother and father and the mitochondrial DNA from the egg of a donor: *in all, the scientists transferred five of the three-parent embryos into the woman.* [13 **Oct.** 2003 *BBC News*]

2 having or regarding three different adults in a parental role: *kids in three-parent homes were at *least* as happy and well-adjusted as those in two-parent ones.* [5 **Sept.** 2001 Usenet: alt.atheism]

tick•et•less /'tikitlis/ ▸ **adjective and adverb 1** not requiring a paper ticket: *with JetBlue, all seats are assigned, all travel is ticketless, all fares are one-way, and a Saturday night stay is never required.* [10 **Oct.** 2003 *Business Wire (press release)*]

2 not in possession of a valid ticket: *Shiv Sena activists on Monday travelled ticketless in suburban trains here to protest the hike in ticket fares.* [15 **Sept.** 2003 *Sify (India)*]

tid•al farm /'tīdl ˌfärm/ ▸ **noun** an installation of turbines used to generate electricity from tidal forces: *the consortium behind it hopes to build a whole set of turbines in the area—a tidal farm.* [16 **June** 2003 BBC News Online]

TIFF /tif/ ▸ **abbreviation** Computing tagged image file format; a format for storing images that is widely used in desktop publishing.

tight•y-whit•ies /'tītē '(h)wītēz/ ▸ **noun** informal men's white cotton briefs: *is it just me, or do any other women find absolutely no turn on to see men in their tighty-whities?* [**2002** bitchblog.com archives]

tip•ping point /'tipiNG ˌpoint/ ▸ **noun** the point at which a series of small ineffective changes acquires enough pressure or importance to cause a larger, more significant change: *a theory that suggests there is a kind of tipping point in society, where X number of criminal types (noncooperators) gets the edge on Y number of honest citizens (basically cooperators).* [**31 May 2003** Usenet: soc.history.war.misc]
■ the point at which the build-up of minor incidents reaches a level that causes someone to do something they had formerly resisted: *this was the tipping point for me. I had just spent about $150 on a CD-RW which wouldn't work under MS-Windows without reading and trying every possibility in a dissertation from HP customer service.* [**4 June 2002** Usenet: comp.os.linux.advocacy]

TLA ▸ **abbreviation** three-letter acronym.

TMJ ▸ **abbreviation** temporomandibular joint.

tor•na•do al•ley /tôr'nādō 'alē/ ▸ **noun** an area of the Great Plains centered on eastern Kansas and Oklahoma and including parts of the surrounding states, where tornadoes are frequent.

touch•point /'təCHˌpoint/ ▸ **noun 1** any point of contact between a buyer and a seller: *extend your applications to every channel and customer touchpoint.* [**2003** PeopleSoft Web site]
2 a device like a miniature joystick with a rubber tip, manipulated with a finger to move the screen pointer on some laptop computers.

tow•el•head /'tou(ə)l ˌhed/ ▸ **noun** informal, offensive a person who wears a turban.

tox•i•drome /'täksiˌdrōm/ ▸ **noun** a group of signs and symptoms constituting the basis for a diagnosis of poisoning: *the toxidrome produced by these agents is essentially the same as for any organophosphate.* [**21 Mar. 1995** Usenet: misc.emerg-services]

toy•book /'toiˌbо͞ok/ ▸ **noun** a children's book with features that enable it to be played with as well as read: *today's bookstore shelves* *spill over with tot-oriented "toybooks" shaped like cats, dogs, hens, horses, lions, elephants, insects and other things.* [**19 Aug.** 2003 *Washington Post*]

TPV ▸ abbreviation THERMOPHOTOVOLTAIC.

trace min•er•al /'trās ˌmin(ə)rəl/ ▸ noun any of a number of inorganic elements (mainly metals) that exist in minute quantities in higher organisms and that are an essential component of nutrition: *vegetarians choose agar, rich in iodine and trace minerals, over animal-based gelatin products.* [**17 Sept.** 2003 *Contra Costa (CA) Times*]

trac•tor beam /'traktər ˌbēm/ ▸ noun (in science fiction) a hypothetical beam of energy that can be used to control the movement of objects such as space ships or hold them stationary: *using the principle that small particles illuminated by a focused light beam are drawn to the light's brightest point, the tweezers could trap a particle and move it around in three dimensions just like a Star Trek tractor beam.* [**June** 2003 *University of Chicago magazine*]

trail•er trash /'trālər ˌtraSH/ ▸ noun offensive poor, lower-class white people, typified as living in trailers: *their parenting style has moved the family from upper-middle class suburban to trailer trash in one generation.*

train•ing ta•ble /'trāniNG ˌtābəl/ ▸ noun a table in a dining hall where athletes in training are served specially prepared meals: *besides their well-publicized stand opposing the elimination of athletic dormitories and training tables, the Southeastern Conference universities have chosen not to back scholarship cuts and recruiting limitations.* [**9 Jan.** 1991 *Chronicle of Higher Education*]

trans•gen•der /tranz'jendər; trans-/ (also **trans•gen•dered**) ▸ adjective identified with a gender other than the biological one: *Leslie Feinberg, an American transgender activist and author, says the movement includes not only drag queens but drag kings and androgynes, bearded women and female weightlifters.* [**27 Mar.** 1995 *Independent (UK)*]

tran•si•ent is•che•mic at•tack /'transHənt is'kēmik əˌtak; 'tran-zHənt / (abbreviation: **TIA**) ▸ noun a technical term for MINISTROKE.

tran•si•tion /tran'zishən/ ▸ verb undergo or cause to undergo a process or period of transition: [trans.] *this new high-capacity network ought to be built by the federal government and then transitioned into private industry* [**21 Dec.** 1992 *Cable World*] | [intrans.] *we have tran-*

sitioned from a high-intensity combat operation to a support role in the community.

tre•tin•o•in /trə'tinō-in/ ▶ noun a drug related to retinol (Vitamin A), used as a topical ointment in the treatment of acne and other disorders of the skin.

tri•fold /'trī,fōld/ ▶ adjective triple; threefold: *an ingenious trifold partnership between government, employers and students to fund a learning bank.* [7 **Feb.** 1995 *Guardian (UK)*]

trip-hop /'trip ,häp/ ▶ noun a style of dance music, usually slow in tempo, that combines elements of hip-hop and dub reggae with softer, more ambient sounds: [as modifier] *Joni Mitchell's quarter-century-old BigYellow Taxi is turned into, of all things, a trip-hop number, with its original backing track replaced by a rap drumbeat.* [29 **Sept.** 1995 *Entertainment Weekly*]

trol•ley dol•ly /'trälē ,dälē/ ▶ noun British informal a flight attendant: *with his sta-pressed smile and slightly tight uniform, the gay trolley dolly is an institution in the travel industry.* [14 **Jan.** 2000 *Independent (UK)*]

tro•phy child /'trōfē ,CHīld/ ▶ noun a child whose birth or achievements are paraded to enhance the parents' status: *those who are appalled that an older woman wants to bear a child saw nothing amiss when Tony Randall and Ben Bradlee fathered trophy children with women young enough to be their daughters or granddaughters.* [16 **Nov.** 1997 *NewYork Times Book Review*]

trust•a•far•i•an /,trəstə'fe(ə)rēən/ ▶ noun informal a rich young person who adopts an ethnic lifestyle and lives in a college town or a non-affluent urban area: *she figures that any discussion of fair in NewYork is absurd, anyway, in a city of $600-an-hour corporate lawyers and trustafarians.* [**date unknown**]
–ORIGIN 1990s: blend of *trust fund* and *Rastafarian*.

T-top /'tē ,täp/ ▶ noun a car with removable panels in the roof: *five years later, GM designers came back with the third design with its round lines, a removable rear window, T-top and popup headlamps.* [6 **Apr.** 1997 *Chicago Tribune*]

TTS ▶ abbreviation text-to-speech, a form of speech synthesis used to create a spoken version of the text in an electronic document: *[the agency] then uses TTS to turn the text into audio within minutes, sav-*

ing the company both time and money. [15 **Sept.** 2003 *Business Wire news release*]

turf bat•tle /'tərf ˌbatl/ ▸ **noun** a conflict or argument between rivals for control of something: *accusations, including from one top Republican, that turf battles inside the administration have bogged down postwar planning.* [14 **Oct.** 2003 *CBS News*]

Tu•ring test /'t(y)o͞oriNG ˌtest/ ▸ **noun** a test of artificial intelligence devices or programs in which the goal is to make a human interacting electronically unable to tell whether it is a machine or another human: *the Turing test was held here at the behest of New York businessman Hugh Loebner, president of restaurant supplier Crown Industries Inc., who has offered a $100,000 prize for the first computer system able to pass it.* [11 **Nov.** 1991 *Wall Street Journal*]
-ORIGIN after mathematician Alan *Turing,* (1912–1954), who proposed it in his 1950 paper, 'Computing Machinery and Intelligence.'

tu•ri•sta /to͞o'rēstə/ ▸ **noun** informal **1** a tourist: [as modifier] *yet the Zócalo in Oaxaca, I would submit, is the apotheosis of Mexican town squares: It's the most magnificent sittable place I've ever sat my* turista *ass in.* [**October** 2001 *Outside*]
2 traveler's diarrhea: *the differences in incidence of turista in visitors from the northern and the southern hemispheres is quite striking in this report.* [5 **May** 1973 *Lancet (UK)*]

turn•speak /'tərnˌspēk/ ▸ **noun** an interpretation of an event or phenomenon that is perceived by detractors as the opposite of what is really the case.
-ORIGIN on the pattern of George Orwell's *newspeak.*
USAGE: At present, *turnspeak* appears to be almost exclusively a polemical term for use in accusations from both sides in the Israeli-Palestinian conflict.

tween /twēn/ (also **tween•ie**) /'twēnē/ ▸ **noun** short for TWEENAGER.

tween•ag•er /'twēnˌājər/ ▸ **noun** informal a child between the ages of about 10 and 14: *[Roundhouse,] the hot Nickelodeon show for tweenagers.* [3 **June** 1994 *Washington Post*]

twelve-step /'twelv ˌstep/ ▸ **adjective** [attrib.] denoting or relating to a process of recovery from an addiction by following a twelve-stage program, especially one similar to Alcoholics Anonymous: *it is heresy in a twelve-step group to question claims of abuse. All claims of*

suffering are sacred and presumed to be absolutely true. [**Oct.** 1993 *Atlantic Monthly*]
▶**verb** [often as noun **twelve-stepping**] (of an addict) undergo such a program: *as we 12-step our way through the dance hall of life, our mantra has shifted: I have a lot of shit to work out, you're codependent.* [**Apr.** 1994 *Spin*]
■ treat (someone) using principles of such programs: *in the days of Bill and Bob, everyone knew a drunk whom you could seek out and Twelve-Step in what used to be your favorite bar.* [**20 Mar.** 1995 *New Yorker*]
-DERIVATIVES **twelve-step•per** noun

24/7 (also **24-7**) /'twentē͵fôr 'sevən/ (also **24/7**) ▶ **adverb** informal twenty-four hours a day, seven days a week; all the time: *in this business you just can't afford to let things get you down, especially when you are on call 24/7.* [**20 Aug.** 1997 *Independent (UK)*]

twig fur•ni•ture /'twig ͵fərniCHər/ ▶ **noun** a rustic style of furniture in which the natural state of the wood is retained as an aesthetic feature: *twig furniture, they call it, made to look as if it grew in the woods.* [1991 Russell Banks, *The Sweet Hereafter*]

twist•ed pair /'twistid 'pe(ə)r/ ▶ **noun** Electronics a cable consisting of two wires twisted around each other, used especially for telephone or computer applications: *we prewired the building with eight-strand twisted pair with half-floor granularity.* [**Sept.** 1991 *Unix Review*]

ty•lo•sin /'tīlə͵sin/ ▶ **noun** an antibiotic that is routinely fed to live-stock as a growth promoter and that may contribute to antibiotic resistance in humans: *contact allergy to tylosin and cobalt in a pig-farmer* [1995 *Contact Dermititis (article title)*]

tza•tzi•ki /tsä'tsēkē/ (also **tza•tzi•ki sauce**) ▶ **noun** a sauce of Greek origin, made from yogurt, garlic and cucumbers: *beef gyro strips over pita bread with tzatziki sauce* [2003 online menu of the Aegean Taverna]

Uu

u•ber- /'o͞obər/ (also **über-** /'ʏbər/) ▸prefix denoting an outstanding or supreme example of a particular kind of person or thing: *an uberbabe | the uberregulator.*
-ORIGIN German *über*, 'super.'

u•biq•ui•tin /yo͞o'bikwit(i)n/ ▸noun a single-chain polypeptide found in living cells that plays a role in the degradation of defective and superfluous proteins: *a small protein called ubiquitin is turning out to be the Clark Kent of cell biology.* [**13 Sept. 2002** *Science*]

u•don /'o͞o͵dän/ ▸noun wide, flat wheat noodles used in Japanese cooking.
-ORIGIN Japanese

Ugg boot /'əg ͵bo͞ot/ (also **Ugh boot**) ▸noun trademark a type of soft sheepskin boot originating in Australia: *if P. Diddy needed a location for a music video set in Marrakesh with models dancing in bare midriffs and Ugg boots, he might consider the SkyBar, the new lounge at the Shore Club hotel in Miami Beach.* [**9 Feb. 2003** *New York Times*]
-ORIGIN 1960s: probably named after *Ugh*, a series of cartoon characters.

u•ma•mi /o͞o'mäme/ ▸noun a category of taste in food (besides sweet, sour, salt, and bitter), corresponding to the flavor of glutamates, especially monosodium glutamate: *the peptide seems to contribute to "umami," the little-known fifth taste sensation that some scientists think is perceived by specific receptors in the mouth.*
-ORIGIN Japanese, literally 'deliciousness.'

um•bil•i•co•plas•ty /͵əm'biliko͵plaste/ ▸noun plastic surgery performed on the navel: *last spring plastic surgeons began reporting a curious spike in the number of women requesting navel reconstruction—or "umbilicoplasty," as the pros call it.* [**15 Dec. 2002** *New York Times Magazine*]

um•rah /'o͞om͵rä/ ▸noun the nonmandatory lesser pilgrimage made by Muslims to Mecca, which may be performed at any time of the year: *Saudi Arabia plans to implement the cooperative health insurance scheme on pilgrims coming to the Kingdom for Haj and Umrah.* [**6 Sept. 2003** *Arab News*]
-ORIGIN Arabic *'umra.*

UMTS ▸ **abbreviation** Universal Mobile Telephone System.

U•na•bomb•er /'yōōnə,bämər/ ▸ **noun** the name given by the FBI to Ted Kaczynski, the elusive perpetrator of a series of bombings (1975–1995) in the United States that killed three and wounded 23. The victims were mainly academics in technological disciplines, airline executives, and executives in businesses thought to affect the environment: *he's one of those back-in-the-woods cabin guys. Like the Unabomber, but sexy.* [**1999** Linda Barnes, *Flashpoint*]

un•aired /ˌən'e(ə)rd/ ▸ **adjective** not previously broadcasted: *Culp stars in a rare unaired TV pilot that rivals any* Twilight Zone *episode.* [**Feb. 1992** *FilmFax (advertisement)*]

un•braid /ˌən'brād/ ▸ **verb** [trans.] untie (something braided): *he knows that she may never see the name Mrs George Middleton engraved upon a visiting card, never unbraid her hair in the soft candle-light of a shared bedroom.* [**1999** R. Tremain, *Music and Silence*] [intrans.] *Susan removed the bobby pins from her left braid and began to unbraid.* [**1990** L. Martin, *Deficit Ending*]
■ [intrans.] become untwisted or unbraided: *Walt looked so old now, but that, too, was to be expected, and he'd aged gracefully, as an old rope will, until it finally unbraids.* [**Jan. 1993** *Science Fiction Age*]

un•clamp /ˌən'klamp/ ▸ **verb** [trans.] remove from, or as if from, a clamp. ■ remove a clamp or clamplike device: *the animal's diet includes white rats, and the zookeeper did not want the animal to think that Mr. Bronstein's feet were dinner. But it attacked Mr. Bronstein's foot anyway. He unclamped its jaws and climbed out of its cage.* [**12 June 2001** *New York Times*]

un•crate /ˌən'krāt/ ▸ **noun** [trans.] an item of merchandise removed from its shipping container: *Clearance Sale. Mark Downs. Closeouts. Discounts. Uncrates. Floor Samples.* [**28 Dec. 2002** *Chicago Tribune*]

un•crease /ˌən'krēs/ ▸ **verb** [trans.] [usually as adjective] (**uncreased**) remove the creases from.

un•der•cling /'əndər,kliNG/ Climbing ▸ **noun** a handhold that faces down the rock face: *above, Erbesfield does reach the undercling, then pops left to a large hold.* [**Feb. 1991** *Climbing*]
▸ **verb** (past and past participle **under•clung**) [intrans.] climb using such handholds.

un•der•stored /'əndər'stôrd/ ▸ **adjective** supplied with fewer retail stores than the market demands: *there are specific market niches in*

which Chicago is understored compared to Los Angeles and New York.
[2003 GreatRealty.com]

un•der•tip /'əndər'tip/ (**un•der•tipped, un•der•tip•ping**) ▸ verb [trans.]
give (someone) an excessively small tip: *to complete the disguise,
always be sure to drink far too much wine at breakfast, lunch, and dinner—and then undertip.* [**Aug.** 1991 *Elle*]

un•der•vote /'əndər,vōt/ ▸ noun a ballot not counted because of unclear marking by the voter: *they were selected because party officials
determined each one had high numbers of "undervotes," the ballots that
the machines did not detect any vote for president.* [13 **Nov.** 2000 *New
York Times*]

un•en•riched /,ənen'riCHt/ ▸ adjective (of uranium) in the natural
state, containing less than one percent of U_{235}: *the company began its life, meanwhile, with a huge stock of its raw material, unen-
riched uranium hexafluoride, a kind of dowry from the government,
and has been selling it, to pay dividends and other costs.* [20 **June** 2000
New York Times]

un•fused /,ən'fyōōzd/ ▸ adjective 1 not fused or joined: *Darwin had
predicted that a proto-bird would one day turn up with unfused wing
fingers, but this exceeded all expectations.* [1992 A. Desmond and J.
Moore, *Darwin*]
2 not fitted or supplied with a fuse: *the Toledo and Orion both had
exposed, unfused electrical terminals that could short and cause a fire
in a front-on crash.* [20 **Oct.** 1992 *Which? (UK)*]

un•grad•ed /,ən'grādid/ ▸ adjective not divided into grades or separate levels: *students are in ungraded classrooms and proceed at their
own pace.* [**March** 1992 *Atlantic Monthly*]

un•ground /,ən'ground/ ▸ verb remove from a grounded state: *on the
decision to ground the fleet he said: "It's easy to jump in and ground
aeroplanes. It's not so easy to unground them."* [26 **Mar.** 2001 *Guardian (UK)*]

un•ground•ed /,ən'groundid/ ▸ adjective a synonym, increasingly frequent in journalism, for unfounded or groundless: *however, immi-
gration support groups say the government is pandering to ungrounded
fears fueled by the populist media.* [27 **Aug.** 2003 *Reuters*]

USAGE: The similarities of ungrounded to the words it is mistak-
enly used in place of—unfounded or groundless—may make it
seem like a serviceable substitute, but it is typically found in direct quotations and rarely in well-edited text.

un•hip /ˌənˈhip/ ▸ adjective (**un•hip•per, un•hip•pest**) informal unaware of or unaffected by current fashions or trends: *I visited there a couple of years ago and found that while it was remote and decidedly unhip, the town was otherwise right up-to-date.* [**Jan. 1990** *Spy*]

un•hol•ster /ˌənˈhōlstər/ ▸ verb [trans.] remove (a gun) from a holster: *Koon said he ordered Powell to unholster his gun in case deadly force was needed.* [**Aug. 1991** *Vanity Fair*]

u•ni•cast /ˈyo͞oniˌkast/ ▸ noun transmission of a data package or an audio/visual signal to a single recipient: [as modifier] *the unicast method wastes a lot of bandwidth by sending duplicate information.* [**1997** *NewsMedia*]
–ORIGIN 1990s: on the pattern of *broadcast.*

u•ni•form re•source lo•ca•tor /ˈyo͞onəˌfôrm ˈrēsôrs ˌlōkātər; lōˌkā-/ (abbreviation: **URL**) ▸ noun a location or address identifying where documents can be found on the Internet.

un•in•stall /ˌəninˈstôl/ ▸ verb (**un•in•stalled, un•in•stall•ing**) [trans.] remove (an application or file) from a computer: *if you wanted to uninstall them, you could never be certain which files could be safely deleted* [**Jan. 1997** *T3 (UK)*] | [intrans.] *the main drawback to Double-Space is that it is almost impossible to uninstall.* [**July 1993** *Computer Shopper*]
▸ adjective denoting a command, function, or capability to remove software: [as modifier] *at a minimum, this means that you use the registry, not add information to WIN.INI or SYSTEM.INI, and provide complete uninstall capability with your application.* [**July 1994** *Microsoft Developer Network News*]
–DERIVATIVES **un•in•stall•er** noun

un•me•tered /ˌənˈmētərd/ ▸ adjective **1** not charged for according to amount or time used: *if you're traveling only in the US, check out the unmetered service from Sprint.* [**18 Sept. 2003** *Linux Journal*]
2 not supplied or fitted with a meter: *outside the station, Malcolm negotiated the fare with an unmetered taxi.* [**1991** R. Mystry, *Such a Long Journey*]
3 not canceled or franked using a postage meter: *the agents warned the public to be on the alert for unmetered packages, especially those posted to business addresses; few companies used stamps to send parcels anymore.* [**1996** N. Gibbs, *Mad Genius: Odyssey, Pursuit & Capture of Unabomber Suspect*]

un•muf•flered /ˌənˈməflərd/ ▸ adjective **1** (of an engine or vehicle) not fitted with a muffler: *from the crescendo of unmuffled 400 horse-*

power engines revving up to 7,000 r.p.m.s to the g-forces of men and machines hurtling around a banked track at 200 mph, no sport electrifies like NASCAR. [2003 twbookmark.com]

2 not restrained, muffled, or suppressed in any way: *are you having unmufflered fun yet, Zippy?* [9 July 2003 Zippy comic strip]

un•pack•aged /ˌən'pakijd/ ▸ adjective chiefly British (of a vacation) not organized as an inclusive package: *why not let us use our considerable knowledge and expertise of these islands to create the unpackaged holiday of your choice.* [Nov. 1992 *Harpers and Queen*]

un•plug /ˌən'pləg/ ▸ verb (**-plugged, -plug•ging**) [trans.] **1** sever the connection between a peripheral device and a computer: *Denny had unplugged the computer keyboard.* [1989 Dean Koontz, *Midnight*]
2 [intrans.] informal relax by disengaging from normal activities: *a garden is certainly a nice thing to have, a place to unplug from a bruising, harried world into someplace ripe and unwired.* [19 June 1995 *Time*]

un•pruned /ˌən'proōnd/ ▸ adjective not subjected to any reducing, trimming, or refining process: *BA work cycles aim to present structured, unpruned data to the domain experts.* [4 Sept. 2003 *Computerworld (Australia)*]

un•staffed /ˌən'staft/ ▸ adjective not provided with a staff or official personnel: *the cones blocked the path through the metal detector, which is now unstaffed, diverting employees and guests into the building unchecked.* [2 Sept. 2003 *Fort Wayne News Sentinel*]

un•stayed /ˌən'stād/ ▸ adjective (especially of masts and rigging) not provided with stays; unsupported: *they carry a large crew for live and transferable ballast on hiking boards to counter the lofty spread of sails on their raked and unstayed masts.* [1994 T.C. Gillmer, *History of Working Water Craft*]

un•sub•scribe /ˌənsəb'skrīb/ ▸ verb [intrans.] cancel a subscription to an Internet newsletter, e-mail list, or discussion group: *once you have tried it out, you can unsubscribe by sending mail to the same address with no subject and "unsubscribe Webtoday-1" in the body of the message.* [Dec. 1999 *Writing Magazine*]

un•vent•ed /ˌən'ventid/ ▸ adjective [attrib.] (of strong, usually negative feelings) not expressed: *with an acerbic explosion of passion, anger and self-inflicted injuries,* This Was Meant to Hurt You *takes all the* *unvented fury of hardcore and wraps it up in the sort of package that keeps all the risky decadence and sense of semi-controlled musical spasms close to the band's surface.* [**2003** Matt Schild, aversion.com]

un•wired /ˌən'wī(ə)rd/ ▸ **adjective** disengaged or disconnected from electronic media: *the only way to truly regenerate yourself enough to be truly creative and inventive again is to be unwired at times in the year and to be in the other part of the world.* [**21 Nov. 1999** *New York Times*]

up•do /'əpˌdōō/ ▸ **noun** (plural **up•dos**) a hairstyle in which the hair is secured at the top and back of the head: *to try this updo, begin by adding extensions that hang 13 inches from the nape.* [**2003** www.behindthechair.com]

up•size /'əpˌsīz/ ▸ **verb** increase in size, extent, or complexity: [intrans.] *American companies are now busy "upsizing," taking on new staff in a feverish attempt to keep customers by improving services.* [**11 Mar. 1998** *Daily Telegraph (UK)*] | [trans.] *Little Caesar's Inc plans to upsize its pizzas by a couple of notches without raising prices.* [**2 Sept. 1997** *Wall Street Journal*]

up•skirt /'əpˌskərt/ ▸ **adjective** having a vantage point up a woman's skirt: *we run an upskirt photo feature every month; it's a very easy and cheap thing to stage.* [**Dec. 1999** *Wired*]

up•weight /'əpˌwāt/ ▸ **verb** [trans.] **1** give increased importance, rank or weighting to: *. . . advertisers pursued different strategies. Renault, for instance, upweighted TV, while Peugeot Citroen upweighted press.* [**30 June 2003** Zenithoptimedia.com] **2** Finance increase the proportion of (an asset or asset class) in a portfolio or fund: *Hansen recommends that investors should use the current pullback in global markets, including South Africa, as an opportunity to upweight equities where feasible within their risk profile.* [**8 Oct. 2003** *MoneyWeb (South Africa)*]

U•ra•ni•an /yōō'rānēən/ literary ▸ **adjective** homosexual.
▸ **noun** a homosexual: *I suppose in his personal life he considered himself a Uranian—a British euphemism for homosexual.* [**2000** Saul Bellow, *Ravelstein*]
–ORIGIN late 19th cent.: with allusion to a reference to Aphrodite in Plato's *Symposium*.

USB ▸ **noun** Universal Serial Bus, an external peripheral interface standard for communication between a computer and add-on devices such as audio players, joysticks, keyboards, telephones, scanners, and printers.

Use•net /'yo͞oz‚net; 'yo͞os-/ ▸ **noun** a part of the Internet that stores and handles the transmission of messages for newsgroups and discussion groups: *for many, Usenet is the heart of the Internet, because it is where the community of its millions of users comes to gather and exchange ideas and views.* [**8 Dec. 1994** *Computer Weekly (UK)*]

us•er in•ter•face /'yo͞ozər 'intər‚fās/ ▸ **noun** Computing the software by which the user and a computer system interact, typically consisting of graphic displays with menus, clickable options, and areas for input: *Macintosh users aren't being ignored here, but they have a much different user interface than either DOS or Unix.* [**Aug. 1989** *Byte*]

Ut•tar•an•chal /‚o͞otə'rənCHəl/ a state in northern India, formed in 2000 from the northern part of Uttar Pradesh; capital, Dehra Dun.

Vv

vac•u•um-pack /ˈvakyo͞o(ə)m ˌpak/ (also **vac•u•um pack**) ▸ noun a hermetically sealed product package: *you will find it soaking in marinade in tubs or vacuum packs in either the refrigerator or the freezer section of many natural food stores.* [29 Nov. 2000 *Washington Post*]

vag•i•no•plas•ty /ˈvajənōˌplastē/ ▸ noun Medicine plastic surgery performed to create or repair a vagina.
–ORIGIN late 19th cent.: from *vagina* + *-plasty*.

vamp /vamp/ informal ▸ verb [trans.] (in fiction) turn (someone) into a vampire: *Yeah I'd like to see Buffy vamped in the final episode, and become a real bad-ass dudette.* [28 Mar. 2001 Usenet: aus.tv.buffy]

van•pool /ˈvanˌpo͞ol/ ▸ noun an arrangement whereby commuters travel together in a van.
–ORIGIN on the pattern of *carpool*.

vari- ▸ combining form various: *variform.*
–ORIGIN from Latin *varius*.

vCJD ▸ abbreviation (sometimes **nvCJD**) variant Creutzfeld–Jakob disease (the human form of mad cow disease).

veg•e•tal /ˈvejitl/ ▸ adjective 1 formal of or relating to plants: *a vegetal aroma.*
2 [attrib.] Embryology of or relating to that pole of the ovum or embryo that contains the less active cytoplasm, and frequently most of the yolk, in the early stages of development: *vegetal cells | the vegetal region.*
–ORIGIN late Middle English: from medieval Latin *vegetalis*, from Latin *vegetare* 'animate.' Sense 2 dates from the early 20th cent.

ve•nous in•suf•fi•cien•cy /ˈvēnəs ˌinsəˈfisHənsē/ ▸ noun Pathology failure of the veins to adequately circulate the blood, esp. from the lower extremities.

ver•bal o•ver•shad•ow•ing /ˈvərbəl ˌōvərˈsHadōiNG/ ▸ noun psychology the tendency of verbalization to impair the recall of visual memories, resulting in unreliable eyewitness accounts.

ver•sion con•trol /'vərzHən kən,trōl/ ▸ noun Computing the task of keeping a software system that consists of many versions and configurations well organized.

ver•tic•al•ly chal•lenged /'vərtik(ə)lē 'CHalənjd/ ▸ adjective jocular not tall in height; short: *that runty, big-mouthed lover of hers . . . O.K. forget runty . . . Vertically challenged. How's that?* [1987 A. Maupin, *Significant Others*]

ver•ti•cal sta•bi•liz•er /'vərtikəl 'stābə,līzər/ ▸ noun Aeronautics a small, flattened projecting surface or attachment on an aircraft or rocket for providing aerodynamic stability.

Ver•y Large Ar•ray /'verē 'lärj ə'rā/ (abbreviation: **VLA**) ▸ noun the world's largest radio telescope, consisting of 27 dish antennas in Socorro, New Mexico.

Vi•ag•ra /vī'agrə/ ▸ noun trademark a proprietary formulation of the male impotency drug SILDENAFIL CITRATE.
-ORIGIN 1990s: apparently a blend of *virility* and *Niagara*.

vi•bra•tion white fin•ger /vī'brāsHən '(h)wīt 'fiNGgər/ ▸ noun Raynaud's disease, which is caused by prolonged use of vibrating hand tools or machinery.

vid•e•o mail /'vidēō ,māl/ ▸ noun 1 an e-mail message with a video clip attached.
2 the facility for creating such messages.

vid•e•o pill /'vidēō ,pil/ ▸ noun a capsule containing a tiny camera that, when swallowed, transmits photographs of the stomach and intestines to a recording device: *video pills can be used to diagnose ulcers.*

vid•e•o•scope /'vidēə,skōp/ ▸ noun a fiberoptic rod, attached to a camera, that transmits images from within the body to a television monitor, used in diagnosis and surgery.

vid•e•o•sur•ger•y /'vidēō,sərjərē/ ▸ noun a minimally invasive approach to surgery using from one to five small incisions, each between ¼ inch and 1 inch in length, through which specially designed instruments are inserted into the body. One of these is a tiny fiberoptic rod attached to a camera, enabling the surgeon to see on a television monitor what is happening inside the body.

vi•nyl /'vīnl/ ▸noun generic term for phonograph records: *he offers the only place anyone can still find country singles on 45 rpm (or what's left of that format since the industry all but abandoned vinyl).* [**Jan. 1992** *Chicago Magazine*]
–ORIGIN in reference to vinyl as the standard material used to make phonograph records.

vi•pas•sa•na /ˌvē'päsänä/ ▸noun the Buddhist name for INSIGHT MEDITATION.

vi•ral mar•ket•ing /'vīrəl 'märkitiNG/ ▸noun a marketing technique whereby information about a company's goods or services is passed electronically from one Internet user to another: *called "viral marketing," it's the trick of getting customers to propagate a product on behalf of the company that creates it.* [**12 Apr. 1999** *Newsweek*]
–ORIGIN 1980s: from the idea of the information being passed on like a computer virus.

vir•tu•al com•mu•ni•ty /'vərCHOОəl kə'myoŏnitē/ ▸noun a community of people sharing common interests, ideas, and feelings over the Internet.

vir•tu•al en•gi•neered com•pos•ite /'vərCHOОəl ˌenjə'ni(ə)rd kəm'päzit/ ▸noun a digitally controlled chemical molding system that uses water pressure to retain the shape of easily manufactured, nonrigid molds.
■ the material used to fabricate objects using this system.

vir•tu•al•ize /'vərCHOОə,līz/ ▸verb convert (something) to a computer-generated simulation of reality: [trans.] *traditional universities have begun to virtualize parts of their curricula* | [intrans.] *our method makes it easy to virtualize.*
–DERIVATIVES **vir•tu•al•i•za•tion** noun; **vir•tu•a•li•zer** noun

vir•tu•al of•fice /'vərCHOОəl 'ôfis; 'äfis/ ▸ noun the operational domain of any business or organization whose work force includes a significant proportion of workers using technology to perform their work at home.

vir•tu•al pet /'vərCHOОəl 'pet/ ▸noun see CYBERPET.

vir•u•lence gene /'vir(y)ələns ˌjēn/ ▸noun a gene whose presence or activity in an organism's genome is responsible for the pathogenicity of an infective agent: *a variant of the* esp *virulence gene could provide a way to prevent the spread of vancomycin-resistant En-*

terococcus faecium—a common cause of US hospital infections—in Europe. [**15 Mar.** 2001 *The Scientist*]

vis•it•a•bil•i•ty /ˌvizitə'bilitē/ ▸ noun a measure of a building's ease of access to people with disabilities: *we endeavor to create a community that is not only accessible to disabled persons, but is also a model of visitability.*
-DERIVATIVES **vis•it•a•ble** adjective

VLA ▸ abbreviation VERY LARGE ARRAY.

vogue /vōg/ ▸ verb [intrans.] (**vogued, vogue•ing** or **vogu•ing**) dance to music in such a way as to imitate the characteristic poses struck by a model on a catwalk.
-ORIGIN 1980s: from the name of the fashion magazine *Vogue*.

voice rec•og•ni•tion /'vois rekəgˌnisHən/ ▸ noun computer analysis of the human voice, especially for the purposes of interpreting words and phrases or identifying an individual voice.

vol•u•met•ric sen•sor /'välyə'metrik 'sensər/ ▸ noun a security device that detects the movement of people or objects by sensing their shapes.

vor•tal /'vôrtl/ ▸ noun an Internet site that provides a directory of links to information related to a particular industry.
-ORIGIN 1990s: blend of *v(ertical)* (as in *vertical industry*, an industry specializing in a narrow range of goods and services), and *(p)ortal*.

Ww

wake•board /'wāk‚bôrd/ ▸ **noun** a board towed behind a motor boat, shaped like a broad waterski and ridden like a surfboard.
▸ **verb** ride a wakeboard: *I have wakeboarded for three years.*
-DERIVATIVES **wake•board•ing** noun

wall•ing /'wôliNG/ ▸ **adjective** (in surfing) pertaining to waves with a high vertical surface: *both posted excellent eight and nine point rides and appeared suited to the long walling waves at Bells.* [**2 Oct.** 2003 *Geelong Advertiser (Australia)*]

wall of hon•or /'wôl əv 'änər/ ▸**noun** a wall on which are inscribed the names of individuals whose acts or achievements are deemed praiseworthy: *a plaque with Johnson's likeness, engraved in bronze, was added to the 6th District's Wall of Honor, which commemorates slain officers.* [**30 Apr.** 1998 *Washington Post*]

wan•ky /'wäNGkē; 'waNG-/ ▸ **adjective** chiefly British vulgar slang contemptible, worthless, or stupid: *I was determined not to end up as some Nigel doing wanky beer ads.*

WAP /wap/ ▸ **abbreviation** Wireless Application Protocol, a set of protocols for connecting cellular phones and other radio devices to the Internet.

war•chalk•ing /'wôr‚CHôkiNG/ (also **war chalk•ing** /'wôr‚ 'wôr‚CHôkiNGmCHôkiNG/) ▸ **noun** Computing the practice of marking chalk symbols on sidewalks and other outdoor surfaces to indicate the location of unsecured wireless network connections: *savvy IT managers check their buildings' facades for signs of warchalking.*

war•driv•ing /'wôr‚drīviNG/ ▸ **noun** the practice of seeking out and taking advantage of free connection to unsecured wireless networks: *management recently heard about wardriving and is very concerned that corporate information is being intercepted by those who don't need to see it.* [**12 Oct.** 2003 *Network World Fusion]*
-ORIGIN 2003: allegedly coined by Pete Shipley, a San Francisco Bay-area IT consultant, from *war* + *driving*, described by him as "driving around looking for unsecured wireless networks."

war•fight•er /'wôr,fîtər/ ▸ noun a soldier in combat: *"the lease proposal balances the urgent needs of the warfighter with the demands of our other vital programs, while staying within our budget," Wolfowitz wrote.* [**23 Sept.** 2003 *Washington Post*]

USAGE: The burgeoning usage of this term with reference to ground troops in Iraq, mostly in sympathetic contexts, suggests that the old-fashioned *soldier* no longer captures the imagination of listeners and readers.

wat /wät/ ▸ noun (in Thailand, Cambodia, and Laos) a Buddhist monastery or temple: [as modifier] *Phra Bhante Kantasilo, a senior monk in Wat Boworniwet.* [**30 Sept.** 2003 *Straits Times (Singapore)*] –ORIGIN Thai, from Sanskrit *vāṭa* 'enclosure.'

Wat•su /'wätso͞o/ ▸ noun trademark a form of shiatsu massage that takes place in water. –ORIGIN 1980s: blend of *water* and *shiatsu*.

weap•on of mass de•struc•tion /'wepən əv 'mas di'strəksHən/ ▸ noun [usu. plural] a chemical, biological, or radioactive weapon capable of causing widespread death and destruction. (abbr. **WMD**)

wear•a•ble /'we(ə)rəbəl/ (also **wear•a•ble com•put•er** /'we(ə)rəbəl kəm'pyo͞otər/) ▸ noun a computer that is small or portable enough to be worn or carried on one's body: *wearable computers are the height of geek chic.*

web•cam /'web,kam/ ▸ noun trademark a video camera that inputs to a computer connected to the Internet, so that its images can be viewed by Internet users: *unnerving stories of video spies abound: an Internet site for voyeurs that has secret webcams mounted in a tanning booth for women.* [**6 July 1998** *Chicago Tribune*] –ORIGIN 1990s: blend of *web* in the sense 'World Wide Web' and *cam(era)*.

web•cast /'web,kast/ (also **Web•cast**) ▸ noun a live video broadcast transmitted across the Internet: *an estimated 1.5 million to 2 million surfers clicked on to the live Webcast of the Victoria's Secret annual fashion show.* –DERIVATIVES **web•cast•ing** noun

web-en•a•ble /'web en,ābəl/ ▸ verb [trans.] make accessible via or compatible with the World Wide Web: *a project to web-enable legacy accounting systems.* | *web-enable your small business.*

–DERIVATIVES **web-en•a•bled** adjective: *though each of these three companies is Web-enabled, their online business has yet to overtake their more traditional customers.*

web host•ing /'web ˌhōstiNG/ ▸ noun the activity or business of providing storage space and access for Web sites.

web•log /'webˌlôg; -ˌläg/ ▸ noun a Web site on which an individual or group of users produce an ongoing narrative: *where, in all the cant about interactive shopping, was the nascent nation of online weblog diarists, pouring out their souls one hyperlinked paragraph at a time?* [**Sept. 2001** *Yahoo! Internet Life*]
–DERIVATIVES **web•log•ger** noun
–ORIGIN 1990s: from *web* in the sense 'World Wide Web' and *log* in the sense 'regular record of incidents.'

web•zine /'webˌzēn/ ▸ noun a magazine published electronically on the World Wide Web.
–ORIGIN 1990s: from *web* in the sense 'World Wide Web' and *(maga)zine.*

wed•ding plan•ner /'wediNG ˌplanər/ ▸ noun someone whose job is to plan and organize weddings.

wedge is•sue /'wej ˌiSHoō/ ▸ noun a divisive political issue, especially one that is raised by a candidate for public office in hopes of attracting supporters to their campaign or in order to alienate an opponent's supporters from their candidate: *gay marriage could emerge as an important wedge issue that Republicans could use in 2004 to woo traditional Democrats, particularly Roman Catholics.* [**28 Sept. 2003** *Boston Globe*]

wedg•ie /'wejē/ ▸ noun informal an act of pulling up the material of someone's underwear tightly between their buttocks as a practical joke: *he was back there grabbing the waistband of their skivvies, preparing to give them the wedgie of a lifetime.*

weed whack•er /'wēd ˌ(h)wakər/ ▸ noun an electrically powered grass trimmer with a nylon cutting cord that rotates rapidly on a spindle.

well-en•dowed /'wel en'doud/ ▸ adjective informal having a strikingly large penis or bosom: *I am a nice-looking, 45 year old woman, 125 lbs, 5' 7", who fantasizes about being taken by a young, slim well-endowed man.* [**14 Nov. 1997** Usenet: alt.sex.swingers]

wel•wit•schi•a /wel'wiCHēə/ ▶ **noun** a gymnospermous plant of desert regions in S.W. Africa that has a dwarf, massive trunk, two long strap-shaped leaves, and male and female flowers in the scales of scarlet cones. It is remarkable for its ability to extract moisture from fog.
•Genus *Welwitschia*, family Welwitschiaceae: one species, *W. mirabilis*.
–ORIGIN mid 19th cent.: modern Latin, named after Friedrich *Welwitsch* (1806–72), Austrian botanist.

West Brit•on /'west 'britn/ ▶ **noun** Irish, derogatory an Irish person who greatly admires England or Britain.

West Nile Vi•rus /'west 'nīl ˌvīrəs/ ▶ **noun** a flavivirus of African origin that can be spread to humans and other mammals via mosquitoes, causing encephalitis and flu-like symptoms, with some fatalities.

what•ev•er /ˌ(h)wət'evər; ˌ(h)wät-/ ▶ **exclamation** informal said as a response indicating a reluctance to discuss something, often implying indifference: *if someone came running to say he'd just seen Jesus preaching, most New Yorkers would reply, 'Whatever.'*

white•list•ing /'(h)wīt,listiNG/ ▶ **noun** Computing the use of antispam filtering software to allow only specified e-mail addresses to get through: *whitelisting sometimes backfires because it filters e-mail from people or companies you might be interested in.*
–ORIGIN on the pattern of *blacklisting*.

white-van man /'(h)wīt 'van ˌman/ ▶ **noun** British informal an aggressive male driver of a delivery or contractor's van: *sales reps and the infamous white van man have to be targeted.*

whole bod•y scan /'hōl 'bädē ˌskan/ ▶ **noun** a CT scan of the torso, especially one obtained for health screening purposes.
–DERIVATIVES **whole bod•y scan•ning noun**

Wi-Fi /'wī'fī/ ▶ **abbreviation** Wireless Fidelity, a group of technical standards enabling the transmission of data over wireless networks.
▶ **verb** (**Wi-Fies, Wi-Fied, Wi-Fy•ing**) [trans.] convert or adapt for Wireless Fidelity compatibility: *what type of electronics will be immune from being Wi-Fied?* [**29 Sept. 2003** *NewsFactor Network*]

wig•ger /'wigər/ ▶ **noun** offensive slang **1** a white person who emulates or acquires African-American behavior and tastes: *Whites who pal around with Blacks are called "wannabes" or "wiggers."*

2 an unreliable or flaky person: *the '80s wigger is the same as the '50s greaser, the '60s hippie, or the '70s burnout.*

wild cane /'wīld 'kān/ ▸ **noun** another name for GIANT REED.

wild•craft /'wīld,kraft/ ▸ **verb** gather herbs, plants, and fungi from the wild, usually for some commercial purpose: [as adjective] *concentrates with wildcrafted goldenseal root.*
▸ **noun** the action or practice of wildcrafting.

wind farm /'wind ,färm/ ▸ **noun** an installation of wind turbines for generating electricity: *the developers of a soon-to-be-constructed wind farm did not sufficiently study the potential harm the site could pose to migratory birds and protected species like bald eagles and Indiana bats, a letter from federal officials said.* [**8 Oct.** 2003 *Evening Sun (PA)*]

win•dow treat•ment /'windō ,trētmənt/ ▸ **noun** interior decoration for a window or window frame: *replacing blinds on the windows in the living room, dining room and breakfast area with curtains or sheers or some other window treatment.* [**13 Sept.** 2003 GoMemphis.com]

wing•span /'wiNG,span/ ▸ **noun** the distance between opposite fingertips of the outstretched arms of an athlete, especially a basketball player: *Hakim Warrick's massive wingspan got in the way of Kansas's national championship hopes.* [**9 Apr.** 2003 *CNN Sports*]

win•ter creep•er /'wintər 'krēpər/ ▸ **noun** an evergreen clinging vine that is native to China and cultivated elsewhere as an ornamental ground cover; it has escaped cultivation and is regarded as an ecological threat in some eastern U.S. states.
•*Euonymus fortunei*, family Celastraceae.

wire•less hot•spot /'wī(ə)rlis 'hät,spät/ ▸ **noun** an area with a usable signal to allow wireless connection to the Internet or some other computer network: *a wireless hotspot where people can surf the Internet and check their e-mail without even plugging in their laptops* [**28 Oct.** 2003 *Democrat and Chronicle (NY)*]

wire•less•ly /'wī(ə)rlislē/ ▸ **adverb** without a wire connection; using a wireless technology: *a patented FM technology which broadcasts music wirelessly from a small transmitter to satellite speakers.* [**9 Mar.** 1992 *U.S. News and World Report*]

WMD ▸ **abbreviation** (plural **WMDs**) WEAPON OF MASS DESTRUCTION.

wood ear /ˈwo͝od ˌi(ə)r/ ▸ **noun** an edible fungus, black or brown in color, that grows on trees and is sold in dry wrinkled shapes somewhat resembling ears.
•*Auricularia auricula*, family Auriculariaceae.

word•robe /ˈwərdˌrōb/ ▸ **noun** informal a person's vocabulary: *once a period is established the appropriate wordrobe for the characters is extensively researched and developed.*

work•book /ˈwərkˌbo͝ok/ ▸ **noun** Computing a single file containing several different types of related information as separate worksheets.

work•ing mem•o•ry /ˈwərkiNG ˈmem(ə)rē/ ▸ **noun** Psychology the part of short-term memory that is concerned with immediate conscious perceptual and linguistic processing: *your conversation depends on another brand of memory: working memory, which enables us to hold fleeting material in our heads so that we can build and understand complex sentences.* [**21 Nov. 1992** *New Scientist (UK)*]
■ Computing an area of high-speed memory used to store programs or data currently in use.

world beat /ˈwərld ˌbēt/ ▸ **noun** Western music incorporating elements of traditional music from any part of the world, especially from developing nations: *the booming sounds of world beat in the background.*

world cit•y /ˈwərld ˈsitē/ ▸ **noun** a cosmopolitan city, with foreigners visiting and residing: [as modifier] *the book charts Hong Kong's path to world city status.*

wran•gler /ˈraNGglər/ ▸ **noun** a person who trains and takes care of animals on a movie set.

wrap /rap/ ▸ **noun 1** a flour tortilla, filled with any of various stuffings and rolled: *it seemed the wrap was front-loaded with the Tabasco mayo, as only that first bite knocked me over; it should have been better distributed.* [**8 Oct. 2003** *Arizona Weekly*]
2 a summarizing conclusion; wrap-up.

wrap•a•round mort•gage /ˈrapəˌround ˌmôrgij/ ▸ **noun** a second mortgage held by a lender who collects payments on it and the first mortgage from the borrower; the lender makes the payments to the original mortgage holder.

wrap•a•round porch /ˈrapəˌround ˌpôrCH/ ▸ **noun** a shallow veranda enclosing two or more sides of a house: *much of the area . . . is new* *development, such as Corolla Light—immense three-story million-dollar houses with wraparound porches perched on pilings.* [**16 June 1996** *Denver Post*]

wrap•per ap•pli•ca•tion /ˈrapər apliˌkāsHən/ ▸ **noun** a computer program that works only with another fully developed program, which it enhances in some way: *we have created a viewer which is a simple wrapper application for the underlying multimedia system.*

wrecked /rekt/ ▸ **adjective** informal **1** very intoxicated on alcohol or drugs: *I'd like to get really wrecked and then go out and find some girls.* **2** exhausted.

wrong•ful death /ˈrôNGfəl ˈdeTH/ ▸ **adjective** denoting a civil action in which damages are sought against a party for causing a death, typically when criminal action has failed or is not attempted: *the family of a Western Kentucky University student who was set on fire and murdered in her dorm room has filed a wrongful death lawsuit.* [**18 Sept. 2003** *WKTY (Kentucky)*]

Wy•o•tan•a /ˌwī-ōˈtanə/ ▸ **noun** informal a region consisting largely of mountain wilderness lying partly in southern Montana and partly in northern Wyoming.

Xx

Xan•ax /'zan͵aks/ ▸ trademark a proprietary formulation of the tranquilizer alprazolam.

Xe•lo•da /zə'lōdə/ ▸ trademark a proprietary formulation of the prescription drug capecitabine; it is used to treat various metastatic cancers by inhibiting tumor growth while sparing most surrounding tissue.

Xen•i•cal /'zeni͵kal/ ▸ noun trademark a synthetic drug that blocks pancreatic enzymes used in the digestion of fats, used to treat obesity.

xen•ol•o•gy /zə'näləjē/ ▸ noun (chiefly in science fiction) the scientific study of alien biology, cultures, etc.: *a race of raucous mucusoids so foul and unloveable that even graduate students in xenology, hardened by years of study among primitive and even disgusting societies, could seldom be found to live near the Porsa and study their ways.* [**1990** S. S. Tepper, *Raising Stones*]
-DERIVATIVES **xen•ol•o•gist** noun
-ORIGIN 1950s: from Greek *xenos* 'stranger, foreigner', (adjective) 'strange.'

xen-phen /'zen ͵fen/ ▸ noun a drug combination of Xenical and phentermine, used to treat obesity.

Xer /'eksər/ ▸ noun a GEN-XER.

XML ▸ abbreviation Extensible Markup Language; a compliant version of SGML that is designed to make a wide variety of documents compatible with the Internet and electronic data exchange: [often as modifier] *unlike the existing HTML format, the XML-enhanced format will support features such as pivot tables in spreadsheets, and revision marks in word documents.* [**25 June 1998** *Computing*]

Yy

yad•da yad•da yad•da /'yädə 'yädə 'yädə/ (also **ya•da ya•da ya•da**)
▸ informal used as a substitute in written and spoken contexts for actual words where they are too lengthy or tedious to recite in full: *boy meets girl, boy loses girl, yadda yadda yadda.*

yah /yä/ ▸ **noun** British informal an upper-class person: *the cafe is full of yahs whose daddies own chateaux in France.*

Ya•sa-sheet /'yäsə ˌSHēt/ ▸ **noun** a specially treated plastic that suppresses the emission of ethylene gas from ripening fruits and vegetables, prolonging their shelf-life: *wrap an apple in Yasa-sheet and it will stay fresh for weeks.* [**9 Aug. 2003** *Science News*]

yet•tie /'yetē/ (also **Yet•tie**) ▸ **noun** informal a young person who earns money from a business or activity that involves the Internet: *he has all the electronic devices that characterize a yettie.*
-ORIGIN acronym from *young entrepreneurial technocrat* (or *tech-based*), on the pattern of *yuppie.*

yield man•age•ment /'yēld ˌmanijmənt/ ▸ **noun** the process of making frequent adjustments in the price of a product in response to market factors such as demand or competition: [as modifier] *Haji-Ioannou is using the same yield management system that made easy-Jet, the low-cost airline, a success.* [**6 Sept. 2003** *Daily Telegraph (UK)*]

yo•gic fly•ing /'yōgik 'flī-iNG/ ▸ **noun** a technique practiced chiefly by adherents of Transcendental Meditation that involves thrusting oneself off the ground while in the lotus position.

yoke /yōk/ ▸ **noun** Irish informal a thing whose name one cannot recall, does not know, or does not wish to specify: *when everything quietened down, yer man, the gobdaw, asks me to get the yoke. 'What yoke?' says I. 'The hammer!' he says as if I should have known.*
▸ **verb** slang rob; mug: *two crackheads yoked this girl. They beat her down and took her jewelry. Punched her in the eye; just cold bashed her.* [**1995** P. Bourgois, *In Search of Respect*]

Zz

za•min•dar /zəˈmēn͵där/ (also **ze•min•dar**) ▸ noun Indian a landowner, especially one who leases his land to tenant farmers: [as modifier] *Tasneem belonged to a famous zamindar family in Lucknow which had contributed to the independence movement.* [**24 Sept.** 2003 *Mumbai Newsline*]
–ORIGIN via Urdu from Persian *zamīndār*, from *zamīn* 'land' + *-dār* 'holder.'

Zel•ig /ˈzelig/ ▸ noun a person who is able to change his or her appearance, behavior, or attitudes, so as to be comfortable in any situation: *a financial Zelig, Allen made banking history by being the only man to advise all four of the major networks on deals in one year.* [**Oct.** 1996 *Vanity Fair*]
–ORIGIN 1980s: from the name of Leonard *Zelig*, central character in the film *Zelig* (1983).

ze•min•dar /zəˈmēn͵där/ ▸ noun variant spelling of ZAMINDAR.

zi•kr /ˈzēkər/ ▸ noun a variant spelling of DHIKR.

Zi•on /ˈzīən/ (also **Si•on** /ˈsīən/) ▸ noun (among Rastafarians) Africa.

zip•cuff /ˈzip͵kəf/ ▸ noun a plastic strip with a loop on one end that is secured with notches on the other end, used as a temporary handcuff.
▸verb [trans.] restrain with zipcuffs: *one cop called someone on the phone while the other one zipcuffed me* | [as adjective] *zipcuffed protestors.*

zo•o•not•ic /͵zōəˈnätik/ ▸ adjective (of diseases) transmissible from animals to humans: *two recent cases of zoonotic transmission are getting plenty of attention—SARS and monkeypox.*

zo•o•phile /ˈzōə͵fīl/, ▸ noun **1** a person who loves animals; an opponent of cruelty to animals.
2 a person who is sexually attracted to animals: [as modifier] *in My Dog Tulip, J R Ackerley owned up to what might be termed interspecific frottage, but the confession was not exactly a rallying cry for zoophile liberation.* [**17 July** 1994 *Independent (UK)*]
–DERIVATIVES **zo•o•phil•i•a** /͵zōəˈfilēə/ noun; **zo•o•phil•ic** adjective

-ORIGIN late 19th cent. (originally in the botanical sense 'a plant pollinated by animals'): from *zoo* + *-phile*. The current senses date from the early 20th cent.

zorb•ing /ˈzôrbiNG/ ▸ noun a sport in which a participant is secured inside an inner capsule in a large, transparent ball that is then rolled along the ground or down hills.
-ORIGIN 1990s: invented word from *zorb* (the name of the ball used in this activity) + *-ing*.

Zy•ban /ˈzīˌban/ ▸ noun trademark the antidepressant bupropion, used to relieve nicotine withdrawal symptoms in people giving up smoking.
-ORIGIN 1990s: an invented name, probably from *ban* or *banish*.

Resources

Finding New Words

YOU'RE READING your favorite magazine, or a new novel, or your local paper, and you come across this sentence: "It was an eerie, crebadative feeling, as if she were being watched." *Crebadative?* You wonder. You check a dictionary (or two, or three) and you don't find it. What you have found is a new word. A classic new word, one that has a completely different arrangement of letters from any other existing word. You understand roughly what it means, from context, but you're not sure, and you file it away in your head as new and unusual. You probably won't write it or speak it yourself, unless you're very playful or adventurous—you don't have a firm grasp on it, and there are plenty of other words in your storehouse that you feel more comfortable with. A little later, perhaps, you read this sentence: "Scientists in Melbourne have discovered a new enzyme responsible for fat digestion, lipafazil." *Lipafazil?* You probably don't check that one at all, slotting it instead into a neat compartment in your brain labeled "science stuff." And you don't use it (unless you yourself are an enzyme-research scientist) because you simply have no need for it.

This kind of new-word-finding experience is what most people think of when they (or if they) think about new words: the unique word appearing out of the blue, especially the unique science and technology word. This kind of new word is often called "coined," and in some cases a particular person can be credited with the invention of the word (as with the word *cyberspace*, which was coined by William Gibson in 1982). Even coined words, though, aren't usually completely original combinations of letters; a combination like *phygrttle* is certainly original, but it looks hard to pronounce and doesn't give readers any clue as to what it means, unlike the word *infomercial*, which is a readily recognizable blend of "information" and "commercial." Many coined words are blended from two already accepted words. One completely original coined words is *googol* "ten raised to the hundredth power (10^{100})," which was invented by the nine-year-old nephew of a mathematician.

However, from the lexicographer's point of view, most new words aren't the careful coinage of a single person, or even the simultaneous independent coinages of several people (which happens more often than you might think, to the frustration of all involved). Many new words are stolen by English from other languages; words like *keiretsu*, from Japanese, or *chicano*, from Spanish. English is very likely to swipe words for food: *chianti, sauerkraut, tandoori*. Sometimes English, instead of taking the word, just transmutes the foreign word into English. German *Übermensch*, for example, became English *superman*. This is called a *calque* (from the French for 'copy') or a *loan translation*. Occasionally, people will hear foreign or unfamiliar words and reanalyze them to fit them into a more familiar form, making new words. This process is called *folk etymology*, and made words like *cockroach*, from Spanish *cucaracha*, and *woodchuck*, from an American Indian word often spelled *otchek*. Occasionally this process is more involved, as with *alligator pear*, "avocado"— given this name because they were supposed to grow where alligators were common.

New acronyms are very common, and occasionally become words whose acronymic origins are all but forgotten by users (words like *scuba* 'self-contained underwater breathing apparatus' and *snafu* 'situation normal, all fouled up' rarely come across as acronyms today, and the origin of a word like *gigaflops*, where the *–flops* is from 'floating operations per second' is not blatantly acronymic). There is even a recent trend towards making *bacronyms*, words that are made acronymically but for which the most important consideration is that the acronym make an appropriate (usually already existing) word or words, such as MADD, "Mothers Against Drunk Driving," or the recent USA-PATRIOT Act, in which USA-PATRIOT stands for "Uniting and Strengthening America by Providing Appropriate Tools Required to Intercept and Obstruct Terrorism."

Although entirely new words are exciting to the lexicographer and the layperson alike, changes to existing words can thrill as well. The meanings of words are no more fixed than any other aspect of human culture, and despite well-meaning efforts by many to make them stand still, they continue to change. Spotting these new meanings takes a more sophisticated approach to language, and one that is more sensitized to shades of definition instead of just knee-jerkishly categorizing a new meaning as 'wrong.'

A favorite kind of lexical change is metaphorical extension: the computer meanings of *mouse* and *virus* are good examples of this, as is the basketball meaning of *dunk*. An unfavorite, though frequent, kind of lexical change is change in grammatical function: the verbing of nouns. Why one kind of change is welcomed and thought clever by logophiles while the other kind is deplored and thought degrading is unclear, but *impact, contact, script, conference,* and other verbs-from-nouns are in very frequent use.

Words' meanings can get worse, a process called *pejoration*. This has happened in a big way to words like *barefaced*, which originally meant just "open, unconcealed," and then became "shameless," and in a small way to words like *poetess* and *actress*, which now seem like lightweights compared to *poet* and *actor*. Words can also improve their meanings, or *ameliorate*. The word *luxury* originally mean "lust," but gradually changed to mean "something desirable but not indispensable."

Besides getting better or worse, meanings can become more or less inclusive. Becoming less inclusive is called *specialization*, as when *amputate* went from meaning "to cut off" to meaning "to cut off a limb or other part of the body." Becoming more inclusive is called *generalization*, as when the word *pants* went from meaning specifically "pantaloons" to meaning almost any kind of lower-body covering.

Some new words are just shorter versions of old words. These are made either through clipping (*fax* from *facsimile, exam* from *examination* are standard examples) or from back-formation (*burgle* from *burglar, bus* from *busboy, edit* from *editor*). This is so common that most people don't register these words as "new" or are astonished to learn the longer word is older, and the shorter word is newer. This is probably because many other new words are formed by derivation, that is, by adding affixes to existing words, lengthening them. (Affixes are prefixes and suffixes, and, in facetious use only, infixes, which are parts inserted in the middle of words. These are usually only used with obscenities: "abso-damn-lutely.") Words like *ascertainable* and *finalization* are derivatives. Many of the new words added to dictionaries are new derivatives, tacked on to the end of existing entries.

Of course, some words are made from proper names, and are then called *eponyms*: *sequoia* and *sihouette* are two well-known examples. Using a proper name to stand for something having an attribute associated with that name is called *antonomasia*, and calling someone especially perspicacious a *Sherlock* is one example. When proper names are treated in this way they are very often added to dictionaries and thus count, for lexicographical purposes, as new words. The genericization of trademarks (like *thermos* and *aspirin*) also falls under antonomasia.

One last method of forming new words is echoing, or onomatopoeia, in which new words are made to resemble real-world sounds, like *bleep*, *bloop*, and *boing!* This might be the most fun way to make new words, but it is also less likely to create words that give off that "new" feel, especially if the sound is familiar.

With this field guide to word formation processes you should now be able to find new words everywhere you look—and possibly create a few yourself.

A Select Bibliography of Oxford Dictionaries and Reference Works

DICTIONARIES

The Oxford English Dictionary. Second Ed. 20 vols. 1989.
The 500-lb gorilla of the dictionary world, also available on CD-ROM, and online by subscription at http://www.oed.com.

The New Shorter Oxford English Dictionary. Fifth Ed. 2 vols. 2002.
Not just an abridgement of the twenty-volume *OED*, the Shorter has its own independent research program. With more than 83,000 quotations, this packs the punch of the *OED's* literary approach in a more manageable format. Also available on CD-ROM.

The New Oxford American Dictionary. 2001.
A completely new dictionary of American English from Oxford, with an innovative arrangement of definitions in which the more prominent core senses are given first, with related senses arranged in blocks underneath. This allows for a nice overview of constellations of meaning not possible with other dictionaries. Also available on CD-ROM.

The Oxford American Dictionary and Thesaurus
(with Language Guide). 2003.
A very good general dictionary with a complete thesaurus and a great deal of extra usage and language information, plus a 62-page Language Guide reference supplement.

The Concise Oxford Dictionary, 10th Ed. 1999.
The classic desk-size dictionary for British English, including the most current words and phrases and scientific and technical vocabulary. Word Formation features identify complex word groups such as *-phobias, -cultures,* and *-ariums.*

DICTIONARIES OF USAGE

Burchfield, R.W. *The New Fowler's Modern English Usage.*
3rd Ed. 1996.
A completely revised and expanded version of the beloved Modern English Usage with examples from modern authors such as Tom Wolfe, Saul Bellow, and Iris Murdoch.

Fowler, H.W. *A Dictionary of Modern English Usage.*
2nd Ed. 1983
The most-beloved language reference book and the one by which all others are judged. And a darn good read!

Garner, Bryan. *Garner's Modern American Usage.* 2nd Ed. 2003.
The new authority for American usage and guidance not only for the grammar-impaired but for anyone who would like to write gracefully and precisely.

OTHER REFERENCE BOOKS

Ayto, John. *Twentieth Century Words.* 1999.
An overview of 5,000 words and meanings of the twentieth century, including *flapper, flower power,* and *road rage.*

Chantrell, Glynnis. *The Oxford Dictionary of Word Histories.* 2002.
This book describes the origins and sense development of over 11,000 words in the English language, with dates of the first recorded evidence from ongoing research for the OED.

Delahunty, Andrew; Sheila Dignan and Penelope Stock.
The Oxford Dictionary of Allusions. 2001.
A guide to allusions most frequently found in literature both modern and canonical. It covers classical myths and modern culture and ranges from "Ahab" to "Teflon," "Eve" to "Darth Vader." Many entries include a quotation illustrating the allusion in use.

Greenbaum, Sidney. *The Oxford English Grammar.* 1996.
A complete overview of the subject, including a review of modern approaches to grammar and the interdependence of grammar and discourse, word-formation, punctuation, pronunciation, and spelling.

Knowles, Elizabeth, ed. *The Oxford Dictionary of Phrase and Fable*. 2000.

Drawn from folklore, history, mythology, philosophy, popular culture, religion, science, and technology, these alphabetically arranged entries include ancient gods and goddesses, biblical allusions, proverbial sayings, common phrases, fictional characters, geographical entities, and real people and events.

Lindberg, Christine. *The Oxford American Thesaurus of Current English*. 1999.

A very good general thesaurus with an exclusive Writer's Toolkit and more than 350,000 synonyms.

Quinion, Michael, *Ologies and Isms: Word Beginnings and Endings*. 2003.

A book about the building blocks of the English language—the beginnings and endings, and sometimes the middles—that help form or adapt many of the words we use.

Onions, C. T. *The Oxford Dictionary of English Etymology*. 1966.

The standard reference for scholars, this dictionary delves into the origins of more than 38,000 words.

Index by Subject

RTFM
run-time
run-time license
save
screenager
script kiddie
secure server
security patch
select
selection
serial port
service pack
servlet
skin
smart dust
sortation
SP
spawn
speech recognition
spider
SSL
status bar
sticky
streaming
subweb
swapfile
syntax error
synthespian
tablet PC
technical support
TIFF
T-1
touchpoint
Turing test
unicast
uninstall
unpruned
unsubscribe
USB
Usenet
user interface
version control
virtual office
virtualize
voice recognition
vortal
warchalking
wardriving

wearable
web-enable
whitelisting
wireless hotspot
wirelessly
workbook
working memory
wrapper application
XML

Food and Clothing
activewear
adobo
airpot
ajinomoto
albondigas
argan oil
asiago
Atkins diet
baguette
ballotin
balsam apple
bammy
bandeau
barbeque
barista
barrique
Bellini
bento
bhuna
Birkenstock
bitter gourd
black bottom pie
bling-bling
boat neck
boba tea
bollito misto
boot-cut
boutique hotel
Brazilian
bresaola
brewski
bridge mix
Brillo
broast
brocciflower
broccoli rabe
bubble tea

Law, Politics, and Government

Nihang
9/11
no-fly
noncustodial
nonjudicial
nonstruck
NU
nuclear threshold
Nunavut
ochlocracy
OIC
Pakhtun
panic room
particle beam
Passamaquoddy
peace order
pepper spray
phishing
Picard
poison pill amendment
POTUS
PQ
prebuttal
protective order
prove
push poll
racial profiling
reasonable woman standard
regime change
Republicrat
right-to-know
rort
safe haven
safe room
Schengen agreement
shopgrifting
situationism
skank
skimming
sleeper cell
SLV
snakehead
spinmeister
stabbing
stench warfare
street-legal
structured settlement
SWAT team

tailgate
tax-and-spend
Teflon
thought leader
turf battle
turnspeak
Unabomber
undervote
ungrounded
unholster
Uttaranchal
wall of honor
warfighter
weapon of mass destruction
wedge issue
West Briton
WMD
world city
wrongful death
Wyotana
zipcuff

Lifestyle
active barrier
advanced placement
aftercare
alt.
ass-backward
assisted living
at-risk
BarcaLounger
barkitecture
basket bingo
basket-weaving
bass-ackwards
bazillion
beater
beef
Belfast sink
birthdate
bizarro
bladdered
blunt
bogart
bomb
boosterish
booty call
bootylicious

subsense
support system
SWF
SWM
sympathetic smoker
thought leader
three-parent
tipping point
TLA
towelhead
toybook
trailer trash
transgender
trolley dolly
trophy child
trustafarian
tween
tweenager
twelve-step
unplug
Uranian
vamp
visitability
wall of honor
wedding planner
West Briton
wigger
wordrobe
xenology
Xer
yadda yadda yadda
yah
Zelig
zoophile

Religion
Abrahamic
acharya
altar call
altar girl
areligious
bardo
bashert
beit din
bhikkhu
bhikkhuni
biblicist
breatharian

cardinal sin
Chrismation
dhikr
discernment
faith-based
Falun Gong
guna
ichthus
iconize
identity politics
insight meditation
Islamophobia
jihadi
jihadist
Nihang
panentheism
powerbeads
prakriti
Raelian
rajas
rajasic
sattva
sattvic
stained-glass ceiling
tamas
tamasic
theoterrorism
theotherapy
umrah
vipassana
wat
yogic flying
zikr
Zion

Science and Technology
access charge
addy
ADSL
ahi
ajowan
Alberta Clipper
alecost
AMBER Alert
ambulocetus
Andrewsarchus
animal
Anthropocene